Political Representation in the European Union

In recent years the financial and economic crisis of 2008–9 has progressed into an equally important political and democratic crisis of the EU. These troubled times have set the framework to re-assess a number of important questions in regard to representative democracy in the EU, such as the normative foundation of political representation, the institutional relationship between representatives and represented, the link between democracy and representation and new arenas and actors.

This book examines the diverse avenues through which different sorts of actors have expressed their voices during the Euro crisis and how their various interests are translated into the decision-making process. It offers a state-of-the-art assessment of what political representation means in this context as well as a contribution to the 'representative turn' in democratic theory. The authors address three key themes:

- The main actors and channels of political representation in the EU.
- Interlocking levels of representation in the EU and the way in which national and supranational representation works.
- How the European institutional system represents EU citizens through law and administration.

Focusing on the importance of representation in the legitimation of democracy, this book will be of interest to students and scholars of European Union politics, European studies, democratic theory, representation studies, civil society and transnational democracy.

Sandra Kröger is a lecturer at the Department of Politics at the University of Exeter, UK.

Routledge advances in European politics

1 **Russian Messianism**
Third Rome, revolution, Communism and after
Peter J.S. Duncan

2 **European Integration and the Postmodern Condition**
Governance, democracy, identity
Peter van Ham

3 **Nationalism in Italian Politics**
The stories of the Northern League, 1980–2000
Damian Tambini

4 **International Intervention in the Balkans since 1995**
Edited by Peter Siani-Davies

5 **Widening the European Union**
The politics of institutional change and reform
Edited by Bernard Steunenberg

6 **Institutional Challenges in the European Union**
Edited by Madeleine Hosli, Adrian van Deemen and Mika Widgrén

7 **Europe Unbound**
Enlarging and reshaping the boundaries of the European Union
Edited by Jan Zielonka

8 **Ethnic Cleansing in the Balkans**
Nationalism and the destruction of tradition
Cathie Carmichael

9 **Democracy and Enlargement in Post-Communist Europe**
The democratisation of the general public in fifteen Central and Eastern European countries, 1991–1998
Christian W. Haerpfer

10 **Private Sector Involvement in the Euro**
The power of ideas
Stefan Collignon and Daniela Schwarzer

11 **Europe**
A Nietzschean perspective
Stefan Elbe

12 **European Union and E-Voting**
Addressing the European Parliament's internet voting challenge
Edited by Alexander H. Trechsel and Fernando Mendez

13 **European Union Council Presidencies**
A comparative perspective
Edited by Ole Elgström

14 **European Governance and Supranational Institutions**
Making states comply
Jonas Tallberg

15 **European Union, NATO and Russia**
Martin Smith and Graham Timmins

16 **Business, The State and Economic Policy**
The case of Italy
G. Grant Amyot

17 **Europeanization and Transnational States**
Comparing Nordic central governments
Bengt Jacobsson, Per Lægreid and Ove K. Pedersen

18 **European Union Enlargement**
A comparative history
Edited by Wolfram Kaiser and Jürgen Elvert

19 **Gibraltar**
British or Spanish?
Peter Gold

20 **Gendering Spanish Democracy**
Monica Threlfall, Christine Cousins and Celia Valiente

21 **European Union Negotiations**
Processes, networks and negotiations
Edited by Ole Elgström and Christer Jönsson

22 **Evaluating Euro-Mediterranean Relations**
Stephen C. Calleya

23 **The Changing Face of European Identity**
A seven-nation study of (supra) national attachments
Edited by Richard Robyn

24 **Governing Europe**
Discourse, governmentality and European integration
William Walters and Jens Henrik Haahr

25 **Territory and Terror**
Conflicting nationalisms in the Basque country
Jan Mansvelt Beck

26 **Multilateralism, German Foreign Policy and Central Europe**
Claus Hofhansel

27 **Popular Protest in East Germany**
Gareth Dale

28 **Germany's Foreign Policy Towards Poland and the Czech Republic**
Ostpolitik revisited
Karl Cordell and Stefan Wolff

29 **Kosovo**
The politics of identity and space
Denisa Kostovicova

30 **The Politics of European Union Enlargement**
Theoretical approaches
Edited by Frank Schimmelfennig and Ulrich Sedelmeier

31 **Europeanizing Social Democracy?**
The rise of the party of European socialists
Simon Lightfoot

32 **Conflict and Change in EU Budgetary Politics**
Johannes Lindner

33 **Gibraltar, Identity and Empire**
E.G. Archer

34 **Governance Stories**
Mark Bevir and R.A.W Rhodes

35 **Britain and the Balkans**
1991 until the present
Carole Hodge

36 **The Eastern Enlargement of the European Union**
John O'Brennan

37 **Values and Principles in European Union Foreign Policy**
Edited by Sonia Lucarelli and Ian Manners

38 **European Union and the Making of a Wider Northern Europe**
Pami Aalto

39 **Democracy in the European Union**
Towards the emergence of a public sphere
Edited by Liana Giorgi, Ingmar Von Homeyer and Wayne Parsons

40 **European Union Peacebuilding and Policing**
Michael Merlingen with Rasa Ostrauskaite

41 **The Conservative Party and European Integration since 1945**
At the heart of Europe?
N.J. Crowson

42 **E-Government in Europe**
Re-booting the state
Edited by Paul G. Nixon and Vassiliki N. Koutrakou

43 **EU Foreign and Interior Policies**
Cross-pillar politics and the social construction of sovereignty
Stephan Stetter

44 **Policy Transfer in European Union Governance**
Regulating the utilities
Simon Bulmer, David Dolowitz, Peter Humphreys and Stephen Padgett

45 **The Europeanization of National Political Parties**
Power and organizational adaptation
Edited by Thomas Poguntke, Nicholas Aylott, Elisabeth Carter, Robert Ladrech and Kurt Richard Luther

46 **Citizenship in Nordic Welfare States**
Dynamics of choice, duties and participation in a changing Europe
Edited by Bjørn Hvinden and Håkan Johansson

47 **National Parliaments within the Enlarged European Union**
From victims of integration to competitive actors?
Edited by John O'Brennan and Tapio Raunio

48 **Britain, Ireland and Northern Ireland since 1980**
The totality of relationships
Eamonn O'Kane

49 **The EU and the European Security Strategy**
Forging a global Europe
Edited by Sven Biscop and Jan Joel Andersson

50 **European Security and Defence Policy**
An implementation perspective
Edited by Michael Merlingen and Rasa Ostrauskaitė

51 **Women and British Party Politics**
Descriptive, substantive and symbolic representation
Sarah Childs

52 **The Selection of Ministers in Europe**
Hiring and firing
Edited by Keith Dowding and Patrick Dumont

53 **Energy Security**
Europe's new foreign policy challenge
Richard Youngs

54 **Institutional Challenges in Post-Constitutional Europe**
Governing change
Edited by Catherine Moury and Luís de Sousa

55 **The Struggle for the European Constitution**
A past and future history
Michael O'Neill

56 **Transnational Labour Solidarity**
Mechanisms of commitment to cooperation within the European Trade Union Movement
Katarzyna Gajewska

57 **The Illusion of Accountability in the European Union**
Edited by Sverker Gustavsson, Christer Karlsson, and Thomas Persson

58 **The European Union and Global Social Change**
A critical geopolitical-economic analysis
József Böröcz

59 **Citizenship and Collective Identity in Europe**
Ireneusz Pawel Karolewski

60 **EU Enlargement and Socialization**
Turkey and Cyprus
Stefan Engert

61 **The Politics of EU Accession**
Turkish challenges and Central European experiences
Edited by Lucie Tunkrová and Pavel Šaradín

62 **The Political History of European Integration**
The hypocrisy of democracy-through-market
Hagen Schulz-Forberg and Bo Stråth

63 **The Spatialities of Europeanization**
Power, governance and territory in Europe
Alun Jones and Julian Clark

64 **European Union Sanctions and Foreign Policy**
When and why do they work?
Clara Portela

65 **The EU's Role in World Politics**
A retreat from liberal internationalism
Richard Youngs

66 **Social Democracy and European Integration**
The politics of preference formation
Edited by Dionyssis Dimitrakopoulos

67 **The EU Presence in International Organizations**
Edited by Spyros Blavoukos and Dimitris Bourantonis

68 **Sustainability in European Environmental Policy**
Challenge of governance and knowledge
Edited by Rob Atkinson, Georgios Terizakis and Karsten Zimmermann

69 **Fifty Years of EU–Turkey Relations**
A Sisyphean story
Edited by Armagan Emre Çakir

70 **Europeanization and Foreign Policy**
State diversity in Finland and Britain
Juha Jokela

71 **EU Foreign Policy and Post-Soviet Conflicts**
Stealth intervention
Nicu Popescu

72 **Switzerland in Europe**
Continuity and change in the Swiss political economy
Edited by Christine Trampusch and André Mach

73 **The Political Economy of Noncompliance**
Adjusting to the single European Market
Scott Nicholas Siegel

74 **National and European Foreign Policy**
Towards Europeanization
Edited by Reuben Wong and Christopher Hill

75 **The European Union Diplomatic Service**
Ideas, preferences and identities
Caterina Carta

76 **Poland within the European Union**
New awkward partner or new heart of Europe?
Aleks Szczerbiak

77 **A Political Theory of Identity in European Integration**
Memory and policies
Catherine Guisan

78 **EU Foreign Policy and the Europeanization of Neutral States**
Comparing Irish and Austrian foreign policy
Nicole Alecu de Flers

79 **Party System Change in Western Europe**
Gemma Loomes

80 **The Second Tier of Local Government in Europe**
Provinces, counties, départements and Landkreise in comparison
Hubert Heinelt and Xavier Bertrana Horta

81 **Learning from the EU Constitutional Treaty**
Democratic constitutionalism beyond the nation-state
Ben Crum

82 **Human Rights and Democracy in EU Foreign Policy**
The cases of Ukraine and Egypt
Rosa Balfour

83 **Europeanization, Integration and Identity**
A social constructivist fusion perspective on Norway
Gamze Tanil

84 **The Impact of European Integration on Political Parties**
Beyond the permissive consensus
Dimitri Almeida

85 **Civic Resources and the Future of the European Union**
Victoria Kaina and Ireneusz Pawel Karolewski

86 **The Europeanization of National Foreign Policies towards Latin America**
Lorena Ruano

87 **The EU and Multilateral Security Governance**
Sonia Lucarelli, Luk Van Langenhove and Jan Wouters

88 **Security Challenges in the Euro-Med Area in the 21st Century**
Mare Nostrum
Stephen Calleya

89 **Society and Democracy in Europe**
Oscar W. Gabriel and Silke Keil

90 **European Union Public Health Policy**
Regional and global trends
Edited by Scott L. Greer and Paulette Kurzer

91 **The New Member States and the European Union**
Foreign policy and Europeanization
Edited by Michael Baun and Dan Marek

92 **The Politics of Ratification of EU Treaties**
Carlos Closa

93 **Europeanization and New Member States**
A comparative social network analysis
Flavia Jurje

94 **National Perspectives on Russia**
European foreign policy in the making
Maxine David, Jackie Gower and Hiski Haukkala

95 **Institutional Legacies of Communism**
Change and continuities in minority protection
Edited by Karl Cordell, Timofey Agarin and Alexander Osipov

96 **Sustainable Development and Governance in Europe**
The evolution of the discourse on sustainability
Edited by Pamela M. Barnes and Thomas C. Hoerber

97 **Social Networks and Public Support for the European Union**
Elizabeth Radziszewski

98 **The EU's Democracy Promotion and the Mediterranean Neighbours**
Orientation, ownership and dialogue in Jordan and Turkey
Ann-Kristin Jonasson

99 **New Democracies in Crisis?**
A comparative constitutional study of the Czech Republic, Hungary, Poland, Romania and Slovakia
Paul Blokker

100 **Party Attitudes Towards the EU in the Member States**
Parties for Europe, parties against Europe
Nicolò Conti

101 **The European Union and Occupied Palestinian Territories**
State-building without a state
Dimitris Bouris

102 **Portugal in the European Union**
Assessing twenty-five years of integration experience
Laura C. Ferreira-Pereira

103 **Governance and European Civil Society**
Governmentality, discourse and NGOs
Acar Kutay

104 **The EU, Migration and the Politics of Administrative Detention**
Edited by Michela Ceccorulli and Nicola Labanca

105 **Political Representation in the European Union**
Still democratic in times of crisis?
Edited by Sandra Kröger

Political Representation in the European Union

Still democratic in times of crisis?

Edited by Sandra Kröger

Routledge
Taylor & Francis Group
LONDON AND NEW YORK

First published 2014
by Routledge
2 Park Square, Milton Park, Abingdon, Oxon OX14 4RN

and by Routledge
711 Third Avenue, New York, NY 10017

First issued in paperback 2016

Routledge is an imprint of the Taylor & Francis Group, an informa business

British Library Cataloguing in Publication Data
A catalogue record for this book is available from the British Library

Library of Congress Cataloging in Publication Data
Political representation in the European Union: democracy in a time of crisis / edited by Sandra Kröger.
pages cm. – (Routledge advances in European politics)
Includes bibliographical references and index.
Representative government and representation–European Union countries. 2. European Union countries–Politics and government–21st century. 3. Global Financial Crisis, 2008–2009–Political aspects–European Union countries. I. Kröger, Sandra, author, editor of compilation.
JN30.P644 2014
341.242'22 -dc23 2013040175

ISBN13: 978-0-415-83514-5 (hbk)
ISBN13: 978-1-138-68353-2 (pbk)

Typeset in Times New Roman
by Wearset Ltd, Boldon, Tyne and Wear

Contents

Contributors

Dario Castiglione is Reader in Political Theory at the University of Exeter. He is currently one of the editors of the ECPR Press. His main research interests are theories of democracy and constitutionalism, with particular application to the European integration process, and the history of political thought. He has held visiting positions at various international institutions, including Georgetown University (Washington, DC), the New School of Research (New York), the University of Turin (where he was the Gaetano Mosca Chair for 2008) and Australian National University (ANU) (Canberra). He has been involved in and directed numerous Europe-wide research projects funded by the EC and the Economic and Social Research Council (ESRC). His recent publications include, as co-author, *Constitutional Politics in the EU* (Palgrave, 2007); and as co-editor, *The Handbook of Social Capital* (OUP, 2008), *The Language Question in Europe and Diverse Societies* (Hart Publishers, 2007), *The Making of European Citizens* (Palgrave, 2006) and *The History of Political Thought in National Context* (CUP, 2001).

Michelle Everson is LLB (Exeter) and PhD (EUI, Florence), and is Professor of European Law in the School of Law, Birkbeck College, University of London. She sits on the editorial boards of *Law and Critique* and the *Journal for Socio-Legal Studies*; and was Vice-Chair of the Academic Board for Social Sciences of the Austrian Academy of Sciences. She has researched widely in the field of European law and has particular interests in the areas of European regulatory law, European administrative and constitutional law and European citizenship. She has published widely on constitutionalism (see *The Making of the European Constitution: Judges and Lawyers Beyond Constitutive Power*, with Julia Eisner (Routledge-Cavendish, 2007)), as well as economic law (see 'The fault of (European) law in (social and political) economic crisis', *Law & Critique*, 2013, 24:59) and citizenship (see 'A very cosmopolitan citizenship; but who pays the price?', in Michael Dougan, Niamh Nic Shuibhne and Eleanor Spaventa (eds), *Empowerment and Disempowerment of the European Citizen* (Hart Publishing, 2012)).

John Erik Fossum is Professor of Political Science at ARENA, the Centre for European Studies at the University of Oslo. His main fields of interest include political theory, democracy and constitutionalism in the EU and Canada, Europeanization and transformation of the nation state. Fossum was co-architect behind, and substitute coordinator for, the FP6-funded Integrated Project Reconstituting Democracy in Europe (RECON) (2007–2011). Recent publications include *The European Union and the Public Sphere*, co-edited with Philip Schlesinger (Routledge, 2008); 'The multilevel parliamentary field – a framework for theorizing representative democracy in the EU', with Ben Crum, in *European Political Science Review* (2009); *The Constitution's Gift: A Constitutional Theory for the European Union*, with Agustín J. Menéndez (Rowman & Littlefield, 2011); *Law and Democracy in Neil MacCormick's Legal and Political Theory*, co-edited with Agustín José Menéndez (Springer, 2011); *Rethinking Democracy and the European Union*, co-edited with Erik Oddvar Eriksen (Routledge, 2012); and *Practices of Inter-Parliamentary Coordination in International Politics – The European Union and Beyond*, co-edited with Ben Crum (ECPR Press, 2013).

Dawid Friedrich is Senior Lecturer at the Center for the Study of Democracy at the Leuphana University Lüneburg, Germany. He studied Political Science, Social Work and European Social Policy at the Universities of Tübingen (Germany) and Bath (UK) and obtained his doctoral degree at the Bremen International Graduate School of Social Sciences (BIGSSS), University of Bremen (Germany). His research interests cover different empirical and normative aspects of European and global democracy, the relation of law and politics and questions of postnational personal rights and citizenship. Recent publications include *Democratic Participation and Civil Society in the European Union* (Manchester University Press, 2011); 'Transnational civil society and the European Union', in David Bailey and Uwe Wunderlich (eds) *The European Union and Global Governance – A Handbook* (Routledge, 2011); and 'Partizipatives Regieren in der EU. Die EU zwischen "laissez-faire" und geregelter Partizipation zivilgesellschaftlicher Akteure', in *Zeitschrift für Internationale Beziehungen* (2008) 2: 209–235.

Christian Joerges holds a part-time senior professorship at the Hertie School of Governance in Berlin and is a Research Professor at the Law Faculty of Bremen University and Co-director of the Centre of European Law and Politics. Until 2007 he held the chair for European Economic Law at the European University Institute Florence. He was Visiting Professor at various law faculties in the US and Europe and Fellow at the Institutes for Advanced Study in Wassenaar, the Netherlands, and Berlin. In 2009 he obtained an Honorary Doctoral Degree in Law from the University of Fribourg, Switzerland. His research deals with the Europeanization of private and economic law, transnational risk regulation governance structures, constitutionalism in the post-national constellation and anti-liberal traditions of German legal thought. His collection *Darker Legacies of Law in Europe* (co-editor Navraj Ghaleigh, 2003) received 28 reviews, and some of his own essays have been published in other languages. Recent publications include *Karl Polanyi, Globalisation and the Potential of Law in Transnational Markets*, co-editor Josef Falke (Hart Publishing, 2011); *Constitutionalism, Multilevel Trade Governance and International Economic Law*, co-editor Ernst Ulrich Petersmann (Hart Publishing, 2011); and the anthology *Jürgen Habermas*, co-editors Klaus Günther and Camil Ungureanu (Ashgate, 2011).

Beate Kohler-Koch is Professor Emeritus, University of Mannheim and project director at the Mannheim Centre for European Social Research (MZES). She has initiated and coordinated large national and European research programmes focusing on European governance. In recent years her research has concentrated on civil society and democracy in the EU and she now focuses on EU lobbying. She is author and editor of numerous publications including: *De-Mystification of Participatory Democracy: EU Governance and Civil Society*, with C. Quittkat (Oxford University Press, 2013); *European Multi-Level Governance: Contrasting Images in National Research*, with F. Larat (Edward Elgar, 2009); *Changing Images of Civil Society: From Protest to Governance*, with B. Jobert (Routledge, 2008); *EU Governance Model*, with H. Zhou (in Chinese: Social Sciences Academic Press, 2008); and *Debating the Democratic Legitimacy of the European Union*, with B. Rittberger (Rowman & Littlefield, 2007). She has held numerous academic positions; among others she was Chairwoman of the German Political Science Association. She is Honorary Professor at Nankai University, China, and doctor honoris causa at Oslo University (2008) and Maastricht University (2011). In 2009, she was presented the award for Lifetime Achievement in Contemporary European Studies by the University Association for Contemporary European Studies (UACES), and in 2011 she received the THESEUS Award for Outstanding Research on European Integration. In 1996 she was honoured with membership of the Berlin–Brandenburg Akademie der Wissenschaften.

Sandra Kröger is Lecturer at the Politics Department of the University of Exeter. She holds degrees in social sciences (Humboldt University of Berlin, Paris VIII) and interdisciplinary French studies (University of Freiburg) and obtained her PhD at the University of Göttingen. From 2008–2011, she was Lecturer at the Jean Monnet Center for European Studies (CEuS) at the University of Bremen, and from 2011–2013 a Marie Curie Fellow at Exeter. Her current research interests include the ways civil society organizations construct and organize political representation across the different levels of governance as well as national parliaments in EU policy-making. Recent publications include: 'Representation and democracy in the EU: does one come at the expense of the other?', a special issue of the *Journal of European Integration*, co-edited with R. Bellamy (2013) 35(5); 'Creating a European demos? The representativeness of European umbrella organizations', *Journal of European Integration* (2013) 35(5): 583–600; 'Democratic representation in the EU: two kinds of subjectivity', with D. Friedrich in *Journal of*

European Public Policy (2013) 20(2): 171–189; *Representation in the European Union: Coping with Present Challenges to Democracy?* co-edited with D. Friedrich (Palgrave Macmillan, 2012); she also edited 'What we have learnt: advances, pitfalls and remaining questions in OMC research', *European Integration Online Papers* (2009), vol. 13, special issue 1.

Gert-Jan Lindeboom is researcher at Panteia, the Netherlands. He holds a cum laude research Master's degree in Political Science from Leiden University, and has published articles on political representation and interest group politics. For Panteia, he has been involved in several Europe-wide research projects, working for the European Parliament, the European Commission and European agencies, primarily in the field of education, labour market and HR policies.

Martino Maggetti (PhD, University of Lausanne) is a lecturer at the Institut für Politikwissenschaft (University of Zürich) and senior researcher at the Institut d'Études Politiques et Internationales (University of Lausanne). He is teaching Comparative Regulatory Governance and Comparative Public Policy at the University of Zürich. His research interests focus on public policy, public administration, regulatory governance and comparative politics. His main research project is currently 'The democratic accountability of transnational private governance', funded by the Swiss National Center of Competence in Research (NCCR) Democracy. His latest books are *Regulation in Practice* (ECPR Press, 2012) and *Designing Research in the Social Sciences*, with Fabrizio Gilardi and Claudio M. Radaelli (Sage, 2012).

Daniel Naurin is Associate Professor of Political Science at the University of Gothenburg. He has previously been a research fellow at the European University Institute (EUI, Florence), Sussex European Institute (UK), Monash European Centre (Melbourne) and the Swedish Institute of International Affairs (Stockholm). His current research projects deal with judicial politics in the EU, negotiations in the EU Council of Ministers, the effects of transparency on decision-making and legitimacy, lobbying and interest group populations in Sweden and Europe. Recent publications include 'The effect of co-decision on council decision-making', with F. Häge in *Journal of European Public Policy* (2013); 'When does transparency generate legitimacy?', with J. de Fine Licht *et al.* in *Governance* (2013); 'Out in the cold? Flexible integration and the political status of Euro opt outs', with R. Lindahl (which received the Sage Award for best article published in *European Union Politics*, Vol. 11, 2010); and 'Most common when least important? Deliberation in the EU Council of Ministers', in *British Journal of Political Science* (2010).

Nieves Pérez-Solórzano Borragán is Senior Lecturer in European Politics at the School of Sociology, Politics and International Relations at the University of Bristol. Her research examines the involvement of civil society and interest groups in EU governance in the context of wider debates on participatory and deliberative democracy. She has written extensively on the impact of EU membership on civil society in the new member states from Central and Eastern Europe and on aspects of interest group participation at EU level. She is co-editor (with Michelle Cini) of *European Union Politics* (Oxford University Press, 2003).

Simona Piattoni is Professor of Political Science at the University of Trento. She holds a PhD from the Massachusetts Institute of Technology, Cambridge, USA. She was European Forum Fellow at the EUI (1999–2001) and is currently Chair of the European Consortium for Political Research (ECPR). Her research focuses on clientelism, Italy in the EU, and multilevel governance. Recent publications include *Clientelism, Interests and Democratic Representation: The European Experience in Historical and Comparative Perspective*, edited (Cambridge University Press, 2001); *Italy in the European Union: Redefining National Interest in a Compound Polity*, co-edited with S. Fabbrini (Rowman & Littlefield, 2008); *Between Europeanization and Local Societies: The Space for Territorial Governance*, co-edited with J. Bukowski and M. Smyrl (Rowman & Littlefield, 2003); and *The Theory of Multi-Level Governance: Conceptual, Empirical, and Normative Challenges* (Oxford University Press, 2010).

Johannes Pollak is Professor at Webster University, Vienna and Head of the Political Science Department at the Institute for Advanced Studies in Vienna. In addition he is a lecturer at the universities of Vienna and Salzburg. Trained as a political scientist in Vienna and the London School of Economics and Political Science, Pollak received a postgraduate degree at the Institute for Higher Studies, and was a Jean Monnet Fellow at the Schuman Centre for Advanced Studies at the EUI, Florence, a Leverhulme Fellow at the University of Reading, UK, and Senior Visiting Research Fellow at the LSE. He has participated in a number of international research projects (e.g. CIDEL, RECON, CONNEX) and supervizes PhD students from various universities. His research focus is devoted to parliamentarism beyond the nation state, theories of political representation and European energy policy. Recent publications include 'The silence of the shepherds: the communication function of national parliaments', in *Journal of Legislative Studies*, 2013; 'Unequal but democratic? Equality according to Karlsruhe', with C. Lord in *Journal of European Public Policy*, 2012/13; 'Representation and accountability: communicating tubes?', with C. Lord in *West European Politics*, 33(5), 968–988, 2010; 'The EU's many representative modes: Colluding? Cohering?', with C. Lord in *Journal of European Public Policy*, 17(1), 117–136, 2010; 'Contested meanings of representation', in *Journal for Comparative Politics*, 5(1), 87–103, 2007.

Anne Rasmussen is Professor at the Department of Political Science at the University of Copenhagen and is affiliated to the Department of Public Administration of Leiden University. Previously, she has been Lecturer at the

University of Leiden, Fellow at the Montesquieu Institute since 2010 and a Max Weber Fellow at the European University Institute in Florence from 2006 to 2008. She has also been a Senior Honorary Research Fellow at University College London, Visiting Scholar at George Washington University, and a Centennial Fellow at the American Political Science Association in Washington, DC. Her current research analyses decision-making, political parties, interest representation and political responsiveness in the European Union and its member states. Furthermore, she has a strong interest in research design and methodology as well as in the US political system. Recent publications include a co-edited special issue of *West European Politics*, 2011, 34(1), entitled 'Linking inter- and intrainstitutional change in the European Union', and the following articles: 'Interest group – party interaction in EU politics' in *Party Politics*, 2012, 18(1), and 'Foreign interests lobbying Brussels: participation of non-EU members in Commission consultations', with Petya Alexandrova in *Journal of Common Market Studies*, 2012, 50(4).

Stijn Smismans is Professor of European Law and Governance at the Law School of Cardiff University and Director of the Cardiff Jean Monnet Centre of Excellence. He holds a PhD from the European University Institute, was Jean Monnet Fellow at the Robert Schuman Centre of the EUI, Marie Curie Fellow at the Institut d'Études Politiques in Paris and Lecturer and Researcher at the Faculty of Sociology of the University of Trento. He has worked on research projects financed by the European Commission, the European Foundation for Living and Working Conditions, the European Economic and Social Committee, and the Italian Ministry for University Education and Research. Publications include *Law, Legitimacy and European Governance* (OUP, 2004); *Civil Society and Legitimate European Governance* (edited) (Edward Elgar, 2006); *The European Union and Industrial Relations* (edited) (MUP, 2012), 'European civil society and citizenship: complementary or exclusionary concepts?' (*Policy & Society*, 2009), 'New modes of governance and the participatory myth' (*West European Politics*, 2008).

Hans-Jörg Trenz is Professor in Modern European Studies at University of Copenhagen and adjunct professor at ARENA, Centre for European Studies at the University of Oslo, where he coordinates research on political communication, public sphere and democracy in the context of European integration. He attained his habilitation at Humboldt University Berlin and a PhD in social and political sciences at the European University Institute in Florence. His main research interests are in the areas of media, communication and the public sphere, civil society, European civilization and identity, migration and ethnic minorities, cultural and political sociology, social and political theory, democracy and constitutionalism in the European Union. His main publications include *Online Euroscepticism: Contesting EU Legitimacy in 2009 European Parliament Election Campaigns*, with Pieter de Wilde and Asimina Michailidou (ECPR Press, 2013); *The Politicization of the European Union:*

Contesting European Integration and Democracy in Public Spheres, with Paul Statham (Routledge, 2012); *The New Politics of European Civil Society*, with Ulrike Liebert; (Routledge, 2010); and *Europa in den Medien. Die europäische Integrationsprojekt im Spiegel nationaler Öffentlichkeit* (Campus, 2005).

Acknowledgements

This book would not have seen the daylight without a number of people whom I would wish to thank, and institutional support that I would like to acknowledge. First, I would like to thank the authors for their dedication to this publication project and the timely delivery of the chapters, which rendered the editorial work as easy as it gets. Second, I would like to acknowledge the financial support of the EU Jean Monnet programme (Grant decision no. 2011–2915/199856), without which I could not have organized a conference that provided the opportunity to discuss first drafts and ideas of the present chapters; the book benefited substantially from the respective discussions. I also gratefully acknowledge the support of a Marie Curie Intra European Fellowship within the Seventh European Community Framework Programme (Grant Agreement Number: PIEF-GA-2010–273514). Third, I am grateful for all the gentle and helpful support that Routledge has given me throughout the publication process. Finally, I would wish to thank a number of people that helped to realize this project at different stages: thanks to Dario Castiglione for help with the organization of the conference and with the original book proposal; to Fiona Raffael for invaluable administrative support before and during the conference; to Katherine Berrisford and Stuart Ingham for proof-reading and editorial work; and to Richard Bellamy for continued feedback, support and encouragement throughout the entire publication project.

Abbreviations

CESR	Committee of European Securities Regulators
CFSP	Common Foreign and Security Policy
CJEU	Court of Justice of the European Union
COPA-COGECA	Committee of Professional Agricultural Organisations and General Confederation of Agricultural Cooperatives
CoR	Committee of the Regions
COSAC	Conférences des Organes Spécialisés dans les Affaires Communautaires (Conference of Community and European Affairs Committees)
CSO	Civil society organization
EAC	European Affairs Committees
ECI	European Citizens' Initiative
EEB	European Environmental Bureau
EFSF	European Financial Stability Facility
EP	European Parliament
ERN	European regulatory network
ERT	European Round Table of Industrialists
ESM	European Stability Mechanism
ESMA	European Securities and Markets Authority
ESRB	European Systemic Risk Board
EU	European Union
FCC	Federal Constitutional Court (Germany)
IPEX	Interparliamentary Information Exchange
NP	National parliament
OHIM	Office for Harmonisation in the Internal Market
QMV	Qualified majority voting
SNA	Subnational authority
TEU	Treaty of the European Union
TFEU	Treaty on the Functioning of the European Union
TSCG	Treaty on Stability, Coordination and Governance
WTO	World Trade Organization

Introduction

The search for democratic representation in times of crisis

Sandra Kröger

Standard accounts of political representation have described and justified democratic political representation in nation states, particularly if not exclusively under the assumption of perfecting its territorially based electoral forms. Democratic representation in the context of nation states was to be realized through two institutions: (1) regular, free and fair elections, based on the rule of one-person-one-vote, which expresses the norm of political equality, and (2) a representative government that follows from the results of these elections, and which publicly aggregates societal interests into a political programme. Elections in this model serve as the start and end points of democratic representation: through them, the represented authorize their representatives and hold the latter to account. Normatively, electoral cycles imply that power is conditional, and that its abuse can be sanctioned. Democratic representation has been understood as a way of establishing the legitimacy of representative institutions and of creating institutional incentives for governments to be responsive to citizens. Representative government so conceived has been a practically feasible and normatively justifiable version of democracy (Hobson 2008: 451).

Indeed, by and large it is accepted today that political representation is a *sine qua non* for the legitimacy of any democratic political system, that representation is the most appropriate means to serve the goal of political equality and to render the exercise of political authority legitimate. Conceptually and empirically, however, this link is not self-evident: 'Through much of their history both the concept and the practice of representation have had little to do with democracy or liberty' (Pitkin 1967: 2). Instead, the close linkage of representation with democracy was a product of contingent historical developments, more specifically of the gradual emergence of territorially confined nation states. The American and French Revolutions offered the intellectual and political context in which democratic government came to be envisioned and institutionalized as representative government (Urbinati 2004; Hobson 2008).

It now seems that contemporary democracies are evolving in ways that increasingly undermine the adequacy of this standard model. Contemporary politics is increasingly defined by transnational arenas such as the European Union (EU) or the World Trade Organization (WTO), where new regional, international and global players operate outside of the reach of territorially defined democratic representation. Similarly, the number of issues that are non-territorial (or trans-territorial) in nature is ever increasing. Moreover, collective decision-making at both the national and the supranational level is increasingly under the control of specialized and expert bodies, with loose connections to the traditional institutions of political representation (Warren and Castiglione 2004; Kröger and Friedrich 2012). In the EU, the relationship between representation and (national) democracy is particularly challenged (Bellamy and Kröger 2013), given the number of competences that have been transferred to it, and given its densely structured multi-level politics, both of which weaken the ability of national democracies to keep decision-making authority in their hands.

Indeed, European integration brings about a transformation of political authority by which the state loses its monopoly on collectively binding decision-making. The result is a transformation of national sovereignty which is occurring empirically, and which scholars are struggling to come to terms with conceptually. Since it took on its modern meaning, national sovereignty provided an account of legitimate rule, within a confined territory and associated to defined functions, in which political authority was 'singular and supreme' (Goodhart 2007: 573). What scholars are struggling with, then, is to detach the notion of sovereignty – and thereby representation – from boundaries that bind together territory, *demos* and the idea of righteous rule of that *demos* within those defined boundaries, leading some to speak of 'methodological nationalism' (Zürn 2000) that does not question the Westphalian state as its point of departure when thinking of normative democratic standards today.

This introduction – indeed, this volume – cannot go into all the issues involved when we speak about representation and democracy in the EU (see: Kröger 2014). Instead, it will focus on two axes of representation – that of channels and that of levels of representation – which, taken together, seem to be the main axes that scholars are interested in when thinking about democratic representation in the EU.

Democratic representation in the EU

Representation is also a central concept in the way in which the EU understands its democratic legitimacy. In Title II on 'Provisions on Democratic Principles', the Lisbon Treaty highlights two key principles. First, Article 9 states the normative basis for democracy in the EU, namely political equality. Second, Article 10 asserts 'the functioning of the Union shall be founded on representative democracy'. Thus, political equality and representative democracy are the self-proclaimed democratic 'meta-standards' of the EU (Lord and Pollak 2010: 126). More concretely, the Treaty stipulates in Title II, Article 10:

1 The functioning of the Union shall be founded on representative democracy.
2 Citizens are directly represented at Union level in the European Parliament. Member States are represented in the European Council by their Heads of State or Government and in the Council by their governments, themselves

democratically accountable either to their national Parliaments, or to their citizens.

3 Every citizen shall have the right to participate in the democratic life of the Union. Decisions shall be taken as openly and as closely as possible to the citizen.

4 Political parties at European level contribute to forming European political awareness and to expressing the will of citizens of the Union.

In Article 11, the Lisbon Treaty states that the European institutions shall give citizens and associations 'the opportunity to make known and publicly exchange their views in all areas of Union action' and to maintain a regular and open dialogue with them. It also introduces the European Citizen Initiative whereby a group of at least a million EU citizens may petition the European Commission to further actions that fall within its competences. The Lisbon Treaty thus distinguishes at least four different channels of representation (see Kröger and Friedrich 2013).

Electoral forms of representation and the democratic crisis of the EU

More often than not, for a few years now, people have been speaking of a debt, Euro and/or financial crisis of the EU. However, by now it seems clear that what originally may have been a financial and economic crisis in 2008–9, has meantime turned into an equally important political and democratic crisis of the EU. For sure, many have contemplated the democratic quality of the EU ever since the Maastricht Treaty, and have found it to be deficient, particularly if assessed against standards of democracy developed in nation states. However, the financial and economic crisis that has strained the EU since 2008–9 has accentuated and made fully evident the deficits and incoherence of the EU's system of representation. To address how far the crisis has affected different actors of political representation in the EU is one of the main goals of this book.

Indeed, the primary representative institutions – parliaments and political parties – have been quite sidelined in the handling of the crisis (see the contributions by Pollak, Rasmussen and Lindeboom, and Fossum to this volume respectively). As is known from the literature, parliaments do not have a direct influence over the European agenda, they cannot initiate legislation, and their powers more generally seem to be weakened. Not surprisingly, the 1990s witnessed the emergence of a 'deparliamentarisation' thesis (Raunio and Hix 2000). This thesis seeks to capture the transfer of policy-making powers to the EU and the resulting loss of power and influence of domestic parliaments as well as the strengthening of executives in EU policy-making, which results in informational asymmetries between the legislature and the executive (Auel and Benz 2005: 373; Raunio and Hix 2000: 145). As a result, national parliaments have no direct control over European policy-making and 'suffer from a lack of authoritative power over transnational policymaking' (Schmidt 1999: 25). Instead, executives have become the 'gatekeepers' in EU policy-making. National parliaments (NPs) have, therefore, often been called the main 'losers' of European integration (Maurer and Wessels 2001; Bellamy and Kröger 2012).

As a reaction to some of the shortcomings of NPs in EU policy-making, NPs are mentioned in the main text of the Treaty for the first time, thereby continuing a trend going back to the Maastricht Treaty and the debate on the EU's democratic deficit, which have seen the empowerment of NPs in EU affairs as one possible mechanism for tackling this issue. Most notably, Article 12 now details the basic rights and functions of NPs in EU matters and introduces an 'Early Warning Mechanism' (EWM), which assigns national legislatures the right to scrutinize proposed EU decisions and initiatives for compliance with the principles of subsidiarity and proportionality. Furthermore, NPs can have a collective legislative influence, in that a majority of them may force, by way of a so-called 'orange card', an early vote on an EU legislative proposal in the Council and the EP (European Parliament). They are also now involved in evaluating measures taken within the area of freedom, security and justice (Articles 70, 85, 88), may block Treaty changes under the simplified revision procedures (Article 48) and must be informed of new applications to join the EU (Article 49). NPs have therefore become actors in their own right in EU policy-making.

And still, the deparliamentarization thesis has found new support through the transfer of some budgetary competences from NPs to the European Commission in the context of the crisis management. The latter now can assess the budgetary plans of governments and may ask for amendments even before they are discussed in parliament, which is a major intrusion into the primary competence of NPs, i.e. competence over the national budget. This is particularly worrying as the Commission's decisions are dominated by quasi-automatic rules set by the Commission itself in close collaboration with another non-elected institution, the European Central Bank. Whilst most Member States' parliaments had to approve of governmental responses to the crisis (with the few exceptions of those Member States where a referendum had to be held), discussion of political alternatives was by-and-large sealed off with the all too simple 'argument' that there 'is no alternative' to what was being proposed (Puntscher Riekman and Wydra 2013), thereby also sidelining political parties competing for power by offering political alternatives. The EP has been completely sidelined in the crisis management. Whilst there is a Euro Group working in the Council, this group has no counterpart in the EP. In fact, there has been almost no word from the EP on the crisis since it first began.

The contribution by Johannes Pollak (Chapter 1) deals particularly with NPs and their potential role and actual delivery in EU policy-making, in particular in regard to the handling of the Euro debt and the financial crisis. Pollak's conclusion is that whilst NPs 'have new instruments at their disposal, those seem to be rather unused'. This is particularly astonishing given that budget policy is the core policy of NPs and that the EU's handling of the crisis needed ratification by NPs – one could have therefore expected them to have played a key role. However, and amazingly, NPs 'do not seem to have been overly concerned about this loss of sovereignty'. Pollak concludes that NPs did not take seriously 'their role of representing those who are most affected by the crisis', and accountability mechanisms also do not seem to function properly. As a consequence, in the context of the Euro debt and financial crisis, 'citizens' capacity to determine their own laws via representatives is thereby undermined'.

In another way, the contribution by Anne Rasmussen and Gert-Jan Lindeboom (Chapter 2) also deals with the electoral channel of representation at the domestic level by addressing the Europeanization of national parties. The authors first discuss the different ways Europeanization can affect national parties in order to then assess parties' interaction with interest groups in the domestic sphere and ask whether this interaction is different at the national level from the European level. Their findings suggest that 'the focus of national parties on interaction with interest groups in areas of EU policy remains marginal despite the increased transfer of national competences to the EU level'. In fact, national members of parliament (MPs) 'purposively limit their interest group contacts in EU policy' because of their interest in *votes* and *office*. And in order to be (re-)elected, say the authors, what domestic politicians need is to be able to show achievements in domestic policies, rather than in the lowly politicized and often unpopular EU policies. Therefore, the stimuli to cooperate with groups in the context of EU policies, which the authors expect theoretically, is not found empirically. The contribution finally reflects that even in the context of the economic and financial crisis, NPs were not inclined to further Europeanize their activities in general or their links with interest groups in particular, as doing so would illuminate the misfit that 'risks manifesting itself between the activities and policies of domestic actors and those of the EU' – overall, a significant problem for domestic political parties in the EU, as the authors conclude.

The European Parliament (EP) is of course the other main channel of electoral representation in the EU. Universal suffrage in the elections for the EP is valid for all who possess EU citizenship, in both other Member States and their own. Yet, not every vote counts equally in EP elections. For instance, the Luxemburgian vote counts for about 80 times more than the German vote. This deviation from a strictly proportionate distribution of seats reflects the principle of 'degressive proportionality', with a minimum threshold of six seats for the smallest Member State and a maximum of 96 for the largest (Art. 14.2 TEU). The official rationality behind this arrangement has been to ensure that the range of political opinion found in even the less populous Member State gets represented. Unlike NPs, the EP does not possess the right to initiate legislative proposals that originate in the European Commission. Co-decision procedures with the Council of the EU over these proposals is the rule by now.

The contribution by John Erik Fossum (Chapter 3) in particular addresses the EP, but also the structure of electoral representation in the EU more generally, and how it has been affected by the current crisis. Fossum lays out the in-built tension in the EU's system of representation between intergovernmentalism and supranationalism. Because of this unique construction, he argues in favour of different standards for representation for the EU than those we know from the domestic sphere and holds that the process of continued constituency-building and constitutionalization holds both risks – such manipulation and blame-shifting – and opportunities – such increased deliberative spaces. He concludes that whilst the crisis seems to render inter-parliamentary coordination more relevant, at the same time it 'appears to have greatly weakened parliaments in relation to executives' and therefore also weakened 'and perhaps even undercut the process of EU democratisation'. In contrast, experts and intergovernmentalism have been strengthened, and the overall complexity of political representation has been increased through even greater differentiation, which is why one of the main challenges now would be to pay 'systematic attention to the democratic implications of increased differentiation'.

If parliaments have been weakened, then because in this situation of crisis, the EU has opted in favour of a depoliticized, technocratic and more intergovernmental form of governance (see in particular Chapter 7 in this volume: Borragán and Smismans). Intergovernmental governance has been strengthened by moving from the 'community method' to what German chancellor Merkel has called the 'Union method', which puts national governments centre-stage. However, not all governments have been on an equal footing in the handling of the crisis. Rather, Germany (and, to a lesser degree, France) has dominated fiscal policy over the last few years, whilst Greece in particular, and to a lesser degree other Southern Member States and Ireland too, were forced to accept the austerity measures that the German Chancellor was and remains so keen on. National governments, specifically those of the highly indebted states, have proved powerless to change the underlying fiscal approach that has been decided in Berlin and Frankfurt. Technocratic governance has been increased by creating the Frankfurt Group and letting it become the main driving body of fiscal policy as well as by supporting the establishment of technocratic governments in both Italy and Greece. A consequence of a politics that is moving towards technocratic governance is that political alternatives are hardly present at the EU level, as effectively as has been the case in Member States. Indeed, the notion of opposition does not even exist with the Union, implying that citizens do not feel that they can change the direction of policy.

In contrast to parliaments, Member States have seen their role increased in the context of crisis management and its drift towards more intergovernmental forms of cooperation. Their representation materializes mainly through the Council of the EU and the European Council. The European Council brings together heads of state or government. It does not legislate but 'defines the general political directions and priorities' of the EU (Treaty of the European Union, art. 15, para. 1). As such, it has become the main agenda-setter of the EU in the recent past – as well as the 'default crisis manager of the EU' (Daniel Naurin, Chapter 4 in this volume). The Council of the EU meets in diverse sectoral configurations, bringing together the respective ministers of national governments. It is the main European legislator, even though most laws are now passed under the co-decision procedure with the EP. Even though qualified majority voting (QMV) is formally the default for decision-making, in practice it operates through consensus wherever possible. Moreover, the planned double-majority rule for QMV from 1 November 2014, involving 55 per cent of Member States representing at least 65 per cent of the population, is designed to ensure that decisions must balance the interests of large and small states by preventing the former imposing a decision on the latter and vice versa.

Daniel Naurin in his contribution to this volume (Chapter 4) addresses the two Council settings and the way they contribute to representation in the EU. As he points out, there are a number of factors preventing the Councils from representing the preferences of European citizens as well as one might wish for. These are:

> [the] sectorial organisation of the Council of Ministers, the lack of party coordination of policy conflicts in the Council of Ministers and the European Council, the practice of consensus decision-making and the lack of transparency of the Councils' proceedings and decisions.

Because of the first two, there is a lack of comprehensive political programmes that could be evaluated by the voters. As Naurin points out, the 'deliberative practices and the consensus norm may contribute to its character of an insulated elite club' whilst the 'lack of transparency ... makes the Councils both less comprehensible and less accountable'. Together, then, the Councils would be rather 'representing national sector interests than general political ideas and values'. However, Naurin also suggests that the Councils have been quite effective in producing agreements between states with highly diverging interests, and the crisis may have had at least one positive effect – namely that EU affairs have become a major issue domestically.

A territorial actor that has so far not attracted considerable academic attention is the Committee of Regions (CoR). The CoR was established in 1994 with the goal of bringing citizens closer to the EU. Today, it has 353 members from the 28 Member States of the EU. Since the Treaty of the European Union (TEU) entered into force, the CoR has had to be consulted throughout the legislative process, involving co-decision procedures in the following areas: economic and social cohesion, trans-European networks, health, education and culture, employment, social policy, the environment, vocational training, transport, civil protection, climate change, and energy.

In Chapter 5, Simona Piattoni asks whether the CoR delivers 'full political and democratic representation'. According to her, this requires addressing whether members of the CoR represent:

> their own *institutional* interests, the *political* interests of the parties they belong to, the *functional* interests prevalent in their territories, the *territorial* interests of their constituents or the general interest of the EU demos at a lower level of aggregation?

In other words, Piattoni asks whether the members of the CoR can balance the different kinds of representation they are involved in. After investigating four recent official documents of the CoR, Piattoni finds that the latter manages to reconcile these different kinds of representative functions and indeed 'to give voice to a "subnational tier" that would not be heard without its representational activity'.

Non-electoral forms of representation in multi-level representation in times of crisis

As the chapters on democratic representation in the EU addressed above suggest, political representation in the EU occurs not only via different actors, but also at different levels of governance. Indeed, the other axis – besides that of channels or actors – that renders any assessment of political representation in the EU extremely difficult is the axis of the level(s) of governance and representation. There are the subnational, national and European levels of governance and representation, and more often than not, it remains disputed which channel of representation should (legitimately) take place at which level, and what sort of representative channels and mix of levels we need in order for the overall system of representation to be democratic. All the contributions mirror this dilemma to a stronger or lesser degree. Some of the respective actors have played a less prominent role during the crisis management of the EU than the actors addressed above, which does not mean that their role in the overall architecture of representation in the EU would be negligible.

One particularly telling and controversial example of the complicated ways of multi-level representation in the EU is committee governance. Committees are generally made up of one or several members that the individual Member States delegate and that are supposed to represent the respective Member State's interest in the committee, whilst the secretariat of the committees is generally provided by the European Commission, which will try and act as a broker between national interests and work in favour of more integration. At times, additional experts are invited to individual hearings of the diverse committees. The theoretical controversy has been whether indeed the delegates were (mainly) representing national interests or whether the committees should primarily be seen as deliberative spaces in which a common 'European interest' can evolve through the force of the better argument and continued processes of mutual socialization.

The contribution by Martino Maggetti (Chapter 6) deals with one example of committee governance, namely with European regulatory networks (ERNs). ERNs were a result of domestic independent regulatory agencies wanting to create transnational groups and of the European Commission's desire to foster the harmonization of European regulation. ERNs are an interesting case in terms of political representation, as they should represent their states of origin whilst formally being independent from their governments. At the same time, 'network members are expected to also represent European actors because they work "at arm's length" from the European Commission'. For the empirical analysis, the Committee of European Securities Regulators (CESR) was selected. The analysis shows that network members 'mainly claim to represent their national regulatory authority'. At the same time, their view of representation seems to evolve over time as members start to represent, 'above all, the viewpoints of a self-referential transnational community of financial regulators'. In the context of the financial crisis, the latter provided a 'window of opportunity' for supranational actors to 'partially reshape the European financial supervisory system'. At the same time, and in reaction to pressures from Member States, the ambitions of the newly created European agency were confined.

Functional representation has addressed mainly the European Commission, even though more recently and with increasing competences, the EP has also become the addressee of lobbying strategies of civil society organizations (CSOs). The Commission is notoriously under-staffed and therefore dependent on external expertise (Bouwen 2002; Broscheid and Coen 2003). Indeed, it has actively engaged in a systematic attempt to promote and develop 'societal representation' at the EU level (Bellamy and Castiglione 2010; Kohler-Koch and Finke 2007; Saurugger 2010). Since the early 1990s, it has massively invested in the creation and survival of some large, non-profit seeking European umbrella organizations, thereby also seeking to increase the legitimacy of its own proposals and to contribute to the construction of a transnational *demos* (Kröger 2013). As a consequence, there is now a distinguished system of interest representation in place in Brussels (Coen and Richardson 2009; Fairbrass and Warleigh 2013; Greenwood 2011). There are a couple of contributions to this volume that address the Commission in general and its role of interest mediation in particular.

The contribution by Nieves Pérez-Solórzano Borragán and Stijn Smismans (Chapter 7) addresses the role of the Commission by focusing on the principle of 'institutional balance', by which the authors refer to the features of the institution itself and to its relations with other institutions. The particular role of the Commission, within the institutional balance, would be to ensure a 'balanced representation of interests in the policy-making process', and to act as an 'institutional broker geared to the realization of the common European interest'. How well the Commission performs the role as a broker 'depends on the way it organizes its consultative processes in terms of transparency and representativeness' – which the authors then describe in terms of standards and practices. With regard to the crisis management by the Member States, they note that Member States have not allowed the Commission 'to play its broader brokering role' between electorally mandated institutions and CSOs. They conclude that under the current conditions, the crisis management – intergovernmental and technocratic governance in sum – might 'ultimately undermine the legitimacy of the entire European construction' if the Commission is no longer to be allowed to play its role as institutional broker and defender of the European interest.

The contribution by Sandra Kröger (Chapter 8) also has as its starting point the ambitions of the Commission to engage in societal representation. Indeed, CSOs have been hoped by many to be able to foster and maintain the mutual trust required for the polity-building project. Her contribution addresses whether these are appropriate perspectives on the role of CSOs in the EU by asking whether European umbrella organizations are representative of the constituencies they claim to represent. She argues that they are representative and make a legitimate contribution to EU policy-making so long as 'they involve their constituencies in the development of policy positions and that the latter enjoy a high degree of acceptance by the constituencies'. Combining qualitative with quantitative research methods, Kröger investigates CSOs active in agricultural, environmental and anti-poverty policy, at the EU, national and regional levels of governance. Her results seem to confirm the message of earlier research that certain CSOs 'are ill-suited to provide the kind of Europeanization of their constituencies that would seem necessary for the creation of a supranational polity ... or for combating the democratic deficit of the EU'. However, this is not because of a lack of internal democratic structures. Rather, these structures are not used by more than a few key national policy officers. More often than not, 'CSOs simply do not seem to mediate between the state and society as hoped by some scholars or Commission officials – not between the EU and national peoples anyway'.

Finally, most recently, the EU also experiments with *direct* forms of representation such as expressed in the European Citizens' Initiative (ECI). This possibility was introduced with the Treaty of Lisbon and only came into force in April 2012. Its legal basis is set out in Article 11, para. 4 of the Treaty of the European Union and in Article 24, para. 1 of the Treaty on the Functioning of the European Union. By way of an ECI, European citizens can invite the European Commission to propose legislation on matters where the EU has competence to legislate. The ECI has to be backed by at least one million EU citizens, coming from at least seven out of the 28 Member States. Once officially registered, the organizers of the ECI have one year to collect signatures. After that, the Commission examines the initiative and decides whether to take action or not. If it decides to put forward a legislative proposal, the normal legislative procedure is in place, and, if the proposal is adopted, it becomes law.

Another form of direct participation are citizens' forums. Dawid Friedrich, in Chapter 9, addresses transnational citizens' forums with which the EU has experimented since the 2000s. In his analysis, he aims to deepen our understanding of both the 'democratic potential and the limitations of deliberative citizen forums in a transnational context by adding a perspective of representation'. The existence of these forums at the EU level may surprise, given that they have so far been the prerogative of local politics and for different reasons seem to suit those best. However, they must also be seen in the context of bringing the EU closer to the people and vice versa, and as an additional attempt to complement the institutions of representative democracy. The screening of secondary literature, however, leads Friedrich to conclude that there are no signs as yet that the online forums had 'led to more publicity, either for the mediated public sphere or for policy-makers of the EU institutions'. As the 'EU did not initiate a viable link between the forums and the EU institutions and policy-makers, it fell short of exploiting the legitimating potential of forums'. Nonetheless, Friedrich hopes that by way of these forums, citizens can 'contribute to stimulating trans-European discussions about specific policy choices' and that thereby 'citizen deliberation may become an important means of strengthening the identity dimension of European democracy'.

In Chapter 10, Hans-Jörg Trenz is also interested in the role the public, or, as he tends to call it, the 'audience' plays in political representation in the EU. Indeed, he perceives of political representation 'as a dynamic communicative process that takes place in the public sphere, filtered and shaped by the media environment', and must therefore be studied in a systemic way. As a consequence, Trenz proposes to focus on 'mass media as the stage of representative politics', and thereby to 'contribute to the understanding of the "making of" political representation'. So far, EU affairs were of low public salience and attracted little public attention. Indeed, the trouble with the EU, according to Trenz, is not so much its institutions and their interplay, but rather the lack of communicative spaces and publicity for and of its activities. Has the current crisis changed this? It does not seem so. On the contrary, the characteristic features of audience democracy 'seem to constrain rather than to enhance the legitimacy of the EU', not least because 'media representations of the crisis are linked to frequent disinformation, a preference of emotional over factual content, unequal chances of political representatives to access the media sphere and an inbuilt nationalism of media frames and interpretations'. As a result, the politicization of EU affairs that did take place in the context of the crisis has 'rather endorsed the renationalization of EU representative politics and strengthened those actors who oppose delegated authority to the EU'.

Another actor that exemplifies perfectly the difficulties of representation across several levels of governance is the Court of Justice of the European Union (CJEU). In Chapter 11, Michelle Everson and Christian Joerges address the difficulty, between the CJEU and national Constitutional Courts, of accommodating the institutional and structural diversity of the various Member States. Indeed, as of today, constitutional guardianship in the EU has both national and European 'masters who may be in disagreement with one another' – legitimate masters, though, since courts are 'the non-majoritarian vanguard and institutions *par excellence* of constitutional democracies. Non-partisanship defines their very ethos'. Still, they build upon a Weberian kind of legitimacy, which they gain through 'rule-bounded, but socially responsive adjudication'. Due to the lack of hierarchical ordering between the Courts, social adjudication between the different levels and Member States is particularly under strain in the context of the current crisis, as is shown by way of example of recent rulings of the German Federal Constitutional Court and the CJEU. In the context of the crisis, both courts have accepted the 'primacy of discretionary politics against the normative dignity of the constitutional order' (Kohler-Koch in Chapter 12, her contribution). Concretely, this has meant that the Courts have accepted the economic orthodoxy of Berlin and Brussels and therefore contributed to the erosion of law and its disciplining functions (see Chapter 12). Overall, they have thereby weakened the prospects for a legal accommodation of the EU's structural diversity in the context of crisis by rendering social adjudication between states even more difficult. Against this development, Everson and Joerges argue for a 'radical "proceduralization" of the integration project in which the European judiciary engages in continuous juris-generative efforts ... that seek responses to Europe's complex conflict constellations'.

No matter which channels and levels of representation the authors of this volume address, they all seem to agree that the handling of the Euro- and debt crisis has amplified the already existing democratic deficits, not least the lack of a transparent, open political process at the EU level in the hands of democratic representative institutions and therefore, in the last resort, of the European peoples and citizens. Instead, peoples have been represented in an untransparent manner by their governments, whilst not all governments have weighted equally, and therefore have not all citizens and peoples been represented equally.

The future of the EU and its Member States may look like Italy or Greece in 2011–12 – Member States governed by technocrats or other Member States, at least indirectly, rather than by party government. Governments may no longer be enforcing partisan electoral promises, but implementing budgetary, economic and other policies decided at the EU level, either in the European Council or, worse, in the Euro-Group, rendering national elections almost irrelevant. Whether a Member State has a right-wing or a left-wing government no longer seems to make much difference for the choice of core policies. What has been said to characterize the EU – policies without politics – may be becoming the dominant governance form in Member States, too. The Euro crisis has certainly increased the opportunity structure for the further hollowing out of national democracy without establishing democratic government at the EU level. Indeed, it so far remains unclear what kind of representative democracy is being developed at the EU level, and with what sort of consequences for Member States.

Lessons of the volume

These troubled times set the framework to reassess a number of important questions in regard to representative democracy, such as what should be the normative foundation of political representation in the EU? Which institutional design captures this foundation best? What kind of relationship can there be between represented and representatives in the EU, and what kind of authorization and accountability mechanisms are in place? Does the European integration project contribute to the strengthening or the weakening of the link between democracy and representation? How do newer arenas and actors, such as regulatory committees and CSOs, manage to 'get in the game', and is their involvement democratically legitimate? This volume makes a contribution to these and other pertinent questions, and particularly the concluding chapters by Beate Kohler-Koch (Chapter 12) and Dario Castiglione (Chapter 13) reflect these questions, not least in light of the foregoing chapters.

Doing so, Beate Kohler-Koch engages in a very thorough discussion of the empirical findings and more theoretical reflections of all the individual contributions and situates them in the context of the existing literature. As she points out, many of the contributions 'conceptualize representation as a relationship between represented and representatives. They examine constellations of interaction and participation and consider whether these live up to the standards of democratic representation'. Looking at them together, it becomes clear that 'institutions and actors legitimize the representation claim on different grounds'. Indeed, that is not very surprising given the different channels of representation in the EU, their different logics and standards and often their lack of interaction with one another. Add to that different conceptualizations of democratic representation by the scholars, and the confusion is perfect. Indeed, what is missing in most of the contributions, and as Kohler-Koch rightly points out, is a systemic view on representation: are the individual channels and actors of representation democratic and complementary, and do they add up to a coherent, democratic overall system of representation, or are they rather conflicting and competing with one another? And by which normative standards should we evaluate this question as well as the possible superiority of some channels over others? These as well as the questions listed above are addressed in the following chapter.

In his concluding essay, Dario Castiglione (Chapter 13) focuses on the different ways in which multilevel governance in the European context challenges the 'standard view' of political representation, and democratic representation in particular. This challenge has given rise to a theoretical development, which has been called the 'constructivist turn', which seeks to combine elements of representative, deliberative and participatory democracy. As he points out, both the principal–agent relationship and the limitation to a territorially bounded, national constituency, are ever more difficult to uphold in the context of internationalization, as is the restriction to electoral forms of representation that the standard view seems to impose. Castiglione suggests that none of the traditional channels of representation examined in this volume offers 'a robust enough link with the citizens for these institutions to be said to represent them at a European level according to the model suggested by the "standard view", with clear authorization and effective accountability'. What is more, for other, non-electoral actors of representation in the EU, 'the agents' understanding of their own representative role and scope is independent of any direct process of authorization, or indeed from ex-post accountability', which is why their representation has a 'self-referential character' in which representation becomes 'increasingly dependent on the agents' own claims … that they are acting as representatives', and is not really linked anymore to responsiveness to the represented. One risk is therefore that constructivist approaches 'encourage the insulation of the representatives from the represented'. Still, according to Castiglione, the constructivist analysis and terminology seems better suited to capture political representation that 'takes place through a variety of forms and channels' in the supranational context. However, it may not address well what we mean by *democratic* representation.

The other test for constructivist approaches, according to Castiglione, is whether they are capable of capturing the systemic aspect of representation. Indeed, he argues that in a complex and supranational context such as the EU, 'democratic legitimacy may depend more on the way in which the overall system of representation operates', rather than on traditional electoral mechanisms of representation. The problem within the overall system, however, seems to be that:

> the two distinct moments of public deliberation and collective will formation, which the representative system tried to bring together, often remain apart, so that the system of political representation becomes more tenuous, informal, dispersed and disaggregated.

In consequence, 'the overall system remains ineffective when looked at from a democratic perspective', because the European public has 'voice' but no 'influence'. For Castiglione, the open question then is whether 'what is lost at a systemic level can be gained at a micro-level, by the promotion in the public sphere of different democratic instances and by the diffusion of more democratic practices operating autonomously'.

There is no easy answer to the question of what democracy in a supranational context does or indeed should look like, or what qualities are needed for representation to be democratic. Therefore, there is likely to be a continued divide in the interested community over what normative standards should be applied to the EU as regards its democratic quality. The EU is a problem for democratic theory insofar as it cannot be democratic on modern accounts of democracy. Why indeed should we expect institutions and norms of democracy that were developed in the national context to retain their meaning if translated to a fundamentally different supranational context? Given the historical contingency of territorial boundaries and the decreasing congruence between the people affected by political decisions and nation state boundaries, democratic theory is not well advised to treat the identity of a people as given (Goodhart 2007). On the other hand, it would be unacceptable not to be guided by normative standards when evaluating the democratic quality of the EU, and citizens are also likely to be inspired in their assessment from what they consider to be democratically legitimate in their respective national contexts.

References

Auel, K. and Benz, A. (2005) 'The politics of adaptation: The Europeanisation of national parliamentary systems', *Journal of Legislative Studies*, 11 (3–4): 372–393.

Bellamy, R. and Castiglione, D. (2010) 'Democracy by delegation? Who represents whom and how in European governance', *Government and Opposition*, 46 (1): 101–125.

Bellamy, R. and Kröger, S. (2013) 'Representation deficits and surpluses in EU policy-making', *Journal of European Integration*, 35 (5): 477–497.

Bellamy, R. and Kröger, S. (2012) 'Domesticating the democratic deficit? The role of national parliaments and parties in the EU's system of governance', *Parliamentary Affairs*, doi:10.1093/pa/gss045.

Bouwen, P. (2002) 'Corporate lobbying in the European Union: the logic of access', *Journal of European Public Policy*, 9 (3): 365–390.

Broscheid, A. and Coen, D. (2003) 'Insider and outsider lobbying of the European Commission: an informational model', *European Union Politics*, 4 (2): 165–189.

Coen, D. and Richardson, J. (2009) (eds) *Lobbying in the European Union: Institutions, Actors and Issues*, Oxford: Oxford University Press.

Fairbrass, J. and Warleigh, A. (2013) *Influence and Interests in the European Union: the New Politics of Persuasion and Advocacy*, Routledge.

Goodhart, M. (2007) 'Europe's democratic deficits through the looking glass: The European Union as a challenge for democracy', *Perspectives on Politics*, 5 (3): 567–584.

Greenwood, J. (2011) *Interest Representation in the European Union*, Basingstoke: Palgrave Macmillan.

Hobson, C. (2008) 'Revolution, representation and the foundations of modern democracy', *European Journal of Political Theory*, 7 (4): 449–471.

Kohler-Koch, B. and Finke, B. (2007) 'The institutional shaping of EU–society relations – a contribution to democracy via participation?', *Journal of Civil Society*, 3 (3): 205–221.

Kröger, S. (2014) 'Political representation and democracy in the European Union', in J. Richardson and S. Mazey (eds) *European Union: Power and Policy-Making*, 4th edn, London: Routledge.

Kröger, S. (2013) 'Creating a European demos? The representativeness of European umbrella organisations', *Journal of European Integration*, 35 (5): 583–600.

Kröger, S. and Friedrich, D. (2013) 'Introduction: the representative turn in EU studies', *Journal of European Public Policy*, 20 (2): 155–170.

Kröger, S. and Friedrich, D. (2012) 'Representation in the EU: The second transformation', in S. Kröger and D. Friedrich (eds) *Representation in the European Union: Coping with Present Challenges to Democracy?*, Houndmills: Palgrave Macmillan, pp. 3–20.

Lord, C. and Pollak, J. (2010) 'The EU's many representative modes: Colliding? Cohering?', *Journal of European Public Policy*, 17 (1): 117–136.

Maurer, A. and Wessels, W. (eds) (2001) *National Parliaments on their Ways to Europe: Losers or Latecomers?* Baden-Baden: Nomos.

Pitkin, H.F. (1967) *The Concept of Representation*, Berkeley, CA: University of California Press.

Puntscher Riekmann, S. and Wydra, D. (2013) 'Representation in the European state of emergency: parliaments against governments?', *Journal of European Integration*, 35 (5): 565–582.

Raunio, T. and Hix, S. (2000) 'Backbenchers learn to fight back: European integration and parliamentary government', *West European Politics*, 23 (4): 142–168.

Saurugger, S. (2010) 'The social construction of the participatory turn: The emergence of a norm in the European Union', *European Journal of Political Research*, 49: 471–495.

Schmidt, V. (1999) 'European "Federalism" and its encroachments on national institutions', *Publius*, 29 (1): 19–44.

Urbinati, N. (2004) 'Condorcet's democratic theory of representative government', *European Journal of Political Theory*, 3 (1): 53–75.

Warren, M. and Castiglione, D. (2004) 'The transformation of democratic representation', *Democracy and Society*, 2 (1): 5–22.

Zürn, M. (2001) 'Politik in der postnationalen Konstellation. Über das Elend des methodologischen Nationalismus', in C. Landfried (ed.) *Politik in einer entgrenzten Welt*, 21 wissenschaftlicher Kongreß der Deutschen Vereinigung für Politischen Wissenschaft, Köln: Verlag Wissenschaft und Politik, pp. 181–203.

Part I

Electoral forms of representation and the democratic crisis of the EU

1 Compounded representation in the EU

No country for old parliaments?

Johannes Pollak

Introduction

Political representation is not only a fuzzy concept; it is also an elusive activity. The higher the institutional complexity of a political system, the more elusive it becomes. While there is not much agreement amongst political scientists on what constitutes good representation there is an agreement that the institutional complexity of the European Union (EU) is a challenge for representative politics. There is also agreement that political representation is one of the key concepts of political science. As such it has undergone considerable changes from its invention in medieval times to the twenty-first century – changes which affected the conceptual dimension as well as the practical–institutional one. Thus, today we are debating new and innovative approaches such as Michael Saward's model of representative claims (2010) as much as we are looking for new forms of representation, bypassing the trodden paths suggested by the all-too-simple standard model that is configured along the lines of the principal–agent format. The questions that representative theory has to answer, however, have remained remarkably stable: Who represents whom and how? What means do principals have to keep agency loss at bay?

This contribution understands democratic representation as 'acting in the best interest of the represented' (Eulau *et al.* 1959: 743; Pitkin 1967: 209; Przeworski *et al.* 1999: 2) by representatives subject to intensive public control. It is of less concern in this definition what kind of selection takes place – by lot, election, appointment – or how potential representatives construct their claims to representativeness. Rather, the focus is on how various agents 'acting in the best interest' can lead to a system that guarantees the central tenets of democracy.

What are those tenets?

1 All citizens must have the equal right to author their own laws either directly or through representatives in order to maximize the extent of public and private autonomy.
2 The public must be able to control the administration of laws, which is usually done through a chain of delegation in which their elected representatives form governments with controlling powers over the rest of the public administration (Strøm 2003).

3 A representative assembly must exist as the central place permitting 'any one view to be justified or challenged in relation to any other' (Mill 1972 [1861]).
4 All citizens must have the equal right to 'form and change the conditions of their common life together, including democracy itself' (Bohman 2007: 66).
5 All citizens have the equal right to question the responsiveness of representatives and recall them via democratic processes (see Lord and Pollak 2010).

Different times and circumstances have given different institutional answers as to how to fulfil those conditions: from parliamentary to presidential democracies, from unitary to federal states, from proportional to first-past-the-post electoral systems, from checks-and-balances systems to horizontal or vertical separation of power systems, and so on. The EU has found an original answer by incrementally and probably also unintentionally developing a compounded system of representation, in which representatives of the same institution can be selected by different methods (e.g. the European Parliament (EP)), where we find different mandates (e.g. in the Council), and different territorial bases (Committee of the Regions) depending on national parliamentary scrutiny rights, political traditions, and state organization.

But what happens to this system if it comes under ever more strain from deepening supranational integration, globalized crises phenomena, and a decreasing trust in democracy's problem-solving capacity? What happens if the congruence between voters, territory, and conceptions of political community breaks down? In order to answer these questions, the EU's compounded system of representation in general, and the role of national parliaments therein in particular, will be addressed.

The contribution proceeds as follows. The second section looks briefly into theoretical developments contrasting the standard view of representation with representation as claims-making. The following section asks, from the perspective of parliamentarism, what specific form of representation has emerged at the European level and what its deficits are. The lack of parliamentary politics is recognized as the most disturbing element of European democracy. The third section charts the role of national parliaments in the EU and analyses whether the new parliamentary constellation of the Lisbon era increases the EU's representative quality and thereby presents itself as a model to reconcile scope and representativity. The fourth section deals briefly with the impact of the financial crisis on parliamentary politics. A final section sums up the argument and concludes.

A challenge for theory and practice

The standard model describes the representative–represented relationship by pointing to four elements: first, territorially defined principals elect agents to stand and act for their interests, thereby separating the sources of legitimate democratic power from those that are beholden to exercise this power. Second, electoral representation identifies a space within which the sovereignty of the people is identified with state power. Third, some measure of responsiveness and accountability is ensured by electoral mechanisms. And finally, the universal franchise endows electoral representation with an important element of political equality (Urbinati and Warren 2008: 389), thereby guaranteeing some measure of self-government. Jennifer Mansbridge (2003, 2009) has called this model the promissory model of representation, or the sanctions model of representation. Arguably, the representative assembly occupies a central place in this understanding of representative democracy: it allows the citizens to fulfill the Kantian requirement of self-government without foregoing their private autonomy. In addition, the existence of a representative body also improves public autonomy to the extent citizens can enjoy greater public control where, instead of attempting the task themselves, they can appoint accountable representatives who are, in turn, specialized and skilled in bringing other power-holders to account for decisions concerning the 'authoritative allocation of values' (Easton 1953) in a polity. As Richard Bellamy (2008: 1) puts it: 'in terms of democratic legitimacy, the system of representation offers a holistic framework within which to embed mechanisms of democratic authorization, control, and accountability.'

There are four generic reasons that make the standard account problematic. First, most of its elements are used in different contexts with various meanings and are theoretically underspecified. Neither is it clear what exactly is meant by authorization, social identity, or accountability, nor is it obvious how the various dimensions of representation work together and what the effects of their different combinations are (Pollak 2007). Thus, conceptual clarity is hard to find. Second, current political communities are remarkably different from the ones for which the standard account was developed – be it the rise of transnational decision arenas and actors, the rise of informal representation by interest groups, the stellar importance of state administrations, or perhaps the ever-decreasing turnout in Western democracies. The dominance of the nation state as the primary form of organizing liberal democracy is being increasingly challenged. Third, the boundaries of political communities have become increasingly fuzzy and porous. International (criminal) law and supranational law penetrate the autonomy of national (including constitutional) law to an extent that self-government becomes an elusive ideal. As a corollary of this porousness the size of political communities renders any direct social relationship between representatives and represented immensely difficult. Fourth, the core assumption of representative government, at least since Edmund Burke and Abbé Sieyès – that all other forms of representation and public decision-making in a polity can be subject to the ultimate regulation of a parliament elected from across the territorial unit as a whole – appears increasingly challenged by a wide range of actors claiming to be representative or claiming to be in a better position to judge the needs of the represented than elected representatives.

Recent developments in representative theory point on the one hand to the tremendously important aesthetic, constitutive factor in representation, and on the other hand criticize the reduction of a complex relationship between representative and represented to the electoral nexus. Political representation is very much about creating (Ankersmit 2002; Saward 2006, 2010) what is represented by condensing, generalizing, sharpening, inventing, and offering an image to an audience. What is represented is always just a fraction of what makes an audience. At the same time the representative is itself an artificial Leviathan, changing shape, form and colour with every angle or audience.[1] Moreover, manifold forms of representation beyond the electoral connection are emphasized, be they clad into deliberative, participative or associative forms of democracy. NGOs, interest groups, citizen initiatives, and so on, all claim their place at the table of political decision-making by pointing to their representativity. Those new theoretical developments reflect changes in the political landscape consisting of increasing deterritorialization, i.e. politics and economics are increasingly decoupled from a territory defining the realm of sovereignty. Moreover, they reflect an increasing heterarchization of politics itself taking place on multiple levels, involving state as well as non-state actors. The prime advantage of the representation as claims-making approach lies in overcoming the inflexibility of the standard account, which focuses on formal representation. Representation is no longer a status conferred upon elected officials: it is an activity open to everyone. As such it captures the rallying cry for more democracy, because everyone can now claim to represent something and demand a place at the decision-making table.[2] This demand is voiced increasingly by civil society groups, NGOs, INGOs, interest groups, and so on. But it is not only the heterarchization of politics or the increasing institutional complexity; it is also the remarkable reluctance of national representative institutions to adapt to a new political environment. In the face of supranational politics and the possibility of majority decisions, EU Member States insist on their sovereignty and uphold the fiction of national representative democracy. Because the national institutions of representation remained largely unbothered in the face of a dramatically changed political landscape, representative democracy no longer enjoys the undivided admiration it once did (Pollak 2007). An increasing gap between the way institutions are designed and their capacity to answer modern needs and demand is evident. On the one hand, this is reflected in a rising scepticism towards established institutions going hand in hand with a newly found penchant for direct democratic elements. On the other hand, this triggers questions about the adaptability of established institutions, and how they can be 'made' to fulfil their representative tasks.

The EU's compounded system of representation

The EU was built by replicating – and in some cases duplicating – national institutions of representation. The result is tension between the scope of responsibility and the scope of representation. While national parliaments are viewed as a central arena of 'public bavardage', party competition and law-making their actual legislative influence on policy-making has shrunk considerably due to European integration (see Maurer 2008; Raunio 2010). They retain the former functions without enjoying the same legislative effectiveness. The hope that by replicating and duplicating or by lumping together existing representative institutions a new supranational representative system will emerge seems to be too optimistic. Thus, we need to ask how to reconcile traditional and new forms of representation with a widening scope of 'representation needs', reaching well beyond what national institutions are able to provide.

Allegations about the EU's democratic deficit are usually met by referring to its complex institutional architecture and its three-tier representation structure. According to Article 10 TEU, EU citizens are directly represented at the Union level in the EP, Member States are represented in the European Council and in the Council, and all the institutions are called upon to maintain an open, transparent and regular dialogue with representative associations and civil society. Indeed, a system seems to be in place that puts executive actors under considerable constraint to refrain from intergovernmental bargaining or purely administrative policy-making via committees of experts. Instead, a complex and fine-tuned web requires balancing a wide range of interests and demands brought forward by a multitude of actors. This increases inclusiveness and promotes ideals of non-arbitrariness that emphasize a need to make decisions with the participation of the effected. The EU sports a system of representation that relies on a mixture of formal and informal representation, while further subdividing the delivery of both into processes that are partially autonomous of one another. Formal representation connotes those institutions or actors with a constitutionally recognized right to represent others in the making of authoritative, collective decisions of a polity. In contrast, informal forms derive from the attempts of groups in civil society to organize themselves for engagement with a polity. They portray themselves as representatives of sometimes very broad membership structures – such as consumer groups or environmental organizations – and therefore claim a place in the collective decision-making process. Crucially, informal representatives do not just lack the authority to speak on behalf of the whole citizenry; they do not seek that authority, preferring, instead, to give voice and influence to specific membership groups. This sets them significantly apart from formally elected representatives, who in order to maximize the common ground of decision-making, whether to minimize transaction costs or to optimize votes, have to present fairly general representative claims (Lord and Pollak 2010). Indeed the mixture between formal and informal representation seems to be a characteristic of the EU's representative system expressed in a highly complex, consensus-oriented institutional set-up.

While this complex and compounded system theoretically does justice to the multitude of interests in modern societies it is by no means obvious that this results in democratic, fair and equal representation. Several indeterminacies pertaining to the executive and the parliamentary dimensions of the EU have to be considered:

1 When it comes to the representation of Member States in the European Council, which has a far greater influence than the Treaties confer, differences in economic weight result in inequality. Again and again commentators

deplore the dwindling driving force of the Franco–German axis. Seen from the point of view of equality this axis was of course always an expression of inequality between the Member States. The hard-to-digest and inconsistently applied principle of digressive proportionality in the Council adds another peculiar twist increasing the inequality between states, which may continue to exist in its current form until 2017. Countering the logic of population numbers and instead rather focusing on the intensity of preferences the Council hardly ever votes and prefers to rely on the negotiating skills of civil servants and ambassadors in the Committee of Permanent Representatives and other upstream committees and working groups. However, the latter are hardly ever subject to detailed scrutiny by national parliaments[3] to ensure 'that the agent (government) behaves according to the instructions of the principal (parliament)' (Raunio 1999: 186).

2 Largely unnoticed by the wider public, the EP has emerged as a major player in the decision-making system. The representative connection with the citizens, however, is still very much tainted by the second-order character of EP elections and the lack of public awareness.

3 Supposed to give voice to the interests of the regions, the Committee of Regions hardly ever crosses the point of having legislative influence beyond having to be asked for an opinion in strictly limited policy areas. Likewise, the Social and Economic Committee (according to its website striving to contribute 'to strengthening the democratic legitimacy and effectiveness of the EU by enabling civil society organisations from the Member States to express their views at European level'[4]) is largely dependent on whatever benevolence the other actors may feel inclined to show.

4 When it comes to civil society groups their ability to bring in additional perspectives and representative claims depends entirely on their resources and, in the case of unions, on the backing from respective national counterparts. Large resource asymmetries between advocates and opponents of whatever cause are coupled with the notoriously opaque system of working groups, agencies and committees.

In short: the compounded system of representation may offer access for a variety of actors but whether they are able to feed representative claims into the decision-making system depends on their legal status as well as on their resources. In order to remedy this situation two suggestions are prevalent in the literature: one can either strengthen the role of national parliaments and enhance their scrutiny rights over governments in order to counter their loss of legislative influence that comes with ever-deepening integration. Or one strengthens the powers of the EP. Interestingly enough, we see both developments: all Member States' parliaments have set up European affairs committees although their formal scrutiny powers range from exceptionally strong (Austria, Denmark) to fairly weak (Greece, Spain); and every treaty reform since the Single European Act has considerably strengthened the EP. culminating in the ordinary legislative procedure or the new EP's budgetary rights stipulated in the Lisbon Treaty.

Thus, the formal conditions for creating a kind of horizontal parliamentarism are given. Horizontal parliamentarism refers to the possibility of national parliaments exchanging information, pooling resources, and coordinating scrutiny work across boundaries. Does it work?

The role of national parliaments in the EU: black-letter law and reality

Within the EU's political system the assessment of the role of national parliaments oscillates between hope and frustration. Their impact on policy-making and thus on EU legislation is regarded as minimal (Kiiver 2006; Maurer 2008; O'Brennan and Raunio 2007; Raunio 2010); their contribution to the EU's representativity and legitimacy is generally expected to be positive (Maurer 2008, 2012), but how exactly so is hardly ever debated (the exception being Cooper 2012); the rising importance of European affairs committees in national parliaments is well demonstrated by a number of studies (Maurer and Wessels 2001; Auel and Benz 2005; O'Brennan and Raunio 2007; Barrett 2008b). However, due to national constitutional stipulations and political cultures the extent and practice of this scrutiny shows wide variety and can be considered to be *ex post* effective rather than policy-creative. Yet the linkage between national parliaments and citizens, the communication function of legislatives, remains widely neglected (Auel and Raunio 2012). First studies dealing with inter-parliamentary cooperation relish in pointing to the obvious: a lack of time, expertise and resources of national parliaments to efficiently coordinate their activities and provide a place for 'public bavardage' limit their impact considerably (Pollak and Slominski 2003; Lord and Pollak 2010; Fasone 2012). Theoretically innovative and empirically informed approaches try to find traces of 'horizontal parliamentarism' (Maurer 2001), a 'parliamentary field' (Crum and Fossum 2012) and even a 'virtual "third chamber"' (Cooper 2012) consisting of all the national parliaments together. If assumptions about an increasing inter-parliamentary cooperation are right then European politics should bear the marks of a parliamentary and representative system. What is the contribution of national parliaments?

There are three ideal type ways for national parliaments to participate in European politics. First, they control national decision-making processes with regard to Member States' European policies. At the latest since the beginning of the 1990s all Member States' parliaments have established European affairs committees (EAC), the last one being the Senate and the Chamber of Deputies in Romania in 2001. They contribute to the formulation of national positions that are then, via governments, negotiated in the Council and have, in some cases, even mandating rights. Since the Lisbon Treaty came into effect the so-called 'Early Warning Mechanism' also allows national parliaments to object to Commission proposals within eight weeks of their publication on the grounds that they breach the principle of subsidiarity. In general EACs serve as the interface between government and parliament. Second, national parliaments have to implement European law. This ranges from implementing EU directives according to Article 288 TFEU, to ratification of treaty changes including EU accessions and certain Council decisions that ask for ratification 'by all Member States in accordance with their respective constitutional requirements' (art. 48 (4), 49 TEU). While the first two forms of participation are regulated at state level and therefore vary considerably, the Lisbon treaty was regarded as a watershed with respect to the third function (Maurer 2002; Rozenberg 2002; Raunio 2005).

National parliaments feature quite a prominent role in the Treaty of Lisbon – at least compared to the predecessor treaties (Barrett 2008a). After two declarations in the Maastricht Treaty (nos 13 and 14) a further enhancement of the role of national parliaments was agreed upon by incorporating a legally binding 'Protocol on the role of National Parliaments in the EU' into the Amsterdam Treaty. The same protocol awards the Conférences des Organes spécialisés dans les Affaires communautaires (COSAC) the right to 'make any contribution it deems appropriate' and address 'to the EP, the Council and the Commission any contribution which it deems appropriate on the legislative activities of the EU'. Furthermore, the 'Declaration on the Future of the Union' in the Treaty of Nice addresses a fundamental question for the institutional fabric of the European polity: what role should be played by national parliaments within the multi-level system of European governance? This question was taken up and enhanced in the Laeken Declaration in December 2001 and also played an important part in the Convention on the Future of the EU. The final report of Working Group IV (CONV 353/02) emphasizes the role of national parliaments in scrutinizing their governments. After the failed constitutional referenda in France and the Netherlands, the role of national parliaments was for the first time ever incorporated in the treaty text itself giving national parliaments the collective power to intervene directly in the supranational legislative process. Article 12 TEU confirms the existing information rights of national parliaments and extends it significantly: all institutions of the Union have to forward all draft legislative acts directly to the parliaments. Apart from the draft legislation from the Commission this now, according to the protocol no. 1, includes initiatives from a group of Member States, initiatives from the EP, requests from the Court of Justice, recommendations from the European Central Bank and requests from the European Investment Bank for the adoption of a legislative act. Substantial new rights for national parliaments were gained in the policy area of freedom, justice and security (arts 70, 71, 85, 88 TFEU). Moreover, national parliaments have to be informed immediately about all treaty amendments (art. 48 TEU) and changes from special legislative procedures to the ordinary legislative procedure intended by the European Council (art. 48/7, TEU).

Most of the political and scholarly attention was directed towards the newly introduced subsidiarity mechanism. National parliaments have the right to issue a reasoned opinion on whether a draft legislative act complies with the principle of subsidiarity within a period of eight weeks instead of six weeks as foreseen in the Constitutional Treaty. In order to facilitate this subsidiarity check a 'fiche de subsidiarité' accompanies all draft legislation, which should contain detailed information about the expected financial effects of the legislation and, in case of a directive, the implications of the rules to be put in place by Member States. The justification for a Union measure should be based on qualitative and quantitative indicators. The protocol on subsidiarity and proportionality (Protocol no. 2 TEU) stipulates that when a reasoned opinion represents at least one-third of all national parliaments[5] the draft must be reviewed by the Commission, which has the right to maintain, amend or withdraw the draft concerned. If, however, the reasoned opinion represents the majority of the national parliaments, the proposal must again be reviewed by the Commission. If it chooses to maintain the draft it has to issue a reasoned opinion and argue why the draft is in accordance with the principle of subsidiarity. If the EP along with the Council considers the proposal compatible with the principle of subsidiarity it can adopt the legislative act. While this so-called early warning mechanism can be regarded as a negative rather than a positive instrument (Sonnicksen 2010: 150) it also reflects the opinion that the EU institutions are probably more inclined to adhere to the principle of subsidiarity by an *ex ante* political review done by national parliaments than a judicial *ex post* review once the legal act has been adopted. However, the treaty foresees the possibility of national parliaments that raise an objection concerning the subsidiarity compatibility of a legislative draft filing an action of annulment with the European Court of Justice.

Within the frame of COSAC, national parliaments started trial runs well before the Lisbon Treaty was in force. The objective of those trial runs was to get national parliaments, especially EACs, accustomed to the new participation rights. A total of eight trials showed considerable difficulties for national parliaments pertaining to the time frame, language, and scrutiny resources. Cooper (2012: 449) has differentiated between three kinds of factors impeding the effectiveness of the new subsidiarity control: incentive problems, logistical problems, and weaknesses inherent to the subsidiarity principle. Add to this the traditional nexus between parliamentary majority and government in most Member States that questions the willingness of national parliaments to scrutinize 'their' respective parliaments, and the lack of a common definition of what subsidiarity actually is,[6] which casts doubt over the justiciability of the principle as such, and the new-won powers seem less impressive. Over the course of 2011, only 64 draft legislative acts were subject to subsidiarity scrutiny – none of them came even close to a chamber majority. Among the national parliaments the Swedish Riksdag (11) and the Luxembourg Chambre des Députés (7) were by far the most active (European Commission 2011). While the number of 64 seems comparably small this poses quite a considerable workload for EACs. To date, there was no majority of reasoned opinions on any draft legislation, nor was there a case where the Court had to annul a measure for breach of subsidiarity.

Parliaments of course need the means to live up to the expectations and tasks formulated in the Lisbon Treaty, which explicitly calls for interparliamentary cooperation (protocol no. 1, art. 9 TFEU). To facilitate cooperation, the Interparliamentary EU Information Exchange (IPEX) website was established in 2006. According to its website, IPEX is a 'platform for the electronic exchange of EU related information between parliaments in the Union' (see: www.ipex.eu), which basically contains two types of documents: first, all documents which are adopted at the EU level, notably Commission proposals, which usually start the EU legislative process and, second, documents uploaded from individual national parliaments that scrutinize EU documents, especially as to whether they are in accordance with the principle of subsidiarity. COSAC runs bi-annual reports on how the cooperation works and how the use of IPEX facilitates cooperation. In the 17th report, 36 out of 40 parliaments and/or chambers responded that their parliamentary staff consults the database on a daily (17) or weekly (19) basis. Members of parliament do so less frequently. National parliaments also expressed the need for improvement of IPEX when it comes to reliability. However, 32 out of 40 parliaments/chambers responded that they upload reasoned opinions the same day, or within two days of adoption.

One has to keep in mind that according to rules stipulated in the Lisbon treaty national parliaments cannot actually veto a legislative proposal. Instead of trying to throw in the monkey wrench, national parliaments seem to have chosen a more promising path using the so-called 'Barroso initiative'. Launched by Commission President Barroso in 2006, the written exchange of opinions and replies between national parliaments and the European Commission has been steadily intensifying ever since. The total number of opinions sent by national parliaments in 2011, including reasoned opinions, reached 622. This represents an increase of some 60 per cent compared to 2010 (387). This trend continues: by June 2012 400 opinions were already sent. The Portuguese (184) and Italian (76) parliaments were the most active in communicating with the Commission. Thus, vertical communication with the European institutions, at least with the pivot in the legislative system, points towards an exchange of thoughts.[7] In fact it can probably be termed 'bavardage' – unfortunately, parliaments fail to communicate their respective activities to the wider public.

But do national parliaments have any impact on supranational legislative activities? Do they have an influence on the European laws and regulations by which citizens are governed? A closer look at the European policy-making process makes it difficult to see such a parliamentary impact on legislation. Rather the 'double democratic deficit', already analysed almost twenty years ago (Lodge 1993, 1994), seems to have been increased to a multiple deficit with every treaty revision (see Maurer 2011):

1 More and more policy areas have been subjected to qualified majority voting in the Council, thereby further sidelining national parliaments unless they are enjoying extraordinary control rights of national executives. Most Member States' parliaments do not enjoy such rights (Auel 2007; Auel and Benz 2005). Moreover, between 70 and 90 per cent of Council decisions are actually taken at Committee level (including the Committee of Permanent Representatives, the Antici Committee, the Mertens Committee) (Hayes-Renshaw and Wallace 1995). Parliaments hardly have the resources to control this policy-making process effectively.

2 Once the Commission has drafted a directive, national parliaments apply the subsidiarity check. But during these weeks, expert working groups from the Commission and the Council do not twiddle their thumbs but start to hammer out the details of the directive, which can substantially alter the content of the draft sent to the parliaments. Thus, the parliaments are always in a race to keep up.

3 The Common Foreign and Security Policy and the Common Defence Policy are explicitly excluded from parliamentary control. The same is true for the European Council as such. Existing reporting obligations of the Presidency towards the EP and national parliaments cannot replace parliamentary involvement. Moreover, when it comes to employment (art. 148 TFEU) and economic policy (art. 121 TFEU), the method of open coordination, which is an intergovernmental coordination mechanism, also sidelines national parliaments (Kröger 2007). In addition, national parliaments are not informed or consulted when it comes to the monitoring of national budgetary situations (art. 126 TFEU).

4 The EU's 'agency fever' (Pollitt *et al.* 2001) has added yet another layer to an already complex executive system. Examples of agencies' activities range from the European Agency for the Management of Operational Cooperation at the External Borders (FRONTEX) providing – together with the Member States – aircrafts, vessels and expert personnel to identify migrants and protect EU borders, to the European Air Safety Authority (EASA), publishing guidelines for flight operations when there is evidence of volcanic ash or certifying the new Airbus A380; from the European Food Safety Authority (EFSA) issuing opinions on the risk connected to Bovine Spongiform Encephalopathy (BSE) or animal health issues including Avian Influenza, and the European Medicines Agency (EMEA) along with the European Centre for Disease Control (ECDC) working together on a risk assessment of BASF's transgenic potatoes, to the EU's Office for Harmonization in the Internal Market (OHIM) collecting fees for roughly 90 000 trademark registrations per annum. Such a network or 'underworld' of agencies raises a question of democratic control and accountability, which is a general requirement of the principle of democracy in Art. 2 and Title II of the EU Treaty (TEU) and of the case law of the European Court of Justice (ECJ).[8]

Fair-weather parliaments?

So far a rather critical account of the capacity of national parliaments to influence European policy-making has been offered. While they have new instruments at their disposal, those seem to be rather unused. One reason for this may be the highly consensual form of policy-making at the supranational level. Another reason may be that the national political circumstances have not asked, required, or allowed for the proper use of those instruments. This has certainly changed with the full onslaught of the economic crises hitting the EU. Have parliaments raised their voice and influenced decisions putting economic burdens on every EU citizen in an unsurpassed way? A glance at the introduction of the European emergency funding instruments since 2010, their stipulations and their national ratification gives a tentative answer.

The economic crises hitting Europe since 2008 seem to have put parliamentary politics on the backburner. Heads of states and governments, finance ministers and central bankers occupy the limelight when it comes to tackling the effects of the crises. In summit after summit they tried to come up with measures to preserve the monetary union as well as national fiscal sovereignty.

While they may have occupied the limelight it has also become clear that heads of state and government have decided for an incremental rather than a big-bang strategy. This was on the one hand due to the enormous complexity of the sovereign debt crisis as such, the fundamentally different conditions in the most affected countries, and widely differing strategic visions of the EU of the future. However, mechanisms such as the European Financial Stability Facility (EFSF)/European Stability Mechanism (ESM) and the Treaty on Stability, Coordination and Governance in the Economic and Monetary Union (TSCG), which set national austerity measures in motion, needed ratification by national parliaments. Thus, national parliaments should have played a key role not only in ratifying those treaties but also in deliberating them. Confronted with a public increasingly sceptical about the EU and the problem-solving capacity of governments, trust in the EU decreased from 50 per cent (Eurobarometer 69, autumn 2008) to 33 per cent (Eurobarometer 78, autumn 2012), for national governments the rate went down from 32 per cent to 27 per cent – the sovereign debt crisis could have presented an opportunity for national parliaments to hold 'their' governments to account. In the eyes of the public this did not seem to have worked very well: trust in the national parliaments declined from 34 per cent to 28 per cent, while support for the European economic and monetary union with a single currency remained almost stable. Hopes that the Lisbon Treaty would help national parliaments to develop a pro-active role with respect to European policy-making were easily undermined by the intergovernmental character of the measures agreed upon to fight the economic crises: already the first €110 billion loan for Greece in May 2010 was based on an intergovernmental declaration of the Eurozone heads of states and governments. This intergovernmental way was continued with the EFSM, EFSF and ESM. The so-called Troika (the European Central Bank, the European Commission, and the International Monetary Fund) is the institution designated to negotiate a memorandum of understanding with the states that request help from the ESM. Only *after* this memorandum is negotiated does the ESM Board of Governors decide about loans and credits (see ESM Guideline on Loans, art. 2).[9] It is not clear to whom this Troika is accountable. There is no role whatsoever foreseen for national parliaments or the EP. Thus, article 12 of the Lisbon Treaty, which lists several ways in which national parliaments can contribute actively to the good functioning of the Union, meets the normative force of the facts.

Some national parliaments are better equipped to deal with these facts, the best example being the German Bundestag which, with the help of the Federal

Constitutional Court[10] has wide-reaching information rights with respect to financial aid in the Eurozone. However, the TSCG goes one step further and potentially limits the effect of such information rights: if a state cannot fulfill its obligations under the Fiscal Compact[11] an automatic correction mechanism is triggered and a budgetary and economic partnership programme needs to be put in place (TSCG art. 5) which has to be endorsed and monitored by the European Commission and the Council. Thus, not only the states that happen to have severe economic problems but also those that violate the principles of the Fiscal Compact can be placed under supranational supervision. National parliaments do not seem to have been overly concerned about this loss of sovereignty. As of March 2013, parliamentary ratification was achieved successfully in all but Bulgaria and Hungary, where the treaty has not yet been submitted to the respective parliaments. Given that the treaty was signed on 12 March 2012 its entering into force on 1 January 2013 shows a quick ratification compared to the Treaty on the EU (21 months between the signing of the treaty and its entering into force), the Nice Treaty (24 months), or the Lisbon Treaty (824 months). It remains doubtful whether such a complex treaty with enormous financial consequences could have been thoroughly discussed in such a short time frame.

To sum up: first, there was no relevant input from national parliaments during the negotiations about the various instruments on fighting the economic crises, since those negotiations were carried out at an intergovernmental level; second, it is not clear how the democratic accountability of the Troika can be ensured; and third, the mechanisms foreseen for the application of the TSCG provisions concerning national fiscal management can undermine national fiscal sovereignty, i.e. parliamentary budgetary sovereignty is hollowed out.

Conclusions

Within the EU's compounded representative system parliaments occupy a central role. In order to live up to the yardsticks of democratic representative theory they are pivotal to ensuring that citizens are the authors of the laws that govern their polity, that they can thereby substantially change the conditions of their common life together if they choose to do so, that electoral processes allow the changing of representatives, and finally, that public bavardage ensures transparency and the exchange of arguments over the best course for reaching collective decisions.

It seems that national parliaments now have a range of instruments available to influence the European policy-making process on behalf of their respective electorates. Those instruments range from the scrutiny of their governments to the subsidiarity check; from the exchange of information via IPEX to COSAC contributions to the European Union's institutions; and from taking part in the revision of the treaties to being notified of applications for accession to the Union. Together with the EP 'multi-level parliamentarism' becomes a possibility. It may well be true that those instruments have to be further developed and parliaments have to get accustomed and interested in their potential new roles.

Parliaments now have the option to exercise more than the mere scrutiny and implementation function at the domestic level. However, so far, this remains a mere option due to the ongoing 'executivization' of European politics. The current economic crisis provides a vivid example. The sovereign debt crisis has shown that parliaments neither play a role in the negotiation of joint European remedies to fight economic emergencies, nor do they actively take over their role of representing those who are most affected by the crisis. Rather, the mantra of austerity politics seems to be widely accepted. In addition, policy fields from which the parliaments are blatantly excluded, national parliaments that do not demand close scrutiny of 'their' governments' for party political reasons, and a widespread clandestine committee, working group and agency system rather raise concerns over the EU's current representative quality. Citizens' capacity to determine their own laws via representatives is thereby undermined; the control of the administration working in a highly complex committee and agency system is highly limited; as seen in the current economic crisis, national parliaments rather succumb to the emergency rhetoric put forward by the European executives instead of discussing various economic options and visions for the future of Europe. What remains is the right to question the responsiveness of the representatives – data about the trust in national and European institutions do not bode well in this area. Electoral accountability is so far limited to those Member States that crumble under the debt crisis. Up to now the EU seems not to be a 'country for old parliaments'.

Notes

1 Compare Saward's (2012) notion of 'shape-shifting'.
2 For a critique of the claims-making approach see Lord and Pollak (2013).
3 The Finnish parliament being the exception starting the scrutiny process as early as possible and also covering the working groups. In Denmark the government is now obliged to inform parliament of the governmental position as early as possible and not just right before the Council meeting.
4 See www.eesc.europa.eu/?i=portal.en.about-the-committee (accessed 24 November 2012).
5 Each national parliament has two votes (art. 7, Protocol no. 2).
6 In the 18th COSAC Bi-Annual Report (see www.cosac.eu/documents/bi-annual-reports-of-cosac, accessed 30 November 2013) 20 out of 40 parliaments stated a need for further clarification of the subsidiarity check criteria used by national parliaments.
7 The 17th and 18th Bi-Annual Reports from COSAC (see link at note 6 above) report, however, that Member State parliaments wish for a swifter and more substantive responses by the Commission.
8 Meroni & Co., *Industrie Metallurgiche, SpA v. High Authority* (Cases 9 and 10/56), ECR 11–48, 53–86, ECJ 1958; *Guiseppe Romano v. Institut national d'assurance maladie-invalidité* [1981] ECR 1241.
9 Available at www.esm.europa.eu/about/legal-documents/index.htm (accessed 14 March 2013).
10 See BVerfG, 2 BvR 1390/12 (12 September 2012), available at www.bundesverfassungs gericht.de/en/decisions/rs20120912_2bvr139012en.html (accessed 14 March 2013).
11 This includes a general budget deficit of less than 3 per cent of GDP, a structural deficit of less than 1 per cent of GDP if the debt level is below 60 per cent, alternatively a structural deficit less than 0.5 per cent of GDP.

References

Ankersmit, F.R. (2002) *Political Representation*, Stanford, CA: Stanford University Press.

Auel, K. (2007) 'Democratic accountability and national parliaments: redefining the impact of parliamentary scrutiny in EU affairs', *European Law Journal*, 13 (4): 487–504.

Auel, K. and Benz, A. (2005) 'The politics of adaptation: The Europeanisation of national parliamentary systems', *Journal of Legislative Studies*, 11 (3–4): 372–393.

Auel, K. and Raunio, T. (ed.) (2012) 'National parliaments, electorates and EU affairs', *IHS Political Science Series*, www.ihs.ac.at/publications/pol/pw_129.pdf (last accessed 30 November 2013).

Barrett, G. (2008a) 'The king is dead, long live the king: the recasting by the Reform Treaty of the provisions of the Constitutional Treaty concerning national parliaments', *European Law Review*, 33 (1): 66–84.

Barrett, G. (ed.) (2008b) *National Parliaments and the European Union: The Constitutional Challenge for the Oireachtas and Other Member State Legislatures*, Dublin: Clarus Press.

Bellamy, R. (2008) 'No delegation without representation', paper presented at the international workshop, A Re-Assessment of Political Representation, University of Reading, UK: 22 February.

Bohman, J. (2007) *Democracy across Borders: From Dêmos to Dêmoi*, Cambridge, MA: MIT Press.

Cooper, R.I. (2012) 'A "virtual third chamber" for the European Union? National parliaments after the Treaty of Lisbon', *West European Politics*, 35 (3): 441–465.

Crum, B. and Fossum, J.E. (2012) 'A democratic backbone for international organisations: the multilevel parliamentary field', in T. Evas, U. Liebert and C. Lord (eds) *Multilayered Representation in the European Union. Parliaments, Courts and the Public Sphere*, Baden-Baden: Nomos.

Easton, D. (1953) *The Political System: An Inquiry into the State of Political Science*, New York: Alfred A. Knopf.

Eulau, H., Wahlke, J., Buchanan, W. and Ferguson, L. (1959) 'The role of the representative: some empirical observations on the theory of Edmund Burke', *American Political Science Review*, 53: 742–756.

European Commission (2011) 'Annual Report 2001 on relations between the European Commission and national parliaments', Brussels, 10 July 2012, COM 375 final.

Fasone. C. (2012) 'Interparliamentary cooperation and democratic representation in the European Union', in S. Kröger and D. Friedrich (eds) *The Challenge of Democratic Representation in the European Union*, Houndmills: Palgrave Macmillan, pp. 41–58.

Hayes-Renshaw, F. and Wallace, H. (1995) 'Executive power in the European Union: the functions and limits of the Council of Ministers', *Journal of European Public Policy*, 2 (4): 559–571.

Kiiver, P. (2006) *The National Parliaments in the European Union: A Critical View on EU Constitution-Building*, The Hague: Kluwer Law International.

Kröger, Sandra (2007) 'The end of democracy as we know it? The legitimacy deficits of bureaucratic social policy governance', *Journal of European Integration*, 29 (5), 565–582.

Lodge, J. (1993) 'EC policymaking: institutional dynamics', in J. Lodge (ed.) *The European Community and the Challenge of the Future*, 2nd edn, London: Pinter, pp. 1–36.

Lodge, J. (1994) 'Transparency and democratic legitimacy', *Journal of Common Market Studies*, 32 (3): 343–368.

Lord, C. and Pollak, J. (2010) 'The EU's many representative modes: Colliding? Cohering?', *Journal of European Public Policy*, 17 (1): 117–136.

Lord, C. and Pollak, J. (2013) 'The pitfalls of representation as claims-making', *Journal of European Integration*, 35 (5): 517–530.

Mansbridge, J. (2003) 'Rethinking representation', *American Political Science Review*, 97 (4): 515–528.

Mansbridge, J. (2009) 'A "selection model" of political representation', *Journal of Political Philosophy*, 17 (4): 369–398.

Maurer, A. (2001) 'National parliaments after Amsterdam: adaptation, re-calibration and Europeanisation by process', Paper for the Working Group Meeting, XXIVth COSAC, 8–9 April.

Maurer, A. (2002) *Parlamentarische Demokratie in der Europäischen Union. Der Beitrag des Europeäischen Parlaments und der nationalen Parlamente*, Baden-Baden: Nomos.

Maurer A. (2008) 'National parliaments in the architecture of Europe after the Constitutional Treaty', in G. Barrett (ed.) *National Parliaments and the European Union: The Constitutional Challenge for the Oireachtas and Other Member State Legislatures*, Dublin: Clarus Press.

Maurer, A. (2011) 'Mehrebenenparlamentarismus – Konzeptionelle und empirische Fragen zu den Funktionen von Parlamenten nach dem Vertrag von Lissabon', in G. Abels and A. Eppler (eds) *Auf dem Weg zum Mehrebenenparlamentarismus. Funktionen von Parlamenten im politischen System der EU*, Baden-Baden: Nomos, pp. 43–64.

Maurer, A. (2012) *Parlamente in der Europäischen Union*, Wien: WUV/UTB.

Maurer, A. and Wessels, W. (eds) (2001) *National Parliaments on their Ways to Europe: Losers or Latecomers?*, Baden-Baden: Nomos.

Mill, J.S. (1972 [1861)] *Utilitarianism, On Liberty and Considerations on Representative Government*, London: Dent.

O'Brennan, J. and Raunio, T (eds) (2007) *National Parliaments within the Enlarged European Union: From victims of integration to competitive actors?*, Abingdon: Routledge.

Pitkin, H. (1967) *The Concept of Political Representation*, Berkeley, CA; Los Angeles, CA; London: University of California Press.

Pollak, J. (2007) 'Contested meaning of representation', *Journal of Comparative Politics*, 5 (1): 87–103.

Pollak, J. and Slominski, P. (2003) 'Influencing EU politics? The case of the Austrian parliament', *Journal of Common Market Studies*, 41 (4): 707–729.

Politt, C., Bathgate, K., Caulfield, J., Smullen, A. and Talbot, C. (2001) 'Agency fever? Analysis of an international policy fashion', *Journal of Comparative Policy Analysis: Research and Practice*, 3 (3): 271–290.

Przeworski, A., Stokes, S.C. and Manin, B. (eds) (1999) *Democracy, Accountability, and Representation*, Cambridge: Cambridge University Press.

Raunio, T. (1999) 'Always one step behind? National legislatures and the European Union', *Government and Opposition*, 34 (2): 180–202.

Raunio, T. (2005) 'Holding governments accountable in European affairs: explaining cross-national variation', *Journal of Legislative Studies*, 11 (3–4): 319–342.

Raunio, T. (2010) 'Destined for irrelevance? Subsidiarity control by national parliaments', Europe Working Paper 36/2010, Real Instituto Elcano.

Rozenberg, O. (2002) 'The involvement of national parliaments in European Union Affairs: An empirical test of two variables', Paper for the ECPR Joint Sessions, Turin.

Saward, M. (2006) 'The representative claim', *Contemporary Political Theory*, 5: 297–318.

Saward, M. (2010) *The Representative Claim*, Oxford: Oxford University Press.

Saward, M. (2012) 'Shape-shifting representation', Paper for APSA 2012 Panel 'Counter-representation and democratic legitimacy', available at http://papers.ssrn.com/sol3/papers.cfm?abstract_id=2104796 (accessed 21 January 2013).

Sonnicksen, J. (2010) 'Die demokratischen Grundsätze', in A. Marchetti and C. Demesmay (eds) *Der Vertrag von Lissabon. Analyse und Bewertung*, Baden-Baden: Nomos, pp. 143–160.

Strøm, K. (2003) 'Parliamentary democracy and delegation', in K. Strøm, W. Müller and T. Bergman (eds) *Delegation and Accountability in Parliamentary Democracies*, Oxford: Oxford University Press, pp. 55–106.

Urbinati, N. and Warren, M. (2008) 'The concept of representation in contemporary democratic theory', *Annual Review of Political Science*, 11: 387–412.

2 Party strategies towards interest groups in a Europeanized Europe

Anne Rasmussen and Gert-Jan Lindeboom

Introduction

To ensure *democratic legitimacy*, a representative democracy needs to be constructed in such a way that it is possible for the views of the citizens to get transmitted to the decision-makers who have been delegated the responsibility for policy making. It needs to be possible for the decision-makers to hear the view of the public, either by giving the public a direct access to them or by ensuring that strong *gatekeepers* are in place that can help transmit the views of the public to the political system.

Political parties are central actors in modern-day Western democracies. They act as some of the important gatekeepers that help transmit the views of the public to the political system (Easton 1957). Political parties are often important for ensuring a high degree of coherence between public opinion and policy, and that political systems end up acting in a politically responsible manner. Hence, it often depends heavily on political parties whether citizen views are channelled to the political system. In this way, the interaction of political parties with individual citizens and interest groups is central to the quality of democracy. Thus they contribute to democratic legitimacy by ensuring that the decisions made reflect the views of the public and have a high problem-solving capacity (Scharpf 1999).

In the European Union (EU), the involvement of partisan actors at the level of EU decision-making shares similarities with the national level in some respects. Examples of how parties aggregate the views of the voters around a set of party platforms and engage in deliberation along traditional left–right conflict lines can clearly be found (Lindberg *et al.* 2008). At the same time, party politics is also different at the EU level. Even if actors with partisan links can be found in all EU institutions, the extent to which these organizations are organized according to an intrinsic partisan logic and decision-making within these bodies is conducted along partisan conflict lines varies (Lindberg *et al.* 2008). Moreover, EU party politics takes place and involves partisan actors from both the national and EU levels.

As a result, studies of EU party politics do not only look at the EU level but also at how the EU affects the behaviour and organizations of parties at the national level. With an increasing number of competences transferred from national governments to the European Commission ('the Commission'), it seems only logical that national political parties adapt to such changes and alter their strategies accordingly. National political parties participate in EU politics by being involved both in the preparation and implementation of EU policy. In fact, even in policy matters that are not strictly about Europe and do not concern EU competence, the EU might still have an effect on national parties by affecting party organizations and how parties interact with other actors.

Broadly speaking, such studies are conducted under the heading of 'Europeanization studies'. We devote the first part of this chapter to a discussion of the *channels* through which Europeanization might affect national parties and an overview of some of the important pieces of empirical work in this literature. As we will show, this literature is still relatively sparse and draws somewhat contradictory conclusions about the extent to which Europeanization has had an effect on national political parties. Moreover, studies are often constructed in such a way that it is difficult to isolate the effect of Europe on national political parties from other effects. Finally, there is still an important gap in this literature when it comes to looking at how parties interact with interest groups in matters of EU policy. Parties play a formal role in legislative decision-making and distinguish themselves from interest groups by running for election to obtain seats in political institutions (Schattschneider 1948). In contrast, an interest group is an 'association of individuals or organizations, usually formally organized, that on the basis of one or more shared concerns, attempts to influence public policy'.[1]

The lack of studies on party–interest group relations in EU policy may seem surprising, since the role of parties is weaker in the political constellation of the EU than in a number of EU Member States. Instead, there is a particularly high emphasis on involving interest groups in EU decision-making processes. This may affect the attractiveness of engaging in interactions between parties and interest groups. Apart from an existing study of how interest groups rate the importance of contacts with national parties for influencing EU policy (Rasmussen 2012), no one has examined how Europeanization affects interest group–party relations and, to date, no studies have approached this issue from the perspective of the national parties.

After our literature review of Europeanization effects on national parties, we therefore dig deeper into a case study of national party strategies towards interest groups in response to Europeanization. We do so by systematically comparing their interaction with interest groups in EU and national policy; thereby we avoid some of the difficulties in existing Europeanization research of isolating the effect of Europe. Our key question is whether parties interact differently or to a different extent with groups at the EU level when compared to their behaviour in national arenas. We do not start from an initial expectation of what the degree or character of cooperation between parties and interest groups should look like in areas of European integration, but conduct a study that is exploratory in nature rather than using a deductive design. Our analysis is based on semi-structured qualitative interviews with all Danish parliamentary parties in 2007–8. In this way, we will be able to examine not only (the lack of) differences in *the degree* and *character* of the interaction between parties and groups in national as opposed to EU policy, but also get closer to the possible causes attributed by our respondents to the identified patterns.

Our case study of Denmark shows that the focus of national parties on interaction with interest groups in areas of EU policy remains marginal despite the increased transfer of national competences to the EU level. The responsibility for interest group relations in EU matters is often delegated to a small subset of politicians in the Parliament specialized in Europe or to the party's members of the European Parliament (EP). This is interesting given that Denmark represents a 'most likely' case for the EU involvement of national members of Parliament (MPs) in EU affairs, owing to its high degree of scrutiny of EU matters. Our evidence shows that national MPs purposively limit their interest group contacts in EU policy. The main reason is that, even though parties operate in an environment affected by European integration, it is still achievements in national rather than EU policy that ultimately help them secure *votes* and *office*.

Europeanization and political parties

The scope of the literature on Europeanization has increased considerably over the last decade and includes many different definitions of Europeanization (Featherstone and Radaelli 2003; Ladrech 2010). A growing literature emphasizes how European institutions and integration more generally influence the processes of institutional adaptation of domestic actors to European integration (see for example Börzel 2009; Ladrech 2002; Mair 2006). Although scholars disagree about the extent of Europeanization's impact on national political parties (compare Poguntke *et al.* 2007b; Almeida 2012), we do know that Europeanization has at least some impact on political parties. Changes in the national electoral or legislative arenas may provide incentives for domestic actors to change preferences and strategies (Van der Eijk and Franklin 2004; Taggart 1998; Hooghe *et al.* 2002). For the present purpose, we study Europeanization by focusing on how *European integration affects political parties and party politics in a top-down manner.*[2]

Studying the Europeanization of political parties is particularly challenging because we are likely to be witnessing primarily the *indirect* effects of Europeanization. As pointed out by Ladrech (2002), 'Europe does not hit parties in a direct manner'. EU legislation gets debated at the national level but is often absent in the primary operating environments and activities of national political parties; as such parties are not impacted *directly* by European integration. Often there is also no clear incentive for national political parties to turn to the EU, because there are neither 'apparent resources that can be transferred nor allies that could be useful for domestic partisan gain, nor are they legally obliged to interact with either EU institutions or operate at the EU level' (Ladrech 2009: 8). On the other hand, since European integration affects the classic party goals of votes, office and policy (see for example Fenno 1973) the national contexts of party structures and strategies are to a significant extent shaped by EU decisions.

'Channels' of Europeanization

We start by discussing how effects of Europeanization on national political parties may be channelled through changes in the classical party goals. In other words, we are interested in how changes in the electorate (*votes*), in parties' relation with the national government (*office*), and changes in patterns of party competition (*policy*) act as channels through which their strategies and preferences are Europeanized.

If we first look at *votes*, changes in the electorate with regard to EU integration are relevant to this study, for these affect individual parties and may thereby also affect broader patterns of party competition. A considerable body of literature has focused on such electoral trends, focusing specifically on Eurosceptic attitudes and resultant party choice or party affiliations (see for example Hooghe and Marks 2007, 2009; de Vries 2007; Kopecký and Mudde 2002; Gabel 2000). More recent studies (Hooghe and Marks 2009) in this tradition now report finding politicization – i.e. a rising salience – of EU issues across different electorates. However, these studies generally concentrate on extreme EU positions rather than the role of pro-EU positions in the electorate.

When looking at *office*, EU integration has also 'changed the game' when it comes to political decision-making. Because an increasing number of political decisions are no longer taken at the national level, the relation between national executives and national Parliament is changing. It has been argued that the current setup of regular legislative meetings of the Council of Ministers and the European Council strengthens the position of the national executive (see for example Moravcsik 1994). A relatively small group of policy experts is included in European decision-making processes, whereas a large number of 'EU outsiders' are left out. In the meantime, the 'EU insiders' enjoy far greater insight and decision-making power in the EU than those politicians that are limited to national political arenas. As such, European integration is argued to 'change the rules of the game', and strengthen the national executive by for instance increasing information asymmetries between government parties and opposition parties in Parliament (Mair 2000; Ladrech 2002).

Finally, in terms of *policy* and competition in national party systems, Mair (2006) even argues that competition becomes hollowed out as the scope of European-level decision-making extends. Any decision taken by the EU can no longer be considered a viable political policy choice in the national arena. As such, the range of policy options and instruments that political parties can compete over in elections is reduced, thereby lowering the stakes of competition between political parties (Mair 2000). Support for this 'policy constraints' thesis is found by comparatively investigating the mention of policy issues in party manifestos (see for example Dorussen and Nanou 2006). Indeed, Dorussen and Nanou found that different political parties in different EU Member States converged in terms of the contents of their manifestos. This effect was found particularly for Eurosceptic parties. As such, since parties promote less divergent positions, policy choices for voters have become more limited.

European integration affects the strategic behaviour and structures of political parties through these three channels. We proceed by discussing a series of relevant studies on how political parties react or respond to these changes that may be attributed to Europeanization (for a comprehensive literature review on the Europeanization of political parties, see Ladrech 2009).

Programmatic change

When the electorate demands more attention is paid to European issues, parties may for instance react by including European issues more prominently in their party programmes, or attributing more importance to such issues in Parliament. Political parties may strategically take a more conscious position *vis-à-vis* other parties on specific EU policy areas, if such issues become relevant in national contexts. On the other hand, Mair (2000) argued that, with more decisions taken at the European level, policy choices for national governments in their national contexts become limited. As such we may also find reduced policy space in national elections. Also, when the government is involved with an increasing number of issues that are discussed and decided upon at the European level, we may also expect certain policies to be removed from the national political agenda.

First of all, the clearest support for a Europeanization effect would be found if national parties refer more or differently to the EU in their party manifestos. Through these references we may get a preliminary idea of the impact of the EU in domestic politics (Ladrech 2002). Looking at the combination of positions and the salience of EU policy areas, Kritzinger and Michalowitz (2005) found in Austria, Finland and Sweden, three relatively new EU Member States, considerable influence of European integration on the programmatic content of parties. Here, the authors were able to account for what Haverland (2006) calls the problem of non-variance, because they investigated the positions and salience of EU policy before and after accession.

Pennings (2006) on the other hand, used a larger dataset, encompassing more Member States to analyse the emphasis on the EU in national party manifestos. He found that the number of references depends greatly on strategic institutional and party factors. This shows the value of analysing Europeanization as a dependent variable across different institutional contexts (see Kulahci 2012). More generally across different countries however, the number of references to Europe in party manifestos is remarkably low, though rising over the years. Even if it is possible that political parties only mention policy areas that are outside EU competence, this may also reflect the wish of political parties to appear 'in charge' of a broad range of policy areas. In similar terms, Poguntke *et al.* (2007b) found little evidence of heavier involvement of EU specialists in drafting party manifestos, beyond the relatively narrow directly EU-related policy areas.

With regard to parties' attention to European issues, the empirical results remain mixed. Steenbergen and Scott (2004) for instance have found increasing attention paid to European issues when political parties were competing in national elections. In Denmark, on the other hand, Green-Pedersen (2012) found that regardless of the increasing prominence of European issues for the Danish electorate, parties tended to weigh their coalition interests carefully against their electoral interest. He shows that EU issues remained largely depoliticized for mainstream parties in Denmark, not because the issues lacked electoral potential, but because the parties would risk exclusion from potential coalitions. As a result, Green-Pedersen concluded that pro-European/mainstream parties in Denmark have no incentive to bring European issues to the public agenda, whereas Eurosceptic parties, which do have an incentive to discuss European issues, usually cannot do so due to the refusal of mainstream parties.

Other studies have focused on the question whether the issue of EU integration represents a new dimension or line of conflict in party competition (Hix 1999; Kriesi 2007), or such issues can be incorporated in existing patterns of party competition (Gabel and Scheve 2007; Hooghe *et al.* 2002). However, Almeida (2012) finds no evidence for a common approach to EU integration in different member states, and shows varying responses to Europe between parties of similar party families across different countries.

Intra party organizational changes

Next to potential programmatic change, scholars also see a potential impact of Europeanization on party structures. Consider for instance the argument that Europeanization may create a division between actors who are involved in European politics and those who are not. Whereas many national MPs negotiate in Brussels and often discuss issues with fellow government representatives, other MPs lack this possibility and are often completely excluded from decision-making at the European level. It may therefore become necessary to improve or alter chains of accountability within national parties. As before, such changes in the organizational structures of political parties may be informed by electoral demands, or by an altered relation with the national executive itself. For instance, if the public is more informed about European issues, it may become necessary for the party to also improve internal accountability within the party.

In this respect, Poguntke *et al.* (2007b) draw attention to the fact that both institutional structures and actual behaviour in these parties may be affected. Primarily, they argue, Europeanization alters the relation of party elites and EU specialists *vis-à-vis* other party members, because they enjoy a prominent role at the centre of (in)formal EU decision making. It is argued that if this arena of decision-making becomes more relevant, then these two groups are likely to gain power and resources within Euro-friendly political parties. Obviously, the strength of this intra-party shift of power is mediated by several important variables, such as different organizational or ideological traditions, or for instance by the incumbency of a party (Poguntke *et al.* 2007b).

In a large cross-sectional empirical analysis, Poguntke *et al.* (2007b) found little or no evidence for changes in the institutional structures of parties that would alter the position of party elites and EU specialists in relation to the rank-and-file of the party. Poguntke *et al.* did find indications of more *informal* changes within parties that favour these two groups even though the variation across parties and countries was considerable. Party elites especially, who have privileged access to EU decision-making arenas where they represent their country, enjoy a greater power base within their party. Raunio (2002) also analysed shifts in the balance of power within parties. He identified greater centralization of power and leader autonomy within political parties in especially countries that have less explicit procedures of parliamentary scrutiny of European affairs. This follows the logic that individual party leaders from different countries need to reach agreements in supranational negotiations, which are generally conducted behind closed doors. Only the results of these negotiations are subsequently reported back to national parliaments and to their parties. Especially when decisions are reached through majority voting, these elites can quite effectively avoid accountability for the decision: '[a]fter all, national party politicians can hardly be held accountable for decisions to which they did not agree!' (Poguntke *et al.* 2007a: 764). A later piece by Carter and Poguntke (2010) also showed that party elites, when involved in EU decision-making, hold a relatively powerful position within their respective national parties, and that their position has been strengthened over time. A notable finding is that, apart from minor differences, these conclusions generally hold throughout all Member States in the EU.

In sum, our review of important pieces of work on the Europeanization impact on national political parties clearly shows that a substantial body of literature has developed, which addresses many different themes. In some respects, a general consensus forms around Mair's thesis of depoliticization (2000). While issues of European integration are growing in importance, parties still seem reluctant to position these issues at the centre of attention. In this way Europe does not affect much the everyday work of national politicians. At the same time, other evidence suggests that the power relations inside parties are in fact adapting to the European integration process.

Political parties and external contacts

Despite considerably more focus on the Europeanization of national parties and party politics, the literature still contains gaps. To date we know little about how Europe has affected the external contacts of political parties. Next to the already-discussed party programmatic changes or new internal party structures, such interaction of political parties with other actors is central for the quality of democracy. The EU is often described as a special type of political system where, due to a less prominent position of political parties, the link to the electorate is weaker (Gaffney 1996). In contrast, interest groups have a more privileged position in EU policy making: the European Commission deliberately seeks to include non-partisan societal actors in the policy process and gives them a prominent role (Greenwood 2011; Mazey and Richardson 1997). Several interest groups receive direct funding from the EU budget and/or are allocated privileged access to the decision-making venues through for example giving them advisory committee seats. In the words of Peter Mair, 'the EU fosters a new version of democratic engagement that may indirectly undermine the conventional party agenda' (2006: 165). Differences in the relative strength of parties and interest groups may affect both the degree and character of the way they interact with each other. Political parties may be reluctant to expand contacts to interest groups, since they often see themselves as the 'main interlocutors' between citizens and politics. However, if their main goal is to influence policy outcomes, maintaining and expanding contacts with interest groups that have direct access to the European Commission may be a key way for them to adapt to the changing political environment in which EU decisions are taken.

Just as the Europeanization of national parties has been examined, an existing body of literature examines how the EU affects interest groups (for an overview of this literature, see Eising 2006). However, Europeanization research has examined interest groups and parties in isolation from each other, just as the majority of studies in the broader political science literature have (for reviews, see Allern 2010; Rasmussen and Lindeboom, 2013). This is surprising given Raunio's prediction (2002: 415) that European integration would not only have an individual impact on national interest groups and parties but also result in a weakening of *the links* between them. He argued that interest groups no longer have incentives to interact with national political parties, because they can target the European Commission directly on an increasing number of issues. The only exception among the studies examining whether Europeanization affects the links between groups and parties is a recent study by Rasmussen (2012) examining the importance interest groups attach to political parties in national and EU policy. However, this study does not deal with these interactions from the perspective of the political parties and therefore does not map whether European integration exerts any effect on party strategies *vis-à-vis* interest groups.

From a rational choice perspective, the relationship between parties and interest groups can be seen as one in which groups provide resources to parties that can help them secure votes and office, while in return parties grant groups access to political decision-making (Warner 2000; Allern *et al.* 2007). We can expect reciprocal interactions between groups and parties when the benefits of repeated interactions outweigh the costs for both actors. Presumably, the ongoing process of European integration has an effect on the pay-offs in this resource exchange model. The idea here is that EU-level stimuli might make parties more or less dependent on the resources of interest groups when it comes to securing *votes* and *office*, and along the same lines, these stimuli might make groups more or less dependent on the national parties when it comes to securing access to political decision-making. As an example, national parties may depend more on groups to influence EU policy than national policy due to the privileged access groups often enjoy in EU policy forums, whereas for interest groups the situation may be the exact opposite of course.

From a historical perspective, the relationship between parties and interest groups is linked less to their rational calculations than to their historical legacies and existing cooperation patterns. Interest groups may not adapt strategically to the new EU opportunity structures, but may be conditioned by their historical legacies and bonds to groups no matter whether the policy matters discussed are EU or national policy. Parties with weak links to groups are likely to keep relations to groups at a low level in both spheres of policy no matter whether or not the EU offers them a new opportunity structure.

Research design

Whereas we have employed a deductive, theory-testing design in previous studies of party–interest group linkage (Rasmussen 2012; Rasmussen and Lindeboom 2013), our specific aim here is to employ a qualitative design that is explorative in nature. Our main reason for doing this is that we are interested not only in mapping the interactions between parties and groups, but also in getting closer to the possible reasons attributed by our party respondents to the (lack of) differences in the degree and character of their interaction with groups. To this end Anne Rasmussen conducted qualitative interviews with key informants from the Danish parliamentary parties in the period 2007–8 (see annex). She asked to speak to the party official with the best overview of both the party's contacts with interest groups that have a general nature and those that focus on specific policy cases. In most parties, this person was the head of its central political–financial unit, which is typically a unit that gives strategic advice to both the party leadership and the individual MPs that serve as spokesperson in specific policy areas.[3] Her interview guide systematically asked the respondents to compare the interaction that national political parties have with interest groups in EU and national policy. In this way, we address some of the criticism of the existing body of Europeanization studies, which have had difficulty isolating the effect of Europe (Haverland 2006). At the same time, we need to bear in mind of course that the borderline between these two 'political spheres' is not always clear-cut. The Danish case is ideal for the comparison, because the likelihood of finding involvement of national politicians in EU policy should be somewhat higher in this context than in many others. First, the degree of parliamentary scrutiny of EU affairs and involvement of national parties in these matters is particularly strong in the Danish case (Bergman 1997; Wessels *et al.* 2003). Second, even if the EU is clearly not a major issue on the Danish political agenda, it has in fact received some attention especially in 1985, 1991 and 1996 in connection with the discussions of new treaties (Green-Pedersen 2012). This also means that the Danish case is not necessarily a representative one of all EU Member States. However, the fact that it is a 'most likely case' means that if we do not find evidence of Europeanization here, the likelihood of finding such evidence elsewhere may be even lower.

Party strategies towards interest groups

It is clear from the interviews that the degree of interaction in EU politics and national politics varies considerably. All respondents agree that, despite increasing

European integration, EU politics accounts for a small share of the contacts between the Danish national parties and interest groups. The following statement from R3 illustrates this very well:

> I know that the number of EU rules has increased but the reality is that the EU plays a marginal role in Danish politics.... EU politics takes place in 'an isolated sphere'. It has clearly lost attention the last 10 years. There was some sort of hype after the referendums, it's over now.

R1 adds, 'It's not my impression that our EU policy officers are flooded with contact requests', and R6 that 'we tell each other how ready for globalization we are, but with regard to EU policy we might not be. How important is the European Committee of the Danish Parliament? The battle is fought elsewhere[.]' The respondents also agree that not only does the intensity of party–interest group contacts in EU and national policy vary, their character is also different. The average EU case is described as more technical and less politicized than an average national one. R3 gives an overview of the different types of cases a party deals with: 'Some cases are in the top of the hierarchy and need to be handled in a strategic manner. Here the core business of the organization is at stake. Ninety-nine point nine per cent of such cases are national'. In addition the respondent points out how not just the character of the EU policies negotiated but also the way the negotiation of EU policy is structured adds to de-politicization. He states how:

> The negotiation of EU policy is shielded from the rest of our business.... It is done by politicians who are specialized in the cases together with representatives from the ministries and employees from the interests groups who are also highly specialized ... the conduct of these matters is systematized and formalized to an extreme degree ... It's a sort of parallel political system.

R5 points out that one reason the EU area is less politicized is the tradition to reach broad compromises in this area, in contrast to a number of other national policy areas, 'There is a fine tradition in the area of the EU to strive for as broad consensus as possible. In EU matters voting in the Danish Parliament is different from national matters.'

When asked to explain the substantial differences in contacts between national parties and interest groups in national and EU policy matters, respondents point to a number of factors. First, several of them emphasize how EU policy distinguishes itself from national policy by being more government-driven. Even if the Danish parliament exerts a certain degree of scrutiny over the Danish government, the negotiations lie in the hand of the government and the Danish parliament often gets involved relatively late in the policy discussion (see also Sousa 2008). This means that the groups themselves put an even stronger emphasis on contacting the government rather than the parliamentary parties in EU matters than they do in national ones. Moreover, national political parties focus their energy on the government if they want to influence a given matter rather than contacting the groups. R3 explains, 'Yes, we have got parliamentary control of EU policy but you know at that stage many matters are settled', and R6 follows up, 'if we need something in an EU legislative area, we need to contact the relevant minister'.

Second, it is clear from more or less all interviews that national politicians have very little incentive to engage extensively with interest groups in EU policy matters, because such contacts do not benefit their career. R3 states how 'such efforts are not what will determine the "political destiny" of the politicians'. National elections are affected by primarily national policy issues rather than European ones, and even those elections that are supposed to be about Europe often are not (see also Reif and Schmitt 1980; Van der Eijk and Franklin 2004). As a result many parties specifically aim at adding a 'Danish angle' to the EU issues. According to R1, 'if EU cases are relevant for Denmark, we try to sell them as an example of how the EU does something for a specific group or business'. In such cases, it is worthwhile for the national politicians to engage, and in such cases there will be more contact with interest groups, but such cases are the exception. Also, experience with EU issues is not necessarily regarded as a stepping-stone for moving up within the party hierarchy. R3 explains how 'there was a phase where many prominent politicians within a party were knowledgeable and had some experience in the EU area. I think that phase is over'.

A third reason emphasized by the respondents for the lower focus on EU policy is the lack of opportunity national political parties have to influence these policy matters. This relates to the point already mentioned, that EU policy is perceived as being more technical and less politicized. R1 explains that 'if it's just a legislative proposal that implements an EU directive where the framework has already been agreed, then we would rarely get involved'.

A fourth reason mentioned is the division of labour between national parties and their Members of the European Parliament (MEPs). MPs simply get less involved and have fewer contacts with interest groups in EU policy, because a lot of the responsibility lies with their MEPs. R1 explains that for them, 'EU policy is something that takes place in the EP'. Moreover, when commenting on the low number of contacts between national parties and interest groups in matters of EU policy, R6 states,

> the answers would be completely different if you asked the Danish Members of the European Parliament (MEPs) rather than the Danish MPs. Most of the contacts between groups and politicians are to the MEPs and to a much lesser extent to the national politicians.

The focus on the MEPs is remarkable in the light that the EP is far from involved in all policy matters and at all stages of the policy processes.

Discussion and conclusion

The academic literature contains ample evidence of how European integration has exerted a substantial impact on national actors, institutions and decision-making processes. However, scholars examining the impact of European integration on national parties and party politics have often drawn more modest conclusions. One of the reasons is that the EU does not affect parties in a direct way by requiring them to live up to certain organizational or behavioural standards, but in an indirect manner by affecting the environment in which they act. At the same time it is clear that research on the Europeanization of political parties is crucial, since it is often the responsibility of these parties that the views of citizens are transferred to the political system. Hence, for a representative democracy to be *legitimate*, mechanisms have to exist for the views of the citizens to get transmitted to the political system and ultimately be reflected in the policy outcomes. In national political systems, political parties have traditionally contributed to democratic legitimacy by facilitating this process. We have identified the channels through which Europeanization might influence national political parties, and reviewed important pieces of empirical work on the Europeanization of national parties. Our review shows that, even though this body of literature has grown, it still draws somewhat contradictory conclusions about the effects of Europeanization. Moreover, it often faces difficulty of isolating the effect of Europe from other factors and still contains empirical gaps.

Our empirical case study focused on one of these, i.e. whether European integration affects how national parties interact with interest groups. Comparing party strategies to groups in national and EU policy in Denmark we show that there are substantial differences in both the degree and character of these strategies in the two policy spheres. Our interviews with key partisan players demonstrate that the focus of national parties on interaction with interest groups in EU policy is marginal despite the increased transfer of national competences to the EU level. The responsibility for relations to interest groups in EU matters is often delegated to a small subset of politicians in the Parliament specialized in Europe or to the party's MEPs. This is interesting, given that the Danish Parliament might be seen as a 'most likely' case for EU involvement of national MPs owing to its strong scrutiny of EU affairs.

The substantial differences that we found in the party strategies towards interest groups in EU and national policy clearly contradict a historical perspective expecting parties to keep doing 'business as usual' in the newer EU policy sphere as the older national one by interacting with groups to the same degree and in the same way in both. This is clearly not the case. EU and national policy are treated and prioritized differently by the national political parties. The question is then whether this means that party strategies towards interest groups instead follow the predictions of the rational exchange model where parties should prioritize groups more when they have more to gain from interacting with them.

At first outset, our evidence is negative. We might have expected national parties interested in influencing policy to prioritize groups more in EU policy due to the prominent role these groups have in EU matters (see for example Mair 2006; Mazey and Richardson 1997; Greenwood 2011; Rasmussen and Lindeboom 2013). However, none of the Danish parties seem to take advantage of this fact or put more pressure on interest groups to get their views heard on EU policy matters. In fact, confronted with this finding, R4 made the following remark about studying politics in general:

> One of the surprising things is that political work is worrying, irrational and unorganized. We spend a lot of time on 'nothing' where people in a business would say, let's reach an agreement and walk out of the door and implement it. However, politicians cannot be managed in such a way and maybe this is something citizens should be pleased about after all.

However, before dismissing the rational exchange model entirely, we need to remember that influencing policy is not the only goal of national politicians. In addition to *policy*, Fenno (1973) drew attention to *votes* and *office.* In other words, national MPs do not care only about putting their fingerprints on policy but also about securing votes and office. When it comes to achieving the latter two, our interviews provided plenty of evidence that a focus on EU policy cannot help them much. EU issues are not politicized and often do not have a character that allows them to be easily 'sold' at home. EU-level stimuli clearly do not make parties more dependent on the resources of the interest groups when it comes to securing some of their primary goals of votes and office relevant to their basic existence. As a result, the pattern we see may not be an irrational one after all. The ongoing process of European integration has not affected the payoffs in the resource exchange model between parties and interest groups positively.

This is unlikely to change in the coming years. In fact we see that even during the current economic and financial crisis national parties do not devote much attention to the EU in their everyday business. The EU is faced with some of its biggest challenges ever by having to make difficult decisions to fight the current economic and financial crisis that will have a substantial impact on the daily lives of millions of EU citizens. However, these developments are handled largely as matters of 'high-level EU politics' and not matters to which an average national political party devotes a lot of attention. Moreover, even if some parties decide to do so, such parties are not likely to engage in extensive dialogue with citizens or interest groups about these matters. As such, the current economic and financial crisis of the EU cannot be expected to affect the Europeanization of party–interest group linkages. In fact, it illuminates the double 'degree of misfit' that risks manifesting itself between the activities and policies of domestic actors and those of the EU (Börzel 2005). This poses potentially significant problems for political parties in the Member States and more generally for the quality of democracy as a whole, both at the national and EU level.

Annex

- Morten Bangsgaard, Secretary General, Conservative Party.
- Bjarne Corydon, Head of the Political–financial Unit of the Social Democrats.
- Jesper Groenenberg, Head of the Political–financial Unit of the Danish Social-Liberal Party.
- Soren Majrup Jensen, Head of the Political–financial Unit of the Danish Liberal Party.
- Turid Leirvoll, Head of the Political–financial Unit of the Socialist People's Party.
- Søren Søndergaard, Head of Public Affairs, Danish People's Party.

Notes

1 See www.britannica.com/EBchecked/topic/290136/interest-group (accessed 30 November 2013).

2 At the same time, we acknowledge that Europeanization is a two-way process (Kulahci 2012). National parties and executives laid down the foundations for the European Union, and national contexts still shape day-to-day European institutions today. Despite this influence, parties primarily exert this influence indirectly (Lindberg *et al.* 2008; Döring 2007). Through party government, for instance, a political party is able to get its points across in the European Council of Ministers. Another option is to use its partisan channels in the European Parliament (Hix *et al.* 2007).

3 We quote the respondents with a number, which does not reflect the alphabetical order in which they are listed in the annex.

References

Allern, E.H. (2010) *Political Parties and Interest Groups in Norway*, Colchester: ECPR Press.

Allern, E.H., Aylott, N. and Christiansen, F.J. (2007) 'Social democrats and trade unions in Scandinavia: The decline and persistence of institutional relationships', *European Journal of Political Research*, 46(5): 607–635.

Almeida, D. (2012) *The Impact of European Integration on Political Parties. Beyond the Permissive Consensus*, London: Routledge.

Bergman, T. (1997) 'National parliaments and EU affairs committees: notes on empirical variation and competing explanations', *Journal of European Public Policy*, 4(3): 373–387.

Börzel, T. (2005) 'Europeanization: how the European Union interacts with its Member States', in S. Bulmer and C. Lequesne (eds) *The Member States of the European Union*, Oxford: Oxford University Press.

Börzel, T. (2009) *Coping with Accession to the European Union. New Modes of Environmental Governance*, Houndmills: Palgrave Macmillan.

Carter, E. and Poguntke, T. (2010) 'How European integration changes national parties: evidence from a 15-country study', *West European Politics*, 33(2): 297–324.

De Vries, C.E. (2007) 'Sleeping giant: fact or fairytale?: How European integration affects national elections', *European Union Politics*, 8(3): 363–385.

Döring, H. (2007) 'The composition of the College of Commissioners: patterns of delegation', *European Union Politics*, 8(2): 207–228.

Dorussen, H. and Nanou, K. (2006) 'European integration, intergovernmental bargaining, and convergence of party programmes', *European Union Politics*, 7(2): 235–256.

Easton, D. (1957) 'An approach to the analysis of political systems', *World Politics*, 9(3): 383–400.

Eising, R. (2006) 'Interest groups and social movements', in P. Graziano and M. Vink (eds) *Europeanization: New Research Agendas*, Basingstoke: Palgrave Macmillan.

Featherstone, K. and Radaelli, C. (eds) (2003) *The Politics of Europeanization*, Oxford: Oxford University Press.

Fenno, R.F. (1973) *Congressmen in Committees*, Boston: Little Brown and Company.

Gabel, M. (2000) 'European integration, voters and national politics', *West European Politics*, 23(4): 52–72.

Gabel, M. and Scheve, K. (2007) 'Mixed messages: party dissent and mass opinion on European integration', *European Union Politics*, 8(1): 37–59.

Gaffney, J. (1996) *Political Parties and the European Union*, London: Routledge.

Green-Pedersen, C. (2012) 'A giant fast asleep? Party incentives and the politicisation of European Integration', *Political Studies*, 60(1): 115–130.

Greenwood, J. (2011) *Interest Representation in the European Union*, London: Palgrave.

Haverland, M. (2006) 'Does the EU *cause* domestic developments? Improving case selection in Europeanisation research', *West European Politics*, 29(1): 134–146.

Hix, S. (1999) 'Dimensions and alignments in European Union politics: Cognitive constraints and partisan responses', *European Journal of Political Research*, 35(1): 69–106.

Hix, S., Noury, A.G. and Roland, G. (2007) *Democratic Politics in the European Parliament*, Cambridge: Cambridge University Press.

Hooghe, E.A.E.B. and Marks, G.W. (2007) 'Understanding Euroscepticism', *Acta Politica*, 42 (2–3): (Special issue).

Hooghe, L. and Marks, G. (2009) 'A postfunctionalist theory of European integration: from permissive consensus to constraining dissensus', *British Journal of Political Science*, 39(1): 1–23.

Hooghe, L., Marks, G. and Wilson, C.J. (2002) 'Does left/right structure party positions on European integration?', *Comparative Political Studies*, 35(8): 965–989.

Kopecký, P. and Mudde, C. (2002) 'The two sides of Euroscepticism: party positions on European integration in East Central Europe', *European Union Politics*, 3(3): 297–326.

Kriesi, H. (2007) 'The role of European integration in national election campaigns', *European Union Politics*, 8(1): 83–108.

Kritzinger, S. and Michalowitz, I. (2005) 'Party position changes through EU membership? The (non-)Europeanisation of Austrian, Finnish and Swedish political parties', *Politique Européenne*, 2(16): 21–53.

Kulahci, E. (2012) *Europeanization and Party Politics*, Colchester: ECPR Press.

Ladrech, R. (2002) 'Europeanization and political parties: towards a framework for analysis', *Party Politics*, 8(4): 389–403.

Ladrech, R. (2009) 'Europeanization and political parties', *Living Reviews in European Governance*, 4, available at www.livingreviews.org/lreg-2009–1 (accessed 7 January 2013).

Ladrech, R. (2010) *Europeanization and National Politics*, Basingstoke: Palgrave Macmillan.

Lindberg, B., Rasmussen, A. and Warntjen, A. (2008) 'Party politics as usual? The role of political parties in EU legislative decision-making', *Journal of European Public Policy*, 15(8): 1107–1126.

Mair, P. (2000) 'The limited impact of Europe on national party systems', *West European Politics*, 23(4): 27–51.

Mair, P. (2006) 'Political parties and party systems', in P. Graziano and M. Vink (eds) *Europeanization: New Research Agendas*, Basingstoke: Palgrave Macmillan.

Mazey, S. and Richardson, J. (1997) 'The Commission and the lobby', in G. Edwards and D. Spence (eds) *The European Commission*, London: Catermill.

Moravcsik, A. (1994) 'Why the European Union strengthens the state: domestic politics and international cooperation', paper presented at the Annual Meeting of the American Political Science Association, New York.

Pennings, P. (2006) 'An empirical analysis of the Europeanization of national party manifestos, 1960–2003', *European Union Politics*, 7(2): 257–270.

Poguntke, T., Aylott, N., Ladrech, R. and Luther, K.R. (2007a) 'The Europeanisation of national party organisations: a conceptual analysis', *European Journal of Political Research*, 46(6): 747–771.

Poguntke, T., Aylott, N., Ladrech, R. and Luther, K.R. (2007b) *The Europeanization of National Political Parties*, London: Routledge.

Rasmussen, A. (2012) 'Interest group–party interaction in EU politics', *Party Politics*, 18(1): 81–98.

Rasmussen, A. and Lindeboom, G.J. (2013) 'Party–interest group linkage in the 21st century', *European Journal of Political Research*, 52(2): 264–289.

Raunio, T. (2002) 'Why European Integration increases leadership autonomy within political parties', *Party Politics*, 8(4): 405–422.

Reif, K. and Schmitt, H. (1980) 'Nine second-order national elections – a conceptual framework for the analysis of European election results', *European Journal of Political Research*, 8(1): 3–44.

Scharpf, F.W. (1999) *Governing in Europe: Effective and Legitimate?*, Oxford: Oxford University Press.

Schattschneider, E.E. (1948) 'Pressure groups versus political parties', *Annals of the American Academy of Political and Social Science*, 259(1): 17–23.

Sousa, M.M. (2008) 'Learning in Denmark? The case of Danish parliamentary control over European Union policy', *Scandinavian Political Studies*, 31(4): 428–447.

Steenbergen, M.R. and Scott, D.J. (2004) 'Contesting Europe? The salience of European integration as a party issue', in G. Marks and M.R. Steenbergen (eds) *European Integration and Political Conflict*, Cambridge: Cambridge University Press.

Taggart, P. (1998) 'A touchstone of dissent: Euroscepticism in contemporary Western European party systems', *European Journal of Political Research*, 33(3): 363–388.

Van der Eijk, C. and Franklin, M.N. (2004) 'Potential for contestation on European Matters at national elections in Europe', in G. Marks and M.R. Steenbergen (eds) *European Integration and Political Conflict*, Cambridge: Cambridge University Press.

Warner, C.M. (2000) *Confessions of an Interest Group: The Catholic Church and Political Parties in Europe*, Princeton, NJ: Princeton University Press.

Wessels, W., Maurer, A. and Mittag, J. (2003) *Fifteen into One? The European Union and its Member States*, Manchester: Manchester University Press.

3 The structure of EU representation and the crisis

John Erik Fossum

Introduction

This chapter focuses on the structure of European Union (EU) representation and how it is affected by the crisis. This focus yields three closely related sets of purposes. The first purpose is to shed light on the nature of the structure of representation that has emerged in the EU. EU democratization has occurred along two dimensions: a vertical dimension pertaining to the effort to establish representative arrangements at the EU level, most closely associated with the development of the European Parliament (EP); and a more horizontal dimension relating to the effort to stabilize democracy across Europe (including through a system of democratic entrance requirements).[1] The point of departure for this chapter is that this two-dimensional effort to establish and/or reinforce representative democracy unfolds in a distinctive manner and unleashes a process of reconfiguring national representative structures, in order to take the new EU level constituency properly into account. The upshot is that this structure has taken on a distinct and unprecedented form in the EU. The first purpose of the chapter, then, is to provide an overview of the nature of this structure as it emerged in the period prior to the crisis.

The second purpose is to provide an assessment of how the present EU (not only financial but also institutional and constitutional) crisis has affected this representative structure. The crisis appears to have greatly weakened parliaments in relation to executives; at the same time the crisis response (consider in particular the European Semester of budget coordination) also appears to make inter-parliamentary coordination more relevant and necessary.

The third and final purpose of the chapter is to assess the democratic implications of these developments. That assessment must run through the entire analysis because the democratic quality of the structure of EU representation pre-crisis is not only a matter of contention but also quite a challenge because of its complexity and unprecedented nature. Paying attention to the status pre-crisis helps to render more explicit how significant the democratic implications of the crisis are.

In the following pages, I first establish what is meant by democracy and discern a set of criteria that informs the democratic assessment. Thereafter I provide a brief overview of the distinctive features of the structure of EU representation as it appeared in the period prior to the crisis. As we will see this system has emerged in a highly dynamic manner, and without a clearly delineated template or familiar *leitmotif*. Even if bits and pieces of Member State representative arrangements have been copied onto or emulated at the EU level the overarching structure has no precedents, because it has emerged in a situation where there has been a constant tension and struggle between two distinctly different conceptions of organizing Europe: through supranational integration on the one hand and through interstate coordination and cooperation on the other.[2] Both conceptions are baked into the present EU structure, which means that the structure of EU representation has been set up to serve both, and is affected by their uneasy interaction. Then I provide an overview of the crisis, what type of crisis it is, and what it has done to the integration process. As part of both assessments, attention is paid to the democratic implications that we can discern from these developments.

Democracy conceptualized

Democracy must be understood foremost as a higher-order legitimation principle (Eriksen and Fossum 2000). As such, it is a principle that spells out the requisite conditions for justification. Laws must be justified to those affected by them. In that sense democracy serves as a critical standard, which in turn also places deliberation at the centre of democracy; deliberation is necessary to get political results right. This reading of democracy does not exclude the use of voting; it underlines that the relevance of such decision-making procedures must be explained and justified.

The two core criteria of democracy can be said to be *autonomy* and *accountability* (Eriksen and Fossum 2000, 2012a, 2012b). Autonomy refers to the notion that those who are affected by laws should be authorized to make them. Accountability is both about making an account and holding to account. It is about 'a justificatory process that rests on a reason-giving practice, wherein the decision-makers can be held responsible to the citizenry, and where, in the last resort, it is possible, to *dismiss*, incompetent rulers' (Eriksen and Fossum 2012a: 20). These principles require representative democratic arrangements and explicit sanctioning mechanisms. The link to representation becomes clearer once we recognize that 'the opposite of representation is not participation. The opposite of representation is exclusion. And the opposite of participation is abstention' (Plotke 1997: 19). This on the one hand means that we cannot pin autonomy on a notion of direct participation because no modern political system can deliver the requisite level of direct participation. On the other hand it means that representation is not inimical to autonomy, when appropriately devised systems of representation can serve autonomy. In modern democracy, representation is deliberatively encoded and is fashioned in such a manner as to be in line with the basic principles and values in the democratic constitutional state (freedom, basic rights, rule of law, and democracy). In actual fact, it should be added that democratic representation is generally understood as that form of democracy and that form of institutional arrangement that best ensures democracy in a modern context. With David Plotke we could say that '(r)epresentation is crucial in constituting democratic practices' (Plotke 1997: 19).

The two core criteria of democracy require institutions and procedures, which must ensure that citizens will be able to affect law-making processes and must provide citizens with opportunities for evaluating whether they find the justifications behind the laws and the decisions to be acceptable. In that sense democracy in the deliberative trapping that I espouse here presupposes a set of arrangements that include: (1) a constitution with a set of inalienable rights; (2) forums for public debate; and (3) institutional mechanisms that are capable of transforming political initiatives into collective commitments in a representative manner.[3]

It follows from the above that whereas democracy is fundamentally a justification principle, in the modern state context it has developed into an institutionalized arrangement with explicit presuppositions of how human beings should relate to each other, and how they should address problems and issues that concern them all, individually and collectively. Democracy is associated with a conception of the relevant community, or *demos*; there are therefore also associated presuppositions of membership (and citizenship); that is, of who are part of the community and of how and in what sense they are part; of identity (people need to identify with the community for it to constitute a community in the first place); and of legitimacy, as people must believe that the community's basic norms are just and valid for it to make up a democracy. Such additional presuppositions are necessary, for at the core of democracy there is a fundamental ambiguity: democracy cannot itself determine the *demos*; that is, spell out precisely who the people shall be. Thus, whereas democracy requires other additional arrangements to establish the specific popular make-up, it not only depends on but also places particular democratic requirements on membership (citizenship), identity, and legitimacy.

At the same time, precisely because democracy is essentially a justification principle, all the criteria for establishing the *demos* have to be open to constant contestation. That means that a central precondition for a democratic order is a viable public sphere. With that is meant a communicative space (or spaces) in which relatively unconstrained debate, analysis and criticism of the political order can take place (Habermas 1989).[4]

This conception of democracy also entails that democracy should not be seen as strictly tied to the state form. There is a strong historical argument for such a link, but it is contingent. The state form has no doubt been able to deliver arrangements that can sustain democracy within a given territory. But there is no need to confine democracy to this particular institutional form or historical configuration. In this connection it should be added that the state plays a central role in sustaining a profound paradox in today's world, namely that the successful entrenchment of democracy in the internal affairs of states is coupled with 'a lust for power [that] marks the relations among countries in which the stronger dominate the weaker' (Archibugi 2008: xiii). One distinctive trait of the EU experience is precisely the attempt to surpass this situation, with the main instrument being a complex tapestry of representative democratic structures.

EU democratization pre-crisis: a brief overview

In order to understand the nature and impact of the structure of democratic representation that has emerged in the complex multilevel EU configuration, the normal point of departure would be the familiar assumption that EU-level democracy is being embedded in two distinct channels of representation that address citizens in their capacity as individual members of a European constituency (embodied in the EP), and in their capacity as members through holding citizenship in a Member State (with national constituencies represented in the Council structure). At first glance the relevant image would be that of a rather conventional two-channelled structure of representation, similar to the kind of structure we find in such federal states as Germany. From this we might surmise that EU democratization would be mainly a matter of 'uplifting' national democracy to the EU level.

This image is however somewhat misleading. Although we see two broad institutional patterns in the EU, they take on a distinct shape. One channel connects the EU directly to the citizens through the EP, and is a vertical process of the EP parliamentarization.[5] This process is far from complete and has its own distinctive features. The structure in place at the EU level falls well short of parliamentarianism, in the sense that the EP election procedure offers no clear safeguard for European citizens' voting preferences through parliamentary elections to carry direct implications for the composition of European government, and the Commission as a non-elected body is endowed with a formal monopoly of proposing legislative acts. It is obvious that insofar as we can talk of a European constituency, the structure in place is imbued with serious autonomy defects: European citizens cannot understand themselves as self-legislating persons under this structure.

The other collective channel actually connects citizens to the EU through *two* sets of collectives: the main one through the many council formations and another through national parliamentary involvement (and inter-parliamentary interaction).

Council formations: chameleons or shape-shifters?

With regard to the Council, it has legislative functions, but deviates in certain respects from a second legislature or upper chamber. Joseph Weiler has noted:

> Community and Union governance perverts the balance between the executive and legislative organs of the state. The executive branch, government ministers, are reconstituted in the Community as the principal legislative organ with [...] an ever widening jurisdiction over increasing areas of public policy.
>
> (Weiler 1997: 274)

It is questionable whether more transparency has done much to alter this (see Naurin, Chapter 4). In this connection it should also be added that the Council has explicit executive functions (see for instance Curtin 2009; Curtin and Egeberg 2008).

Part of the reason for the distinctness of the Council structure is that it has roots in or is at least still endowed with significant vestiges of such institutional arrangements and procedures that we associate with international diplomacy, rather than domestic representative democracy. That in turn has rendered it particularly germane to distinctive representative roles, such as for instance the notion of 'shape-shifting representation'. By shape-shifting is meant that representatives adopt distinct representative roles that they strategically adjust to the particular settings they are addressing or relating to (cf. Saward 2012). I propose here to extend the notion from the level of representative to the level of body, in order to claim that certain bodies are almost shape-shifting by nature. The European Council and the Council configurations receive and mediate between two sets of institutional inputs, one from the European level and the other from the Member State level (individual Member States and the collective of Member States). Naurin (Chapter 4, citing Wallace 2002), labels the Council a 'complex and chameleon-like beast', and notes that:

> It is both-and, and depending-on: Both executive and legislative in its functions, both national and European in its interests and incentives, both intergovernmental and supranational in its procedures, much depending on the policy area and the policy agenda of the day.

A similar argument applies to the European Council, which lacks the legislative role but still occupies a range of different roles directed to different constituencies: as a strategic driver of the integration process and directed to the European constituency; as a national champion because each head of government is elected by and responsible to its respective national constituency; and as a second-order constitutional agent, because it is the key body in charge of constitution-making and at the same time the aggregate of national constitutional agents, each of which has a veto over constitutional change proposals. The many roles that the Council and the European Council are supposed to fulfil in relation to their various contexts leave considerable scope to representatives for shape-shifting: how much scope depends on the specific elements of the representative relationship, such as whether they are instructed to act as delegates or, more freely, to act as trustees. The Danish representatives face the strongest national constraints (with clear instructions from the national parliament) and are considered delegates. Other representatives with weaker national constraints can more easily play the role of trustee and adapt that role strategically to the several contexts they relate to. It is obvious that such bodies are notoriously difficult for citizens to programme and to hold to account, given that they serve several constituencies. To whom should they (and do they) give accounts, and what should (and do) these accounts contain?

Inter-parliamentary coordination

The other form of collective representation pertains to a growing web of arrangements that increasingly tie national parliaments to the decision-making processes at the EU level. In today's EU, national parliaments are increasingly tied together with the institutions at the EU level (notably the Commission and the EP) through formal arrangements such as the provisions in the Lisbon Treaty on national parliaments and subsidiarity, and the so-called Early Warning Mechanism.[6] There are specific arrangements for collecting and publishing information, such as the Inter-Parliamentary EU information eXchange (IPEX) and the European Centre for Parliamentary Research and Documentation (ECPRD). There are specific arrangements that secure ongoing parliamentary interaction, such as the Conference of Parliamentary Committees for Union Affairs of Parliaments in the European Union (Conférence des Organes Spécialisés dans les Affaires Communautaires: COSAC). We also find a range of informal arrangements where parliamentarians meet, interact and exchange information and knowledge. There is, not the least, considerable interaction among parties at different levels (Crum and Miklin 2013).

This structure contributes on the one hand to bringing national parliaments closer into contact with what is taking place at the EU level. The structure makes it possible to express national concerns through parliaments at the EU level and not only through the executives that occupy the Council structure. In that sense the structure leaves more space for representing a multitude of national positions at the EU level.

The best manner of conceptualizing this system is not to think of it as an added – third – channel but rather through the notion of a multilevel parliamentary field that encompasses the EP and the national parliaments (MLPF) (Crum and Fossum 2009, 2013). This notion implies that parliamentary systems share certain structural similarities and are connected across states and levels of governance. They have the same overarching function, namely to represent their citizens. What marks this field is that it unites horizontal and vertical processes. The notion of field helps us to understand how these processes work together, or at least relate to each other.

What we see then is that since the Maastricht Treaty the process of democratizing the EU has exhibited an ever-greater set of horizontal features, in line with the development of a number of formal and informal arrangements for promoting stronger relations of cooperation, coordination and learning among national (and to a far more limited extent sub-national) parliaments. In this manner the EU system is in the process of establishing a structure that links citizens and the EU system, through direct representation in the EP as well as through two forms of collectives: the Council formations and national parliamentary involvement. These, especially the EP and the national parliaments, are becoming increasingly interwoven or imbricated. This in turn reflects how a distinctive feature of the integration process, namely what we may term the 'fusion of levels'[7] has worked its way into the representative–democratic dimension (see Wessels 1997;

Wessels and Rometsch 1996): the process wherein representative bodies try to catch up with executives and integration is one that weaves representative bodies more closely together, both across levels and across states.

Within this field structure, national parliaments become more readily activated in relation to what is taking place at the EU level. This in turn might increase accountability. At the same time, this structure of representation also lends itself to *cooptation*. Since national parliaments are consulted by the Commission and directly involved in what goes on at the EU level they can prevent an issue from being dealt with there, and come to assume co-responsibility for those decisions that are made there. Even if an issue ends up being decided at the EU level, national parliaments have been consulted, and can in this sense also be said to be co-responsible for EU decisions. This in turn complicates or dilutes the lines of accountability back to the citizens.

To sum up thus far, we see that whereas the EU system in the period pre-crisis was made gradually more subject to representative–democratic procedures; these were not programmed in a traditional parliamentary manner, or according to the key tenets of a division-of-powers system. It appears more reasonable to consider this a comprehensive system of consultation, interaction, and sounding out. As already noted, a distinctive feature of multilevel EU representation is that it involves national parliaments increasingly in EU-level decision-making.

When we look at the broader context, we see that the EU integration process was skewed in favour of executives and experts, as is generally the case with the internationalization of politics. EU democratization has always been a matter of catching up with that dynamic integration process.

Further, it is important to recall that the European integration process takes place in a setting of already existing states, and EU democratization unfolds within this system of states. Democratization accompanies polity formation; the two processes proceed in parallel (at least they have been doing so for a considerable period of time). It is *not* just a matter of democratizing an already established and existing system, but of establishing and democratizing a supranational system at the same time. This supranational system is so configured as to remain solidly anchored in the Member States, many of which prefer interstate interaction and cooperation over supranational integration. The strong Member State presence in the institutions at the EU level also structures the integration process: it is a matter of fusing levels (EU and Member State) and sharing competencies rather than singling out a distinct European level of government with exclusive competencies. States cede sovereignty not to a distant entity but to a common unit in which they all participate directly.

These observations go to show that it is difficult to offer a fast and ready assessment of how well this system delivered on the two criteria of autonomy and accountability pre-crisis, because the EU failed to settle conclusively that it was a matter of supranational polity formation rather than a highly distinct version of international organization. If we are to take this EU experiment seriously we cannot simply rely on domestically derived conceptions of autonomy and accountability but must be willing to ‘stretch’ these notions. At the same time and in particular since the EU affects national systems so deeply that we need to be clear on how EU developments affect nationally based democracy. In retrospect, it appears to have been quite commonplace to suspend final judgement on the quality of the system as long as there appeared to be a positive link between integration and democratization and defects were being addressed.

The critical issue now is whether the crisis undermines this assumption. If we can no longer assume a positive relationship between integration and democratization, it is no longer possible to suspend judgement on the defects of the structure in place. It might even be that the crisis and the way it has been handled has amplified these defects and brought in new problems.

The crisis and Europe's conundrum

The first thing to establish when considering the effects of the crisis is to clarify what kind of crisis it is. It is clearly not only a financial or even a public debt crisis; any designation of the crisis in economic terms would ignore the important political and institutional – even constitutional – dimensions of the crisis. The crisis is therefore not simply a mere response to an externally generated problem in the global financial markets; it is more encompassing and severe and reflects deep structural faults built into the EU construct. It should be added that its handling has not only exposed, but also exacerbated, structural flaws in the EU (Scharpf 2010).[8]

The crisis has deleterious democratic effects. Some also argue that democratic failures are among the root causes of the crisis. Miguel Maduro has recently noted that 'the origins of the financial and economic crisis of the Euro system are state and market based democratic failures that the original regime of Euro governance did not adequately address' (Maduro 2012: 1). Two widely espoused accounts attribute much of the responsibility to national representative democracies. One of these accounts attributes failure to some states' inability to pursue responsible fiscal policies, which in turn has generated negative externalities for other states. In other words, the representative systems in these countries have rewarded politicians who have pursued fiscally irresponsible policies. This account locates the democratic problems basically within debtor states and a lack of fiscal prudence.[9] The EU in turn has shown itself incapable of addressing these problems. The other account holds that the crisis is a combination of market forces and states' inability to control capital flows; the source of the problem stems mainly from financial markets and creditor states' supply of cheap capital. Both accounts underline Member States' inadequate recognition of, as well as inability to handle, complex interdependence and integration. The obvious solution is to reform the system of EU governance to rectify these shortcomings.

There is a bit of truth to both accounts. With regard to the first some countries have pursued fiscally irresponsible policies, if we use the Maastricht convergence criteria and the Growth and Stability Pact as the benchmark, but then Germany and France also violated the conditions that these agreements had specified (and precipitated their change). But it is hard to pin these problems to working representative systems without taking properly into account deeper structural failures, as appears to be the case with Greece, of significant structural failures in the Greek state that exceed well beyond its representative system (and were known outside Greece but not addressed), and biases and limitations in the EU, as well. The deeper question that is better addressed in the second account is whether democracy plays any causal role in the crisis, or is better thought of as the main casualty of the crisis.

Democracy appears foremost as a victim of the crisis; there is little credence in accounts that hold democracy as part of the cause. It is also important to note that the two accounts are inadequately attentive to the institutional context, and to the distinct features of democracy in the multilevel constellation that makes up the EU, which I have highlighted above. Maduro's main democratic recommendation, namely to render the Commission more directly accountable to the EP by establishing closer links between the Commission's composition and the outcome of EP elections, is intended to strengthen EU-level democracy and to leave more space for EU politics. But when considered in light of the structure of representation already in place in the EU it is also implicitly a recommendation to strengthen the multilevel parliamentary field and not only the EP, precisely because Maduro's recommendation is tailored to the present EU (it is not premised on the need for treaty changes). The following assessment of the democratic effects of the crisis seeks to pay attention to the complex and composite system of democratic representation that has already been instituted in the multilevel EU configuration.

There is no doubt that the crisis, and the way it has been handled to date, has had negative effects on EU democracy and on democracy in the Member States. The EP has noted that 'the democratic credibility of European integration has suffered enormously from the manner in which the Euro crisis has been dealt with to date' (European Parliament 2011).

The first point of note is that the crisis has in many instances weakened the role and political influence of parliamentary assemblies, notably, but far from exclusively, in the Eurozone. Their ability to serve the interests of their citizens has clearly been weakened, as has their citizens' ability to hold those who are really responsible to account for the policies that afflict them also weakened. The pattern is however far from even across Member States in the Eurozone; the impact is clearly greater in debtor than in creditor countries. Several debtor countries have seen technocrats temporarily taking over governments. In Germany, a creditor country, the German Constitutional Court has bolstered the power of the Bundestag, even if the German Bundestag is also facing the short deadlines and market and executive 'imperatives' that emanate from the handling of a complex, multifaceted and highly dynamic crisis.

From a democratic perspective, it is also important to keep in mind that some creditor state parliaments (notably Germany's) determine *de facto* many of the operating conditions of debtor state parliaments (notably Greece, Portugal, and Ireland) (Benz 2013). This expands some democratic constituencies' decision-making ability beyond their authorized bounds and procedures, whilst at the same time delimiting others', with potentially profound implications for citizens' ability to govern themselves across Europe. It is difficult to understand this as anything but dominance. It violates the democratic requirement of autonomy – that those that are affected by laws should be authorized to make them.

Other measures with negative bearings on citizens' autonomy can be seen in those instances where Eurozone debtor countries' parliaments, especially those needing bail-outs, are subject to very stringent EU and troika (the European Commission, the European Central Bank (ECB), and the International Monetary Fund (IMF)) budgetary requirements, coupled with demands for deep budget cutbacks and deeply unpopular fiscal restraint measures. The economic philosophy underpinning much of the crisis management, coupled with the lopsided monetary union, generates policies with strong distributional effects (wage reductions, welfare and pension reductions). All Member States are subject to strict budget requirements that constrain their parliaments' leverage, place strong constraints on budgetary policy, and subject them to sanctions in cases of non-compliance. This system is now coordinated at the EU level under the so-called European Semester procedure. The EU and the Eurozone coordinate their budgetary and economic policies *ex ante*, and on this basis specific policy recommendations are issued to each state. This has reduced the budgetary scope for national parliaments, which in turn constrains their citizens' autonomy. The EP's role in this system is quite marginal, which also delimits the autonomy of EU citizens. Given its limited role the EP will not be able to control these processes at the EU level. Thus, for parliaments to reassert themselves in such a structure, inter-parliamentary coordination appears necessary (and is also listed in Article 13 in the Treaty on Stability, Coordination and Governance in the Economic and Monetary Union (TSCG)).

Second, the onus on instituting constitutional spending brakes, if necessary at the national level (cf. Article 3.2 TSCG) is not only a major imposition, but raises questions of constitutional authority and legitimacy. What constitutional authority can the European Court of Justice (ECJ) claim to justify sanctions against Member States that are in violation of the spending brakes? Without a properly democratically authorized constitution at the EU level ECJ action would constitute a clear violation of citizens' autonomy, as spelled out in their respective Member State constitutions.

Third, the crisis leads to a further strengthening of the role and salience of executives and experts at the behest of legislatures. As such, the crisis appears to reinforce certain built-in path dependencies in the EU structure, in particular in terms of executive prominence or even dominance (Fossum and Laycock 2012; Habermas 2012: viii discusses this latter aspect as a form of executive federalism). The crisis also appears to reinforce greatly the role of technocracy, or government by experts, not only within the Union (through strengthening the ECB, the ECJ and the Council structure), but through the central role of such international bodies as the IMF (as part of the troika). The prominent role of technocrats in turn suggests that the crisis and its handling will, owing to framing effects, be described and assessed as technical issues, with a strong onus on market imperatives and efficiency considerations. Such accounts tend to distort or conceal fundamental issues of political accountability. This in turn means that parliaments – if they are to bounce back and operate as chaperons of citizens' autonomy and as enforcers of political accountability – must actively consider such framing effects and propound alternative crisis interpretations and ways of handling them. If not, their role will be further marginalized and their legitimacy in the eyes of increasingly disgruntled citizens will likely be further diminished.

Fourth, the crisis appears to be ushering in a general relative strengthening of the European Council. When coupled with a strong onus on handling the crisis through intergovernmental means (the so-called Merkel method),[10] including fashioning intergovernmental treaties (cf. the TSCG in the Economic and Monetary Union (EMU)), and striking informal intergovernmental bargains through extensive summitry (including bilateral meetings between Germany and France),[11] the net effect is to weaken the integrity of the supranational Community system and the EP's ability to subject it to democratic requirements.

The more informal intergovernmental approach to crisis handling appears to weaken the supranational structure by making it more trans-governmentalized.[12] This would not only weaken the credibility and legitimacy of the supranational structure but also render it more readily accessible to and serving of certain core governments, to carry out their particular conceptions of how the crisis is to be dealt with. It clearly exposes the Commission, which is attributed with a very salient role, including the instituting of sanctions (according to the undemocratic reverse quality majority voting system)[13] to such fissiparous pressures.

The negative implications we can discern from this strengthening of the more intergovernmental components of the EU do not only apply to the EP but also to national parliaments (NPs). When much of the crisis is handled through intergovernmental bargains – to deal with issues that are either outside of the treaties, or where the treaties are not considered helpful to fashion adequate responses and are therefore effectively violated – the law's bite is reduced.

It might be added that this intergovernmental turn has in some instances been a matter of moving forward when certain Member States (notably the UK) veto treaty changes. But it is also exposing a deeper structural problem,[14] namely the discrepancy between the problem structure and the decision-making structure. Simply put, the 17-member Eurozone relies on the 27-member EU institutions to foster binding decisions. It raises the question of how, and in what respect, non-Euro Member States should participate in decisions pertaining to the euro, which will clearly affect them, but differently from the manner in which Euro countries will be affected. One problem is how to sort out what are common concerns and what are concerns specifically pertaining to the Eurozone. Another is that of representation: how to devise a democratic decision-making structure that can accommodate these different concerns? How can such a structure be rendered accountable?

A fifth and readily apparent element is a great increase in citizens' distrust and rising opposition. As part of this we see a rise in extreme left- and right-wing populism. Representative democracies may find themselves increasingly enmeshed in a highly toxic mixture of market-oriented technocracy and extreme populism.

Sixth, even before the crisis struck, the political processes leading up to and the nature and status of the Lisbon Treaty have increased uncertainty and ambiguity as to the EU's constitutional nature and status (Fossum and Menéndez 2011). This has arguably made it easier for leaders to violate and/or sidestep legal provisions in their efforts to handle the crisis. Combined with the intergovernmental handling of the crisis and the general trend towards transgovernmentalization of the EU structure this issue is altering the EU's constitutional construct.

Towards permanent differentiation?

A final observation is that the crisis appears to raise fundamental questions about the nature of the EU and the direction it is taking. This does not necessarily mean that the crisis has brought up these questions. It might equally well be that the main effect of the crisis is to expose and highlight features that have marked the EU well before the crisis but that have not been adequately recognized as problems before the crisis struck. One such is the differentiated nature of the EU. Whereas a core tenet in the *acquis communautaire* has been that the same policies should apply in the same way at the same time in all participating countries; differentiation is legion and takes many forms and shapes (Leuffen *et al.* 2012[15]). The most notable elements today are monetary union, in which only 17 out of the EU's 27 Member States are full members, and Schengen in which only 22 out of the 27 are full members.[16] Thus not only is EU democratization legally encoded – taking place within a densely institutionalized system of interstate coordination and cooperation – this system is far from uniform.

This problem is, if anything, exacerbated by the crisis. Prior to the crisis it was widely thought that differentiation was mainly a matter of different speeds:[17] all states were integrating, and would reach the same destination, but would do so at different rates. Through the crisis differentiation may instead be a matter of member states occupying permanently different statuses. States, for various reasons, have obtained exemptions, but they have generally not been thought of as *permanently* different roles. The crisis, however, compels us to think of an EU composed of states with different *statuses* within the European order. In addition, we also see efforts at renegotiating relationships with the EU, as is notably the case with the UK. Thus, rather than further integration, we may see the rolling back of integration, or even dis-integration (still possibly including a break-up of the Eurozone). When efforts to reinforce integration within the Eurozone combine with efforts to renegotiate membership status, we face a situation of simultaneous differentiated integration and differentiated disintegration. There is integration and there is rolling back, and both processes vary according to country or issue-area. There are many possible combinations of such processes. Table 3.1 provides an illustration of these different possible combinations.

Table 3.1 Different developmental trajectories for the EU

	Integration	*Disintegration*
Uniform	1	3
Differentiated	2	4

Cell 1 depicts the standard integrationist assumption. Cell 2 depicts a situation of differentiated integration. Cell 3 depicts a process of rolling back the EU, whether partially or completely, but across the EU and in the same manner across all issue-areas. Cell 4 depicts a situation of differentiated disintegration, meaning that some Member States in some issue areas disintegrate more than other ones.

Much of the EU debate has tended to focus on the cell 1 as the dominant pattern, but some have also discussed the scenarios in cells 2 and 3. Recent developments, in particular, compel us to pay more systematic attention to cell 4, and different possible cell combinations. The comments above on the effects of the crisis suggest the need to consider more carefully what happens when there is a combination of cells 2 and 4: differentiated integration combined with differentiated disintegration.

This combination in particular (but also other ones) raises thorny democratic challenges. How for instance can one ensure autonomy and accountability in a situation where there is differentiated integration combined with differentiated disintegration: that is, where there is a combination of cells 2 and 4?

I have already suggested that the crisis forces us to rethink the core assumption that has animated research on the EU, namely that there is a positive relationship between democratization and integration. Which of the scenarios and combinations of scenarios that we can discern from the table will help to sustain that assumption, and which ones will undercut it? Which scenarios are most likely to result from the crisis? What does appear clear is that a move in the direction of greater permanent differentiation – whether through a combination of cells 1 and 3 (through the singling out of a hard core and a periphery along all functional domains) or through various combinations of 2 and 4, differentiated integration and differentiated disintegration – raises fundamental questions pertaining to autonomy and accountability. Who authorizes decisions in a system where voter control is differentiated according to territory and function? Who is to hold whom accountable for decisions within such a structure? These are fundamental questions for political and normative theory.

Conclusion

The above analysis has revealed that EU democratization is a matter of establishing a system of representation at the EU level; the process in turn redirects and reprogrammes national systems of representation. The process is distinct, given that it is both about establishing supranational representative democracy, and rendering interstate relations democratic, because the EU has a built-in tension between supra-nationalism and intergovernmentalism. Faced with such a configuration we cannot establish the EU's democratic quality simply by relying on standard ways of conceiving of autonomy and accountability, as these principles have been devised and applied for the domestic realms of political systems. The development of the EU's representative structure and its multilevel parliamentary field represents a dynamic process of constituency construction and reconstruction. The process opens up scope for manipulation, with representatives shifting blame to others, and it opens up space for cooptation. But it also opens up scope for parliaments to capitalize on their unique deliberative qualities, which may be enhanced through such systems of interparliamentary interaction.

These observations pertaining to the putative democratic merits of the EU's multilevel representative structure, as we have seen, are being challenged by the present crisis. At this stage it is clear that the crisis has seriously weakened and perhaps even undercut the process of EU democratization. As suggested above, a critical benchmark would be the assumption of a positive relationship between integration and democratization. The key question is whether this relationship has been thoroughly undermined or whether it can still be rescued. We have seen that the crisis has weakened parliaments, enhanced the role of experts and executives, reinforced transgovernmentalism at the behest of supra-nationalism, and raised the prospect of added complexity through greater differentiation.

These comments suggest that we need to pay more systematic attention to the democratic implications of increased differentiation. For instance, can the 17/27 tensions be reconciled in a democratic manner? These observations underline the need to subject to close ongoing scrutiny what the crisis is doing to the EU, not least what it is doing to the complex representative configuration that presently characaterizes it.

With regard to how the EU system appears to be handling the crisis, there appears to be a penchant for greater multilevel parliamentary imbrication. Such a penchant must also be made subject to close critical scrutiny. What is clear is that such a configuration, were it even to become occupied with viable parliamentary systems at all relevant levels, will still raise serious questions pertaining to developing viable representative structures that are sufficiently attentive to the criteria of autonomy and accountability.

Notes

1 Cf. article 49 of the Treaty of European Union.

2 Lionel Jospin sums it up thus: 'Europe is an original political structure, a unique precipitate, an indissoluble mixture of two different elements: the federalist idea and the reality of European Nation States' (2001: 6).

3 For more details on this institutional version of deliberative democracy, see Eriksen and Fossum (2012b).

4 For assessments of the EU's public sphere, see for instance the various contributions in Fossum and Schlesinger (2007).

5 For a comprehensive account of the development of the EP, see Rittberger (2005). See also Hix *et al.* (2007); Smith (1999).
6 For overviews of these, consult for instance Neunreither (1994); Crum and Fossum (2009); and the various contributions by Buzogany, Knutelska, Cooper, Crum and Miklin, Pollak and Slominski, Garibay, and Wagner *et al.* in Crum and Fossum (2013). Cooper (2012) argues that the Early Warning Mechanism can be understood as a kind of 'virtual third chamber' for the EU.
7 The theory of institutional fusion brings this out very clearly.
8 Many of the measures are set out in the intergovernmental Treaty on Stability, Coordination and Governance T/SCG/en 1 of 2 March (2012) and the so-called 'six-pack', a bundle of five regulations and one directive that cover fiscal surveillance and macroeconomic surveillance under the new Macroeconomic Imbalance Procedure.
9 This account is at most a partial not a very credible explanation of the crisis as such. For one thing there is no one-on-one relationship between fiscal prudence and severity of crisis. The central government of Spain is a case in point.
10 *Spiegel International*, 18 November 2011. Available at www.spiegel.de/international/europe/phoenix-europe-how-the-eu-can-emerge-from-the-ashes-a-797626.html (accessed 3 October 2012).
11 For an overview of types and frequency, see Dinan (2012).
12 Transgovernmental:

> connotes the greater intensity and denser structuring … where EU member governments have been prepared cumulatively to commit themselves to rather extensive engagement and disciplines, but have judged the full EU institutional framework to be inappropriate or unacceptable, or not yet ripe for adoption.
> (Wallace 2005)

13 See http://ec.europa.eu/economy_finance/articles/governance/2012–03–14_six_pack_en.htm (accessed 30 November 2013).
14 See Barroso (2012).
15 The authors depict differentiated integration through three sets of categories: level of centralization, functional scope, and territorial extension.
16 There is a provision for 'constructive abstention' under the Common Foreign and Security Policy (CFSP). There are provisions for reinforced cooperation in the Treaties. Many decisions are subject to derogations, and differential transition periods. Further, *non*-Member States may also participate in Union policies. This applies to the European Economic Area (EEA). It also applies to the Customs Union. Some states have special association agreements with the EU. Other states form part of the Neighbourhood Policy. Others participate in the CFSP, and others in Schengen.
17 For different versions of differentiated integration considered in terms of multiple speeds, see Piris (2011).

References

Archibugi, D. (2008) *The Global Commonwealth of Citizens: Toward Cosmopolitan Democracy*, Princeton, NJ: Princeton University Press.

Barroso, J.M.D. (2012) 'State of the Union 2012 Address', Speech/12/596, Plenary session of the European Parliament/Strasbourg, 12 September.

Benz, A. (2013) 'An asymmetric two-level game: Parliaments in the Euro crisis', in B. Crum and J.E. Fossum (eds) *Practices of Inter-Parliamentary Coordination*, Essex: ECPR Press.

Cooper, I. (2012) 'A "virtual third chamber" for the European Union? National parliaments after the Treaty of Lisbon', *West European Politics*, 35 (3): 441–65.

Crum, B. and Fossum, J.E. (2009) 'The multilevel parliamentary field – a framework for theorising representative democracy in the EU', *European Political Science Review*, 1 (2): 249–71.

Crum, B. and Fossum, J.E. (2013) (eds) *Practices of Inter-Parliamentary Coordination in International Politics – The European Union and Beyond*, Essex: ECPR Press.

Crum, B. and Miklin, E. (2013) 'Interparliamentary Coordination in Single Market Policy-Making: The EU Services Directive', in Crum, B. and J.E. Fossum (eds) *Practices of Inter-Parliamentary Coordination in International Politics – The European Union and Beyond*, Essex: ECPR Press, 71–85.

Curtin, D. (2009) *Executive Power of the European Union: Law, Practices and the Living Constitution*, Oxford: Oxford University Press.

Curtin, D. and Egeberg, M. (eds) (2008) *Multilevel Union Administration: The Transformation of Executive Politics in Europe*, Basingstoke: Palgrave Macmillan.

Dinan, D. (2012) 'Governance and institutions: impact of the escalating crisis', *Journal of Common Market Studies*, 50 (Annual Review): 85–98.

Eriksen, E.O. and J.E. Fossum (eds) (2000): *Democracy in the European Union – Integration through Deliberation?*, London: Routledge.

Eriksen, E.O. and Fossum, J.E. (2012a) (eds) *Rethinking Democracy and the European Union*, Abingdon: Routledge.

Eriksen, E.O. and Fossum, J.E. (2012b) 'Representation through deliberation – the European case', *Constellations*, 19 (2): 325–39.

European Parliament (2011) 'Report on the European Semester for ECONOMIC POLICY COORDINATION', 2011/2071[INI] of 15 November.

Fossum, J.E. and Laycock, D. (2012) 'Representation and democratic legitimacy: comparing the European Union and Canada', mimeo.

Fossum, J.E. and Menéndez, A.J. (2011) *The Constitution's Gift: A Constitutional Theory for the European Union*, Place?: Rowman and Littlefield.

Fossum, J.E. and Schlesinger, P.R. (eds) (2007) *The European Union and the Public Sphere: A Communicative Space in the Making?* London: Routledge.

Habermas, J. (1989) *The Structural Transformation of the Public Sphere*, Cambridge: MIT Press.

Habermas, J. (2012) *The Crisis of the European Union – A Response*, Cambridge: Polity Press.

Hix, S., Noury, A.G. and Roland, G. (2007) *Democratic Politics in the European Parliament*, Cambridge: Cambridge University Press.

Jospin, L. 'On the future of an enlarged Europe' (2001) Address given by Lionel Jospin, 28 May, Paris: Ministère des Affaires étrangères (Ministry of Foreign Affairs), p. 6. Available at http://www.cvce.eu/obj/address_given_by_lionel_jospin_on_the_future_of_an_enlarged_europe_paris_28_may_2001-en-642dc4c9-b224-4ea7-a77b-7e4d894b3077.html (accessed 6 January 2014).

Leuffen, D., Rittberger, B. and Schimmelfennig, F. (2012) *Differentiated Integration. Explaining Variance in the European Union*, Houndmills: Palgrave Macmillan.

Maduro, M. (2012) 'A new governance for the European Union and the Euro: democracy and justice', Report prepared for the European Parliament, Committee for Constitutional Affairs, PE 462.484.

Neunreither, K.H. (1994) 'The democratic deficit of the European Union: towards closer cooperation between the European Parliament and the national parliaments', *Government and Opposition*, 29 (3): 299–314.

Piris, J.C. (2011) *The Future of Europe: Towards a Two-Speed EU?*, Cambridge: Cambridge University Press.

Plotke, D. (1997) 'Representation IS democracy', *Constellations*, 4 (1): 19–34.
Rittberger, B. (2005) *Building Europe's Parliament*, Oxford: Oxford University Press.
Saward, M. (2012) 'Shape-shifting representation', APSA 2012 Annual Meeting Paper, available at http://papers.ssrn.com/sol3/papers.cfm?abstract_id=2104796 (accessed 30 November 2013).
Scharpf, F.W. (2010) 'The asymmetry of European integration, or why the EU cannot be a "social market economy"', *Socio-Economic Review*, 8 (2): 211–50.
Smith, J. (1999) *Europe's Elected Parliament*, Sheffield: Sheffield Academic Press.
Wallace, H. (2005) 'An institutional anatomy and five policy modes', in Helen Wallace, William Wallace and Mark Pollack (eds) *Policy-Making in the European Union*, 5th edn, Oxford: Oxford University Press.
Weiler, J. (1997) 'Legitimacy and democracy of Union governance', in G. Edwards and A. Pijpers (eds) *The Politics of European Union Treaty Reform: The 1996 Intergovernmental Conference and Beyond*, London: Pinter.
Wessels, W. (1997) 'An ever closer fusion? A dynamic macropolitical view on integration processes', *Journal of Common Market Studies*, 35 (2): 267–99.
Wessels, W. and Rometsch, D. (eds) (1996) *The European Union and Member States: Towards Institutional Fusion?*, Manchester: Manchester University Press.

4 Representation in the Councils of the EU[1]

Daniel Naurin

Introduction

The Councils of the European Union (EU) are the institutions in the EU system where the most powerful actors – the Member States' governments – reside. They perform key legislative and executive tasks for the EU, which means that they are central to any account of representation and democracy in the EU.

The European Council, comprised of the heads of state and governments, has gradually developed into the main agenda setter of the larger developments of the EU, in spite of the Commission's monopoly of legislative initiative. According to the Treaty of the European Union (TEU) the European Council 'shall provide the Union with the necessary impetus for its development and shall define the general political directions and priorities thereof' (Article 15.1 TEU). In practice, the European Council has become the default crisis manager of the EU, handling events such as the constitutional crisis of 2005 and the economic crisis of 2008 and onwards. Having such a role in a political system that tends to find itself in a more or less perpetual crisis implies important executive powers.

The Council of Ministers (or simply the Council, as it is formally referred to in the treaties) is where ministers and national officials meet to negotiate and decide on the bulk of the EU's day-to-day businesses. The Council of Ministers holds both legislative and executive functions, although it has seen the latter increasingly sliding upwards towards the European Council in the last years. It is still the prime legislative institution of the EU – no legislation is passed without the consent of the Council – but it has had to get used to sharing legislative power with the European Parliament (EP) on most issues.

When speaking of representation this chapter adopts the simple notion of making citizens' voices, opinions and perspectives 'present again'. In Pitkin's classic definition this means that representatives are 'acting in the interest of the represented, in a manner responsive to them (Pitkin 1967: 209). However, formally the members of the Councils represent states. Each Member State has a seat around the table. The Commission is present at the meetings, explaining and defending its proposals, but only the Member States have a formal vote when the decision is taken. The Member States' representatives in turn weigh differently depending on the size of the populations they represent. In this sense representation of peoples is also part of the institutional construct, although the voting rules have implied that citizens of smaller states have been overrepresented. The population criterion has been given increasing weight in the voting rules, in particular after the Lisbon Treaty.

While the EP has a direct link to the citizens of Europe the path to the Councils is longer and more indirect. The representative chain goes via national elections to the formation of governments, and to the formulation of instructions to civil servants in the Council committees and working groups, where most of the negotiations take place. The quality of this representative chain is to a large extent determined at the national level, and depends on the institutions created for parliamentary monitoring and control of ministers, ministerial routines and practices concerning the permanent representations in Brussels, and the interest and focus of political parties and national media with respect to European affairs. In most Member States national elections historically have not dealt with European issues to any larger degree, which means that the political mandates from the voters that ministers have brought to Brussels have been fairly vague.

However, the Eurocrisis has clearly increased the attention of European issues at the national level, and a range of governments has had to leave office in its aftermath. The increasing integration of economic policy – a core state policy area with a high salience among voters – is likely to keep Europe relatively high on the agenda in national elections for the foreseeable future. Whether it is a good idea for Europe and its Member States to move towards a fiscal union is of course a matter for discussion, and a variety of views exists. From the point of view of the representation of citizens via governments in the Councils, however, the increase in attention should be a positive factor if fiscal policy finally takes the EU above the 'threshold of visibility' for Europeans (Scharpf 1999).

The voting rules and the fact that the quality of the representative chain is largely determined at the national level implies that some European citizens will be better represented than others in the Councils. There are also however some more general factors that affect the ability of the Councils to represent the preferences and ideas of Europeans. This chapter will discuss in particular four interrelated factors that are important: the sectorial organization of the Council of Ministers, the lack of party coordination of policy conflicts in the Council of Ministers and the European Council, the practice of consensus decision-making and the lack of transparency in the Councils' proceedings and decisions. It is argued that taken together these factors make the Councils better at representing national sector interests than general political ideas and values.

What are the Councils?

Just like the EU itself the Council of Ministers is not easily classified into any pre-existing political science category. Not because it performs unfamiliar tasks, or does so in unfamiliar ways, but because the combination of tasks and procedures is rare. The Council is a 'complex and chameleon-like beast' (Wallace 2002: 342). It is 'both–and', and 'depending-on': Both executive and legislative in its functions, both national and European in its interests and incentives, both intergovernmental and supranational in its procedures, much depends on the policy area and the policy agenda of the day.

The two Councils differ both in functions and in working methods. The European Council is more clearly intergovernmental than the Council of Ministers, although the new Presidency function introduced by the Lisbon Treaty has implied more of supranational coordination. The Council of Ministers is, literally, intergovernmental, but also closely attached to and dependent on the supranational institutions of the EU, in particular in its legislative capacity. The Council of Ministers is a forum for intergovernmental negotiations, but one that is deeply embedded into a political system with polity-like ambitions. The output is much more than intergovernmental agreements – it is legislation with direct effect and supremacy over national law. The commitments made are binding, monitored by the Commission and the Court of Justice, and usually complied with.

The frequency of the Councils' meetings, in all their different configurations, is intense. The Councils are a permanently operating negotiation machine, with hundreds of officials meeting every day. Formal and informal rules of procedure have developed to oil the machinery, including more or less supranational functions, such as the General Secretariat, the Presidency and the High Representative for Foreign Affairs and Security Policy. Inter-institutional meetings with the EP and the Commission also add to the agenda, in particular within the ordinary legislative procedure.

All this leads to interactions being influenced both by social experiences and a long shadow of the future. The Member States' representatives recognize that they are in the same boat, and are likely to remain so for the foreseeable future. This insight has contributed to the development of a cooperative bargaining style, and a sometimes relaxed attitude towards formal rules. Consensus behaviour – being prepared to compromise more than you have to – is an important norm (at least among some Member States) (Wallace 2002). The main mission of the chief ambassadors of the Member States' permanent representations (the Coreper) is to reach agreement, rather than stubbornly defend their national positions at all costs (Lewis 2005).

In many respects, therefore, the Councils are more than arenas for intergovernmental negotiations. They are institutions, with institutional memories and institutional preferences. Compared to other intergovernmental organizations the Councils also deal with policy issues normally handled in national rather than in international politics, including distributive and regulative policies with sometimes high domestic salience.

Sectorial organizational structure

The Council of Ministers deals with a broad range of legislative and non-legislative issues. This includes the ordinary legislative procedure, but also macro-economic coordination and decision-making within the Common Foreign and Security Policy (CFSP). It meets in ten different configurations, with different ministers attending depending on the items on the agenda. The meeting frequency of the different configurations varies, and reflects the weight of different policy areas on the EU agenda.

The meetings of ministers are only the tip of the Council iceberg, however. Responsible for the preparation of the meetings are the permanent representatives committee (Coreper), made up of the chief ambassadors of the Member States' representations. Their meetings in turn are prepared by some 150–200 working groups and committees consisting of Member State representatives, and attended also by the Commission officials responsible for the particular dossiers under discussion.

Different ministerial configurations for different policy areas, and a large number of specialized committees and working groups preparing the ministers' meetings, give the Council an organizational structure that is highly sectorial. Environmental, agricultural, justice and home affairs issues, etc. have their own independent set of decision-making forums, with few occasions for crossover. The General Affairs Council, a Council configuration of the ministers of European or foreign affairs, has a coordinating role, but it is a fairly weak counterweight to the line committee structures.

The sectorial structure has important implications for decision-making and representation in the Council. When there is little coordination between policy areas there is also little room for comprehensive political programmes and ideas to drive the decision-making. Issues are dealt with one at a time, with national sectorial interests forming the basis for the preferences and positions that go into the process. A symptom of this state of affairs is that the Councils rarely use issue linkages across policy areas as a bargaining tool (Naurin *et al.* forthcoming).

The European Council is the most important coordinating institution on the intergovernmental side of the EU system. It has four regular meetings per year, but can meet more often if circumstances so require. That has indeed been the case for the last few years, owing to the economic crisis. In 2011–2012 the European Council met 13 times (with an additional four meetings of the heads of state or government in the Euro area). The many meetings recently mirror the increasing importance of the European Council's role of crisis manager of last resort. When the EU needs to respond to some important event, the call is usually the European Council's.

The European Council does not formally legislate, but policy issues that become too contentious to be solved by the line minsters may be referred up to the European Council for problem-solving. At this more aggregate level cross-issue agreements and coordination of policy is easier to achieve than in the compartmentalized committee structures. However, the bulk of the day-to-day legislation in the Council never reaches the European Council. The lack of coordination therefore tends to lead to fragmented policy, which is more difficult for voters to evaluate comprehensively.

Delegation and bureaucratic power

Delegation of decision-making power to bureaucrats is inevitable in all political systems, but the EU is clearly an outlier in this respect. Not only is the power to propose legislation delegated to an independent agency (the Commission), a large part of the actual decision-making – the negotiations in the Council – is conducted by unelected officials. This means that the representative chain is highly vulnerable to principal–agent problems, and that mandate-giving and the accountability of bureaucrats is crucial for representation to succeed.

Under the ordinary legislative procedure, after the Commission has forwarded its proposal to the Council the proposal is normally first addressed by a lower-level working group. If agreement is found already at this stage the proposal is passed up through the Council hierarchy for formal adoption by the minsters without further ado. On other occasions a proposal may travel up and down the Council system. After a Coreper, or a ministerial discussion, the proposal may come back to the working group for final polishing before it returns to the minsters for formal adoption.

Agendas are prepared and meetings are chaired by the rotating Presidency, with the assistance of the General Secretariat. The agendas of the ministers' meetings consist of two types of items: A-points and B-points. The A-points concern proposals that have already been concluded at a previous meeting, and the ministers' role is only to adopt them formally. The B-points, on the other hand, are items that are open for discussion by the ministers. What should become an A- or a B-point is decided at lower levels in the Council hierarchy, and in particular in the Coreper. That decision needs to balance the risk of Council ministerial meetings becoming too overcrowded against that of politically sensitive decisions being taken at the civil service level.

The exact degree of bureaucratic power in the Council is difficult to measure, however. The most thorough attempt so far to answer the question 'Who decides in the Council?' found that the ministers were seriously involved in somewhere in between 35 to 48 per cent of all dossiers. The Coreper and other higher-level committees were decisive in about 22 per cent of the proposals, while the lower level working parties were the primary decision-makers in 31 to 43 per cent. This study was based on 180 legislative proposals adopted in 2003, and it avoids the pitfall of counting the same proposal several times (Häge 2008). One caveat with respect to these figures is that while the ministers seem to be involved in relatively many proposals they are likely to focus only on some details of each proposal. The total share of legislative text being discussed by ministers is clearly much lower than 48 per cent. On the other hand, those details are likely to be the politically sensitive parts of the proposal.

A further complicating factor for anyone trying to gauge the degree of bureaucratic power in the Council is the fact that the negotiations in the committees and working groups are (or at least should be) based on instructions given to the officials by the ministries. A well-organized ministry will make sure that the political values and preferences of the minister are transformed into clear and timely instructions to the permanent representation in Brussels. This is key to upholding the representative chain from elections and government formation to European policy-making in the Council. Having clear instructions is also an advantage for the representatives in the negotiations as it gives a platform for making arguments and building alliances. It is also easier to reach integrative agreements if the negotiators are able to put their preferences clearly on the table (Fisher *et al.* 1997).

Voting practices and accountability

The general trend historically has been a continuous extension of the application of the qualified majority voting (QMV) rule in treaty revisions. The Lisbon Treaty, which made QMV the default rule, includes 113 articles where QMV applies. During 2010–2011 about 90 per cent of the legislative decisions were formally adopted under the ordinary legislative procedure, i.e. with qualified majority as the rule in the Council (and co-decision in the EP).

The relative voting weights were one of the toughest issues in the discussions leading up to the Lisbon Treaty. In particular the Polish and Spanish governments, who had previously negotiated favourable weights, tried to fight proposals with the effect that the population criteria should be allowed to weigh heavier. The compromise eventually moved away from the old weighted votes formula and established a new 'double majority' system, whereby a qualified majority has to include at least 55 per cent of the members of the Council (comprising at least 15 Member States), representing at least 65 per cent of the population of the Union. A blocking minority has to include at least four Council members (Article 16.4 TEU). The new rules take effect from 1 November 2014.

Voting rules are important, as evident by the tough negotiations preceding the revisions of the rules. They are controversial because they define the formal powers of the Member States in the decision-making process. They also influence negotiation behaviour, and ultimately decision outcomes. Voting is also important for representation. The vote is the clearest and most concrete manifestation of the governments' positing-taking, which in turn can be evaluated by the voters. Without formal and explicit votes indicating the real positions taken in the process, it becomes harder to hold representatives to account.

But formal rules are only one part of the story of voting and decision-making in the Council. Legal texts and rules of procedure alone give a misleading picture of how voting is practised and decisions are taken. According to the Council Rules of Procedure the Presidency has a key role in deciding whether or not to call a vote, although it may also be required to do so by a majority of Member States. In practice, however, roll calls are very rare. Although the shadow of the voting rules looms over the parties in every negotiation the Council almost never 'votes', in the simple sense of letting the decision be determined by explicit statements of positions, for example in the form of raising hands. The voting records that are published by the Council are produced *after* the real decision has been taken, and by a different decision-making technique. The records therefore are questionable as indicators of Member States' preferences, and of winners and losers in the negotiations, and consequently also as accountability devices.

Instead, what normally happens is that the Council uses a decision-making technique that is called apparent consensus (Urfalino 2006; Novak 2012). This is a method for taking collective decisions that is distinct from unanimity and an alternative to roll call voting. Typically, when a decision is taken in the Council, the Presidency, after having listened to the discussions, having had bilateral talks with the most concerned Member States, and having 'taken a sense of the meeting', *declares* that the threshold has been reached and notes if there are any objections to this view. Such a statement may take different forms, such as 'Ok, so, everybody can live with the text?' or 'Can we consider this text as adopted then?' (Novak 2007: 5). A Member State that is against the proposal only speaks up at this stage if it disagrees with the Presidency's judgement that the threshold has been reached. This is rare, and would indicate that the Presidency has not done its job properly, as it should not take this step if a blocking minority still existed.

A Member State that is unhappy with the proposal but accepts the defeat remains silent. The formal adoption of the decision usually comes as an A-point at a Council meeting a few weeks later, and may be done by a different Council configuration. It is only at this later stage that votes are registered. This is why, according to the records, fisheries ministers may have voted on legislation concerning emissions from cars, working-time regulations or other issues they have not been involved in and know nothing about. In the period between the apparent consensus decision by the responsible Council configuration, or the Coreper, and the formal adoption of the text at a following Council meeting, Member States inform the General Secretariat on whether they intend to register a no-vote, or an abstention, or if they wish to add a formal statement in the records.

This routine means that a Member State's choice of whether or not to signal discontent publicly is distinct from its choice on whether to support the proposal during the negotiations. Since indicative votes are normally not carried out the situation surrounding the apparent consensus decision is relatively non-transparent even to the parties involved. The Presidency, assisted by the General Secretariat, has a key role in determining whether the threshold has been met. The information asymmetry to the Presidency's advantage, in combination with its procedural privilege to choose when it is time to go to a decision, gives it a powerful position in this process.

Why has the Council settled for this relatively non-transparent decision-making technique that is vulnerable to manipulation and works against well-functioning representation, instead of following the roll-call procedure set out in the Rules of Procedure? Apparent consensus is related to the international organization side of the Council. In fact, it is a decision-making technique that is common in international organizations. For example, in the WTO, roll call voting is formally possible, but in practice decisions are taken by consensus. If no one objects to the chairman's proposition that an agreement exists the deal is done (Steinberg 2002).

The rationale for apparent consensus lies in its ability to secure the basic interests of both more powerful and less powerful actors. Smaller states normally have a less valuable BATNA (Best Alternative To a Negotiated Agreement) than larger states, which makes them more willing to compromise on relative gains in order to secure an absolute gain. At the same time the international norm of state sovereignty says that Member States should be treated officially as equals. The apparent consensus procedure makes it possible for the smaller states to make concessions to the larger ones without losing face. The method has been described as organized hypocrisy (Steinberg 2002). The fact that some are more equal than others is covered up by consensus. The informality of the procedure makes it possible for the more powerful actors to take advantage of their power resources and push for concessions.

The particular version of apparent consensus decision-making applied in the Council also maximizes the flexibility for governments when it comes to the difficult task of communicating defeats. Registered votes in the Council are signalling devices, primarily to domestic constituencies, and may not reveal genuine preferences. There may be both costs in terms of embarrassment and benefits in terms of constituency support involved in signalling. The present procedure lets the Member States decide whether they want to signal discontent or not.

It follows that the voting records are unreliable for voters and parliamentarians who try to monitor the behaviour of their governments in the Council. They should be treated with care also when it comes to drawing conclusions on how decisions are made in the Council. If wrongly used the voting data available from the Council will underestimate the level of conflict surrounding the proposals. The practice of using apparent consensus as the decision-making technique gives the Member States a chance to gloss over conflicts and avoid pointing out losers in the negotiations. Being seen afterwards on paper to be in favour does not necessarily mean that one supported the winning proposal during the negotiations.

Deliberation and consensus

The Councils are first and foremost forums for negotiation between representatives of the Member States' governments. Sometimes these negotiations are characterized by hard bargaining tactics and threats of veto and exit. Most often, however, and in particular in the Council of Ministers, the negotiations are conducted in a cooperative mode. A cooperative attitude – searching for common solutions, considering each other's preferences, sharing information and being prepared to compromise – increases the chances of finding agreements that all or most parties can accept. In negotiation theory such negotiations are called integrative (Walton and McKersie 1965) or problem-solving (Fisher *et al.* 1997). The form of cooperation may have important consequences for representation.

Negotiations in the Council are even claimed to go beyond cooperation in some respects. For example, there has been quite a lot of attention given to the idea of deliberation as a mode of interaction. According to the normative story of deliberative democracy, politics should be more about giving good reasons than forcing or striking deals. 'Arguing', rather than bargaining or voting, is said to be at the heart of democracy. Also within international relations arguing has been upheld as a possible and normatively compelling alternative to unmasked power politics (Risse 2000). In the EU 'deliberative supranationalism' has been promoted as a solution to the problems of democratic legitimacy (Eriksen and Fossum 2000).

A number of studies of deliberation in the EU have tried to test the relevance of this theory to the empirical realities on the ground (Naurin 2010; Warntjen 2010). Differences in how the key concepts of deliberation, arguing and bargaining have been conceptualized and measured contribute to variation in findings in the field. One general pattern nevertheless is that deliberation seems to be present during less politically heated conditions (non-politicized and technical issues, soft law, advisory committees, pre-negotiation phases), but absent under more demanding political circumstances. This condition clearly limits the overall significance of deliberation in the Council.

Another common claim is that Council negotiations are characterized by generous consensus behaviour on the part of the Member States' representatives (Heisenberg 2005). Council negotiators are not only willing to compromise on their ideal positions, according to this view, they are even prepared to do so more than what would be optimal for them in the short run, given the formal rules and the preference distribution in the issue at hand. Consensus behaviour means giving something extra, while possibly (but not necessarily) expecting that this will generate other gains later.

The clearest expression of consensus behaviour is when it is practised by a winning majority or a blocking minority. When the voting rule is qualified majority, consensus behaviour means that an existing majority gives something extra to the states in the non-blocking minority, even if they could rely on their votes to get all of what they want. If a blocking minority exists, or if the rule is unanimity, consensus behaviour is practised by states that refrain from blocking the decision in order to achieve a compromise solution, even if they would prefer the status quo. In more technical terms it means that the agreement does not have to be Pareto-optimal.

Consensus behaviour thus implies refraining from taking advantage of the formal rules and the distribution of preferences to optimize one's short-term gains. The opposite of consensus behaviour therefore is to push for one's own interests in the issue at hand, without considering the preferences of others beyond what is necessary for achieving one's goal. It means building minimum winning coalitions, blocking non-optimal proposals and using formal rules to achieve as much as possible in the short run.

Not all observers agree that consensus behaviour is particularly widespread in the Council. Häge, for example, argues that the main motivation of the Member States is to build coalitions to form a non-blocking minority in order to avoid being outvoted (Häge 2012; see also Novak 2010). Still, there is quite convincing evidence that not only cooperative negotiation behaviour in general, but consensus behaviour as defined here, is practised in the Council.

The evidence is found both among insiders' accounts of the procedures and in systematic qualitative and quantitative research. The picture drawn by Lewis from qualitative interviews with more than a hundred officials from the permanent representations is that appropriate behaviour in Council negotiations includes refraining from pushing for a qualified majority and practicing 'mutual responsiveness' (Lewis 2005: 939). The research by Thomson and colleagues, including 331 controversial issues that were negotiated over the years 1999–2008, also contains evidence of consensus behaviour (Thomson 2011; Thomson *et al.* 2006; see also König and Junge 2009). Thomson evaluates the predictive accuracy of a range of different bargaining models, some of which emphasize the formal procedures and some of which are based on informal bargaining. Interestingly, none of the more sophisticated models, which include information on relative power, salience, reference points and procedural rules, are able to outperform the simplest compromise model. The latter base line model predicts that the outcome will be the mean position of all Member States, the European Commission and the EP.

What explains consensus behaviour? Why would Member States give favours, rather than try to get the most out for themselves of every single proposal? Often this type of behaviour is assumed to be norm-driven, which means that there is a commonly recognized informal rule that guides actors. Adhering to this norm implies respecting the equality or legitimate ranking of the actors involved, while trying to find solutions that are as inclusive as possible. If the norm is internalized the actors genuinely believe that consensus behaviour is the morally right way to act. Actors who have not reached such an elevated moral standard may follow the norm anyway in order to avoid reputational costs.

There may be both economic and sociological sources of a consensus norm. From a rational self-interested point of view paying a little extra today may generate larger gains tomorrow. A general belief in European integration as beneficial overall, although sometimes costly in the short run, provides a powerful underlying rationale in favour of cooperation. Given such a rationale actors involved in repeated games may solve collective action problems by learning over time that a cooperative strategy is more beneficial in the long run. Few, if any, other international organizations have so many repeated games, and such a long shadow of the future, as the EU.

Furthermore, while pooling sovereignty by allowing for qualified majority decisions increases collective decision-making efficiency it also implies risks for Member States that they will be outvoted on important issues. Nurturing a consensus norm – an informal procedure that allows for some flexibility *vis-à-vis* the formal rules – may function as an insurance against that risk. Compromising more than you have to when others are in trouble can be seen as the premium you pay for that insurance.

Although deliberation and consensus behaviour have several advantages for both legitimacy and effectiveness they also have some clear disadvantages with respect to representation. As in consociational and corporatist systems too much compromising and too little conflict at the elite level may leave the voters without a clear picture of what alternatives exist, who is responsible for what, and where accountability for the decision lies. In a similar vein, although deliberative processes within committees may strengthen both the epistemic rationale and the legitimacy of the decisions among the decision-makers, if it means putting instructions aside the representative chain will be weakened.

Conflict dimensions in the Councils

Consensual elite behavior, failing to project any clear conflict dimensions, may be a thing of the past, however, according to an important claim in the literature. The proposition is that the EU in general, including the Council, is approaching 'normal' politics, meaning in particular left–right politics, as at the national level (Hix 2008; Lindberg *et al.* 2008). As the EU becomes increasingly state-like in its tasks, so does its politics, it is argued.

Earlier accounts of the Council have often asserted that coalitions between the Member States' governments are fluid and tend to shift from issue to issue (Spence 1995: 380; Nugent 1999: 474). No over-arching structure in the Member States' preferences has contributed to building long-term and cross-cutting coalitions, according to this view. Two countries that are on the same side with respect to farm subsidies may just as well be on different sides when it comes to working time regulations. The 'normal politics' thesis, on the other hand, assumes that the increasing number of Member States and the more frequent use of qualified majority voting have increased the importance of forming alliances in the Council. And, according to Hix, 'the main basis for any such alliance is the Left–Right policy position of each government' (Hix 2008: 125).

Furthermore, the 'normal politics' thesis is proposed not only as an empirical claim but also as a normative goal. Connecting the politics of the EU to the dominant conflict dimensions of national party politics and election campaigns would anchor the EU more firmly in the normal democratic lives of European societies. If policy alternatives and actor alignments were formed along well-known dimensions, EU politics could also become more accessible to a broader public (Hix 2008; Føllesdal and Hix 2006). The alternative is intergovernmental nation-state diplomacy governments engaged in foreign policy – which has always been remote from political parties, social movements and public opinion.

The 'normal politics' thesis clearly would have important implications for representation in the Council, as it gives a stronger role for the political parties and their crucial function of connecting voters' preferences with representatives' policy-making. Parties also provide general political programmes based on broader values and ideologies, something that does not come naturally to the sectorially organized Council committee system.

However, empirical research on the Council gives little support to the 'normal politics' thesis. While some early studies before the Eastern enlargements based on voting records found traces of left–right alignments in the Council (Mattila 2004), latter research has concluded that alliances in the Council are more or less unrelated to party ideology. This applies to studies of both bargaining positions and cooperation behaviour (Thomson 2009; Naurin 2008; Tallberg and Johansson 2008 for the European Council). Instead geographical proximity – coalitions of neighbouring states – is the most visible pattern, regardless of which party is in government. National sectors' interests largely determine these patterns.

Thomson's study of bargaining positions finds that the geographical patterns are the most common, but that they show up significantly only in about a quarter to a third of all issues (Thomson 2011: 76). It is clearly the case that although coalition-building has become more important, and that geographical patterns based on national interests, rather than political ideologies, are the most common, there is still quite a lot of fluidity in the existing alliances. The fact that different blocs are not permanently depicted against each other is important for the stability and legitimacy of the EU as a political system. The backside, however, is that it makes it more difficult for voters to orient themselves, when the conflicts played out do not match the cleavages that they are used to from the domestic level. The promise of the 'normal politics' thesis of political parties connecting citizens with their representatives in the Council has yet to be fulfilled. The lack of transparency of these representatives' actions, as we shall see in the next section, further complicates communication between citizens and the decision-makers in the Council.

The transparency deficit

The Council of Ministers has an impressive track record with respect to producing agreements among governments with heterogeneous preferences. Only about 10 per cent of the Commission's proposals never see the end of the tunnel as adopted legislation. This is partly because the Commission anticipates the reactions of the Member States, and refrains from making proposals in areas where common ground is lacking. But it is also indicative of the effectiveness of the Council machinery. Its norms and institutions are set on getting to 'Yes'.

Effectiveness is not the only important value of political institutions, however. A downside of the Council's mode of decision-making is a lack of transparency, and links with political debates that are familiar and comprehensible to citizens. The Eurobarometer surveys indicate that the Council is the least trusted of the EU institutions involved in legislation. In the period 2008–2012 about 35–40 per cent of the Europeans say they trust the Council, which is about 5 percentage points lower than the Commission and ten percentage points lower than the EP (Standard Eurobarometer nos 69–78).

The European Council, with its purely executive role, is the least transparent of the Councils. Although its meetings are often closely monitored from outside by the media, especially when there is a new 'crisis' to be addressed, the negotiations are held strictly behind closed doors. Some of the heads of government like to make a few statements to the cameras before they proceed into the building, but after that it is difficult to follow what happens. Leakages to the press occur, and are sometimes part of the bargaining strategy, but can hardly compensate for the lack of transparency. In some Member States (such as Denmark and Sweden) the EU committee of the parliament has a direct line open with its prime minister during the meeting for real-time anchoring of positions at the national level. How tightly connected to the domestic level the ministers are varies considerably between the Member States.

According to Thomson 'there is no other legislative body in the free world that meets in such secrecy' as the Council of Ministers (Thomson 2011: 223). More transparency in Council affairs is a commonly suggested recipe for enhancing the democratic legitimacy of the EU. However, for the foreseeable future at least, the Council of Ministers is unlikely to become as transparent as 'normal' domestic legislatures. Over the last two decades the Council of Ministers has implemented a range of transparency reforms, some of which are in fact more radical than in many national parliaments. Thousands of documents have been released, and legislative deliberations are regularly broadcasted live on the Internet. The Council is surprisingly transparent in some ways, but not in those ways that make people perceive it as transparent, and therefore find it legitimate.

Three conceptual distinctions are useful for shedding light on the paradox of why transparency reforms in the Council do not seem to lead to more perceived transparency. First, one needs to distinguish between *transparency* and *publicity* (Lindstedt and Naurin 2010). While transparency means that there is information available about actions and processes within an institution for those who are willing and able to seek it, publicity means that the information is actually spread to and taken in by people outside the institution. There will be no publicity, i.e. no actual exposure of behaviour to a public audience, no matter how transparent the process or the institution in question is, if the available information about these actions is left unattended.

A second important distinction is that between *transparency in process* and *transparency in rationale* (Mansbridge 2009). Transparency in process refers to information on actions, such as deliberations, negotiations, and votes that took place during the decision-making process, and were thus directly fed into the decision. Transparency in rationale, on the other hand, refers to information on the substance of the decisions and of the facts and reasoning on which they were based. Conclusions, declarations, press conferences after meetings, and, crucially, public debates, are measures for achieving transparency in rationale.

The third distinction that needs to be taken into account here is that between the two faces of 'normal' legislatures – *committees* and *plenary debates*. In parliaments there is a clear division of labour between the two. The committees perform the deliberations and negotiations in the law-making process, while the plenary takes care of the vote and the public debate. The behavioural logic that applies in committees prescribes focus on common ground, compromise and agreement. The logic of plenary debates is the opposite – to clarify differences between parties and positions. Committee meetings focus on problem-solving and concrete technical details, plenary debates on principles and ideologies.

A national democratic legislator normally has all of these components to some extent. It has committees and plenary debates. The plenary debates, where majority and minority parties defend their positions and emphasize weaknesses of the other side, when they work well, produce both transparency in rationale and publicity. They make the technical details of the committee meetings understandable to a broader audience by highlighting their political content, the ideologies that support different alternatives and the principles raised.

The Council of Ministers, however, only has two components. It has committee meetings in abundance. Committee decision-making is what the Council does all the time, on all levels. The search for common ground among diverse interests is part of the Council's DNA. It also has considerable transparency in process after the last years' reforms. Agendas and minutes of preparatory meetings are published, although the minutes may, on request, exclude the names of the Member States that raised objections in the process. Position-taking in ongoing negotiations is broadcast live (although within strict parameters), something that hardly happens in parliamentary committees.

But the Council does not have the three interrelated components of clarifying plenary debates, publicity and transparency in rationale. When the Council decision-making machinery is done, and the legislation is adopted as an A-point, the ministers go home to their capitals. The winning majority never needs to justify its position and sharpen its arguments in public debate against the minority. If in some Member States there is a debate at the national level where the government needs to justify the legislation it is far from certain that this debate is held along the same conflict line as in the Council, as previously discussed.

The Council is transparent in one way (process), but not in the way that makes people beyond a small circle of EU experts understand why the decision-makers decided the way they did (rationale). To explain why the Council is lacking transparency in rationale one has to take into account that it has in many respects more in common with an international organization than a legislative chamber of a democratic polity. The members of the Council are representatives of states rather than parties. The conflicts played out in the Council concern national interests at the sector level, rather than general political ideas. The problem in this context is that it becomes difficult to have the type of public plenary debates that parliaments have, that create transparency in rationale and publicity. Real post-decision debates in the Council would not show left vs right, or liberals vs conservatives, but Germans vs Greeks, Poles vs Italians, and so on.

The reason why we do not have these debates is the fear among the members of the Council that the Europeans are not European enough to handle it. We do not have the democratic infrastructure in Europe to handle divisive public debates, according to this view (Bartolini 2005). There is not enough of a European public sphere and a European demos to deal with it. Public debates in the Council may give transparency in rationale and publicity, i.e. understanding of who won and who lost and why, but rather than helping legitimacy it will destroy it, it is argued, because people will not accept being outvoted by 'others' on salient issues.

Conclusions

The Councils of the EU are the most powerful institutions in the EU political system, and therefore key to any account of democracy and representation in the EU. The link to EU executive and legislative policy-making in the Councils goes via national elections, parliamentary control over government, and ministerial instruction-giving and monitoring of the unelected national officials that make up the mass of Council negotiations in working groups and committees. Primarily, it is the Member States that are responsible for the functioning of mandate-giving and accountability through this route. However, there are also some general characteristics of the Councils that affect representation.

Policy-making in the Council lacks coordination through comprehensive political programmes that may be evaluated by the voters. This is partly due to the sectorial organization of the Council, and partly due to the weak status of party politics. Parties perform a key role in representative democracy by coordinating policy at an aggregate level and presenting comprehensive programmes to the voters. In the Council the positions of the Member States' representatives are instead largely determined by national sectors' interests, rather than the programmes of political parties. The lack of transparency, and in particular transparency in rationale, makes the Councils both less comprehensible and less accountable, while the deliberative practices and the consensus norm may contribute to its character of an insulated elite club.

Clearly, there are reasons to lament some aspects of how representation works in the Councils. However, it should be remembered that compared to the EP the governments' mandates in the Councils are based on a substantially higher voter turnout. Furthermore, any normative calculation must take into account the fact that over the years the Councils have proven to be remarkably effective in producing agreements among sovereign nation states, with often highly diverging interests.

Paradoxically, the economic crisis of the last years may have improved the conditions for representation in the Councils in one respect: European affairs have – finally – become a major issue at the national level, and now regularly make and break governments in European countries. When (or if) the crisis becomes less acute this attention is likely to fade. But for the Euro countries, at least, the move towards fiscal union may take the EU over the threshold of visibility once and for all, which means that the conditions for representation in the Councils will have altered substantially.

Note

1 Parts of this chapter are based on Naurin (2014).

References

Bartolini, S. (2005) *Restructuring Europe*, Oxford: Oxford University Press.

Eriksen, E.O. and Fossum, J.E. (2000) *Democracy in the European Union: integration through deliberation?*, London: Routledge.

Fisher, R., Ury, W. and Patton, B. (1997) *Getting to Yes: negotiating an agreement without giving in*, 2nd edn, London: Arrow Business Books.

Føllesdal, A. and Hix, S. (2006) 'Why there is a democratic deficit in the EU: a response to Majone and Moravcsik', *Journal of Common Market Studies*, 44 (3): 533–562.

Heisenberg, D. (2005) 'The institution of "consensus" in the European Union: formal versus informal decision-making in the Council', *European Journal of Political Research*, 44 (1): 65–90.

Hix, S. (2008) *What's Wrong With the European Union and How to Fix it*, Cambridge: Polity.

Häge, F.M. (2008) 'Who decides in the Council of the European Union?' *Journal of Common Market Studies*, 46 (3): 533–558.

Häge, F.M. (2012) 'Coalition building and consensus in the Council of the European Union' *British Journal of Political Science*, 1 (1): 1–24.

König, T. and Junge, D. (2009) 'Why don't veto players use their power?' *European Union Politics*, 10: 507–534.

Lewis, J. (2005) 'The janus face of Brussels: socialization and everyday decision making in the European Union', *International Organization*, 59 (4): 937–971.

Lindberg, B., Rasmussen, A. and Warntjen, A. (2008) 'Party politics as usual? The role of political parties in EU legislative decision-making', *Journal of European Public Policy*, 15 (8): 1107–1126.

Lindstedt, C. and Naurin, D. (2010) 'Transparency is not enough: making transparency effective in reducing corruption', *International Political Science Review*, 31 (3): 301–322.

Mansbridge, J. (2009) 'A "selection model" of political representation', *Journal of Political Philosophy*, 17 (4): 369–398.

Mattila, M. (2004) 'Contested decisions: Empirical analysis of voting in the European Union Council of Ministers', *European Journal of Political Research*, 43 (1): 29–50.

Naurin, D. (2008) 'Choosing partners. Coalition-building in the Council of the EU', Paper presented at the American Political Science Association Annual Meeting, Boston, MA: 28–31 August.

Naurin, D. (2010) 'Most common when least important: deliberation in the European Union Council of Ministers', *British Journal of Political Science*, 40 (1): 31–50.

Naurin, D. (2014) 'The Councils of the EU: Intergovernmental bargaining in a supranational polity', in J. Richardsson (ed.) *European Union: Power and Policy-making*, London: Routledge.

Naurin, D., Hayes-Renshaw, F. and Wallace, H. (forthcoming) *The Council of Ministers*, 3rd edn, Basingstoke: Palgrave Macmillan.

Novak, S. (2007) 'The mystery of consensus in the EU Council of Ministers', Paper presented at the Midwest Political Science Association, Chicago, IL: 12–15 April.

Novak, S. (2010) 'Decision rules, social norms and the expression of disagreement: the case of qualified-majority voting in the Council of the European Union', *Social Science Information*, 49 (1): 83–97.

Novak, S. (2012) 'Transparency versus accountability? The case of the EU Council of Ministers', Paper presented at the Transatlantic Conference on Transparency Research, Utrecht: 8–9 June.

Nugent, N. (1999) *The Government and Politics of the European Union*, 4th edn, Basingstoke: Palgrave Macmillan.

Pitkin, H. (1967) *The Concept of Representation*, Berkeley, CA: University of California Press.

Risse, T. (2000) '"Let's argue!": communicative action in world politics', *International Organization*, 54 (1): 1–39.

Scharpf, F.W. (1999) *Governing in Europe: Effective and Democratic?*, Oxford: Oxford University Press.

Spence, D. (1995) 'Negotiations, coalitions and the resolution of inter-state conflicts', in M. Westlake (ed.) *The Council of the European Union*, London: Cartermill.

Steinberg, R.H. (2002) 'In the shadow of law or power? Consensus-based bargaining and outcomes in the GATT/WTO', *International Organization*, 56 (2): 339–374.

Tallberg, J., and Johansson, K.M. (2008) 'Party politics in the European Council', *Journal of European Public Policy*, 15 (8): 1222–1242.

Thomson, R. (2009) 'Actor alignments in the European Union before and after enlargement', *European Journal of Political Research*, 48 (6): 756–781.

Thomson, R. (2011) *Resolving Controversy in the European Union*, Cambridge: Cambridge University Press.

Thomson, R., Stokman, Frans N., Achen, C.H. and König, T. (2006) *The European Union Decides*, Cambridge: Cambridge University Press.

Urfalino, P. (2006) 'Apparent consensus and vote: two modes of collective decision-making', Paper presented at the workshop on 'The mechanisms of collective decision-making' at the Adriano Olivetti Foundation, Rome: 29 April.

Wallace, H. (2002) 'The Council: an institutional chameleon', *Governance*, 15 (3): 325–344.

Walton, R.E. and McKersie, R.B. (1965) *A Behavioral Theory of Labor Negotiations; an Analysis of a Social Interaction System*, New York: McGraw-Hill.

Warntjen, A. (2010) 'Between bargaining and deliberation: decision-making in the Council of the European Union', *Journal of European Public Policy*, 17 (5): 665–679.

5 The Committee of the Regions as representative assembly

Mission impossible or miracle in the making?

Simona Piattoni

Introduction

In the literature on the European Union (EU), the Committee of the Regions (CoR) is sometimes considered as a (potential) third representative chamber and sometimes as a talk-shop with little or no political weight. Assessments of its significance range from enthusiastic to sceptical (Christiansen 1996; Hooghe 1995, 1996; Jeffery 1995; Loughlin 1997; Warleigh 1997). Both positions are defensible. Those who like to think of it as a potential third representative chamber cannot but notice its weaknesses: (1) it does not have legislative (co-decision) powers, not even in the areas of specific competence; (2) its members are representatives of sub-national authorities of different economic, political and institutional weight; (3) among the regions therein represented there are purely administrative regions as well as regions with legislative powers; (4) some members do not hold a direct representative mandate, but are only 'accountable to a representative assembly', and in the past there were even career administrators nominated directly by central governments. These structural 'cleavages' have been perceived as weakening the CoR and condemning it to a minor role.

Initially, this situation induced the CoR to look inward, that is, to issue 'own opinions' addressing broad constitutional issues and claiming greater powers, rather than to participate in the EU decision-making process within the limits of its competences. With time, however, the CoR's remit has been significantly expanded and its opinions have exerted a certain influence, thus making the enthusiasm for the CoR's potential role less far-fetched than it might have appeared initially: (1) The range of its opinions has steadily increased, now covering the entire Common Market and more; (2) A 'memorandum of understanding' has been signed between the Commission and the CoR facilitating consultation between these two institutions in the early stages of policy-making; (3) Its composition has been changed so that now all CoR members have a (direct or indirect) 'representative mandate' at the subnational level and its term has been brought in line with that of the other EU institutions; (4) It has defined its own institutional profile vis-à-vis other EU institutions and has managed to assert its role as representative of the subnational tier against existing competitors (such as regional associations or ad-hoc consultative committees).

The White Paper on Multi-Level Governance (WPMLG) (CoR 2009) can be seen as the crowning moment of this evolution: in this important document the CoR proudly states its political nature and claims a prominent role in EU policy-making. If the political and representative nature of the CoR seems to be now beyond doubt, it is fair to ask what kind of representation the CoR actually delivers.

In this chapter I adopt as a benchmark Pitkin's (1967) definition of representation as 'substantive acting for others', that is, 'acting in the interest of the represented in a manner responsive to them' (ibid.: 209) in order to discuss whether the CoR can secure political representation. I further submit that Pitkin's notion of political representation is akin to Urbinati's (2006) notion of democratic representation, 'a middle path between an unconditional delegation and the refusal of any delegation, or between electoral authorization of an aristocracy and direct democracy' (ibid.: 11). I will, therefore, ask whether the CoR, despite its internal fractures and its institutional weaknesses, can nevertheless be seen as delivering full political and democratic representation. Adopting these standards will lead me to ask who precisely CoR members represent; whether their own institutional interests, the political interests of the parties they belong to, the functional interests prevalent in their territories, the territorial interests of their constituents or the general interest of the EU demos at a lower level of aggregation? Can CoR members balance institutional, functional, political and territorial representation and deliver full political and democratic representation? Is this an impossible mission? This chapter will examine the legitimacy of the claim that the CoR performs a full and democratic representative function and will explore what type of representation, if any, CoR members can provide with reference to a particular question: the Euro crisis.

Full political and democratic representation

Pitkin's notion of full (as opposed to partial) political representation implies that 'the representative must pursue his constituents' interests in a manner at least potentially responsive to their wishes, and that conflict between them must be justifiable in terms of those interests' (Pitkin 1967: 213). Responsiveness to the constituents' interests is therefore central to her notion of representation. Mere authorization will not do: the relationship between represented and representative must be ongoing, and must make sure that the interests of the former are pursued in a manner consistent with their own understanding of their interests. This definition entails 'discretion and judgement' both on the part of the representative and on the part of the represented. The represented, therefore, do not divest themselves of their capacity for independent judgement and even direct action. Should the actions of the representative be at odds with the wishes of the represented without good reason or explanation, then the relationship would come under stress. Indeed, disagreements between representative and represented are justifiable only insofar as the representative can claim that his actions are inspired by the pursuit of the interests of the represented.

This notion of representation implies that people – and not 'unattached interests' (as Burke would argue, Pitkin 1967: Chapter 8) – are represented, otherwise disagreement would be inconceivable. Therefore, 'their [of the represented] say in their interest is relevant' (ibid.: 210). It may be possible that decisions must be made in areas in which the represented know absolutely nothing, and that consequently representatives must decide uniquely on their own wits. In this case, however, we 'leave the realm of representation altogether and we end up with the expert deciding technical questions and taking care of the masses as a parent takes care of a child' (ibid.: 210). Such a technocratic, aristocratic and ultimately paternalistic notion of representation – only the representatives know what is good for the represented – is clearly not democratic. But even the statement that there might be technical questions about which the represented know nothing and that, in this case, the representatives can indeed decide solely on their own wits can be challenged: behind most 'technical questions' are often more political questions that everyone can understand and form an opinion on (Føllesdal and Hix 2006; Piattoni 2013):

> Political issues, by and large, are found in the intermediate range, where the idea of representing as substantive acting for others does apply. Political questions are … questions about action, about what should be done: consequently they involve both facts and value commitments, both ends and means.… It is a field in which rationality is no guarantee of agreement.… But this is precisely the kind of context in which representation as substantive activity is relevant. For representation is not needed where … no judgment is needed.
>
> (Pitkin 1967: 212)

If 'disagreement remains despite deliberation and justification and argument', then 'the possibility of a substantive acting for others breaks down'. In this case, the represented may fall back onto 'formal and institutional arrangements even when they seem devoid of substantive content' (ibid.: 213).

Representation has been seen with suspicion by many political theorists as a poor substitute for direct participation and, moreover, as an inherently aristocratic mechanism for selecting the rulers. Urbinati (2006) thinks otherwise. According to Urbinati, Pitkin examines representation as a form of political agency but does not really inquire into its relationship to sovereignty and democracy and into the kind of political participation that representation brings about in a democratic society. Despite their different argumentative strategy, Pitkin's notion of full political representation and Urbinati's notion of democratic representation are surprisingly similar. Urbinati starts by claiming that 'representative democracy is neither an oxymoron nor merely a pragmatic alternative for something we, modern citizens, can no longer have, namely direct democracy; and, second, that it is intrinsically and necessarily intertwined with participation and the formal expression of popular will' (2006: 10). She then proposes to 'stretch' the meaning of representation and to see it as 'a political process and as an essential component of democracy' (ibid).

Urbinati highlights three aspects of representation. First:

> public discourse is one of the main features that characterize and give value to democratic politics, ancient and modern, direct and representative.... Regardless of the form of decision-making, voice involves two kinds of active doing – positive as activating and propositive, and negative as receptive and surveilling.... Second, indirectness ... plays a key role in forging the discursive democratic character of politics, and aids rather than obstructs participation. Third, I sustain that representation highlights the idealizing and judgmental nature of politics, and art by which individuals transcend the immediacy of their biographical experience and social and cultural belongings and interests, and educate and enlarge their political judgment on their own and others' opinions.
>
> (Ibid.: 5)

In sum:

> political representation ... entails a complex political process that activates the 'sovereign people' well beyond the formal act of electoral authorization. Representative politics has the power of unifying and connecting the 'fluctuating atomic units' of civil society by projecting citizens into a future-oriented perspective.
>
> (Ibid.: 5)

The articulation of voice, in addition to the expression of will, is a fundamental component of Urbinati's notion of democratic representation. This explains why also Urbinati insists that the represented should not give up their right to participation and judgement after elections and so comes to share Pitkin's conviction that political representation must imply a continuous dialogue between represented and representatives. The idea, in both cases, is that representation is not exhausted by the choice of the represented (through elections), but that the represented must always be continuously involved in judgement, surveillance and, if necessary, revocation.

It is clear that while CoR members actively participate in the discussion of many EU policy and political issues – that is, they are fully involved in the activation, proposal, reception and surveillance associated with voice (which gives substance to the democratic principle of isegoria, the equal right of all to speak) – they are not at all involved in the activities that express will (which brings about isonomia, the equal right of all to participate in the expression of will). Moreover, while they are partially involved in surveillance – particularly through their ancillary role to national parliaments in guarding the principle of subsidiarity – they are not, unlike members of the European Parliament (EP), directly involved in judgement and revocation. Given the fairly strict standards set by

Pitkin and Urbinati, is it reasonable to argue that the CoR might deliver full political and democratic representation? Is not the most basic ingredient of representation, namely acting in the interest of the represented, beyond the CoR's purview? What kind of concrete actions can the CoR take on behalf of its constituents? And how reasonable is to say that CoR members are responsive to their constituents' interests and wishes? In answering these questions I will concentrate particularly on Urbinati's treatment of democracy as isegoria. While subnational constituencies (of various sizes, wealth and powers) may appear to be rather disempowered when it comes to directly influencing decisions (isonomia), I will argue that they are surprisingly powerful when it comes to expressing their constituents' interests and wishes (isegoria) by performing all four actions identified by Urbinati: activating, proposing, receiving, surveilling. In fact, I will argue that the CoR's relative legislative powerlessness amplifies its expressive powers.

The Committee of the Regions between consultation and representation

The CoR was established in 1994 to provide the Commission with the input from those governmental institutions – subnational authorities (SNAs) – that were closer to the ultimate receivers of EU policies. The Commission had been shaken by the results of the referendums on the Treaty on the European Union (TEU) in the Netherlands and in France, which signalled 'distance and alienation' between EU citizens and EU institutions, and had tried to elaborate in the White Paper on European Governance (WPEG) (European Commission 2001) the lessons to be drawn from those events. The WPEG very clearly assigned to subnational authorities and civil society organizations the task of collecting and conveying the desires of European citizens (input), without however allowing them to be directly involved in the decision-making process for fear that they might derail EU decision-making from community-wide goals by attempting to subject them to localized constraints. Their role in the output side of politics, however, was acknowledged as they were enlisted in the final implementation and delivery of community policies (output).

The CoR was conceived as a consultative committee, along the lines of the much older Economic and Social Committee (ESC), which provided opinions from the workers' and employers' point of view and, later, from that of civil society. For the Commission it was clear that neither committee held a 'proper' representative mandate, but that they nevertheless 'represented' European citizens according to two different principles: territory and function. The capacity of both, therefore, was strictly limited to that of a consultative committee: not of the specific and ad hoc nature like the many committees that the Commission creates and consults with before drafting policy proposals, but endowed with a more general mandate to represent the view from functional groups and civil society (the ESC) and the view of the periphery (the CoR). Member States' representatives in the Council, considering themselves as the true representatives of European national constituencies, would never have agreed to anything more than that, and even the EP, which had been favourable to the creation of the CoR, remained envious of its direct representative mandate.

The events leading to the creation of the Committee of the Regions have been recounted several times (Warleigh 1999). They have been interpreted by some as an attempt on the part of the Commission and the subnational authorities of Europe to create direct links with one another that could bypass the 'gate-keeping' powers of national governments (Hooghe and Marks 1996; Jeffery 2000). This was the hope of the stronger subnational authorities (SNAs) – such as the German *Länder* and the Spanish regions, which were losing at the EU level the policy-making prominence that they enjoyed domestically – and of the main European associations of regional and local authorities. The goal of these SNAs was to recoup at the European level the powers that they enjoyed at home. The creation of the Single European Market in 1986 and the reform of European Regional Development Policy (ERDP) in 1988 had shifted decision-making powers upwards, towards central governmental actors (Keating and Hooghe 1994; Loughlin 1997): central governmental actors decided in the Council of the EU the amount of funds to be devoted to this policy line and the criteria according to which the funds should be allocated, thus *de facto* disempowering those regional authorities which, domestically, would (in some Member States, at least) have been necessarily involved in such decisions.

In the hope of these regional representatives, the goal of the CoR would be to speak for 'the man in the street' and to provide the 'grass-roots' of European Community democracy (Van der Knaap 1994; Schöbel 1997). Because most CoR members were holders of a regional or local representative mandate, they considered it only natural to perform this representative function at the European level also. It was not by chance that the first CoR President and Vice-President were chief executives of two of the most powerful and vocal regional and local authorities of Europe.[1] Hence, the reaction of the regions and local authorities and the creation of a consultative committee was to release a series of their own opinions suggesting that the CoR should be empowered and given a more direct say in the expression of EU will. Some scholars venture so far as to suggest that, behind the decision to create a consultative Committee of Regional and Local Authorities (as the CoR was originally called), lay the attempt of the Commission to forge direct linkages with regional and local representatives who, directly or indirectly, through party linkages and thanks to their sometimes prominent role in policy-making, could access their national governments and steer their position in favour of given European policies. For others, the strategy of the Commission was part and parcel of a conscious strategy to create a 'Europe of the Regions' (Tömmel 1998; Jeffery 2002) by involving the regions in European-level decision-making and trying to obtain for them greater institutional powers from their national governments.

The letter of the TEU, however, is very clear: the Committee of the Regions had a consultative role and could not – not even under any stretch of 'federal' imagination – be considered as a 'third' representative chamber alongside the

Council and Parliament. Too many institutional and legal impediments stand in the way: the CoR is a selection of regional and local representatives drawn from very different national institutional contexts, domestically endowed with very different institutional powers, and ultimately performing their role in widely different manners. The very European institutions that had sustained its creation – the Commission and the EP – were ultimately sceptical of the attempts of some to turn the CoR into a third representative chamber: the Commission, because while forging important alliances with the peripheral governments of Europe, it was cautious not to upset the institutional setup of the Member States; the Parliament, because while favourably predisposed towards the injection of greater doses of political representation in the Union, it was somewhat envious of its role as sole authentic representative assembly (Piattoni 2008).

The CoR, then, was founded upon an inherent contradiction (Hönnige and Kaiser 2003; Christiansen and Lintner 2005): while mostly composed of political representatives from a broad spectrum of political, functional and institutional interests parcelled at a lower level of territorial aggregation (Piattoni 2011b), it was endowed solely with consultative powers 'as if' it could contribute just a particularistic point of view and not rather a different aggregation of the general interest of the EU demos. Admittedly, CoR members are selected through national procedures, which reflect both the territorial articulation and the institutional setup of the different Member States. In addition to federal and quasi-federal states like Germany, Belgium and Spain, at the time of CoR's creation, were present; also unitary states like Britain (at least until the devolution of the late 1980s and early 1990s), the Netherlands, Greece and Portugal, and regionalized states like Italy and, to a lesser extent, France. Therefore, in the CoR at the beginning sat subnational representatives who wielded real political power (such as the Ministerpräsidenten of German *Länder*) as well as subnational representatives who did not even have an elective mandate (such as the representatives of English counties). The situation has since improved, as the Treaty articles regarding the CoR have been progressively changed to indicate that only subnational representatives who 'hold an elective mandate or are accountable before an elected assembly' can be members of the CoR.[2] In time, CoR members have come to emphasize more and more their representative role and de-emphasized their role as consultants (see WPMLG). The questions raised at the end of the first section, then, are not so far-fetched and will be answered in the following section with reference to the European economic crisis.

The Committee of the Regions and the financial and economic crisis

The financial and economic crisis that hit Europe with full force in 2009 is a particularly tough test-case to determine whether the CoR can deliver full political and democratic representation. The CoR has no formal competence on financial and monetary issues, so the question of whether CoR members can act on behalf of those they represent appears to be decided from the start in the negative. I have argued elsewhere (Piattoni 2010: Chapter 5) that the policy areas in which subnational authorities, and hence the CoR, can be expected to be most active are those with a clear territorial dimension and for which the territorial impact of a given policy is clearly felt. Financial and monetary issues slice up Euro-area citizens along national, not regional or local borders: the democratic role of subnational representatives should logically be rather minimal. Still, the impact of the crisis and of the fiscal policies implemented as a response to it is felt unevenly across regions and localities; hence, subnational representatives have a legitimate claim to make their voice heard in defence of economic, social and territorial cohesion and against the potential distorting effects that remedies for the crisis might engender locally.

The CoR has the possibility of getting involved in financial and fiscal matters, which formally lie outside its remit, if it so wishes, in three ways. First, it can release own opinions on broad political matters, thus making its voice heard even if no one has an obligation to listen. Second, it can produce opinions on macroeconomic matters. For example, the CoR may intervene in the debate on the so-called Fiscal Compact insofar as, for example, the constitutionalization of the balanced budget clause extends also to subnational authorities, particularly in federal and regionalized states.[3] Third, the CoR can get mobilized in defence of subsidiarity, should this be imperilled by decisions that unduly limit subnational prerogatives. For all these reasons, it is plausible to look at the representative role that the CoR may play in the current economic and financial crisis.

In assessing the CoR's contribution to full political and democratic representation, I will look particularly at four issues to see whether the CoR exerts all four functions pertaining to the voice side of democratic representation: activating, proposing, receiving, and surveilling. First, I will look at the role of the CoR in activating other EU institutions, particularly the Commission, in favour of desired actions. Second, I will assess the capacity of the CoR to contribute to EU policy-making by providing its own distinctive point of view – the 'view from the periphery' – and by proposing specific policy measures. Third, I will evaluate the role of the CoR in warning against potentially undesired effects of EU legislation at the subnational level, thus exerting its receiving function. Fourth, I will highlight the CoR's commitment to stand guard over established Treaty principles (subsidiarity, proportionality, partnership), and over important democratic dimensions (inclusion, transparency, accountability), by reminding the other EU institutions of existing commitments and fundamental principles (surveilling). Moreover, I will gauge the capacity of the CoR to perform these discursive functions by striking a balance among the many interests that are therein represented and transcending 'the immediacy of their biographical experience and social and cultural belongings and interests' (Urbinati 2006: 7), thereby representing the general interest of EU citizens.

In what follows, I will draw on the opinions that the CoR issued between August 2009 (when the crisis first hit the EU) and March 2013 (at the time of writing), which relate to the economic and financial crisis and to measures enacted by the European Council and/or the Commission in order to counter its effects. Although they represent a small proportion of the CoR's activity – only four opinions were prepared by the CoR expressly addressing the economic and monetary crisis over a total of 220 opinions during this period – I find these documents very telling. References to the crisis are obviously present in a much larger number of opinions having to do with the Structural Funds or the multi-annual financial framework or in communications about multi-level governance. Nevertheless, precisely because monetary and financial issues fall outside the purview of the Committee, it is still significant that the CoR would bother to prepare four opinions on this specific issue, two of which still exist only in draft form.

These opinions[4] cover a number of issues, such as: (1) the increased territorial disparities engendered by the crisis and the need to keep promoting territorial cohesion; (2) specific suggestions on financial and fiscal measures in order to counter these disparities without impacting differentially on regions and localities; (3) greater coordination of budgetary and financial measures in order to relaunch growth without sacrificing subnational autonomy, but rather protecting local banks and small and medium-sized enterprises (SMEs); (4) greater involvement of subnational governments in the discussions on how to attack the crisis. In reviewing these opinions I will assess how the CoR performed the four voice functions recalled above and how it defended the general interest and right of the subnational tier to be better informed and more closely consulted when national governments and EU institutions take decisions regarding the crisis that may have an impact on local and regional communities.

Promotion of territorial cohesion

The CoR often remarks in Opinion 2 (CoR 2011) that the crisis has had an uneven impact on European regions, and that there is a need to monitor more effectively the effects of the measures taken to counter it on territorial cohesion, 'a new policy objective enshrined in the Lisbon Treaty, [which] has become a priority alongside economic and social cohesion' (ibid.: 6). This surveillance function is often coupled with recommendations aimed at improving the coordination among various levels of government in order to redress consequences of the crisis (activation function). In particular, Opinion 2 stresses 'the increased imbalances between and within Europe's regions' (ibid.: 2) and remarks that 'disadvantaged regions are less able than more prosperous ones to bring their own resources into play, and that this accentuates their vulnerability to external shocks and, in a period of crisis' (ibid.: 4). The need to promote the development of Europe's regions is all the more urgent in the current context of shrinking public finances, which in turn means seeking to maximize effectiveness and efficiency.

In order to measure territorial discrepancies correctly, per capita GDP at the regional level is insufficient. To measure economic growth, the CoR proposes that 'complementary indicators [can] be developed in cooperation with local and regional authorities … thus providing a truer picture of each region's level of development and specific social and territorial cohesion-related problems' (ibid.: 4). This proposal is complemented by a specific appeal to the Commission to the effect that, in determining a region's eligibility for the new EU Cohesion Policy from 2014 onwards, it uses indicators that fully reflect the impact of the crisis. The CoR consequently activates the Commission to make use of more up-to-date regional GDP and GDP-trend data in allocating resources (ibid.: 5).

When prompting EU institutions to 'maximise the impact of investments aimed at reducing disparities in growth' (ibid.: 5), the CoR does not fail to exert its reception and surveillance functions by reminding the Commission that:

> The different systems for implementing European cohesion policy depend on the specific circumstances of each Member State and are affected by the institutional context and the division of responsibilities and, more specifically, the level of decentralisation, the extent to which the principles of multi-level governance have been implemented, as well as regional and local experience in the area of territorial development and the scale and geographical scope of programmes.
>
> (Ibid.: 6)

The activating function of the CoR can be further evinced from its recommendations that the Commission should also make all efforts in setting up a Common Strategic Framework that would include all European territorial cohesion funds, i.e. the European Regional Development Fund (ERDF), the European Social Fund (ESF), the Cohesion Fund, the European Agricultural Fund for Rural Development (EAFRD) and the European Fisheries Fund (EFF), albeit each with their own resources and specific rules. Moreover,

> partnership contracts must, *in accordance with the principles of multi-level governance, be drawn up and developed with the full involvement of regional and local authorities*, which are the institutions responsible for implementing and managing the measures on the ground, and not simply between the Member States and the European Commission.
>
> (Ibid.: 8, emphasis added)

In sum, the CoR fears that the current crisis, by imposing restrictive measures on national governments and by reinforcing the intergovernmental nature of the Union, will take a toll on both territorial cohesion and multi-level governance. These are two democratic concerns – the former more substantive, the latter more procedural – that the CoR protects vocally in times of crisis.

A common system of financial transaction tax

In Opinion 3 (CoR 2012), the CoR proposes the introduction of a European financial transaction tax (FTT) as a further 'important step towards the urgently needed re-establishment of *the supremacy of democratic politics* over the serious discrepancies which have occurred in the functioning of financial markets' (ibid.: 2, emphasis added), if necessary 'by using the enhanced cooperation instrument, to encompass the Euro area at the very least' (ibid.: 4). The financial sector was a major cause of the crisis and received substantial government support at the beginning of the crisis, which then started to have major effects on national debts and the real economy.

To ensure that the financial sector makes a fair contribution to public finances thus relieving citizens, enterprises and Member States from the worst consequences of the crisis, the European Commission, on 28 September 2011, put forward a proposal for a financial transaction tax (European Commission 2011).[5] Despite fundamental agreement with the Commission on FTT, the CoR criticizes the European Commission's impact assessment published in September 2011 as 'biased and imprecise', and the conclusions of the models therein contained as 'vague and indecisive' (ibid.: 2). The CoR also opposes to 'the proliferation of uncoordinated national tax measures', which would undermine 'harmonisation in this area, necessary in order to prevent fragmentation of the internal market in financial services, as well as for the operation of the internal market in this area and the prevention of distortions of competition' (ibid.). Both statements reflect the CoR's contribution to EU policymaking (proposal function).

At the same time, the CoR reminds the Council and the Commission of the differentiated impact of financial regulation and highlights the need to take particular account of 'the possible consequences of introducing a common financial transaction tax system on the tax revenues of municipalities and regions' (ibid.: 3). It also makes other specific recommendations aimed at making the impact of FTT less territorially distorting, such as exempting primary market transactions 'as this will reduce undesirable effects on the real economy' (ibid.: 4). As we can see, the CoR here fully contributes to the debate on FTT, hence fully exerts its proposal function by calling attention to the adverse effects that these measures might have on the subnational level (receiving function).

Also in this case the CoR pays attention to the way in which legislation is passed and, although aware of the intergovernmental nature of financial regulation, it still argues in favour of opening the decision-making process to the other institutions of the EU, which represent supranational, subnational and infranational interests – arguably providing a fuller representation of the general interest. While it welcomes the application of the FTT directive, the CoR regrets that:

> The Commission is required to report only to the Council, as this *fails to take account of the Parliament's role in the legislative procedure*, under which the directive is adopted by the Council with the participation of the European Parliament; also considers that this restriction *undervalues the role of the Committee of the Regions*, as the European Union's assembly of local and regional authorities, and the European Economic and Social

> Committee, whose main task under the Treaty is to advise the legislative institutions.
>
> (Ibid.: 3, emphases added)

The CoR moreover takes a strong regulatory stance and:

> [w]elcomes the fact that the rates proposed are minimum rates, allowing the Member States to set higher rates, which is fully in keeping with the subsidiarity principle; at the same time, however, requests that surveillance should be exercised so that higher tax rates in certain Member States do not in fact generate the kind of damaging tax competition between Member States which the directive was specifically supposed to prevent.
>
> (Ibid.: 4)

As a consequence, it calls for the tax rates applied to shares, bonds and derivatives to be reviewed so as to uphold the principle of 'fairness in taxation'. The CoR believes that 'further measures are urgently needed going beyond the fiscal policy sector, ranging from significant strengthening of European coordination of national economic and fiscal policies to effective, institutionalised and *democratically legitimate* EU-level economic guidance' (ibid.: 5, emphasis added).

Greater coordination across levels in managing budgets and funds (Europe 2020)

After underscoring that 'local and regional authorities are responsible for a substantial share of public expenditure in Europe' and that 'in 2011 subnational public sector expenditure accounted for 16.7 per cent of GDP and 34.0 per cent of all public spending in Europe', in Opinion 4 (CoR 2013: 2), the CoR reminds the Commission and the other EU institutions that:

> subnational public investment tends to be concentrated in a number of key priority sectors that are critical for the success of the Europe 2020 strategy … meaning that the impact of austerity measures will have knock-on effects to delivering Europe 2020 goals.
>
> (Opinion 4: 2).

These facts justify paying particular attention to 'creating synergies' among EU, Member State and local and regional budgets. However, the 'synergies discussions' should in no way be used as a 'Trojan horse' to justify cutting the proposed Multiannual Financial Framework nor should it be used as an excuse to 'renationalize' the financing of some elements of the EU budget (for example, the Structural Funds in so-called 'richer' Member States) or to 'legitimate macro-economic conditionality' (ibid.: 2). In other words, greater efficiency in the use of the EU budget should not be achieved to the detriment of multi-level governance.

Achieving the overarching objectives of the Europe 2020 strategy requires effective mobilization of public and private finances at Member-State and sub-state level. The CoR underscores how the Common Strategic Framework (CSF) Funds, which are delivered and implemented at the territorial level in many cases by local and regional authorities, generate an important 'multiplier effect' on the economy.

> During the economic crisis EU funding, in particular from the CSF Funds, has provided stable and secure finance to local and regional authorities, and in many cases has been 'the only money in town' to support public investments and key initiatives, where local, regional and national budgets have been slashed.
>
> (Ibid.: 3)

This is all the more important since the European Commission estimates that, for the 2000–2006 programming period,

> EU Structural Funds had an average leverage-effect of EUR 2.1 for every EUR 1 of EU money contributed; for 2014–2020 the European Commission has set a target of EUR 4.2 per EUR 1 invested through the Cohesion Policy
>
> (Ibid.: 4)

Moreover, the Commission plans to exert additional 'policy leverage' by aligning local and regional strategic priorities around EU level priorities.

Among the new projects and initiatives that could deliver 'transformational change' are the creation of:

> single territorial investment funds (bringing together the various EU, Member State and sub-State funds) or creating a 'one-stop shop' for accessing funds with harmonized rules, comprehensive and clear guidance, including thematic programs such as Horizon 2020, Erasmus for All, the Programme for Social Change and Innovation (PSCI), the Connecting Europe Facility (CEF), etc.
>
> (Ibid.: 4)

In an effort to defend the voice of subnational governments in this debate (proposal function), the CoR further regrets that:

> the current debate around strengthening economic, monetary and political union in the Economic and Monetary Union (EMU) and wider EU, is limited to the main EU institutions and Member State governments, with little or no consideration given to the sub-State level,

and 'regrets also the continuing *failure … to effectively engage local and regional authorities* across the EU in a meaningful way in the European Semester' (ibid.: 5, emphasis added).

The same concerns are expressed also *vis-à-vis* the debate on the completion of a 'genuine' EMU and the possibility that this might trigger 'a drive towards greater centralization of powers and decision-making *without effective engagement of sub-State authorities in this discussion*' (ibid.: 6, emphasis added). The CoR 'notes that the European Commission's 2012 Report on Public Finances in EMU highlights the soundness of a fiscal federalist model that devolves revenue-raising as well as expenditure responsibilities to sub-State authorities' (ibid.: 6). Far from that, changes to the EU's economic governance (introduced through the European Semester, the Six-Pack, the Treaty on Stability, Coordination and Governance, and the Two-Pack proposals) have resulted in the 'development of *stricter rules to oversee local and regional public finances at Member State level* (through transposition of the so-called "golden rule" from the Member State level to the sub-State level in several Member States)' (ibid.: 6, emphasis added). Once again, the CoR acts on its receiving and surveilling functions.

In particular,

> the transposition of rules included in intergovernmental initiatives such as the Treaty on Stability, Coordination and Governance (or Fiscal Compact) into national constitutions or law were done without any proper prior consultation of the Committee of the Regions on the regional and local dimension of the issues at stake and proposes a closer adherence to the community method in further steps towards a Fiscal Union.
>
> (Ibid.: 6)

This mention of the 'community method' as the appropriate legislative procedure to pass fiscal and budgetary measures is particularly telling, as it shows the CoR's activity in defence of the role of the EP and the European Court of Justice to, respectively, legislate and enforce fiscal and budgetary measures (not to mention the role of consultative committees). To rectify the excessive intergovernmentalism embedded in the current procedures heavily centred on the European Council, the CoR:

> calls for … *a more transparent and effective engagement of sub-State authorities with budgetary powers* in the ongoing discussions on these issues, as well as for *a formal involvement of the Committee of the Regions* in the possible subsequent Treaty changes.
>
> (Ibid.: 6, emphases added)

In other words, the CoR fears that fiscal austerity measures will be carried out at the expense of and without the involvement of subnational authorities. The CoR considers with favour the 'principle of solidarity' at the core of EU's fiscal union, but it notes that:

> There cannot be any genuine fiscal union *without a definition of the rights and responsibilities of the different levels of government (fiscal federalism)*,

> a more explicit link between policy alignment and budgetary decision-making, and an ambitious vision on how to enhance vertical synergies between EU, national and local/regional budgets through proper coordination mechanisms.
>
> (Ibid.: 7, emphasis added)

To this end, it 'calls on the European Commission to publish a Green Paper during the first half of 2013 addressing these issues', and the additional principles of fiscal autonomy, fiscal transparency and partnership, thus fulfilling once again its activating function.

In doing this, the CoR argues:

> Respecting subsidiarity and the budgetary rights of local and regional authorities (their role in decision making and scrutiny) [means respecting] their democratic accountability to the communities that elect them, and ensuring the autonomy of each level of governance in determining priorities and spending.
>
> (Ibid.: 8)

Fiscal transparency is equally important as it allows having 'accurate and reliable data and analysis available at the EU level on public finances and budgetary processes down to the sub-Member State level' (ibid.: 8), without which accountability would be unattainable. By invoking the principles of subsidiarity, accountability and transparency, the CoR takes a strong position in favour not just of the institutional prerogatives of subnational authorities, but also of the right of local constituencies to exert their surveillance function and stand guard over the democratic temper of the entire Union.

Greater involvement of the subnational tier in policy-making

The themes of the greater involvement of the subnational tier in discussing and implementing measures aimed at countering the effects of the economic crisis are abundantly present also in Draft Opinion 1 (CoR 2010) which, however, was not approved in the plenary, as it also contained rather contentious statements against financial institutions and their management. The Opinion was discussed during the first phase of the crisis, when the damage done to the world economy by the speculative bubble induced by derivatives and toxic bonds had been exposed with full force. In this draft opinion, the CoR takes too strong a stand against large financial firms, thus probably causing its failure to gain approval.

The CoR has scornful words for the financial industry, which harbours bodies that are deemed 'too big to fail' and/or 'too interconnected to fail'. 'Across the EU, commercial banking should in future be subject to strict regulation with an emphasis on safeguarding customer deposits and corporate credit supply'. Therefore, the CoR is 'not averse to regulating investment banks more strictly' (CoR 2010: 4). The general tone of this CoR opinion is one of criticism of 'global finance', which runs roughshod over the concerns, activities and wealth of the EU citizens who, mostly, live on 'the periphery'. Some of its remarks express a concern that financial globalization may represent a danger for local economies and societies, since, in the end, taxpayers foot the bill.

The CoR would like the Commission and the other financial agencies to take strict measures to prevent similar crises in the future, thus performing a particularly strong activating function. It calls for the creation of an EU public rating agency and the introduction of a worldwide – or at least EU-wide – financial transaction tax, a proposal which, as we saw, was eventually proposed by the Commission and endorsed by the Committee in Opinion 3. The CoR concludes that 'in a nutshell, the overall point at issue is to restore the *primacy of democratically mandated policy* over the financial industry, and the *primacy of law* over the self-righteousness of the financial market players' (ibid.: 6, emphases added). One of the concluding passages of this Opinion is worth quoting at length, for it suggests a rather radical measure that was probably responsible for its dismissal:

> [The CoR] calls for a reform of the remuneration systems in the management of publicly owned companies. Any salaried manager earning just as much as a company owner who carries personal liability for a business should be legally obliged to bear the same risks. Practices such as management liability insurance paid for by the company and golden parachutes awarded on termination of employment contracts even in the event of failed business performance, run counter to the 'spirit of capitalism' (Max Weber) and the principle of rewarding performance. Such practices encourage people to overestimate their own capabilities and they foster irresponsible business policy: as such, they should be banned.
>
> (Ibid.: 7)

More generally, however, in this as well as in other Opinions, the CoR draws constant attention to the insufficient involvement of the subnational tier in the discussion and implementation of measures aimed at countering the crisis. Regretting the relative paucity of information on local and regional public finances across the EU, the CoR 'welcomes the inclusion in the European Commission's 2012 Report on Public Finances in the EMU of a dedicated chapter on Fiscal Decentralization in the EU for the first time' (ibid.: 8). It also calls for the removal of 'other bottlenecks with regard to the budgetary procedures and cycles within the EU, which are exacerbated by the "heterogeneity" of sub-State budgetary processes' (ibid.: 8) as local and regional budgeting is based predominantly on annual cycles rather than multiannual planning, which instead characterizes the EU budgetary framework. Consequently, according to the CoR, it would be advisable to move towards:

> greater harmonization of budgetary cycles within the EU, [and] promoting and encouraging use of medium-term budgetary frameworks at sub-State

> level (in line with measures introduced in the Six Pack), including clarification on how this could work within the annual European Semester cycles.
>
> (Ibid.: 9)

The CoR warns against using the crisis to introduce regulations that might curtail the prerogatives of subnational authorities. Thus, it:

> warns Member State governments against consolidating public budgets on the backs of the local and regional authorities; and also points out that it is precisely in the current situation, where public finance efficiency is paramount, that greater regional and local fiscal autonomy in terms of legislative powers and the raising and availability of resources could improve the control of public spending and the quality of the services provided, which would at the same time *raise the accountability of government levels and therefore restore public confidence in the institutions and in politics.*
>
> (Ibid.: 8, emphasis added)

The CoR underscores that:

> increasing charges and levies raised at local and regional level and cutting back on local services hits the public indiscriminately and thus, in proportional terms, places the biggest strain on people with low incomes; moreover, this is liable to have negative repercussions, especially in cases where central governments apply these levies across the board to local and regional authorities, with no regard for territorial specificities.
>
> (Ibid.: 9)

If this trend continues, it concludes, 'it will severely jeopardise social cohesion and social harmony', whose protection is the CoR's specific mandate.

To this end, the CoR recommends not closing down local savings banks and loan associations and claims that regional banks, such as savings banks and cooperative movements, have a stabilizing influence in the crisis. The conclusion is a bold reminder of the fundamental role of subnational representatives in preserving democracy. 'Elected local and regional authority representatives will – as they always do when times are tough – need drive and persuasiveness *to keep the public on board and political extremism at bay*' (ibid.: 10, emphasis added). Unfortunately, the Communication from the Commission to the EP and the Council entitled *Long-term Sustainability of Public Finances for a Recovering Economy* fails to take account of 'the particular pressures placed on regional and local authorities and of the considerable mismatch between local and regional responsibilities for spending … and fiscal powers, which are still predominantly in the hands of the national authorities' (ibid.: 10). Because of this mismatch between fiscal powers and spending responsibilities, 'multilevel governance is liable to remain a concept with no real bearing' (ibid.: 10).

The representative function of the CoR: mission impossible or miracle in the making?

As these documents demonstrate, in its opinions specifically dedicated to the economic and financial crisis, the CoR manages to strike a balance among the many interests it represents that could fragment its voice. Rather, the CoR manages to 'upgrade' its institutional, political, economic and territorial interests (Piattoni 2011a) by arguing in favour of greater equity and solidarity all while standing guard of democratic principles such as participation, transparency, accountability and subsidiarity. In performing this representative function, it does not merely report the desiderata of its constituencies nor does it simply reflect its internal disparities. Rather, it manages to give voice to a 'subnational tier', 'the periphery' or 'the man in the street', which would not be heard without this representational activity. Is it too bold to conclude that it *succeeds in doing this precisely because it is not directly involved in shaping the will of the Union, but merely in articulating its voice?* It is possible that, being barred from directly contributing to securing isonomia, it may better concentrate on guaranteeing isegoria? I think not. In fact, I would like to submit that these two activities might be inversely related – but this is the object of another inquiry.

Notes

1 Jacques Blanc, the right-wing president of the Languedoc-Roussillon region and president of the Assembly of European Regions (AER), was the first President of the CoR, while Pasqual Maragall i Mira, the leftist mayor of the city of Barcelona and president of the Council of European Municipalities and Regions (CEMR), was the first Vice-president,

2 The principle that CoR members should hold a *representative* mandate was enshrined in the Treaty of Nice (2003), still its formulation – 'The Committee of the Regions shall consist of representatives of regional and local bodies who either hold a regional or local electoral mandate or are politically accountable to an assembly elected by universal suffrage' (Art. 263) – is ambiguous and practically creates the possibility for circumventing it. The Treaty of Lisbon provision on CoR membership (Art. 300.3 TEU, consolidated version) has perhaps taken a step backwards as it states:

> 'The Committee of the Regions shall consist of representatives of regional and local bodies who either hold a regional or local authority electoral mandate or are politically accountable to an elected assembly', thus suggesting that the assembly to which they are politically accountable may be composed of representatives accountable to lower-level assemblies elected by universal suffrage.
>
> (TEU 2007, 6655/7/08 REV 7: 233)

3 The text of the Treaty on Stability, Coordination and Governance in the Economic and Monetary Union, as the Fiscal Compact is more precisely called, can be found at the web-page: www.consilium.europa.eu/media/1478399/07_-_tscg.en12.pdf (accessed 6 January 2014).

4 Full details are listed in the bibliography; the following notation indicates how these opinions will be quoted in the remainder of the chapter: henceforth CoR 2010 is draft Opinion 1; CoR 2011 is Opinion 2; CoR 2012 is Opinion 3; CoR 2013 is Draft Opinion 4.

5 The Commission had explored the idea of taxing the financial sector at EU level for several months already. On 29 June 2011, the Commission announced, in the context

of the multiannual financial framework, that it would propose a financial transaction tax as an own resource for the EU budget, and so it did in September of the same year. The CoR supported this proposal and highlighted that

> the financial transaction tax is an important tool for ensuring that the financial sector plays its part in achieving greater solidarity and fairness, and for curbing speculation, as the CoR noted in its opinion on the new Multiannual Financial Framework post-2013.
>
> (Ibid.: 2)

During the Ecofin meetings in June and July 2012, however, it was ascertained that there was no unanimous support within the Council for a common system of FTT in the Union as a whole, as proposed by the Commission. During these Ecofin meetings several delegations pointed out that progress could be made on the issue in a more restricted group of Member States in the context of enhanced cooperation between interested Member States. In September 2012 the Commission received requests from 11 Member States asking it to submit a proposal for a Council Decision to authorize enhanced cooperation. It was requested that the objectives and scope of this proposal should be based on the original Commission FTT proposal. On 23 October 2012 the Commission proposed to the Council to authorize the enhanced cooperation in the area of financial transaction tax (COM/2012/799). The Council will have to decide since that the European Parliament gave its consent to the latter proposal on 12 December 2012. A subsequent Commission proposal for a Directive implementing the enhanced cooperation in the area of financial transaction tax should follow in due course.

References

Christiansen, T. (1996) 'Second thoughts on Europe's "third level": the European Union's Committee of the Regions', *Publius: The Journal of Federalism*, 26 (1): 93–114.

Christiansen T. and Lintner, P. (2005) 'The Committee of the Regions after 10 years: lessons from the past and challenges for the future', *Eipascope*, 1: 7–13.

CoR (2009) White Paper of the Committee of the Regions on Multilevel Governance, CoR 89/2009.

CoR (2010) Draft opinion (based on Art. 307 TFEU) *Lessons from the financial crisis for financial supervision and public finances* (discussed at the 87th plenary session on 1–2 December 2010, rapporteur Karl-Heinz Klär, DE/PES).

CoR (2011) Opinion, *The complementarily of national and EU interventions aimed at reducing the disparities in economic and social growth* (approved at the 92nd plenary session on 11–12 October 2011, rapporteur Francesco Musotto, IT/EA).

CoR (2012) Opinion, *A common system of financial transaction tax* (approved at the 94th plenary session on 14–15 February 2012, rapporteur Ralf Christoffers, DE/PES).

CoR (2013) Draft opinion on *Creating greater synergies between EU, national and sub-national budgets*, tabled for the 99th plenary session on 31 January–1 February 2013, rapporteur Rhodri Glyn Thomas, UK/EA).

Council of the European Union (2012) Consolidated versions of the Treaty on European Union and the Treaty on the functioning of the European Union – Charter of Fundamental Rights of the European Union (Brussels, 12 November 2012, 6655/7/08 REV 7) consulted online on 16 August 2013 at http://register.consilium.europa.eu/pdf/en/08/st06/st06655-re07.en08.pdf (accessed 30 November 2013).

European Commission (2001) *European Governance: A White Paper* (COM 2001(428) final).

European Commission (2011) 'Financial Transaction Tax: making the financial sector pay its fair share', IP/11/1085, 28 September, available at http://europa.eu/rapid/press-release_IP-11-1085_en.htm?locale=en (accessed 6 January 2014).

Føllesdal, A. and Hix, S (2006) 'Why there is a democratic deficit in the EU: a response to Majone and Moravcsik', *Journal of Common Market Studies*, 44 (3): 533–562.

Hönnige, C. and Kaiser, A. (2003) 'Opening the black box: decision-making in the Committee of the Regions', *Regional and Federal Studies*, 13 (2): 1–29.

Hooghe, L. (1995) 'Sub-national mobilization in the European Union', *West European Politics*, 18 (3): 175–198.

Hooghe, L. (1996) 'Building a Europe with the Regions: the changing role of the European Commission', in L. Hooghe (ed.) *Cohesion Policy and European Integration: Building Multi-Level Governance*, Oxford: Clarendon Press, 89–127.

Hooghe, L. and Marks, G. (1996) '"Europe with the Regions": channels of regional representation in the European Union', *Publius: The Journal of Federalism*, 26 (1): 73–91.

Jeffery, C. (1995) 'Whither the Committee of the Regions? Reflections on the Committee's "Opinion of the Revision of the Treaty on European Union"', *Regional and Federal Studies*, 5 (2): 247–257.

Jeffery, C. (2000) 'Sub-national mobilization and european integration: does it make any difference?', *Journal of Common Market Studies*, 38 (1): 1–23.

Jeffery, C. (2002) 'The Europe of the Regions from Maastricht to Nice', *Queen's Papers on Europeanization*, 7.

Keating, M. and Hooghe, L. (1996) 'By-passing the nation state? Regions and the EU policy process', in J. Richardson (ed.) *European Union: Power and Policy-Making*, London: Routledge, pp. 216–229.

Loughlin, J. (1997) 'Representing Regions in Europe: The Committee of the Regions', in C. Jeffery (ed.) *The Regional Dimension of the European Union*, London: Frank Cass.

Marks, G., Nielsen, F., Ray, L. and Salk, J.E. (1996) 'Competencies, cracks and conflicts: regional mobilization in the European Union', *Comparative Political Studies*, 29 (2): 164–192.

Piattoni, S. (2008) 'The Committee of the Regions: multi-level governance after Enlargement' in E. Best, T. Christiansen and P. Settembri (eds) *The Institutions of the Enlarged European Union: Continuity and Change*, Cheltenham, UK: Edward Elgar, pp. 162–182.

Piattoni, S. (2011a) 'The Committee of the Regions and the "upgrading" of subnational territorial representation in the EU', in S. Kröger and D. Friedrich (eds) *Democracy and Representation in the EU,* Houndmills; Basingstoke: Palgrave-Macmillan.

Piattoni, S. (2011b) 'The problematic coexistence of functional and territorial representation in the EU', *Journal of European Integration*, 33 (4): 369–384.

Piattoni, S. (2013) 'Representation as delegation: a basis for EU democracy?', *Journal of European Public Policy*, 20 (2): 222–242.

Pitkin, H. (1967) *The Concept of Representation*, Berkeley, CA: University of California Press.

Schöbel, N. (1997) *The Committee of the Regions: A Preliminary Review of the Committee's Work During its First Two Years of Operation*, Tübingen: European Centre for Research on Federalism (ECRF).

TEU (2007) Treaty of the European Union (Lisbon Treaty), European Commission, available at http://register.consilium.europa.eu/doc/srv?l=EN&t=PDF&gc=true&sc=false&f=ST%206655%202008%20REV%207&r=http%3A%2F%2Fregister.consilium.europa.eu%2Fpd%2Fen%2F08%2Fst06%2Fst06655-re07.en08.pdf (accessed 6 January 2014).

Tömmel, I. (1998) 'Transformation of governance: the European Commission's Strategy for a "Europe of the Regions" ', *Regional and Federal Studies*, 8 (2).

Urbinati, N. (2006) *Representative Democracy: Principles and Genealogy*, Chicago, IL: University of Chicago Press.

Van der Knaap, P. (1994) 'The Committee of the Regions: the outset of a "Europe of the Regions"?', *Regional Politics & Society*, 4 (2) (Summer): 86–100.

Warleigh, A. (1997) 'A committee of no importance? Assessing the relevance of the Committee of the Regions', *Politics*, 17 (2): 101–107.

Warleigh, A. (1999) *The Committee of the Regions: Institutionalising Multi-Level Governance?*, London: Kogan Page.

Part II

Non-electoral forms of representation in multi-level representation in times of crisis

6 Representation and network governance in Europe

Martino Maggetti

Introduction

In this chapter, a broad definition of democratic representation is adopted to make sense of the shift from 'government to governance' (Rhodes 1996). In this view, democratic representation occurs when representatives are authorized to act, promote the interests of the represented, and are held accountable for their actions (Pitkin 1972). This comprehensive conceptualization includes new, non-electoral forms of representation that are 'increasingly important to expanding and deepening democracy' (Urbinati and Warren 2008: 389), such as those at work in governance networks. To begin with, the concept of representative government embodies a number of principles that, following Manin, are assumed to be invariable over time: the appointment of those who govern through regular elections, the relative autonomy of decision-making from the wishes of the electorate, the liberty to express political opinions, and public scrutiny of political decisions (Manin 1996). These principles are traditionally embodied by democratic, representative institutions such as parliaments and collegial–governmental cabinets. Nevertheless, political representation faces a crucial challenge in modern times. Democratic, representative institutions are said to become less and less important following 'denationalzation', a phenomenon epitomized by the reallocation of sovereignty and policy-making capacity from nation states to less representative supranational institutions (Føllesdal and Hix 2006), which goes along with a concomitant process of delegating decision-making capacity to unelected actors (Vibert 2007).

As a consequence, the role of elected politicians in policy-making is becoming less relevant, while the influence of 'technocratic' actors (Papadopoulos 2003) and non-majoritarian bodies that are not electorally responsive to citizens increases (Coen and Thatcher 2005; Majone 1996a; Thatcher and Stone Sweet 2002). A prominent example of 'sideward denationalization' is offered by the cross-sectoral establishment of independent regulatory agencies (IRAs), which are increasingly widespread in European Member States and beyond (Gilardi 2008; Jordana *et al.* 2011; Levi-Faur 2005; Majone 1996b). At the domestic level, IRAs do not rely on any explicit claim of representativeness and act as a separate power consistent with a Madisonian model of democracy (Maggetti

2010). However, they have to comply with the accountability requirements of democratic institutions through ministerial hearings, reports to parliamentary committees, and so on (Mulgan 2003; Schillemans 2008; Strom *et al.* 2003; Verschuere *et al.* 2006). This institutional complexity was complicated further by the creation of European networks of IRAs in the early 2000s (Eberlein and Newman 2008; Eberlein and Grande 2005). European regulatory networks (ERNs) were established following two parallel developments (Coen and Thatcher 2008b): On the one hand, domestic IRAs decided to create transnational groups to exchange information and coordinate operations at the international level; on the other hand, the European Commission promoted networks as a second best solution to favour the harmonization of European regulation and disseminate pro-competition rules due to Member States' unwillingness to dismiss their national regulatory authorities.

This process implied another step away from democratic institutions, one that can be conceptualized as a 'double delegation' – upward from national regulatory authorities and downward from the European Commission (Coen and Thatcher 2005). In this setting, patterns of representation are particularly intricate. Which form of representation is at work? Is any legitimate type of non-electoral representation possible in this context? Whom are the network members actually representing? These questions are crucial to understanding the nature of regulatory networks, and more broadly, to understanding the functioning of the 'new governance' architecture of the European Union (EU) (Donnelly 2010; Héritier 2003; Héritier and Eckert 2008). In that regard, three main expectations about patterns of representation can be derived from different theories of European integration: according to an intergovernmental perspective (Moravcsik 1995; Rittberger and Schimmelfennig 2006), IRAs participating in ERNs represent national actors and interests; from a supranational viewpoint (Quaglia 2007; Stone Sweet and Sandholtz 1997), ERNs are expected to endorse European policies and represent the views of EU institutions; alternatively, in line with the literature on multilevel governance (Hooghe and Marks 2001; Hooghe and Marks 2003), there are theoretical arguments that posit the idea that ERNs could become a powerful, hybrid layer of governance that is increasingly autonomous both from national actors and European institutions. In that case, network members would not represent other actors in ERNs, but would instead create a transnational community of regulators with a distinctive decision-making capacity and goals. To explore these questions, this chapter proposes a study of IRAs' patterns of representation in the most institutionalized ERN, the Committee of European Securities Regulators (CESR).

After the introductory section, the first part of this chapter presents the main features of network governance in Europe. The second section illustrates theoretical expectations about representation claims in networks. The following two sections focus on the empirical study of the patterns of representation in the CESR by using official documents and semi-directive interviews, with special attention given to the context of the financial crisis as a critical juncture that allowed supranational actors to partially reshape the European financial supervisory system. Conclusions follow.

European regulatory networks

Recent research has focused on transnational networks as the cornerstone of a 'new world order', wherein different political actors interact to respond to the challenges of interdependence in boundary-less issues such as human rights, the environment, finance, trade, and organized crime (Slaughter 2004a; Slaughter 2004b). According to this argument, global governance is crucially shaped by the transnational activity of regulators, judges, and legislators who are exchanging information, coordinating policies, enforcing laws, and regulating markets in an informal, specialized, decentralized, and network-based way. In this context, the EU is considered a particularly advanced networked polity that functions as a regulatory state (Majone 1994; Moran 2002), coordinates policies through informal instruments of 'soft law' (Christiansen and Piattoni 2003; Eberlein 2003), and advances its integration through an experimental architecture based on autonomy granted to lower-level entities and learning platforms that promote reporting, peer review, and deliberative procedures (Radaelli 2000; Sabel and Zeitlin 2010). In particular, EU scholars emphasize that European institutions encourage informal network governance for functional and instrumental reasons; that is, to enhance consensus-building capacity, harmonization, and convergence in areas that are resilient to 'hard' integration and Europeanization (Djelic and Sahlin-Andersson 2006; Donnelly 2010; Héritier 2003; Héritier and Eckert 2008; Radaelli 2003). Accordingly, networks account for a horizontal level of governance, which is expected to become more and more important over time because political power is increasingly fragmented and dispersed (Hooghe and Marks 2001, 2003). Nation states and their bureaucracies are said to lose centrality, while other actors – independent regulators, 'civil society', business representatives, experts, and so on – are becoming more relevant (Bache *et al.* 2005; Piattoni 2010). What is more, networks are seen as catalysts of diffusion processes (Gilardi 2010, 2012) that offer channels for cooperation and the exchange of information, foster innovative policies, and disseminate 'best practices' among Member States and beyond (Dolowitz and Marsh 2000; Radaelli 2000).

There are five main ERNs, and they are charged with the regulation of finance, energy, telecoms, competition, and broadcasting: the CESR; the Council of European Energy Regulators/European Regulators' Group for Electricity and Gas (CEER/ERGEG); the Independent Regulators Group/European Regulators Group (IRG/ERG); the European Competition Network (ECN); and the European Platform of Regulatory Authorities (EPRA). The first two have recently acquired the legal status of European agencies, thus becoming more institutionalized and resourceful, but they still rely on national regulatory authorities for implementation and are organized in a network-based way (Levi-Faur 2011). Concretely, these transnational groups federate the regulatory authorities of EU Member States, as well as of that of some non-Member States such as Iceland,

Norway, and Switzerland. The EU Commission is usually represented at ERN meetings, too. The ERNs' organizational model normally comprises a secretariat; a management board, which is ultimately responsible for decision making; and a number of permanent committees and ad hoc working groups, whose members convene on a regular basis. Committees and working groups frequently involve academic experts and business representatives, and are in charge of preparatory meetings and day-to-day meta-regulatory functions such as reporting, rule setting, and peer-review assessments.

ERNs were promoted by national regulatory authorities, and by European institutions, in order to favour the harmonization of European regulation, provide technical advice, and improve cooperation and information exchanges among national regulatory authorities (Coen and Thatcher 2008a; Kohler-Koch 2002; Yesilkagit 2011). They are in charge of producing and disseminating non-binding standards, guidelines, and recommendations. The goal of these soft rules is to promote 'best practices', achieve coordination among regulatory authorities, and ensure the consistent application of harmonized, pro-competition rules across Europe. ERNs have an official, defined, stable, durable, resourceful, and horizontal structure, and also possess the competency to make decisions that involve the use of soft power to ensure implementation. Therefore, ERNs are a prototypical case for the study of network governance. They are sophisticated, networked organizations disposing from their own resources, and have separate administrative entities set up specifically to manage and coordinate their networks (Provan and Kenis 2008). What is more, ERNs federate representative, relatively homogeneous, and mutually interdependent actors with similar beliefs about the core properties of the policy at stake (Maggetti and Gilardi 2011).

Representation patterns in networks

In this context, patterns of representation are very intricate. If we follow the classical argument of Pitkin anticipated in the introduction, political representation occurs when political actors 'speak, advocate, symbolize, and act' on the behalf of others in a political arena (Pitkin 1972). In the case of ERNs, the question is: 'Whom do network members stand for?' A paradox arises, as regulators formally represent their countries at transnational level and yet, for the vast majority of cases, they are formally independent from their government. At the same time, network members are also expected to represent European actors as they interact in European networks under the shadow of the European Commission. A straightforward way to deal with these issues is to conceive of representation as 'a process that involves the making of claims to be representative' (Saward 2005: 184). This conceptualization is helpful when examining representation patterns in governance arenas wherein even the most advanced theories of parliamentary representation – such as Mansbridge's gyroscopic view of legislators (Mansbridge 2011) – can hardly apply. Therefore, for the sake of the present discussion, we will limit the scope of our analysis to claims of representativeness that are expressed by network-level actors. Indeed, examining the viewpoints of insiders is important to make sense of 'post-parliamentary' governance arenas such as ERNs, which are hardly accessible and quite opaque regarding governance settings and decision-making processes (Papadopoulos 2008).

Three main expectations regarding patterns of representation can be derived from theories of European integration. First, following an intergovernmental position, national governments are the most influential actors in the process of European integration. The liberal variant of this approach emphasizes the fact that integration is the result of a series of repeated games in which national governments bargain to pursue their interests. In this view, European institutions are Member States' agents (with limited supranational capacity) (Moravcsik 1995; Rittberger and Schimmelfennig 2006). When studying European regulatory networks, there is a difference with this model; that is, domestic preferences are aggregated (at the domestic level) and articulated (at the European level) not by governments, but by independent regulatory agencies. As IRAs are formally independent from their political principal, they do not necessarily reflect the preferences of their governments. But, from a liberal, intergovernmental perspective, the logic at work is expected to be quite the same: interactive decision-making processes at the level of European networks are expected to follow the interests of prevailing domestic groups. Therefore, individual network members are expected to express the claim of representing their national regulatory authority and/or of their national interest groups.

Second, according to a supranational approach, integration mainly follows the functional dynamics facilitated by European actors (Quaglia 2007; Stone Sweet and Sandholtz 1997). The first step of this argument is that cooperation in specific economic policy sectors leads to greater economic integration in Europe, and then to wider political integration through so-called functional spillovers from one policy area to another. The second step is that supranational actors are interested in pushing the integration process forward to extend their powers over the EU polity. The application of this theory to European regulatory networks would imply that networks function as arenas promoting a progressive Europeanization of their individual members (that is, representatives of independent regulatory agencies), who are independent from domestic governments and therefore footloose with respect to national interests. As a consequence, network members are expected to express the claim of representing European institutions and/or European interest groups.

A third perspective is also pertinent, corresponding to a 'new' variety of the multilevel governance theory. The core idea is that power and authority are increasingly dispersed in Europe, and that sovereignty has moved away from national governments, not just to the supranational level, but also to other intermediary layers that gain progressive autonomy (Hooghe and Marks 2001, 2003). Earlier theories of multilevel governance situated these additional levels of governance mainly on a territorial scale (for example, with regions and cities). Newer theories suggest instead that the existing gap between the need for EU rules and the persistence of national-level competencies leaves room for the emergence of functional–transnational spaces that are partially self-ruling

(Eberlein and Grande 2005) and populated by transnational groups of actors (Djelic and Quack 2010). These actors are public officials, sectorial experts, business lobbyists, and so on, acting as a cohesive epistemic community sharing similar policy beliefs (Haas 1992). According to this expectation, one would suppose that network members would make claims of primarily representing the network itself and/or sector-specific, transnational interests. The arguments underlying these three expectations are not necessarily mutually exclusive, but the predicted phenomena can hardly occur at the same time.

The case of the Committee of European Securities Regulators

The case of the CESR was chosen to illustrate the patterns of representation in transnational networks. The CESR is a network of the 'harder' type in terms of competencies, powers, and formalization of its structure (Coen and Thatcher 2008b), thus representing a case in which members should consider the network level to be very important and relevant to policy (Maggetti and Gilardi 2011). Moreover, it perfectly exemplifies the problem of double delegation because it was set up by the European Commission, whereas some other networks were self-initiated, at least at their inception. The CESR holds a leading role in the Lamfalussy process, which is the implementation of the new system of regulation of European financial markets (Baker *et al.* 2005; Chaher 2005; De Visscher *et al.* 2007; Lütz 2004). The life span, evolution, and termination of this network can be summarized with the help of publicly available official documentation. In 1999, the European Commission adopted the Financial Services Action Plan, which triggered the formal establishment of the CESR in 2001. The Market Participants Consultative Panel was created in 2002. This panel met regularly to exercise peer pressure on CESR members. The participants in this panel included representatives of the private sector, such as banks and other financial institutions. In 2004, the so-called Himalaya report was published under the impulsion of CESR. This document discussed the tools considered necessary to improve financial supervision in Europe. A crucial point is that the level of market integration varied from case to case, and that there were still significant differences in the competencies of the national regulators. In 2007, the Lamfalussy process was evaluated. Suggestions on how to give CESR a more direct role included simplified procedures, better allocation of roles to the different participants, consideration of the customer's view, and more systematic collection of evidence. In 2008–9, following the financial turmoil, proposals for transforming the CESR in the de Larosière report included upgrading and reforming the network. These reform proposals were endorsed by the European Commission and discussed by the European Parliament (EP). In 2010, the restructuring of CESR began to enable a smooth transition to the European authority, named the European Securities and Markets Authority (ESMA). ESMA became operational in 2011. Its mission is to protect investors, promote a stable and well-functioning market, and foster harmonization and convergence.

CESR (then ESMA) is in charge of improving coordination among securities regulators, acting as an advisory group to assist the EU Commission, and ensuring consistent and timely implementation of community legislation in the Member States. Each EU Member State is represented by the head of the national regulatory authority in the field of securities. The Director General of the DG Market participates as the representative of the European Commission. The securities authorities of Norway and Iceland are also represented. To accomplish these tasks, the CESR develops standards that consist of sector-specific corporate governance measures to promote harmonized, pro-competition rules in the securities markets of Member (and some non-Member) States (Maggetti and Gilardi 2011). They seek to improve transparency and investor protection while eliminating market barriers and reducing costs for investors and fund management companies. The standards and guidelines are not mandatory because they do not have Community law status, which means that CESR members introduce them in their day-to-day regulatory practices on a voluntary basis. However, the review panel of the CESR assesses the overall process of implementation and offers recommendations about specific problems in the implementation process encountered by individual members. It encourages self-assessment procedures in order to obtain a first picture of the practice of supervision in a given area. Most importantly, it exercises group pressure through peer reviews carried out by other members on implementation in all concerned jurisdictions, and sets up so-called benchmarks that are used to evaluate compliance, not unlike the open method of coordination (Radaelli 2004; Schäfer 2004).

The most important soft rules developed by this network are the following: the standard for investor protection (2002) provides harmonized business rules for retail investors in standards and rules of general application, customer information, 'know your customer' and duty of care standards, customer agreements, dealing requirements (including the 'best execution' standards), and individual discretionary portfolio management. Standard 1, on financial information (2003), represents a contribution to the task of developing and implementing a common approach to the enforcement of International Financial Reporting Standards in Europe. It provides for principles by which harmonization of institutional oversight systems in Europe may be achieved. Standard 2, on financial information (2004–5), aims to contribute to the consistent enforcement of International Accounting Standards Board standards within Europe. It was implemented in 2005 by providing a formalized structure and a number of common principles to national supervisors. Finally, the Undertaking for Collective Investment in Transferable Securities Directives (UCITS) guidelines (2006) aims to simplify the notification procedure of UCITS; that is, the use of passports for facilitating the cross-border activities of investment funds. In particular, these guidelines offer a common approach to domestic authorities to bring greater simplicity, transparency, and certainty to the notification process.

The empirical analysis of representation patterns in the CESR

According to the Commission decision of 6 June 2001, 'Establishing the Committee of European Securities Regulators', article 3:

> The Committee shall be composed of high-level representatives from the national public authorities competent in the field of securities. Each Member State shall designate a high-level representative from its competent authority to participate in the meetings of the Committee. The Commission shall be present at meetings of the Committee and shall designate a high-level representative to participate in all its debates. The Committee shall elect a chairperson from among its members. The Committee may invite experts and observers to attend its meetings.

IRAs are primarily represented at CESR meetings, along with Commission representatives and sectorial experts. But for whom are individual network members actually standing? To study network-related issues, including patterns of representation, we conducted a survey targeting all network members. After the second wave of questionnaires, however, we noted that the response rate was not satisfactory (about 35 per cent of the sample), and that the quality of answers was uneven. When we compared this result with a similar inquiry conducted in parallel with members of parliaments in European countries, we observed that both the response rate and the quality of answers were higher in the latter case. This difference between elected and unelected actors could be interpreted as a first sign of lower pressure for public accountability in the case of actors representing non-majoritarian regulators in transnational networks. They are appointed by national regulatory authorities that are formally independent from elected politicians and insulated from the electoral cycle; at the same time they are interacting in a hybrid transnational space situated at the interface between the national and the European level. In this context, a process of autonomization is likely to happen, an *esprit de corps* develops, and outsiders are kept at a distance to reinforce internal cohesion and avoid controversy (Boyt *et al.* 2005; Schmitter and Streeck 1985).

As a second step, we conducted six very focused semi-directive interviews with key CESR players to complete our analysis of official documents by examining actual representation patterns. The main goal was to collect claims of representativeness made by network members. The first set of questions concerned the wide-ranging aims of participant actors when interacting in CESR meetings. It emerged quite clearly that the initial goals of members at the time of network creation were primarily directed toward the protection of national interests (Interviews 1, 5, and 6). Above all, according to our interviews, CESR members unequivocally represented their national regulatory authorities in plenary sessions and network working groups when attending network meetings. They took policy decisions, approved draft guidelines, and wrote official documents at a network level, acting as representatives of their national regulatory authorities (Interview 4). To be precise, according to a former CESR senior manager, participants in a network meeting are senior officials mandated by national regulatory authorities, and their participation in the network is considered very important by their domestic counterparts (Interview 2). Since the vast majority of national regulatory authorities of European Member States correspond to independent regulatory agencies, their autonomy from elected politicians is always emphasized, and very much valued, by all respondents. Conversely, any claim of directly representing their governments has been disregarded.

However – and this is another key point – it seems that over time, network members no longer acted merely as the 'agent' of their 'principal'. Instead, following an endogenous dynamic, the CESR progressively acquired powers and autonomy that went far beyond the initial aims of the network. The prelude of the above-mentioned Commission decision of 2001 described the role of the CESR as to 'serve as an independent body for reflection, debate, and advice for the Commission in the securities field', and to 'contribute to the consistent and timely implementation of Community legislation in the Member States by securing more effective cooperation between national supervisory authorities, carrying out peer reviews, and promoting best practice'. It also stated: 'The Committee of European Securities Regulators should organise its own operational arrangements and maintain close operational links with the Commission and the European Securities Committee'. Nevertheless, the network developed considerable meta-regulatory functions that were not limited to technical advice and coordination, which were concurrent with Commission's powers. In that regard, a former CESR executive noted that every member wanted to contribute to the evolution of the network. A team spirit has emerged, to the point that CESR has been very influential in developing the rules, which has displeased some governments and led them to question the legitimacy of the network (Interview 1).

The CESR developed soft rules that gained influence at the domestic level and were consistently adopted by Member States. In this way, the network evolved into a genuine 'new governance' arena, able to shape regulatory policy regarding European financial markets by making the most of its hybrid position at the interface between the national and European levels. Network members were able to play a sort of 'two-level game' that placed the network in a prominent position in this policy area. As a respondent remarked, this new role was regarded quite suspiciously by European institutions, and by the governments of some important Member States, which feared a loss of democratic control over the network (Interview 1). With regard to European institutions, the criticisms of CESR's evolution came from members of the EP in particular, who decried the weak accountability schemes for this powerful European regulatory network (Interview 1). At this point, the network as a whole became (or at least was perceived as) self-referential, and developed the role of an active political player in European governance. The network started acting as a cohesive policy community representing, above all, the sector-specific viewpoints of increasingly transnationalized financial regulators (Interviews 1 and 4).

The rising discontent, combined with the Commission's long-term goal of promoting EU-level 'agencification', triggered the CESR's transformation into a European agency with increased resources, powers, and competencies. It also had a new name: ESMA (European Securities and Markets Authority). This agency, operational since 2011, is much more formally accountable to the EP than the CESR; it has to appear regularly before the committee in charge of formal hearings (ECON). ESMA is also more formally accountable to the Council of the EU and the European Commission, through periodic reports of its activities and a publicly available annual report. ESMA's establishment is part of a wider reform of financial market supervision that also introduces European supervisory authorities for banking, insurance, occupational pensions, and the creation of a European Systemic Risk Board (ESRB). This package of supervision follows the famous report on the problems of the European financial supervision system in the context of the financial crisis from 2008 by the de Larosière group (de Larosière *et al.* 2009), and the concomitant EU Commission's announcement of a new regulatory framework in May 2009 (Fischer-Appelt 2011; Kull 2011). Following our interviews, this process of agencification is seen mostly as a positive development by network members, as previously informal 'accountability relations' are being formalized and written into the law (Interview 1). This improves the democratic accountability of the transnational group of financial regulators formerly known as the CESR to the EU parliament and Member States' governments.

At this point, ESMA members are expected to represent European interests more directly. To fully understand the process of agencification, it is important to note that the financial crisis constituted the crucial window of opportunity for European actors to establish the ESMA. This point was explicitly acknowledged by all interviewees, but it was most forcefully put forward by a former CESR executive, who said that the crisis has made the transformation of CESR into ESMA acceptable (Interview 1). This is because members realized that 'supervisory arbitration' was detrimental to investors and market confidence. However, when actual decisions about the new agency were forthcoming, Member States came back, as they were not willing to delegate excessive powers to European institutions in a sector considered the lifeblood of advanced industrialized democracies (Mügge 2006). Therefore, the goals of the initial proposal – a more powerful pan-European regulator of financial markets – were reduced and, in practice, ESMA is still working as a networked organization federating national regulatory authorities. Actors involved in the process interpreted this final evolutionary step as the return of intergovernmentalism. In that regard, a former CESR member confirmed that the ESMA was granted much less authority and independence than the authors of the de Larosière report expected (Interview 3).

To sum up, the first step toward this network was taken following a process of double delegation – from national regulatory authorities and from European institutions, respectively. CESR members then began interacting with the goal of protecting national interests. In this context, individual network members represented their national regulatory authorities, which mainly consisted of independent regulatory agencies supporting domestic interest groups. In the second step, the network developed new functions endogenously, acquired progressive autonomy, and started developing its own goals. At this point network members were (also) representing the viewpoints of an increasingly integrated transnational community of financial regulators. In the third step, the financial crisis provided a window of opportunity for European institutions to develop an ambitious project for the reform of the architecture of financial market supervision, which Europeanized the hybrid level of governance that emerged from actors' interactions within CESR. Eventually, however, in a last step, Member States were able to reduce the scope of the reform in order to maintain their domestic influence on European financial regulation. Therefore, existing evidence supports a dynamic view of representation patterns at the network level. When we come back to our hypotheses, we observe that CESR started to work as an intergovernmental arena. Then, over time, it became more and more active and acquired increased autonomy from both the national level and from EU institutions, as expected by multilevel governance theory. Eventually, the financial crisis was a critical juncture that allowed European institutions to Europeanize financial supervision to a certain extent, but Member States were able to retain their domestic powers of supervision and partially reduce supranational ambitions.

The financial crisis

The opening and closing of the 'window of opportunity' provided by the financial crisis deserves special attention to aid understanding of the nature of this form of institutional change. The financial crisis, which originated from the so-called US subprime mortgage crisis, put the spotlight on the failure of devices designed to supervise the financial system and on the 'crisis of knowledge and ideas' it produced, casting doubts on the capacity of the regulatory framework to prevent systemic crises (Hutter *et al.* 2008). The management of the crisis involved a series of massive public intervention measures to prevent the system's collapse. Governments promoted a colossal public rescue of the big financial players in many countries by offering huge amounts of cash and even by partial nationalization of companies of 'national interest' – reinvigorating a 'dirty word, designating a bad old past' (Miller 2008: 7) – through a spectacular violation of international accounting standards. In the immediate aftermath of the crisis, the solution to the problem was politically and societally framed in terms of 'more regulation' (Hofmann 2008; Lodge 2008). In this context, the de Larosière report suggested the creation of a European Systemic Risk Board (ESRB) to collate and analyse issues and information relating to systemic risk and financial stability, and a new 'European System of Financial Supervisors' to provide central coordination for regulators (de Larosière *et al.* 2009). Correspondingly, the establishment of a new independent authority with regulatory powers was proposed at a European level, an authority that would have consisted of 'a standard setter and overseer in the area of supervision, [that] would be involved, alongside central banks, in macro-prudential analysis' (Turner 2009).

Afterward, however, ESMA was established with reduced institutional breadth and enforcement powers, at least in terms of the initial proposals (Moloney 2011; Sasso and Kost De Sevres 2012). This, as our interviews have illustrated, was due to the pressure exerted by Member States in the European Council of Ministers. At the end of the day, policy makers treated the crisis as an epiphenomenon, and the window of opportunity for reform was quite volatile. European actors successfully used it to push the integration of financial market regulation forward. But the momentum for reform weakened over time, and the architecture of European financial supervision experienced a 'gradual transformation', rather than a radical shift, following this critical juncture (Streeck and Thelen 2005).

Conclusion

This chapter aimed at untangling patterns of representation in a particularly intricate case, that of ERNs. These groups, federating IRAs, endorse crucial regulatory functions, and yet they are located very far from democratic representative institutions. They were created following a process of 'double delegation' from national regulatory authorities and from European institutions. On the one hand, domestic IRAs decided to establish transnational groups to exchange information and coordinate their operations at the international level. On the other hand, the European Commission promoted networks as a second best solution to favour the harmonization of European regulation in the single market given Member States' unwillingness to dismiss their national regulatory authorities. There is a paradox of representation in this context, as regulators should represent their countries at transnational level, but they are formally independent from their government. At the same time, network members are expected to also represent European actors because they work 'at arm's length' from the European Commission. The case of the CESR is selected for the empirical analysis of the patterns of representation in European regulatory networks as an example of a particularly relevant network that exemplifies the problem raised by the process of double delegation.

Evidence, based on a small number of very focused interviews, shows that individual network members claim to represent mainly their national regulatory authority. Representation in networks is understood in a way that is largely consistent with the encompassing conceptualization of Pitkin (1972); that is, to be authorized to act, to promote the interests of the represented, and to be held accountable for their actions. This finding confirms that the concept of democratic representation may be broadened to include new non-electoral forms of representation (Urbinati and Warren 2008). Our analysis also points to an evolutionary view of representation. Members started their participation in networks by supporting domestic interests. Then, over time, they have brought into being a new, distinctive, and quite autonomous level of governance wherein members represented, above all, the viewpoints of a self-referential transnational community of financial regulators. The financial crisis provided a 'window of opportunity' for European institutions that feared this uncontrolled development to institutionalize a multilevel system, a process that remains unfinished. In the last step, following pressures from Member States, national regulatory authorities were able to retain their prerogatives, thus reducing the ambitions of the newly created European agency. This last development implied the normalization of the CESR, now ESMA, as a less autonomous and more accountable governance arena. Whether this is good or bad for the democratic quality of representation remains an open question.

References

Bache, I., Flinders, M.V. and Flinders, M. (2005) *Multi-level Governance*, USA: Oxford University Press.

Baker, A., Hudson, D. and Woodward, R. (2005) *Governing Financial Globalization: International Political Economy and Multi-Level Governance*, Oxon: Routledge.

Boyt, T., Lusch, R. and Mejza, M. (2005) 'Theoretical models of the antecedents and consequences of organizational, workgroup, and professional esprit de corps', *European Management Journal*, 23 (6): 682–701.

Chaher, Santiago J. (2005) *Is Lamfalussy Falling from the Third Floor (Level)?*, London School of Economics and Political Science Working Paper Series.

Christiansen, T. and Piattoni, S. (2003) *Informal Governance in the European Union*, Cheltenham: Edward Elgar Publishing.

Coen, David and Thatcher, Mark (2005) 'The new governance of markets and non-majoritarian regulators, governance', *An International Journal of Policy, Administration, and Institutions*, 18 (3): 329–46.

Coen, D. and Thatcher, M. (2008a) 'Network governance and multi-level delegation: European networks of regulatory agencies', *Journal of Public Policy*, 28 (1): 49–71.

Coen, D. and Thatcher, M. (2008b) 'Reshaping European regulatory space', *West European Politics*, 31, 1.

De Larosière, J., Balcerowicz, L., Issing, L., Rainer M., Mc Carthy, C., Lars Nyberg, Pérez, J. and Ruding, O. (2009) *The High-Level Group of Financial Supervision in the EU*. Report. Brussels: The de Larosière Group.

De Visscher, C., Maiscocq, O. and Varone, F. (2007) 'The Lamfalussy reform in the EU securities markets: fiduciary relationships, policy effectiveness and balance of power', *Journal of Public Policy*, 28 (1): 19–47.

Djelic, M.L. and Quack, S. (2010) *Transnational Communities: Shaping Global Economic Governance*, Cambridge: Cambridge University Press.

Djelic, M.L. and Sahlin-Andersson, K. (2006) *Transnational Governance: Institutional Dynamics of Regulation*, Cambridge: Cambridge University Press.

Dolowitz, D.P. and Marsh, D. (2000) 'Learning from abroad: the role of policy transfer in contemporary policy-making', *An International Journal of Policy and Administration*, 13 (1): 5–23.

Donnelly, S. (2010) *The Regimes of European Integration: Constructing Governance of the Single Market*, New York: Oxford University Press.

Eberlein, B. (2003) 'Formal and informal governance in single market regulation', in T. Christiansen and S. Piattoni (eds), *Informal Governance in the European Union*, Cheltenham: Edward Elgar.

Eberlein, B. and Grande, E. (2005) 'Beyond delegation: transnational regulatory regimes and the EU regulatory state', *Journal of European Public Policy*, 12 (1): 89–112.

Eberlein, B. and Newman, A.L. (2008) 'Escaping the international governance dilemma? Incorporated transgovernmental networks in the European Union', *Governance*, 21 (1): 25–52.

Fischer-Appelt, D. (2011) 'The European Securities and Markets Authority: the beginnings of a powerful European securities authority?', *Law and Financial Markets Review*, 5 (1): 21–32.

Føllesdal, A. and Hix, S. (2006) 'Why there is a democratic deficit in the EU: a response to Majone and Moravcsik', *Journal of Common Market Studies*, 44 (3): 533–62.

Gilardi, F. (2008) *Delegation in the Regulatory State: Independent Regulatory Agencies in Western Europe*, Northampton, MA: Edward Elgar.

Gilardi, F. (2010) 'Who learns from what in policy diffusion processes?', *American Journal of Political Science*, 54 (3): 650–66.

Gilardi, F. (2012) 'Transnational diffusion: norms, ideas, and policies', in Walter Carlsnaes, Thomas Risse and Beth Simmons, *Handbook of International Relations*, Thousand Oaks, CA: 453–77.

Haas, P.M. (1992) 'Introduction: epistemic communities and international policy coordination', *International Organization*, 46 (1): 1–35.

Héritier, A. (2003) 'New modes of governance in Europe: increasing political capacity and policy effectiveness', *The State of the European Union*, 6: 105–26.

Héritier, A. and Eckert, S. (2008) 'New modes of governance in the shadow of hierarchy: self-regulation by industry in Europe', *Journal of Public Policy*, 28 (1): 113–38.

Hofmann, J. (2008) 'Cyclic dreams of a strong state', *Risk & Regulation, Financial Crisis Special*, 9.

Hooghe, L. and Marks, G. (2001) *Multi-Level Governance and European Integration*, Lanham, MD: Rowman & Littlefield Publishers.

Hooghe, L. and Marks, G. (2003) 'Unraveling the central state, but how? Types of multi-level governance', *American Political Science Review*, 97, 2: 233–43.

Hutter, B., Lodge, M., Miller, P. and Power, M. (2008) 'CARR on crisis, risk and regulation', *Financial Crisis Special*, 3.

Jordana, J., Levi-Faur, D. and i Marín, X.F. (2011) 'The global diffusion of regulatory agencies', *Comparative Political Studies*, 44 (10): 1343–69.

Kohler-Koch, B. (2002) 'European networks and ideas: changing national policies?', *European Integration online Papers* (EIoP).

Kull, D. (2011) 'Legal implications of the establishment of the European Securities and Markets Authority', Available at SSRN 1948071.

Levi-Faur, D. (2005) 'The global diffusion of regulatory capitalism', Annals, AAPSS, 598: 12–32.

Levi-Faur, D. (2011) 'Regulatory networks and regulatory agencification: towards a Single European Regulatory Space', *Journal of European Public Policy*, 18 (6): 810–29.

Lodge, M. (2008) 'Towards a new age of regulation?', *Risk & Regulation: Financial Crisis Special*, 11–2.

Lütz, S. (2004) 'Convergence within national diversity: the regulatory state in finance', *Journal of Public Policy*, 24 (2): 169–97.

Maggetti, M. (2010) 'Legitimacy and accountability of independent regulatory agencies, a critical review', *Living Reviews in Democracy*, 2: 1–9.

Maggetti, M. and Gilardi, F. (2011) 'The policy-making structure of European regulatory networks and the domestic adoption of standards', *Journal of European Public Policy*, 18 (6): 830–47.

Majone, G. (1994) 'The rise of the regulatory state in Europe', *West European Politics*, 17 (3): 77–101.

Majone, G. (1996a) 'Temporal consistency and policy credibility: why democracies need non-majoritarian institutions', EUI Working Paper SPS, 96 57.

Majone, G. (1996b) *Regulating Europe*, London; New York: Routledge.

Manin, B. (1996) *Principes du gouvernement représentatif*, Paris: Flammarion.

Mansbridge, J. (2011) 'Clarifying the concept of representation', *American JCMS: Political Science Review*, 105: 621–30.

Miller, P. (2008) 'When markets and models fail: rethinking risk, regulation and the state', *Risk and Regulation, Financial Crisis Special*, 6–7.

Moloney, N. (2011) I. 'Reform or revolution? The financial crisis, EU financial markets law, and the European Securities and Markets Authority', *International and Comparative Law Quarterly*, 60 (2): 521–33.

Moran, M. (2002) 'Review article: understanding the regulatory state', *British Journal of Political Science*, 32: 391–413.

Moravcsik, A. (1995) 'Liberal intergovernmentalism and integration: a rejoinder', *Journal of Common Market Studies*, 33 (4): 611–28.

Mügge, D. (2006) 'Reordering the marketplace: competition politics in European finance', *Journal of Common Market Studies*, 44 (5): 991–1022.

Mulgan, R. (2003) *Holding Power to Account: Accountability in Modern Democracies*, Basingstoke: Palgrave Macmillan.

Papadopoulos, Y. (2003) 'Cooperative forms of governance: problems of democratic accountability in complex environments', *European Journal of Political Research*, 43: 473–501.

Papadopoulos, Y. (2008) 'Assessing the claims of "post-parliamentary" governance', in B. Jobert and B. Kohler-Koch (eds) *Changing Images of Civil Society: From Protest to Governance*, London: Routledge.

Piattoni, S. (2010) *The Theory of Multi-level Governance: Conceptual, Empirical, and Normative Challenges*, USA: Oxford University Press.

Pitkin, H.F. (1972) *The Concept of Representation*, Berkeley, CA: University of California Press.

Provan, K.G. and Kenis, P. (2008) 'Modes of network governance: structure, management, and effectiveness', *Journal of Public Administration Research and Theory*, 18 (2): 229–52.

Quaglia, L. (2007) 'The politics of financial services regulation and supervision reform in the European Union', *European Journal of Political Research*, 46 (2): 269–90.

Radaelli, C.M. (2000) 'Policy transfer in the European Union: institutional isomorphism as a source of legitimacy', *An International Journal of Policy and Administration*, 13 (1): 25–43.

Radaelli, C.M. (2003) 'The open method of co-ordination: a new governance architecture for the European Union', Report No. 1/2003, SIEPS.

Radaelli, C.M. (2004) 'Who learns what? Policy learning and the open method of coordination', paper prepared for the ESRC Seminar Series: Implementing the Lisbon Strategy: Policy Learning Inside and Outside the Open Method, European Research Institute. University of Birmingham, 26 November.

Rhodes, R.A.W. (1996) 'The new governance: governing without government', *Political Studies*, 44: 652–67.

Rittberger, B. and Schimmelfennig, F. (2006) Explaining the constitutionalization of the European Union, *Journal of European Public Policy*, 13 (8): 1148–67.

Sabel, C.F. and Zeitlin, J. (2010) *Experimentalist Governance in the European Union: towards a new architecture*, Oxford: Oxford University Press.

Sasso, L. and Kost De Sevres, N. (2012) 'The new European financial markets legal framework: a real improvement? An analysis of financial law and governance in European capital markets from a micro and macro economic perspective', *Capital Markets Law Journal*, 7 (1): 30–54.

Saward, M. (2005) 'Governance and the transformation of political representation', *Remaking Governance: Peoples, Politics and the Public Sphere*, Bristol, UK: Policy Press, pp. 179–96.

Schäfer, A. (2004) 'Beyond the community method: why the Open Method of Coordination was introduced to EU policy-making', *European Integration online Papers*, 8 (13).

Schillemans, T. (2008) 'Accountability in the shadow of hierarchy: The horizontal accountability of agencies', *Public Organization Review*, 8 (2): 175–94.

Schmitter, P. and Streeck, W. (1985) *Private Interest Government: Beyond Market and State*, London: Sage.

Slaughter, A.M. (2004a) 'Disaggregated sovereignty: Towards the public accountability of global government networks', *Government and Opposition*, 39 (2): 159–90.

Slaughter, A.M. (2004b) *A New World Order*, Princeton, NJ: Princeton University Press.

Stone Sweet, A. and Sandholtz, W. (1997) 'European integration and supranational governance', *Journal of European Public Policy*, 4 (3): 297–317.

Streeck, W. and Thelen, K.A. (2005) *Beyond Continuity: Institutional Change in Advanced Political Economies*, Oxford, New York: Oxford University Press.

Strom, K. Bergman, T. and Müller, W.C. (2003) *Delegation and Accountability in Parliamentary Democracies*, Oxford, New York: Oxford University Press.

Thatcher, M. and Stone Sweet, A. (2002) 'Theory and practice of delegation to non-majoritarian institutions', *West European Politics*, 25 (1): 1–22.

Turner, A. (2009) 'The Turner review. A regulatory response to the global financial crisis', London: The Financial Services Authority.

Urbinati, N. and Warren, M.E (2008) 'The concept of representation in contemporary democratic theory', *Annual Review Political Science*, 11: 387–412.

Verschuere, B., Verhoest, K., Meyers, F. and Peters, B.G. (2006) 'Accountability and accountability arrangements in public agencies', in T. Christensen and P. Laegreid (eds) *Autonomy And Regulation: Coping With Agencies in the Modern State*, Cheltenham: Edward Elgar.

Vibert, F. (2007) *The Rise of the Unelected: Democracy and the New Separation of Powers*, Cambridge: Cambridge University Press.

Yesilkagit, K. (2011) 'Institutional compliance: European networks of regulation and the bureaucratic autonomy of national regulatory authorities', *Journal of European Public Policy*, 18 (7): 962–79.

7 The European Commission and political representation

A new inter-institutional perspective

Nieves Pérez-Solórzano Borragán and Stijn Smismans

Introduction

Focusing on the European Commission when talking about political representation in the European Union (EU) seems a *contradictio in terminis*. The Commission is not directly elected and does not clearly represent a particular constituency. In this book the Commission is mentioned neither among the 'actors of representation', such as political parties, civil society organizations and citizens, nor among the 'levels of representation', which focus on forms of electoral territorial representation (EU Council, European Parliament (EP), Committee of the Regions). There are two ways to bring the European Commission into the political representation equation. The first one relates to the inter-institutional relationship between the Commission and those institutions that are the expression of electoral territorial representation. The second one requires the reconceptualization of 'political representation' to take account of the multiple meanings and dimensions of representation in the political process and in democratic design.

The first strategy is the more traditional option. Most scholarly debate on political representation in the EU has not attributed any 'representative value' to the Commission as such, but has focused on the Commission's relation, in terms of delegation, degrees of independence and accountability, with the 'representative institutions' that are the EU Council and the EP. The advantage of this approach is that it allows for normative suggestions regarding (inter-) institutional (re-)design. However, it only offers a very partial picture of the multiple dimensions of representation at work in the political structure of the Union. This focus on electoral or territorial representation is in no way unique to the EU's debate. Although 'representative democracy' is the predominant frame of reference for modern democracies, the complex and multi-dimensional nature of representative processes remains surprisingly understudied and under-theorized. Hanna Pitkin's *The Concept of Representation* (1972) provided an important and influential contribution to identifying multiple aspects of representation in the political process, but ultimately equated democratic representation with electoral representation and remained therefore mainly a conceptual clarification rather than a revolutionary rethinking of democratic design. Political theory's turn to deliberative democracy over the last two decades has not been favourable to developing our understanding of the many aspects of political representation further, as the focus has been on the quality of the deliberative process rather than on the question of who deliberates and what, whom and how they represent. However, as this edited collection also illustrates, there is a renewed attention in political theory for the question of representation; including an increasing willingness to unravel the multiple dimensions of political representation, other than through electoral mandate. The most important contribution in this new debate so far is Michael Saward's conceptualization of political representation as processes of 'representative claims-making' (Saward 2010). One of Saward's key arguments is that

> many more people and groups – in civil society as well as the state – make representative claims, on varied grounds and in varied styles. Conventionally elective claims are not as secure or accepted as many think; many non-elective claims are not as readily rejected as some think (and as many political theorists would like).
>
> (Saward 2010: 138)

Saward's analysis deepens our understanding of the multi-dimensional nature of processes of political representation, going far beyond claims based on electoral mandate. However, Saward's approach has to be dealt with cautiously as it also entails risks. If pushed too far, Saward's approach may lead to 'micro-analysis' by focusing on certain actors' representative claims rather than on inter-institutional design. Similarly, it may lead political theory into empiricism with scholars focusing on the empirical testing of representative claims made by political actors, with the normative grounding and assessment being based on the audience's acceptance (or rejection) of the representative claim. Social legitimacy, i.e. the empirically determined generalized degree of trust of the governed in a polity or system of political representation[1] is indeed the ultimate criterion without which no political system can survive, but it is a rather thin guidance and guarantee of democratic design. Democratic theory would lose much of its normative guiding function if it were reduced to measuring the (majoritarian) acceptance of structures of political representation. As Neil Walker argues (2001), one has to distinguish between the 'internal or social dimension of legitimacy', which refers to social acceptance, and the 'external or normative dimension', which is concerned with the justifiability of a polity in accordance with 'external standards', including the attractiveness and efficacy of its objectives and whether or not its institutions are just.[2]

Therefore, to analyse the position of the European Commission within the EU's system of political representation, this chapter combines the two strategies set out above, but without falling into their pitfalls. We take on board Saward's contribution by acknowledging other processes of political representation beyond those based solely on electoral mandate. However, our starting point is not the empirical assessment of representative claims but rather a more normative stand regarding the EU's inter-institutional design. To do so, we will address the Commission's role in the system of political representation in the EU by focusing on the principle of institutional balance.

We do not aim here to provide an exhaustive definition of political representation, which includes multiple processes involving representation by both individual actors and institutions and in different ways, such as 'standing for' and 'acting for'. Our focus here is on the representative nature of political institutions, in particular the European Commission, which should be understood both through the features of the institution itself and through its relations with other institutions.

In the first section we will address the 'traditional use' of the concept of institutional balance by both political scientists and legal scholars and then propose in the second section an alternative reading of institutional balance as a checks-and-balances system of interest representation that can be used as normative guidance. In the third section, we address the particular role of the Commission in this 'institutional balance of interest representation'. The Commission is identified as the promotional broker of 'the general interest of the Union' within this institutional balance. In the fourth section we address the procedural consequences of this function in relation to the Commission's regulation of interest representation. As institutional broker of the European interest, the Commission is not just a neutral bureaucracy but has a role in ensuring a balanced representation of interests in the policy-making process. At the same time, such interaction implies risks of regulatory capture. Thus, the Commission's approach to regulating interest representation has been hovering between the objectives of ensuring transparency and representation. In the final section we address the consequences of the economic crisis on the Commission's position within the institutional balance of interest representation and on its role as promotional broker of the European interest. We argue that the EU's answer to the economic crisis is based on a combination of intergovernmental crisis management and technocratic management relying on an independent European Commission, which undermines the institution's capacity to act as promotional broker of the European interest.

The traditional institutional balance

The concept of institutional balance is neither mentioned in the Treaty on European Union (TEU) nor in the Treaty on the Functioning of the European Union (TFEU). Not even the 'Provisions on democratic principles' introduced by the Lisbon Treaty mention the concept, let alone define it. That the concept has taken a place in the institutional thinking about the EU is foremost due to the Court of Justice, which introduced the concept as early as 1957. The case law of the Court of Justice (cf. *Meroni*[3] and *Chernobyl*[4]) has defined the institutional balance as 'a fundamental guarantee granted by the Treaty', which consists of a system for distributing powers among the different EU institutions, assigning a precise role to each institution in the institutional structure and in the accomplishment of the tasks entrusted to the Union. The Court ensures respect of the rule of law by monitoring the observance of the institutional balance, i.e. each of the institutions must exercise its powers with due regard for the powers of the other institutions.

However, the institutional balance is not just about the respect of the rule of law, it also relates to normative considerations about the democratic and representative nature of the European institutional design. It is not accidental that the principle of institutional balance has been formulated by the Court most extensively in a case (*Chernobyl*) concerning the prerogatives of the EP. In that case the Court even took a corrective action *contra legem* in order to ensure the EP's prerogatives within the institutional balance (Lenaerts and Verhoeven 2002: 37). Although the Court has never worked out in detail the democratic added value of the institutional balance, the combination of respect for the institutional balance and the democratic input via the EP has largely dominated legal debate on the European democratic deficit (Mancini and Keeling 1994; O'Neill 1995; Ress 1994); and it concurs with the dominance of the parliamentary model in the broader academic and political debate on the issue (Dehousse 1998: 601). Thus the 'traditional' interpretation of the institutional balance built on the case law of the Court is characterized by three elements:

- it is above all a legal principle, namely it is a Treaty-based guarantee: the balance of power among the institutions as enshrined in the Treaties;
- it concerns the main EU institutions – the EP, the Council, the Commission, the European Council, the Court of Justice and the Court of Auditors – and especially the balance of powers among the first three institutions as ensured by the Court of Justice;
- as a normative argument for legitimate EU governance the traditional interpretation of institutional balance links the rule of law with an assumed democratic input via territorial representation either expressed via the *Masters of the Treaty* and the (European) Council (as especially stressed in the inter-governmental interpretation) or via the EP (as stressed in the prevailing parliamentary view).

Political scientists use the concept of institutional balance in a rather different way from legal scholars. Legal scholars tend to conceive of the institutional balance as static and give a normative value to it. Institutional balance is set out in the Treaties and needs to be respected in order to ensure the rule of law, and underlying this, the democratic credentials of the EU, based on electoral representation. Political scientists, instead, use the concept of institutional balance mainly to analyse change in the power relations between the EU institutions, in particular the Commission, the EP and the Council. Treaty change in particular incites political scientists to revive the concept of institutional balance to analyse the changed power relations among the institutions,[5] and sometimes, by extension, among the Member States.[6] Although often acknowledging that one is dealing with processes of political representation, these analyses tend to focus on power, and are reluctant to engage in detailed normative considerations.[7] When normative considerations on the institutional design are made, the main frame of reference is the parliamentary model; focusing on the increased role of the EP while stressing the remaining shortcomings of the EU in democratic terms.

From this perspective, the political scientists and the legal scholars share a strong common ground in their approach to the institutional balance, namely neither of them work out a strong normative argument or assign a strong democratic value to the principle of institutional balance as such. At best it ensures the rule of law and respect of an institutional setting whose democratic representative nature is ensured by parliament (and national territorial representation).

Institutional balance as democratic guidance and balance of interest representation

Contrary to the 'traditional' analysis of institutional balance, some scholars, mainly in the legal field, have defined the concept in a more normative way, and assigned it a central place in the democratic design and system of political representation in the EU. Lenaerts and Verhoeven (2002) most explicitly distinguish between institutional balance as a *legal principle*, the respect of which is ensured by the Court of Justice, and as a *political principle*, which is a broader normative guide in the democratic design of the European institutional set-up. It thus refers to a norm beyond the Treaty that is sought in political and democratic theory. A proper understanding of institutional balance is said to 'contribute to more democracy since it focuses on issues of *interest representation* and fair procedure' (emphasis added):

> The institutional balance requires the makers of the European constitution to shape institutions and the interactions between them in such a manner that each interest and constituency present in the Union is duly represented and co-operates with others in the frame of an institutionalized debate geared towards the formulation of the common good. At the same time, the formulation of the common good should never lead to an unequal and unnecessary sacrifice of individual liberty.
>
> (Lenaerts and Verhoeven 2002: 47)

Similar definitions of institutional balance in terms of fair interest representation have been suggested by Craig (1999), de Búrca (1999), Curtin (1996), and Joerges and Neyer (1997). The common argument is that each institution represents a different interest or constituency, and that their interaction ensures deliberation geared to the attainment of the common good.

The historical and intellectual roots of such a concept of institutional balance lie according to Lenaerts and Verhoeven (2002) in the doctrine of *trias politica*. However, the idea of institutional balance as a system of interest representation is considerably different from the idea of *trias politica*. The first interpretation of *trias politica* is the strict separation of powers commonly attributed to Montesquieu. In this interpretation each institution ensures a particular function –

legislative, executive and judicial. In the EU such an organic understanding of the principle of separation of powers is not possible[8] (though a functional definition of the separation of powers can be provided (Lenaerts 1991)).

In a second step the focus is more on a balance of powers than on a strict separation of powers. As Lenaerts and Verhoeven (2002) suggest, even Montesquieu's *trias politica* can be read in that sense (also see Witteveen 1991: 34; Vos 1999: 86). It was, however, the thinking of the US Founding Fathers that best developed the idea of a system of checks and balances as a way of protecting the liberties of individuals against a concentration of powers in one single authority and as a tool to prevent factions acting adversely to the rights of other citizens or to the aggregate interests of the community (Craig 1990: 58). This system of checks and balances rather than a *trias politica* seems apt for the EU. It stresses the idea of distributing power by creating different institutions that control each other via necessary cooperation, rather than the idea that the legislative, executive and judiciary powers need by definition be divided among three institutions and that each institution should be identified with one function. Although the institutional balance in the Treaty seems to derive more from power interests – and more precisely from the Member States' desire to retain control – than from a liberal or pluralist political ideology (Dehousse 1994: 771), there is much to say for the European institutional balance as a democratic guarantee against the concentration of power. However, this general interpretation of a system of checks and balances gives few indications as to which institutions should be created and how they should relate to each other. As soon as these questions are formulated, the issue of interest representation comes to the fore, which brings us to the third step in the argument.

There is a *saut qualitatif* in the way authors like Lenaerts and Verhoeven, and Craig and de Búrca, address the issue of interest representation compared to the traditional readings of *trias politica* and *checks and balances*. Lenaerts, Verhoeven, Craig and de Búrca attribute to each of the EU institutions a particular interest, identifying each as representative of a particular constituency.[9] Instead of a negative formulation of checks and balances as a guarantee against concentration of power, a positive formulation of 'mixed government' can be made according to which any decision should have the support of institutions representing different interests.

For Montesquieu, however, the issue of interest representation was entirely addressed by the legislative body that had to represent the aristocracy in one chamber and the people in another chamber. For Madison, 'national representatives operating above the fray would be able to disentangle themselves from local pressures and deliberate on and bring about something like an objective public good' (Sunstein 1985–1986: 42).[10] The emphasis was placed on the need to establish a large republic so that factional interests would be so heterogeneous that they could not dominate the institutions (Craig 1990: 332–333; Pitkin 1972: 191–196). Checks and balances were a sort of safeguard in case national representatives did not have the virtue to disentangle themselves from factional interests, rather than a clearly balanced system of interest representation in which various institutions representing different constituencies interact and ensure deliberation on the common good.[11]

The reconstruction of the argumentation retracing institutional balance to the theories of *trias politica* and *checks and balances* suggests that one has to be cautious in using old theories to legitimize new ones. Neither *trias politica* nor *checks and balances* were primarily thought of in terms of interest representation. However, there remains normative value in the concept of institutional balance as a system in which balanced interaction between institutions representing different interests ensures deliberation on the common good.[12] Such an approach makes most sense when taking into account the multiple forms and dimensions of political representation, and not limiting the idea of political representation to electoral territorial representation.

Political representation and the Commission's position in the institutional balance

It is relatively straightforward to identify the representative role of the EP and the (European) Council within the institutional balance. The EP is said to represent the European citizens,[13] while the Council and the European Council represent the Member States (art. 10 TEU). In these cases representation does not only mean standing for such abstractions as 'the interests of the citizens', and 'the interests of the Member States', but it refers also to the direct or indirect electoral mandate of respectively the EP and the (European) Council. As the Lisbon Treaty clarified, these two forms of electoral representation are the basis for arguing that the EU is founded on representative democracy. Although the exact nature and complex character of the representative processes that take place through the EP and the (European) Council could further be developed, for instance in terms of representative claims-making,[14] we focus our attention here on the more difficult position of the Commission as representing an interest within the institutional balance.

According to Article 17 TEU 'the Commission shall promote the general interest of the Union'. On the Europa server the claim is made that 'the Commission represents and upholds the interests of the EU as a whole'.[15] Or as Commission President Barroso put it recently in his Nobel Peace Prize speech, 'the Commission protects the general European interest, defends the European common good and embodies the community of destiny' (Barroso 2012). On what basis can this representative claim be made, given that the Commission cannot rely on a direct electoral mandate?

Traditionally the Commission is said to represent 'the European interest' because of its composition, its role set out in the Treaties and the way it operates. Thus according to Article 17 (3) TEU:

> The members of the Commission shall be chosen on the ground of their general competence and European commitment[16] from persons whose independence is beyond doubt. In carrying out its responsibilities, the Commission

> shall be completely independent. The members of the Commission shall neither seek nor take instructions from any Government or other institution, body, office or entity. They shall refrain from any action incompatible with their duties or the performance of their tasks.

Although the idea of having at least one Commissioner for each Member State reflects also the need to be able to draw on the different national experiences and make the Commission acceptable to the Member States, the original inspiration for the High Authority and European Commission was indeed for it to act as an independent regulatory authority. Jean Monnet, the High Authority's first President, expressed the constitutional philosophy behind the institution as follows:

> The independence of the Authority vis-à-vis government and the sectional interests concerned is the precondition for the emergence of a common point of view which could be taken neither by governments nor by private interests. It is clear that to entrust the Authority to a Committee of governmental delegates or to a Council made up of representatives of governments, employers and workers, would amount to returning to our present [intergovernmental] methods, those very methods which do not enable us to settle our problems.[17]

This independent authority was given strong powers, although originally limited to a narrow set of policy areas. Core to the Commission's role as driver of the European interest are its exclusive right of legislative initiative, and its role as guardian of the Treaties. The principle of the collegiality of Commission decision-making is the operational expression of how this independent authority would deliver decisions in support of the common European interest.

However, while independence, legislative initiative and collegiality remain core features of the Commission, the institutional environment in which the Commission operates has changed drastically over time. As the Union has become involved in more policy areas, the idea of the Commission as an independent authority neutrally implementing a limited amount of competences delegated by the Member States is proving inadequate. European decision-making has become more political in nature increasing the role of the Council, and later EP and European Council. In the Treaty of Rome a unanimous vote was still required in the Council to change a Commission's proposal. Today the Commission operates much more as a broker, with both the Council and the EP profoundly amending Commission proposals. Moreover, while the Commission remains in the driving seat for drafting legislative proposals, only 10 per cent of these proposals still result from autonomous Commission initiatives.[18] More than ever, the Commission is a complex organization 'between an executive authority and a bureaucratic structure' (Cram 2002: 311), and caught between independent regulatory authority and parliamentary accountability. Its increased politicization has steered it away from an independent regulatory authority, but its appointment, role and functioning keep it clearly distant from traditional understandings of an executive accountable to parliament.

There are different ways then to conceive of the Commission as promoter of the general interest of the Union. The first one is to focus on its independence, which sees the Commission as an independent authority as described above. In this case, political representation takes place through the Member States, which delegate well-defined tasks to the independent regulatory authority. While the current Commission and European institutional set-up appear not to correspond to that model, there are still aspects of European governance that are clearly inspired by it, as we will illustrate below in relation to the economic crisis.

The second way of conceiving of the Commission as representing the interest of the Union as a whole focuses on the independence of the Commission as counterweight to the Union being dominated by the larger Member States. Some authors then see dangers in the Lisbon Treaty regime regarding the composition of the Commission expected to come into force on 31 October 2014, as the reduction of the number of Commissioners to two-thirds of the number of Member States is said to undermine the Commission's credibility in its role as a policy-formulator in the Union's general interest (Temple Lang 2004: 544; and Devuyst 2007–2008: 300).

The third way to envisage the role of the Commission as representing the general interest of the Union is to focus on its role as a broker between the Member States. All Commission initiatives are indeed strongly based on an initial assessment of the Member States' positions and redrafting in the light of this assessment. By extension, the Commission operates as a broker between the Council and the EP. The 'European interest' is then the outcome of that balancing act between Member States' interests and interests of the European citizens. The focus on the latter has been strengthened by the introduction of the European Citizens' Initiative in the Lisbon Treaty. As in the vision of an independent Commission, this interpretation of the Commission's role as a broker does not give any representative status to the Commission itself. The Commission operates more as a 'neutral facilitator', while representation is primarily the role of the Council and EP.

The fourth option is to recognize that there is far more to the Commission's brokering role than balancing the interests expressed by the Council and the EP and allowing the Commission to play a more proactive role as promotional broker of the general interest of the Union. For most of its activities, the Commission is indeed not just a 'neutral facilitator' or a 'secluded' independent authority, but it consults widely and interacts with a wide diversity of experts, interests groups and civil society actors (see also art. 11 TEU). The role of the Commission as promotional broker of the general interest of the Union is based on these combined factors: its composition, its role in ensuring the implementation and objectives of the Treaties, its institutional position as broker between the institutions, and its wider consultative processes. Although not based on electoral mandate, the Commission thus plays a unique representative role within the institutional balance, besides the Council and the EP.

Above we have defined the institutional balance as a system in which balanced interaction between institutions representing different interests ensures deliberation on the common good. This is only possible due to the proactive role of the Commission aiming at representing the general interest of the Union by playing an active brokering role between the other institutions and ensuring wider consultation in the light of the objectives and tasks set out in the Treaties.

Brokering and regulating interest representation

If the Commission is indeed not entirely 'secluded' as an independent authority, but aims to act as a promotional broker of 'the general interest of the Union' by balancing a plurality of interests, the way in which it regulates its interactions with interest groups becomes quintessential. Two concerns are central in that case. First, if the Commission deduces the general interest both from its brokering between the other institutions and from its wider consultative practices, the latter should be 'balanced' or representative. Second, such participation creates worries about bias, regulatory capture and unfair lobbying practices, hence the need for transparency.

For long the relation between interest groups and the Commission has been ad hoc and hardly regulated. While the claim of 'an independent Commission' was still dominating normative debate on the EU, the Commission's practice was one of wide ad hoc and largely informal interaction with interest groups and civil society organizations. It is only from the early 1990s that the Commission has started to develop a discourse on the added value of this participation and conceptualizes its particular institutional role in this regard. As a consequence it also starts to take some broader regulatory measures to shape this participation. The role of the Commission as promotional broker within the institutional balance, based on wider consultative practices, is thus both acknowledged and given shape by some regulatory initiatives.

Yet, the Commission's approach to regulating interest participation has changed over the two decades since 1992 and has hovered between the two concerns; namely transparency and representation. In 1992 the Commission adopted at the same moment a set of 'twin communications', one on transparency, another on the Commission's interaction with interest groups. The philosophy of these two intertwined communications was that by increasing the transparency of its own functioning the Commission would facilitate the participation of interest groups, which was argued to contribute to more efficient policy-making. In exchange the Commission suggested that interest groups might adopt a voluntary code of conduct to avoid unfair lobbying practices. This suggestion, however, was met with very little success.

A drastic change in discourse and approach emerges with the Commission's 2001 White Paper on European Governance (WPEG) and a conceptual shift from 'interest groups' to 'civil society organizations'. Compared to the 1990s paradigm that focused on transparency, the WPEG is much more concerned about structuring the representative nature of interest intermediation, even if the concept of 'interest representation' is not used. The WPEG's objectives are threefold: (1) ensuring the transparency of the system of interest representation as a question of accountability, which is mainly referred to in terms of 'openness' (as opposed to the predominent effectiveness driven transparency concept during the 1990s); (2) ensuring a more balanced overall system of interest representation; and (3) creating privileged partnership arrangements with European civil society organizations on the basis of representativeness criteria. The concern about the representative nature of interest intermediation, and in particular the introduction of representativity as a structuring criterion, constitutes an important change from the 1990s. This change is related to the normative assumptions underlying the concept of civil society. The idea that civil society organizations have particular democratic credentials opens the way to structuring interest intermediation through the creation of privileged access for those organizations that show particular 'representativeness' (see Pérez-Solórzano Borragán and Smismans 2012). However, in this way the WPEG has also introduced a dual approach, distinguishing between civil society organizations to which representativeness would apply as a way to justify extensive partnership arrangements, and 'other interested parties', which may be consulted without taking representativeness into account. Such 'extensive partnership arrangements' have never been developed and the Commission has failed to put into practice this dual approach.

With the European Transparency Initiative (ETI) set on track in 2006 the Commission appears to change again drastically its approach to interest group regulation. There is a conceptual return to interest groups rather than civil society and, as its title suggests, the ETI is primarily concerned with transparency rather than with representation. Yet, unlike the effectiveness driven concern of the 1990s where the focus was on increasing transparency of the Commission to stimulate interest group participation, the ETI builds on the WPEG's attention to transparency as an accountability measure and takes it a step further by extending it not only to the overall system of interest representation but to the interest groups themselves, in particular by requiring them to disclose their financial resources. However, while the focus appears to be on transparency as an accountability mechanism, the main instrument of the Transparency Initiative, namely the 'Transparency Register', provides the Commission (and other EU institutions) with an instrument that can be used to structure consultative practices taking into account elements of representativeness. Although the concept of representativeness is not used, the register provides more data on the organizational features of interest groups than the Institutions ever had available before (e.g. in the earlier Consultation, the European Commission and Civil Society (CONECCS) database). This information can be used at the discretion of the Commission when selecting interest groups for targeted consultations or advisory committees or when giving weight to opinions received in general online consultations. Moreover, while the register deals with all interest groups, and no longer only civil society organizations as CONECCS did, it provides five different entry categories: professional consultants and law firms; 'in-house' lobbyists and trade associations; NGOs; think-tanks; and 'other organizations' (including academic and religious organizations and associations of public authorities). This distinction is a practical consequence of the different financial means and organizational infrastructure of these different interest group categories, and is not meant to provide any of these categories with a particular 'bonus in participation' related to an assumed particular added democratic value of that category, like the WPEG intended to do in relation to European civil society organizations. Yet, while the WPEG aimed at a dual approach but failed to provide the instruments for it, the register seems to provide the instrument for such an approach in case it might reemerge as an objective in the future. Since the Transparency Register has appeared to be relatively successful in making a large number of interest groups register (although still voluntary), it provides for the first time an overview of all sorts of interest groups in different types of categories, which could facilitate the structuring of interest intermediation by way of requiring representativeness for certain categories as opposed to others.

The Commission and the institutional balance in times of economic crisis

The profound economic crisis that we are witnessing today is demanding for any system of political representation. For the EU in particular, the economic crisis amplifies all the main characteristics of the European democratic deficit (Smismans 2013). Although the origin of the crisis is not to be sought in the Eurozone construction, but in the lending and speculative practices of the banking sector and the lack of regulation of global financial transactions, the inherent limitations of the European Monetary Union (EMU) and the difficulties in reacting to the crisis have undermined the output legitimacy of the EU. Moreover, the way in which the EU has finally taken action to address the crisis tends to strengthen the technocratic nature of European governance, in particular by undermining democratic debate on ever more aspects of socio-economic governance and thus also compromising the EU's input legitimacy.

Seen from the perspective of institutional balance, both the 'immediate' crisis management and the longer-term new macroeconomic governance design put forward by the EU dilute at once the parliamentary debate and the role of the Commission as promotional broker of the general interest of the Union in the participatory and pluralist sense, as described above. The EU's crisis management has first been characterized by non-action and a delayed policy response centred on a nearly endless series of European Council and EU Council meetings. This intergovernmental decision-making has not only proved to be slow and ineffective, it has also sidelined parliamentary debate and bypassed the Commission in its role of promotional broker, based on wide consultation. The new macro-economic governance design that was finally put into place confirms this pattern.

The 'six pack' on economic governance adopted in Autumn 2011 and the Treaty on Stability, Coordination and Governance (TSCG) in the EMU adopted on 2 March 2012 constitute the most important transfer of sovereignty to the EU since the Maastricht Treaty, limiting the Member States' sovereignty to decide on their own budgets. Decisions on a state's budget are amongst the most important political decisions, which should be open to democratic input and control. However, while the new rules formally state that the national parliaments retain sovereignty to decide over the national budgets, this is in fact strongly limited by the margins of budgetary deficit accepted by the EU and the robust policy guidance on budgetary choices. Although national parliaments retain their formal role in adopting national budgets, the budgetary margins and policy options will be increasingly drafted at the European level, particularly by the European Commission, without intervention from either the EP or the national parliaments, and with only the Council acting as potential intergovernmental blocking authority. Moreover, the new macroeconomic governance design conceives of the Commission mainly as an independent authority, which (if needed in collaboration with the Court of Justice) has to enforce the austerity dictate set by the Member States in an intergovernmental way. There is hardly any space in this technocratic design[19] for the Commission to act as a broader broker carefully crafting the 'general interest of the Union' out of a widely consultative and participatory practice (within and particularly beyond the European institutions).

It may be argued that one should avoid generalizing these conclusions about the new macroeconomic design to the entirety of European governance. With all the media attention on the macroeconomic difficulties of the Eurozone one may tend to forget that much of daily governance business in Brussels goes on, with the 'Community Method' delivering its usual output of product and market regulation and the Commission in its role of promotional broker as set out above. However, the economic crisis reaches beyond the area of macroeconomic governance, and is destined to affect the Commission's role as promotional broker more generally, independently of its efforts to shape that role by way of regulating transparency and representativeness in its interactions.

The economic crisis puts a strong burden on any ideas of solidarity within the EU, and the route of austerity has knock-on effects on many policy areas. Several civil society organizations that were previously relatively 'embedded' within the consultative processes of the Commission now wonder whether participation in minor regulatory aspects can weigh up against the overall austerity policies the EU has embarked on. The European Anti-Poverty Network (EAPN), for instance, wonders whether participation in Commission consultations still makes sense if minor regulatory interventions are emptied of significance by the overall macroeconomic policy on which they are not consulted.[20] Also for the trade unions, 'cosy' involvement in some minor social regulatory issues in the context of the European social dialogue may no longer weigh up against the negative consequences of Europe's macroeconomic governance. Trade unions traditionally struggle with the tension between proposing European solidarity and solutions within a market-oriented EU on the one hand and the demands of rank and file on the other hand. Heiko Pleines, for instance, argues that the engagement of trade unions from the new Member States in EU-level action has the potential to weaken the representative link between constituency and representatives (Pleines 2012: 254). Similar trends can be identified in the old Member States. Parsons (2012), for instance, shows the difficulties for UK trade unions in defending European solidarity when pressured by nationalist discourses such as 'British jobs for British workers'. As the economic crisis intensifies it becomes increasingly difficult to defend common European action and solidarity within an EU that appears increasingly as the guardian of austerity. The European Union Trade Union Confederation still defends 'more Europe' rather than 'less Europe', but both the pressure from rank and file and the direction of Europe's macroeconomic policy have led to a European trade union that is increasingly vocal in its protest against the current EU, and relying more and more on organized protest rather than consultative interaction with EU institutions. The economic crisis has thus not only had an effect on the new macroeconomic design but also threatens the legitimacy of European governance more generally, as civil society actors consider existing patterns of participation as inadequate compared to the broader macroeconomic design on which they have hardly any impact.

For the Member States, the new macroeconomic design, with the Commission as independent guardian of austerity policies, may appear as an easy way to use the EU as scapegoat for austerity policies they do not want to take the blame for. However, this can ultimately undermine the legitimacy of the entire European construction. If 'more Europe' is the answer to the crisis, it can only function if the Commission can play its role as promotional broker of the general interest of the Union properly, by relying on wide consultation, rather than being consigned by Member States to the role of technocratic independent guardian of austerity.

Conclusion

In this chapter we have provided an inter-institutional perspective on the question of political representation in the EU. Political representation is a complex process that involves both individual actors and institutions. Focusing on the representative role of institutions, we have argued that it is too limiting to conceptualize political representation as confined to the institutions that are based on a territorial and representative electoral mandate, and assuming that other political institutions are 'neutral' and 'non-representative', standing in a simple relation of delegation and accountability towards the 'representative electoral institutions'. We have argued that the European Commission has a particular representative function within the European institutional balance, based on its composition, role in the institutional set-up and functioning. The Commission has a particular role as institutional broker geared to the realization of the common European interest. This role is based both on its brokering functioning among the institutions that have an electoral mandate (direct or indirect), namely the EP and the (European) Council, and on its wider consultative functioning.

Like all forms of political representation, the Commission's representative role also has its weaknesses. Thus it depends on the effectiveness with which it can play a brokering role between the electorally mandated institutions, and whether Treaty policy-making provisions indeed provide a balanced interaction between these institutions. Moreover, not being a 'neutral bureaucracy', the Commission's representative role as broker of wider societal interests depends on the way it organizes its consultative processes in terms of transparency and representativeness. From this perspective, the current economic crisis constitutes a double challenge for the democratic design of the EU. The first crisis management reaction has been intergovernmental, not allowing the Commission to play its broader brokering role, and the new economic governance design subsequently put on track has cornered the Commission into the role of enforcer of EU austerity as agreed by the Member States, rather than that of a broker between electorally mandated institutions and based on broader consultations with civil society.

Notes

1 For a similar definition of 'social legitimacy' see: J.H.H. Weiler (1991).

2 It would be wrong to accuse Saward of empiricism. Yet, it must be noted that the main considerations on legitimacy and democracy and some considerations on desirable democratic design in *The Representative Claim* come only in the sixth and final chapter of the book. There is surely something to say for his argument that 'it is not the role of political theorists to *make* first-order judgements about democratic legitimacy of representative claims using some set of substantive or even presumptively universal criteria' as the politics of representation varies across cultures, contexts and social standpoints (Saward 2010: 146, emphasis added). For Saward the political theorist may act as the well-informed interpreter of political claims, and is more normatively advised 'to look especially at the citizen standpoint with respect to least favoured citizens' (Saward 2010: 146). Yet, there remains a large gap between this position and making concrete suggestions for democratic design. Saward finally finds a normative yardstick in the idea that 'provisionally acceptable claims to democratic legitimacy across society are those for which there is evidence of sufficient acceptance of claims by appropriate constituencies under *reasonable conditions of judgment*' (Saward 2010: 144, emphasis added). Ironically enough, and without mentioning it, this brings Saward's renewed attention to the issue of representation very close to arguments put forward by theories of deliberative democracy. In particular, aiming at elaborating the conditions under which appropriate constituencies are able to form and make assessments of representative claims, Saward focuses on 'the open society', a concept that 'pivots around openness of criticism, claim and response', rather than on 'democracy', which 'pivots around comparatively specific institutional arrangements' (Saward 2010: 153). While Saward makes some normative claims on the nature of the open society, and pays some attention to the relationships between wider political representation, societal democratic representation and state-based 'representative democracy' (Saward 2010: 141), he steers away from normative claims on specific institutional design and particularly pays hardly any attention to inter-institutional design.

3 Case 9/56, *Meroni v. High Authority*, 1957 and 1958 ECR 133, at 152.

4 Case 70/88, *European Parliament v. Council*, 1990 ECR I-2041, at I-2072, paras. 21 and 22.

5 See for instance: Nentwich and Falkner (1997) following the Amsterdam Treaty, and the special issue 'The Institutional Balance and the Future of EU Governance: The Future of the Union and the Trap of the 'Nirvana Fallacy', *Governance*, 15 (3): 2002.

Following the Nice Treaty. Legal scholars obviously also dealt with the impact of Treaty change on the institutional balance (e.g. Yataganas 2001, post-Nice; and Devuyst 2007–2008, post-Lisbon), and were even more inclined than political scientists to stress that there is not 'one institutional balance', but that the balance strongly differs according to the legal basis of Union action. Yet, their view is more 'static' in looking at the institutional balance as a guarantee of the rule of law, rather than a power battle.

6 See for instance: Yataganas (2001).

7 The concept of institutional balance is itself part of the power relations between the institutions, as shown in the way the institutions use the concept both in the context of Treaty change, and in proceedings in the Court of Justice. See Prechal (1998: 274).

8 An organic interpretation of the European institutional balance has been given by Pescatore (1978) who identified an organic 'quadripartite institutional balance' within the European Communities rather than a *trias politica*. However, such an organic interpretation – even if 'quadripartite' – is ever more problematic, not at least since the Council's increasing involvement in implementation (via comitology) makes Pescatore's identification of the Commission as the one and only real executive body more difficult.

9 In the words of Lenaerts and Verhoeven: 'each institution represents a particular interest and particular views' (2002: 41). According to de Búrca 'Since each of the institutions ... represents a different constituency, the notion of institutional balance can be presented as a way of ensuring the adequate participation and representation of different constituencies within the European Community process' (1999: 60).

10 Pluralist theorists tend to read Madison as the forefather of the idea of interest group competition, by focusing on his theory of the 'problem of factions'. By pluralizing and ensuring interest group competition, the public good would be identified. See Dahl (1956), Chapter 1.

11 Gargarella (1998: 264–269) however, gives a reading of Madison in which *checks and balances* and interest representation concur. He argues that Madison did indeed recognize the variety of factions in society but was also convinced that a division between two groups was omnipresent in society, namely the division between those who hold property (the minority) and those who are without property (the majority). The main idea of the system of *checks and balances* was to give equal power to both 'the few' and 'the many', as two separate and opposite groups. The House of Representatives (based on direct elections) would express the interests of the majority, while the interests of the minority would be expressed and protected by the executive power, the Senate, and the judiciary (based on indirect elections).

12 This corresponds more with a republican than with a pluralist reading of Madison's idea of checks and balances. Republican theorists argue that the pluralist idea that the result of interest group competition *is* the public good is absent from Madisonian and Federalist thought. They stress that Madisonian thought includes the idea of a common good, and that checks and balances serve as a restraint against factional tyranny in the event that national representatives fail to fulfil their responsibilities (Sunstein 1985–1986: 44 and Craig 1990: 333).

13 Prior to the Lisbon Treaty, the Treaty stated more ambiguously that the EP represents 'the peoples of the States brought together in the Community'.

14 The weak European public sphere, and the particular nature of European political parties, for instance contribute to the complexity of the representative nature of the electoral process. See Sigalas and Pollak (2012).

15 See http://europa.eu/about-eu/institutions-bodies/european-commission/index_en.htm (accessed on 6 December 2012).

16 'European commitment' is an interesting extra requirement introduced by the Lisbon Treaty.

17 Letter from Jean Monnet to Edwin Plowden, 25 May 1950, cited in Stirk and Weigall (1999: 77), and Devuyst (2007–2008: 262).

18 Commission 'Improving and simplifying the regulatory environment', 2001.
19 See also Erne (2012).
20 Interview with EAPN Director, June 2012.

References

Barroso, J.M.D. (2012) *From War to Peace: a European tale*, online, available at http://europa.eu/rapid/press-release_SPEECH-12–930_en.htm (accessed on 6 December 2012).

Craig, P. (1990) *Public Law and Democracy in the United Kingdom and the United States of America*, Oxford: Clarendon Press.

Craig, P. (1999) 'The nature of the community: integration, democracy, and legitimacy', in P. Craig and G. De Búrca (eds) *The Evolution of EU Law*, Oxford: Oxford University Press, 1–53.

Cram, L. (2002) 'Introduction to Special Issue on the institutional balance and the future of EU Governance: the future of the Union and the trap of the "Nirvana fallacy" ', *Governance* 15 (3): 309–324.

Curtin, D. (1996) 'Civil society and the European Union: opening spaces for deliberative democracy', *Collected Courses of the Academy of European Law*, Florence, 185–280.

Dahl, R.A. (1956) *A Preface to Democratic Theory*, Chicago, University of Chicago Press.

De Búrca, G. (1999) 'The institutional development of the EU: a constitutional analysis', in P. Craig and G. De Búrca (eds) *The Evolution of EU Law*, Oxford: Oxford University Press, pp. 57–60 and 73–75.

Dehousse, R. (1994) 'Comparing national law and EC law: the problem of the level of analysis', *American Journal of Comparative Law*, 42: 761–781.

Dehousse, R. (1998) 'European institutional architecture after the Amsterdam Treaty: parliamentary system or regulatory structure?', *Common Market Law Review*, 35: 595–627.

Devuyst, Y. (2007–2008) 'The European Union's institutional balance after the Treaty of Lisbon: "community method" and "democratic deficit" reassessed', *Georgetown Journal of International Law*, 39: 247–325.

Erne, R. (2012) 'European industrial relations after the crisis: a postscript', in S. Smismans (ed.) *The European Union and Industrial Relations. New procedures, new context*, Manchester: Manchester University Press, pp. 225–235.

Gargarella, R. (1998) 'Full representation, deliberation, and impartiality', in J. Elster (ed.) *Deliberative Democracy*, Cambridge: Cambridge University Press, pp. 260–280.

Joerges, C. and Neyer, F.C. (1997) 'From intergovernmental bargaining to deliberative political processes: the constitutionalization of comitology', *European Law Journal*, 3: 273–299.

Lenaerts, K. (1991) 'Some reflections on the separation of powers in the European Community', *Common Market Law Review*, 28: 11–35.

Lenaerts, K. and Verhoeven, A. (2002), 'Institutional balance as a guarantee for democracy in EU governance', in Christian Joerges and Renaud Dehousse (eds), *Good Governance in Europe's Integrated Market*, Oxford: Oxford University Press, pp. 89–108.

Mancini, G.F. and Keeling, D.T. (1994) 'Democracy and the European Court of Justice', *Modern Law Review*, 57: 191–205.

Nentwich, M. and Falkner, G. (1997) 'The Treaty of Amsterdam: towards a new institutional balance', *European Integration online Papers* (EIoP) 1 (5).

O' Neill, M. (1995) 'Democracy and the EU: legal perspectives on the political debate', *Irish Journal of European Law*, 1: 48–67.

Parsons, N. (2012) 'The European Union and posted workers: industrial relations disputes framed by European policy nick parsons', in S. Smismans (ed.) *The European Union and Industrial Relations: New procedures, new context*, Manchester: Manchester University Press, pp. 175–189.

Pérez-Solórzano Borragán, N. and Smismans, S. (2012) 'Representativeness: a tool to structure interest intermediation in the European Union?', *Journal of Common Market Studies*, 50: 403–421.

Pescatore, P. (1978) 'L'exécutif communautaire: justification du quadripartisme institué par les traités de Paris et de Rome', *Cahiers de droit européen*, 4: 387–406.

Pitkin, H.F. (1972) *The Concept of Representation*, 2nd edn, Berkeley, CA: California University Press.

Pleines, H. (2012) 'Representing workers of presenting EU Prescriptions? Trade unions form post-Socialist Member States in EU multi-level governance', in S. Kröger and D. Friedrich (eds) *The Challenge of Democratic Representation in the European Union*, Basingstoke: Palgrave, pp. 241–258.

Prechal, S. (1998) 'The institutional balance: a fragile principle with uncertain contents', in T. Heukels, N. Blokker and M. Brus (eds) *The European Union after Amsterdam. A Legal Analysis*, The Hague: Kluwer Law International, pp. 273–294.

Ress, G. (1994) 'Democratic decision-making in the European Union and the role of the European Parliament', in D. Curtin and T. Heukels (eds) *Institutional Dynamics of European Integration*, Dordrecht: Martinus Nijhoff Publishers, pp. 153–176.

Saward, M. (2010) *The Representative Claim*, Oxford: Oxford University Press.

Sigalas, E. and Pollak, J. (2012) 'Political parties at the European level: Do they satisfy the condition of programmatic convergence?', in S. Kröger and D. Friedrich (eds) *The Challenge of Democratic Representation in the European Union*, Basingstoke: Palgrave, pp. 23–40.

Stirk, P.M.R. and Weigall, D. (eds) (1999) *The Origin and Development of European Integration: A Reader and Commentary*, London: Pinter.

Smismans, S. (2013) 'Democracy and legitimacy in the European Union', in M. Cini and N. Pérez-Solórzano Borragán (eds) *European Union Politics*, Oxford: Oxford University Press, pp. 341–353.

Sunstein, C. (1985–1986) 'Interest groups in American public law', *Stanford Law Review* (38): 29–87.

Temple Lang, J. (2004) 'The main issues after the convention on the Constitutional Treaty for Europe', *Fordham International Law Journal*, 27: 544–589.

Vos, E. (1999) *Institutional Frameworks of Community Health and Safety Regulation – Committees, Agencies and Private Bodies*, Oxford: Hart.

Walker, N. (2001) 'The White Paper in constitutional context', Jean Monnet Working Paper, No. 6/01, Symposium: Commission White Paper on Governance.

Weiler, J.H.H. (1991) 'Problems of legitimacy in post-1992 Europe', *Aussenwirtschaft*, 46: 179–205.

Witteveen, W.J. (1991) *Evenwicht van Machten*, Zwolle: W.E.J. Tjeenk Willink.

Yataganas, X.A. (2001) 'The Treaty of Nice: the sharing of power and the institutional balance in the European Union – a continental perspective', *European Law Journal*, 7 (3): 242–291.

8 The involvement of the constituencies of European umbrella organizations in EU affairs

Sandra Kröger

Introduction

There is a large literature running from de Tocqueville to Truman and Putnam that applauds civil society organizations (CSOs) for mediating between citizens and the state and its government. Broadly speaking, the argument holds that a dense and pluralistic web of civil associations balances out deficiencies in political representation and contributes to the creation of the social capital required to sustain a vibrant democracy. It is also hoped that non-electoral, more direct kinds of representation can help alleviate the crisis that traditional representative actors are facing more generally in Western democracies: decreasing trust as expressed in declining electoral turnout, decreasing party membership, increasing voting abstention, and the growing success of extremist parties, particularly of the right. The hope is based not only on non-electoral forms being more direct, but also on their potentially addressing issues that have traditionally been sidelined or neglected in party politics or by governmental majorities, such the environment or the interests of weak or disadvantaged citizens.

This reasoning has found fertile soil in some of the European integration and Europeanization literature that seeks to find support for the European Commission's hope that CSOs might somehow help overcome the democratic deficit of the European Union (EU). Indeed, it is in the context of supra- and transnational policy-making, which is increasingly decoupled from a clearly recognizable and distinct constituency, and in the quest for supranational polity-building of the EU, that CSOs have increasingly attracted both political and scholarly attention (Kohler-Koch and Edler-Wollstein 2008).[1] The hope is that CSOs and their interactions and input into policy-making could provide the mutual trust that is needed under circumstances of mutual (inter-)dependence as we find them in the EU and help legitimate the governance of the EU itself as it expands its competencies. The lack of a well-developed European public sphere, the weakness of European party federations and of the European Parliament (EP) leaves little room for citizens to participate in will formation, problem formulation or political contestation. The idea is that CSOs could function as transmission belts that bring the interests and values of citizens to the EU (Nanz and Steffek 2004). From this perspective, the role attributed to civil society is to 'mediate between the national and the supranational, thereby connecting national society to transnational governance' (Rumford 2003: 32). Another perspective has focused on the EU as an emergent polity. Here, scholars focus on the link between a social constituency and active citizenship and the creation of a *demos*-equivalent outside the framework of the nation state (Eriksen and Fossum 2000). As an emergent polity, a political community-in-the-making, the EU requires trust: trust in the reciprocity of rule-conforming behaviour by others and mutual solidarity. And civil society and its organizations are hoped to be able to foster and maintain the mutual trust required for the polity-building project.

This contribution will address whether these are appropriate perspectives on the role of CSOs in the EU by asking whether European umbrella organizations are representative of the constituencies they claim to represent. Why is this an important question to ask? The answer is fourfold.

First, the European Commission finds it expedient to consult CSOs in general and their European umbrellas in particular. It also funds a large number of umbrella organizations in Brussels in a structural way, with some of them receiving up to 90 per cent of their total funding from the Commission. In fact, this mounts up to approximately 1 billion Euros per year (Maloney 2007: 77). It does so in order to strengthen non-state actors, which it can in turn consult in order to increase both the effectiveness – by pooling experiences, and ideas, by collectively searching for the best solution, and by securing loyalty to decisions through the involvement of the actors in the process, all of which would help to overcome problems of implementation – and the legitimacy of its own proposals, ultimately aimed at deepening integration. If the Commission can argue that its position is based upon broad consultation with CSOs, its bargaining power *vis-à-vis* the Council will be increased (Bauer 2002; Greenwood 2010; Kohler-Koch 2010).

Second, European umbrellas often pride themselves on the (high) numbers of citizens they represent, which confers legitimacy on their activities and positions. Indeed, one of my interviewees, who works for a European umbrella, declared:

> We have 30 member groups around Europe with a total actor membership or supporter base of something around 600 000 members. So obviously we have quite a responsibility to those individual members and their local groups to be their voice, or transmit their voice, to the European institutions.[2]

Similarly, some authors claim that CSOs could provide the EU with democratic legitimacy by bridging the gap between Brussels and citizens. Both claims merit empirical confirmation.

Third, this chapter contributes to closing a gap in the literature by addressing CSOs both at the EU level and their degree of Europeanization in the domestic sphere. We now have a fairly good understanding of how CSOs are included in policy-making at the EU level (Kröger 2008). From another body of literature, we have some insights into how far CSOs have actually Europeanized themselves and why they may or may not choose to do so. Whilst both literature streams provide novel and interesting insights into how CSOs participate in and adapt to EU policy-making, they have not concerned themselves with issues of political representation and democratic legitimacy and whether European umbrellas are actually representative of their claimed constituencies. Scholars have addressed mainly how far CSOs could potentially contribute to an abstract European *demos*, but not investigated the micro-politics of *representation* via CSOs. This is where the present contribution comes in. It is interested in how representative European umbrella organizations are of their members and therefore of the citizenry they claim to represent. In doing so, it combines insights from representation theory and from the Europeanization literature.

Fourth and finally, there is a theoretical case to be made for the necessary input by the constituency, rather than just by the European umbrella, if that input is to be legitimate. The ontological position adopted here is that in order for there to be democracy, there needs to be a *demos* (Weiler 1995), and that the latter precedes its representation. It is therefore essential to address the national constituencies of supranational representation in order to assess whether these are actually being represented. Normatively, societal involvement is considered essential for the generation of democratic legitimacy. I shall expand this theoretical discussion in the next section.

The argument unfolds as follows. The next section will review recent developments in representation theory and situate the research question within it: namely, whether European umbrella organizations are representative of the constituencies they claim to represent. More specifically, it will be argued that non-electoral representation by European umbrellas crucially requires involvement by its constituencies in order to make a legitimate contribution to EU policy-making. The ensuing section will present the case choice and the data used for this contribution. CSOs active in agricultural, environmental and anti-poverty policy were chosen for this study since they represent different kinds of constituencies. The empirical section will provide fresh data on the degree to which nationally grounded CSOs are linked to their respective European umbrella structures. I shall discuss whether the related practices reflect – or not – the theoretical models according to which the organizations were chosen in the first place and how the findings might be explained. The concluding section sums up, and discusses the prospects of CSOs contributing to (1) creating a European *demos* and (2) legitimate representation in EU policy-making.

Non-electoral representation and the need for societal involvement

To link CSOs to *representation* rather than to participation or deliberation may seem counter-intuitive given the traditional prevalence of parliaments and political parties when it comes to political representation. Still, non-electoral representation has of late gained considerable attention. Two main threads of the debate have been that (1) non-electoral representation and (2) process matter. Let me address both in turn.

There are trends in western liberal democracies that seem to call for additional modes of representation, rather than sticking exclusively to electoral representation. Among these trends, the heterogeneity of societies increasingly challenges parties and parliamentarism, as does supranational governance. Across Europe, albeit to differing degrees, there has been a steady, decades-long decline in electoral turnout, falling party membership and identification, growing volatility in voter preferences and, hence electoral outcomes, greater difficulty in obtaining and sustaining majority support for governments, a decrease in trust in politicians, parties and political institutions more generally, a diminution in the centrality of parliament, and increased devolution of authority to non-state actors and administrative bodies. At the same time, both organized and unorganized civil society have attracted considerable support and engaged in manifold contentious activities.

Some authors in fact argue that party politics is in some structural sense exclusive and that therefore additional forms of representation are required (Mansbridge 1999). Functional representation can contribute to bringing weak interests into the political process, thereby helping to address issues of equity and exclusion (Truman 1951; Young 2000). Iris Marion Young has shown that representative institutions include as well as exclude. Indeed, providing representation for some citizens and/or groups comes at the expense of others' exclusion. From such a perspective, representation is as much about *presence* as it is about *absence* (Young 2000; Kymlicka 1995). Others have placed the emphasis on the representation of discourses through non-electoral representation, suggesting that some discourses and ideas are represented less effectively by traditional representative actors than others, particularly on a supranational or global level (Dryzek and Niemeyer 2008; O'Neill 2001).

The EU, and the Commission in particular, as noted above, have drawn increasingly upon CSOs in the hope of generating effective and legitimate policy-making, as a way of dealing with the absence of the standard model of representation at the EU level (see the contributions by Kröger and Pollak in this volume). With the European White Paper on Governance (COM 2001), the EU has officially adopted a pro-active stance towards civil society organizations (CSOs), perceiving functional representation as a welcome additional source of legitimacy generation (Kohler-Koch and Finke 2007; Saurugger 2010).

As regards process, traditionally the representative relationship has been seen to consist of authorization and accountability. The typical institutional translation of representation has been for the constituents periodically to elect representatives who are, in some way, accountable to the constituency. Political representation so conceived was understood to establish the legitimacy of democratic institutions. More recently, scholars have argued that representation is not just electoral and about outputs, but also about input and process or throughput (Disch 2011; Saward 2010; Schmidt 2013; Urbinati and Warren 2008, see the contribution by Pollak in this volume).

Amongst others, Michael Saward also has emphasized process. He understands representation as claims-making, a constantly changing social dialogue in which different actors make claims to audiences which discuss, reject, or amend them 'in, between, and outside electoral cycles' (Saward 2010: 36). His work is grounded in three assumptions. First, representation is not a relationship expressed at precise moments, like authorization and accountability, but must be thought of as a continuing process that evolves over time. Second, at the core of representation is the practice of claims-making to be a representative. Third, constituents and representatives need not be members of electoral districts or elected parliamentarians, respectively. Saward insists on the dynamic nature of the relationship and on the performative (rather than the institutional) side of representation, in which both represented and representative play active roles. Such a conception of representation, according to Saward, is well suited to capture power and interests in political representation.

A dynamic political process also figures prominently in the work of Nadia Urbinati (2006). She argues that the significance of political representation lies in the perpetuation of the public debate about competing political programmes and in the permanent making present of the represented in choices about public policies. To her, representation is a circular and mutual process between representative institutions and society, which cannot be reduced to the formal act of legal authorization. Similarly, Jane Mansbridge has argued that democratic representation should not be conceived as monolithic but as a multiform concept that includes a variety of forms: promissory, anticipatory, gyroscopic and surrogative representation (Mansbridge 2003), focusing on the nature of the relationship between the representative and the represented beyond official moments of electoral representation, and pointing that it is more than a simple, territorially based principal–agent relationship. In short, with the constructivist turn in representation theory, what happens in between the formal moments of authorization and control in terms of communication, public debate and (inter)action between the represented and the representative is moving centre stage (see: Mansbridge 2004). The advantage of this shift is that it opens the conceptual room for non-identity, conflict, interpretation of and judgement about how well the representative has actually performed his or her task (Urbinati 2006).

However, there are also drawbacks to the constructivist shift. Issues such as the will of the people, the common good, political equality, authorization and control, democratic institutions and inter-institutional design receive less attention. In short, the constructivist perspective is not particularly interested in *democratic* representation – even though scholars typically insist that there needs to be a functioning public sphere in order for representation to take place legitimately. More specifically, the traditional ontology of democratic representation considers that if there is no *demos*, then there can be no democracy – or, for that matter, no constituency, no representation of that constituency (Pitkin 1967). Some of the constructivist approaches to representation dispute this claim and argue that there is no constituency prior to the act of representation. Instead, the represented is constituted and defined '*within* the process of political representation itself, and not somehow apart from or prior to it' (Saward 2005: 181; see also: Disch 2011). In my view, such a perspective focuses too strongly on performative aspects of representation, and risks reversing the representative relationship to the point where the represented only exists by virtue of the representative (Severs 2010), where the representatives constitute the represented by offering claims of representation without which the represented do not exist.

Contrary to such a perspective, I conceive of democratic representation as a principal–agent relationship and join Andrew Rehfeld in holding that there needs to be a constituency in order for it to be represented: 'no object of representation, no representation at all' (Rehfeld 2011: 637). This disagreement notwithstanding, both perspectives perceive of representation as a dynamic, two-way relationship. No matter which stance one has in regard to the ontology of representation, it is a *conflictual relationship* between the represented and the representative, in which both sides enjoy some degree of agency.

How can we transfer these insights to the functioning of CSOs in general and European umbrellas and their representativeness and legitimacy in particular? The question is not only how do we conceptualize process within CSOs, but also what makes that (process of) representation legitimate? The preceding discussion suggests that in order for their contribution to EU policy-making be fully legitimate, certain criteria have to be met. This is particularly so in a context in which such an input is used to legitimize European action and legislative proposals. In a nutshell, I will argue that such legitimacy requires the active involvement of the constituencies of the European umbrellas in the development of policy positions.

Operating on different terms than the standard model of representation does not free CSOs from the requirement of some sort of authorization and acceptance by their respective constituencies if their contribution to policy-making is to be legitimate. Along these lines, it has been argued that 'if something ... is legitimate, that means it is accepted as proper by those to whom it is supposed to apply' (Dryzek 2010: 21; similarly Saward 2010: 145), mirroring Max Weber's notion of social legitimacy. Indeed, output legitimacy is insufficient for legitimacy if the outputs have not been considered in terms of how they 'resonate with the constituencies' substantive values ... and interests' (Schmidt 2013: 11). Only when the constituent parts of the organization have 'the opportunity to reflect for themselves, speak of their factual immediacies and defend their judgments, can they bring to light the specifics that need to be perceived and recognised' (Maia 2012: 435). In *conflictual* representative relationships, what is thus necessary is an *ongoing* interaction between the claims representatives are making and the subjective experiences of the represented, and the mutual adjustment of both. Input legitimacy alone is insufficient, since it does not ensure that the interests of the constituencies are not being deterred or corrupted on the way to output legitimacy. This holds particularly true in the multi-level system of the EU, in which 'the legitimizing criteria of input and output are largely split between the EU and national levels of governance' (Schmidt 2013: 9), with input being generated in the domestic sphere, and output at the EU level.

The above implies that there must be some communication about European policy processes and some involvement of the constituencies in the development of policy positions on those processes, so that the constituencies have the opportunity to consent to or reject specific propositions and positions. If policy positions of European umbrellas are not to be merely formal, the constituency-to-be-represented must (1) be aware of those positions and (2) accept them. Only such an involvement of the respective constituencies will produce the internal legitimacy that is necessary for the claims that European umbrellas bring into EU policy-making to be representative and legitimate. Without such involvement, claims-makers may simply be speaking for themselves or, worse, refusing to take into account the views of those they are supposedly speaking for, either of which would be problematic as regards the legitimacy of the representation.

This holds true both for CSOs that follow a delegate model of representation, i.e. authorize their representatives via elections as sectoral organizations often do, and for organizations that follow more a discursive, interactive way of authorization, as can be assumed for example of global cause groups that represent discourses rather than a people (Dryzek and Niemeyer 2008). More concretely: first, it implies that there are traces of involvement of the constituencies of European umbrellas in the development of policy positions. The minimum condition for this to be the case is that the constituencies actually entertain some links to the European umbrellas, be it directly, or be it by means of a national umbrella, which in a second step would be in touch with the European umbrella. Similarly, at the very minimum the 'public' sphere, which renders representation legitimate, has to exist within the organizations themselves, implying an existing discourse on EU affairs within the organizations. Second, it demands that the constituencies have some degree of satisfaction with the work the umbrellas are performing in their name.

Case choice and data

The cases in the present study are organizations that have different constituencies and are therefore assumed to organize their representation in different ways. They are present in different policy fields, some of which are more, others less integrated. As a result, they have different kinds of incentives to Europeanize some of their activities and constituencies. The existence of a European umbrella structure was a further criterion for their selection. Finally, the selected organizations are all consulted by the European Commission, and are the object of redistributive policies – either by the nature of the policy field or by the Commission structurally subsidizing it. What are these cases?

Conventional studies of non-electoral representation have focused on members as the source of a legitimate role for groups, thereby mirroring the criteria of representative democracy. 'Members', as I shall call this kind of non-electoral representation, are available to constituencies that are human, capable of presence and voice. In such instances, ultimately, individuals are members of the organization, authorize their representatives and hold them to account. Members of such organizations are identical to the constituency whose interests are being advocated (Binderkrantz 2009; Halpin 2006; McLaverty 2002: 309–310). We can therefore expect these CSOs to focus on existing members (as the constituency is structurally limited), and on including their members in will formation as a means of retaining them as members. Member-based, sectoral CSOs typically organize and mobilize professional interests, often with (re)distributive effects that directly concern the membership. Such CSOs are typically well resourced, not least due to the membership fees. We can also expect that members themselves have a strong personal incentive to influence will formation within the CSOs as the success of the organizations' activities will (more or less) directly influence members' (economic) well-being. In such a delegate model of representation, representation is legitimate if and so long as the constituency – the members – have chosen and authorized the representative and can hold the latter to account. In this type of organization, delegation chains from the local/regional to the EU level typically exist. Mechanisms are typically in place to assure that what the European umbrella organization does is linked to what the nationally grounded organizations and their members ask it to do. For this type of CSO, I look at groups that are organized under the framework of COPA-COGECA[3] in order to influence the Common Agricultural Policy (CAP). These organizations are active in a highly Europeanized policy field, and because of its redistributive character, a high salience can be assumed amidst national agricultural organizations.

Second, particularly with regard to supranational institutions, a proposition has been that representation does not have to be grounded in a people in order to be legitimate. *Discursive representation* suggests that representatives should represent discourses rather than peoples (Dryzek and Niemeyer 2008), and be authorized through rational public discussion within a deliberative democracy rather than through a vote. For discursive representation, it is not people per se that matter, but the views and interests they hold, and the claim is that supranational or global institutions do not adequately represent the totality of the relevant views, which is why discursive representation is necessary and legitimate. Specifically in politics beyond the nation state, discursive representation is required (ibid.: 491) as it forces intergovernmental institutions to justify their actions in light of different discourses and thereby renders them more democratic.

I shall dub organizations engaging in such kind of non-electoral representation as representing a 'cause', such as the environment, animals or future generations (Halpin 2006). Those supporting the organization are not those for whom the organization acts as an advocate, they are not *immediately* concerned by the results of the organizations' activities, not least as no (re-)distributional issues are at stake that directly involve them. Therefore, they will be less interested in influencing will formation in the organization; for them, it is sufficient to support the abstract cause by affiliating with the organization in some more or less direct way, e.g. by donating money (Binderkrantz 2009), signing a petition or supporting a campaign.

As a consequence, such organizations are typically not grounded on members who authorize representatives and hold them to account (this does not preclude such organizations offering membership to supporters). Instead, 'cause' organizations seek to gain their legitimacy and authorization from the force of the better argument, ideally supported by scientific expertise, leading to the ability to attract supporters via broad public communication strategies (or members) (Binderkrantz 2008). Therefore, while direct authorization by members plays a less important role in this theoretical model (public) debate and expertise are crucial for the legitimacy of these groups. For this 'cause' type of CSO, I am looking at interest groups that are organized in the European Environmental Bureau (EEB) in order to influence European environmental policy.

The third kind of representation is 'weak interests'. Here, there are human constituencies such as the poor and socially excluded, children or prisoners, who generally do not enjoy the various sorts of capital necessary to organize themselves. From a democratic theory perspective, the representation of weak interests is deemed important given they are generally underrepresented in electoral representation (Young 2000). An unresolved issue is who can or should legitimately represent weak interests, as is mirrored in the debate on 'descriptive representation' (Mansbridge 1999). Descriptive representation refers to representation by people who resemble their constituency in some important way, such as class, gender, ethnic background, religion, and so on. The argument is that these specific identities and social perspectives influence people's political views and choices, and that their representation has so far been systematically skewed in electoral politics. Unless disadvantaged people themselves are more consistently present in policy-making, it may not be possible to push sufficiently on to the political agenda the issues necessary to overcome their disadvantages. Bringing the structurally and historically disadvantaged peoples and views into the political process may lead to fairer outcomes. Thus, descriptive representation has a distinct goal: namely, a fairer and more just society (Phillips 1995; Williams 1998; Mansbridge 1999; Dovi 2002; Young 2000). Groups with a focus on a specific disadvantage can either act as proxies for the disadvantaged or often try to involve the disadvantaged themselves in their political and other activities. One could expect such organizations to combine elements of 'members' and 'cause' representation. Their legitimacy particularly depends on the involvement of those touched by poverty or discrimination and on the respective CSOs bringing issues to the table that would otherwise be excluded from representation. For the 'weak interests' type of CSO, the groups selected are organized under the head of the European Anti-Poverty Network (EAPN) in order to influence European anti-poverty policy.

The larger research project of which this contribution forms a part follows an inductive research strategy, which is why hypotheses are not tested. Also, for this contribution, I am drawing exclusively on information that emerges from the data. The three above-mentioned European umbrellas were contacted, as well as all their national member organizations, both in Germany and in the UK. Contacts with the regional governance levels were established through the interviewees at the national level. Overall, 63 questionnaires were returned and 60 interviews carried out – the former were entered into SPSS, the latter coded and analysed with the help of Atlas.ti. The object of both forms of data analysis was the understanding of representation, the internal workings of the organizations, their broader political environment, and the ways they participate in EU policy-making, and how this potentially affects their work. For the present contribution, the five questionnaires and interviews from the EU level were cleared from the data, given that I am interested here in how nationally grounded organizations relate to their European umbrella, and, more generally, to the EU. This leaves us with 12 questionnaires and interviews for the agricultural organizations at national and regional levels, 20 for the environmental organizations, and 26 for the anti-poverty organizations.[4]

Are there domestic constituencies behind European umbrellas?

In this section, I shall look at how well nationally grounded organizations are linked to their European umbrellas, and how much of an issue the EU is for them. Let me begin with the agricultural organizations, the example of the 'members' type. These groups have an entire chain of delegation from the regional level to the European umbrella. All interviewees agree they havse the right to participate, and all but one agree that not only is the participation of members highly institutionalized, but also regularly practised. Accordingly, 91.7 per cent found the link to the European umbrella to be either strong and regular (75 per cent) or rather strong if irregular (16.7 per cent) whilst only one regional actor said they did not have any link to the EU level.[5] This is complemented by the strong links regional organizations have to their national umbrella – all respective interviewees agreed this was the case.[6] Not only are the links between the national organizations and their European umbrella strong, but also this is complemented by a high degree of satisfaction. Of the interviewees 91.7 per cent said they were happy (33.3 per cent) or rather satisfied (58.3) with the way COPA-COGECA represented them whilst only one (8.3 per cent) did not know. Actors agree that they are being 'informed regularly and quickly, on a weekly basis, and if we need to discuss something, we get support immediately, contacts and meetings are being arranged, it's all to the best' (Interview regional actor, 16 April 2012), not least because 'they have really good people there' (Interview regional actor, 24 April 2012), a 'really, really well staffed office, with super experts' (Interview regional actor, 19 April 2012). These findings are supported by the importance the EU seems to enjoy in nationally grounded agricultural organizations. Asked what importance dealing with EU processes had in their organizations (possible answers being high – medium – low – none), 83.3 per cent thought the importance was 'high' whilst 16.7 per cent thought it was 'medium'. Unsurprisingly, then, 91.7 per cent said the EU was regularly an issue in their work, whilst only 8.3 per cent said this was rarely the case.[7]

The investigated 'members'' organizations clearly mirror a delegate model of representation as theory would have one expect. There are delegation chains in place, and the national and regional constituencies of the European umbrella are strongly and regularly involved in the development of positions on EU processes. The high level of involvement is no surprise given the degree of integration of agricultural policy and its distributive nature, which directly concerns the economic well-being of members. Their high degree of satisfaction signals that their views are regularly taken on board. Insofar as satisfaction with the representation through COPA-COGECA was limited, this was because the European umbrella can represent the interests of their constituencies only at the lowest common denominator:

> In principle the representation is also good. The European umbrella has the problem that it assembles around 60 different organizations, from Cyprus to Northern Ireland, from Finland to Gran Canaria, and then you often have the lowest common denominator as a formulation that is generally acceptable as a result which is not really helpful when looking closer at things. It is rather unsatisfactory, but no one has come up with something better yet.
>
> (Interview regional actor, 16 April 2012)

This is likely to be the case in policy fields with distributive policies such as agricultural policy, and given the important differences of farming within the national identities and economies of the member states. It reflects a structural feature and limitation of the EU, rather than the umbrella not listening to its constituencies. Therefore, we can conclude that COPA-COGECA is representative of its constituency as defined above and that its activities at the EU level therefore enjoy a high degree of legitimacy.

Turning to the 'cause' type of organizations, all but one indicated that members had the right to participate in the organization's business. However, only 63.3 per cent thought that this was actually happening on a regular basis, whilst 36.7 per cent said the right to participate was weakly institutionalized and that participation was irregular. Indeed, this seems to have repercussions on the link the national organizations entertain with their European umbrella. Fifty per cent thought the link was either strong and regular (25 per cent) or rather strong if irregular (25 per cent), whilst 25 per cent said it was weak and rare and another 25 per cent had no link at all. The link between regional and national organizations and the national umbrella that is responsible for EU coordination issues shows similar weaknesses:[8] only 43.8 per cent said they either had a strong and regular (18.8 per cent) or a rather strong if irregular (25 per cent) link to the national umbrella organization, whilst for 31.3 per cent, the link was weak and rare and for 25 per cent, there was no link at all. The mixed results in terms of links to the European level – either direct or through the national umbrella where it exists – are mirrored in the degree of satisfaction with the representation by the European umbrella where 60 per cent are either happy (30 per cent) or rather satisfied (30 per cent), whilst 10 per cent were unsatisfied and another 30 per cent did not know because they had no contact with the European umbrella. These findings correspond with the findings in regard to what interviewees thought of the importance of dealing with EU processes for their organizations, where 35 per cent thought it was high, 45 per cent medium and 20 per cent low. Reflecting these findings, 50 per cent said the EU was regularly an issue in their own work, 20 per cent said irregularly, and 30 per cent rarely. For 'cause' CSOs, attracting supporters outside of their organization is particularly important. Is this reflected in the efforts they undertake in their communication with the larger public? The answer is a conditional 'yes' – 68.2 per cent communicate about EU policies and related activities on their website, 31.8 per cent do not.

These findings that suggest 'cause' groups in part mirror what theoretical models would have one expect. As regards the interaction between represented and representative, they in part reflect a gyroscopic kind of representation (Mansbridge 2003). In gyroscopic representation, the represented selects a representative with similar policy preferences whom (s)he trusts will stay committed to his or her known principles and where therefore no ongoing communication is needed. Transferred to functional representation, this means that once an organization has gained the support of a given person, engagement in regular deliberation with this person is no longer necessary as the CSO is being trusted by the citizen to work in accordance with her or his views. Indeed, two interviewees who indicated that they had no links with the European level nevertheless expressed their satisfaction with the representation by their European umbrella, suggesting that satisfaction with them may stem from the awareness of their activities rather than from being involved in them. Other interviewees declared that the purpose of being a member of the European umbrella was to provide it with legitimacy, trusting that it was doing good work – not necessarily to be involved in it.

However, contrary to what is sometimes suggested, the findings show that 'cause' organizations also have democratic structures in place. They are just not used as consistently as in 'members'' organizations. Another important factor for the comparatively limited connection of environmental groups with their European umbrella appears to be that the European umbrella in question here, the EEB, is only one among other channels that CSOs use when seeking to influence EU policies. For the 'cause' organizations, national ministries and the European Commission as well as another European umbrella (Birdlife International) stand out in particular as other venues:

> BirdLife has only one partner in every Member State, in Germany that's NABU. The EEB has many member organizations in every Member States. It is a huge network which is composed of many large and small organizations, it has many more members, and therefore is a much heavier structure. The EEB decides a lot more on its own, simply because it cannot easily consult its members all of the time, because there are so many of them, whilst BirdLife has exactly 27 member organizations in 27 Member States which you can consult rather quickly. So BirdLife is a bit more powerful in regard to its issues, I would say.
>
> (Interview national actor, 17 February 2012)

Overall then, the evaluation of the representativeness of the EEB and therefore its legitimacy appears mixed, as both involvement in and the satisfaction with the representation by the European umbrella are limited.

In the third, 'weak interests', kind of organizations, 81.5 per cent of the interviewees reported that they enjoyed the right to participate in the organization's business, while for 18.5 per cent, this was not the case. While 73.1 per cent thought that members de facto participated regularly, 26.9 per cent said that this only happened irregularly and in weakly institutionalized forms. By and large, therefore, democratic structures are in place and also regularly used. Do these organizations actively seek to involve poor people themselves in the interest representation, as some theory suggests they should do in order to gain legitimacy? In 23.1 per cent of cases this was regularly the case, in 57.7 per cent of the cases irregularly, and 19.2 per cent of the organizations do not involve the poor.[9] As regards the link that 'weak interests' organizations entertain with their European umbrella, only 7.7 per cent said this was strong and regular, with 26.9 per cent evaluating it as rather strong if irregular; 30.8 per cent found the link weak and rare, and 34.6 per cent had no link at all. Are these weak to absent links to the European umbrella compensated by strong links to the national umbrella? Only partly it seems: 38.5 per cent said they had strong and regular links with the national umbrella, 3.8 per cent rather strong if irregular links. However, 38.5 per cent found their link to the national umbrella to be weak and rare, and some 19.2 per cent percent said they did not have any link at all. Nonetheless, some 42.3 per cent said they were happy (23.1 per cent) or rather satisfied (19.2 per cent) with the way the European umbrella represented them, whilst some 11.5 per cent were rather unsatisfied. Not surprisingly, 46.2 per cent said they did not know how well EAPN represented them. As with the agricultural organizations but in the opposite direction, these findings are mirrored in the role the EU plays for CSOs active in anti-poverty policy. Of these, 19.2 per cent thought dealing with EU processes in their organization had an important role, and 30.8 per cent evaluated it as medium. However, 34.6 per cent said the importance was low, and some 15.4 per cent thought it was not important at all. Accordingly, 30.8 per cent said the EU was regularly an issue in their work, for 15.4 per cent this was the case irregularly, for 34.6 per cent rarely and for 19.2 per cent never. This comparatively low salience of the EU is mirrored in their communication strategy with the larger public – 77.8 per cent had no information on the EU and related activities on their website while 22.2 per cent did.

Similar to the environmental groups, 'weak interests' organizations also have affinities to gyroscopic representation. Sharing a specific background and specific values with a representative can be a reason to support that representative without closely following her political activities. Indeed, also in this case, more responded that they were happy or rather satisfied with the representation by the European umbrella than those who actually entertained close or even irregular links with it. Overall, the involvement of the constituencies in the development of policy positions for 'weak interests' is rather low, as is their awareness of what the European umbrella is actually doing in their name. The representativeness of EAPN, therefore, also seems rather limited, and hence so is its legitimacy.

Three main factors seem to explain the results. First, as for 'members'' organizations, the policy field acts as an incentive. Important parts of social policy, particularly anti-poverty policies, remain in the competence of member states. Indeed, it does not seem reasonable for the related groups to Europeanize their activities given the rather low degree of integration in the field, as mentioned by several interviewees, so long as they can achieve most of their goals in the domestic sphere. This seems particularly logical in view of the second factor, which is that resources matter. Obviously, it is much easier for well-equipped groups to Europeanize their activities than for resource-poorer, which need to deal carefully with their limited resources and may find it more important – in fact crucial for their survival – to keep a strong link with their constituency intact (Dür and Matteo 2012). Indeed, many of the interviewees in the anti-poverty field mentioned that they simply lack the capacity to engage with EU politics:

> We simply can't afford to satisfy these structures. It's a question of capacities. I have only just withdrawn from the next delegates' conference because I simply can't make it. If you're busy locally, talking with the citizens about small things, you almost can't balance the act between the local and the national level, because we don't have the capacities for it.
>
> (Interview local actor, 26 April 2012)

The third factor that seems to account for the rather low degree of representativeness of EAPN is that it can only represent the interests of its constituencies at the lowest common denominator. This is particularly the case with redistributive policies such as anti-poverty policy, where we have a high degree of heterogeneity in welfare levels in the Member States. This was especially true of German CSOs, which seek to protect the comparatively high welfare standards in Germany. Linked to this structural feature is the fact that the European umbrella in question here – EAPN – is only one of many channels that national constituencies use when seeking to influence EU policies. Most importantly, groups seek to address the European Commission directly. Furthermore, German CSOs in particular organize themselves – not only in regard to EU politics, but also in regard to national politics – in another structure (BAG FW),[10] which is not a member of EAPN. This has historical reasons – the BAG FW has existed much longer than EAPN or its German member, the Nationale Armutskonferenz (nak) – as well as substantial reasons. The nak tends to focus on issues of monetary poverty, and ultimately on employment issues, whilst the BAG FW is much broader in the range of topics it is concerned with. But also, several interviewees have pointed out that the heterogeneity between Member States was simply too big for the EAPN to be a meaningful venue to use for their lobbying activities, given that welfare standards in Germany are so much higher than in Eastern states. This leads them to prefer to use a German structure and lobby via that instead:

> I do think that EAPN follows up the Commission's policies very well and also comments on them very critically. Of course it is very difficult for EAPN to take on board German interests, interests of the German Red Cross. EAPN is a European network, and the social standards and policies in Germany are of course far more developed than in Rumania. And accordingly, we in Germany have very high standards which still need to be created in other EU Member States. And so of course it's clear that German positions and demands do not always play the greatest role.... So often, representation via the BAG FW is simply closer to our interests, in the end.
>
> (Interview national actor, 10 February 2012)

Conclusion and discussion

This chapter has asked whether European umbrellas of civil society organizations (CSOs) are representative of the constituencies they claim to represent. It was argued that this was crucial in order for their contribution to EU policy-making to be legitimate, and that they are representative so long as they involve their constituencies in the development of policy positions and that the latter enjoy a high degree of acceptance by the constituencies. Three different types of organizations were chosen for the empirical analysis, 'members', 'cause' and 'weak interests', with the latter two being particularly important cases of non-electoral representation, given they tend to reflect those (views) that are normally not sufficiently represented by parties and legislatures.

The analysis showed that the 'members' ' organizations, here sectoral agricultural groups, are very active over the different governance levels and consistently involve their constituencies in EU affairs. Their representation by way of a European umbrella organization therefore is highly legitimate. Less involvement with EU policy-making was found for the constituencies of the umbrella representing a 'cause', and comparatively little involvement was found for 'weak interests' groups, casting doubts on the representativeness of the respective European umbrella organizations. True, some of their constituencies are happy to be members of the European umbrellas, without being involved precisely so as to provide them with more legitimacy by way of their membership. But such membership can at best provide 'façade representativeness', as it involves no real involvement in the development of policy positions.

The results are partly in line with what theoretical models would expect, mirroring delegate and trustee/gyroscopic kinds of representation. They also show that the degree of integration of a policy field acts as an incentive to Europeanize groups' activities, and suggest the difficulty, for non-sectoral CSOs, of overcoming the national boundaries of traditional constituencies – still one would need larger-n research in order to appreciate whether the data here generated is representative of the different kind of umbrella groups active in Brussels, and therefore can be generalized, and some important institutional factors that explain for the structure and workings of umbrella organizations may simply have not come up in the interviews I conducted (see: Kohler-Koch and Buth

2013). Finally, the results seem to confirm the message of earlier research that certain CSOs are ill-suited to provide the kind of Europeanization of their constituencies that would seem necessary for the creation of a supranational polity (Warleigh 2001) or to combat the democratic deficit of the EU. However, this is not because internal democratic structures are not in place, but because they are not used by more than a few key national policy officers. Many CSOs simply do not seem to mediate between the state and society as hoped by some scholars or Commission officials – not between the EU and national peoples anyway. Does this imply that 'cause' and weak interests' organizations have no legitimate role to play in EU policy-making? Not necessarily so, if they bring issues to the table that otherwise would be neglected. However, their democratic legitimacy seems somewhat limited.

Acknowledgements

I acknowledge the support for this research of a Marie Curie Intra European Fellowship within the 7th European Community Framework Programme (call reference FP7-PEOPLE-2010-IEF). I would like to thank my interviewees without whom this research would not have been possible, as well as Richard Bellamy for very constructive and helpful feedback on the previous version of this text.

Notes

1 In EU studies and political discourse, 'civil society organization' has become more and more become synonymous with 'interest groups'. They will be used interchangeably in this chapter.
2 Interview Friends of the Earth Europe, 21 January 2012.
3 Committee of Professional Agriculural Organisations and General Confederation of Agricultural Cooperatives.
4 The reason for the substantially lower figure of questionnaires and interviews in the agricultural sector is their organization structure under COPA-COGECA, which differs from the two other sectors in that it only allows for one to two national members, whilst in the environmental and anti-poverty field, the European umbrellas at times have a multitude of national members which in turn have a multitude of regional members.
5 In this particular case, this is likely to be due to the comparatively low position of the interviewee in the respective regional organization.
6 For this question, two (British) interviewees said there was no national umbrella, whilst the reply from the German national umbrella organization has been cleared from the data.
7 Possible answers being regularly – irregularly – rarely – never.
8 Of the 20 questionnaires considered here overall, four had to be cleared for this question, one being a national umbrella employee, and three because they answered that there was no national umbrella structure – which is the case in the UK.
9 Involving the poor in interest representation is much more of a tradition in the UK than in Germany, where, however, organizations have also begun to involve them more actively in their political activities.
10 Bundesarbeitsgemeinschaft der Freien Wohlfahrtspflege.

References

Bauer, M.W. (2002) 'Limitations to Agency Control in EU Policy Making: The Commission and the Poverty Programmes', *Journal of Common Market Studies*, 40 (3): 381–400.

Binderkrantz, A. (2008) 'Different groups, different strategies: how interest groups pursue their political ambitions', *Scandinavian Political Studies*, 31 (2): 173–200.

Binderkrantz, A. (2009) 'Membership recruitment and internal democracy in interest groups: do group-membership relations vary between group types?', *West European Politics*, 32 (3): 657–678.

Commission of the European Community (2001) 'European governance: A White Paper', COM (2001) 428 final.

Disch, L. (2011) 'Toward a mobilization conception of democratic representation', *American Political Science Review*, 105 (1): 100–114.

Dovi, S. (2002) 'Preferable descriptive representatives: or will just any woman, black, or Latino do?' *American Political Science Review*, 96: 745–754.

Dryzek, J. (2010) *Foundations and Frontiers of Deliberative Governance*, New York: Oxford University Press.

Dryzek, J. and Niemeyer, S. (2008) 'Discursive representation', *American Political Science Review*, 102: 481–493.

Dür, A. and Mateo, G. (2012) 'Who lobbies the European Union? National interest groups in a multilevel polity', *Journal of European Public Policy*, 19 (7): 969–987.

Eriksen, E.O. and Fossum, J.E. (2000) 'The EU and post-national legitimacy', ARENA Working Papers – WP 00/26.

Greenwood, J. (2010) 'Regulating NGO participation in the EU. A *de-facto* accreditation system built on "representativeness"?', in K. Hahn and J. Steffek (eds) *Evaluating International NGOs. Legitimacy, Accountability, Representation*, Houndmills; Basingstoke; Hampshire: Palgrave Macmillan, pp. 200–219.

Halpin, D.R. (2006) 'The participatory and democratic potential and practice of interest groups: between solidarity and representation', *Public Administration*, 84 (4): 919–940.

Kohler-Koch, B. (2010) 'Civil society and EU democracy: "astroturf" representation?' *Journal of European Public Policy*, 17 (1): 100–116.

Kohler-Koch, B. and Buth, V. (2011) 'Der Spagat der europäischen Zivilgesellschaft – zwischen Professionalität und Bürgernähe', in B. Kohler-Koch and C. Quittkat *Die Entzauberung partizipativer Demokratie. Zur Rolle der Zivilgesellschaft bei der Demokratisierung von EU-Governance*, Frankfurt; New York: Campus, pp. 167–210.

Kohler-Koch, B. and Edler-Wollstein, S. (2008) 'It's about participation, stupid. Is it? Civil-society concepts in comparative perspective', in B. Jobert and B. Kohler-Koch (eds) *Changing Images of Civil Society: From Protest to Governance (Routledge Studies in Governance and Public Policy)*, London: Routledge, pp. 195–214.

Kohler-Koch, B. and Finke, B. (2007) 'The institutional shaping of EU–society relations – a contribution to democracy via participation?' *Journal of Civil Society*, 3 (3): 205–221.

Kröger, S. (2008) 'Nothing but consultation: The place of organised civil society in EU policy-making across policies', European Governance Papers (EUROGOV) No. C-08–03, online, available at www.connex-network.org/eurogov/pdf/egp-connex-C-08–03.pdf.

Kymlicka, W. (1995) *Multicultural Citizenship: A Liberal Theory of Minority Rights*, Oxford: Oxford University Press.

Maia, R.C.M. (2012) 'Non-electoral political representation: expanding discursive domains', *Representation*, 48 (4): 429–443.

Maloney, W. (2007) 'The professionalization of representation: biasing participation', in B. Kohler-Koch, D. de Bièvre and W. Maloney (eds) *Opening EU Governance to Civil Society: Gains and Challenges*, Connex Report Series 5, pp. 69–86.

McLaverty, P. (2002) 'Civil society and democracy', *Contemporary Politics*, 8 (4): 303–318.

Mansbridge, J. (1999) 'Should blacks represent blacks and women represent women? a contingent "yes" ', *Journal of Politics*, 61 (3): 628–657.

Mansbridge, J. (2003) 'Rethinking representation', *American Political Science Review*, 97 (4): 515–528.

Mansbridge, J. (2004) 'Representation revisited: introduction to the case against electoral accountability', *Democracy and Society*, 2 (1): 12–13.

Nanz, P. and Steffek, J. (2004) 'Global governance, participation and the public sphere', *Government and Opposition*, 39 (2): 314–335.

O'Neill, J. (2001) 'Representing people, representing nature, representing the world', *Environment and Planning*, 19: 483–500.

Phillips, A. (1995) *The Politics of Presence*, Oxford: Oxford University Press.

Pitkin, H.F. (1967) *The Concept of Representation*, Berkeley, CA: University of California Press.

Rehfeld, A. (2011) 'The concepts of representation', *American Political Science Review*, 105 (3): 131–141.

Rumford, C. (2003) 'European civil society or transnational social space? Conceptions of society in discourses of EU Citizenship, governance and the democratic deficit: an emerging agenda', *European Journal of Social Theory*, 6 (1): 25–43.

Saurugger, S. (2010) 'The social construction of the participatory turn: the emergence of a norm in the European Union', *European Journal of Political Research*, 49 (4): 471–495.

Saward, M. (2005) 'Governance and the transformation of political representation', in J. Newman (ed.) *Remaking Governance: Peoples, Politics and the Public Sphere*, Bristol: Policy Press, pp. 179–196.

Saward, M. (2010) *The Representative Claim*, Oxford; New York: Oxford University Press.

Schmidt, V.A. (2013) 'Democracy and legitimacy in the European Union revisited: input, output *and* throughput', *Political Studies*, 51: 2–22.

Severs, E. (2010) 'Representation as claims-making. Quid responsiveness?', *Representation*, 46 (4): 411–423.

Truman, D.B. (1951) *The Governmental Process: Political Interests and Public Opinion*, New York: Knopf.

Urbinati, N. (2006) *Representative Democracy: Principles and Genealogy*, Chicago, IL: University of Chicago Press.

Urbinati, N. and Warren, M.E. (2008) 'The concept of representation in contemporary democratic theory', *Annual Review of Political Sciences*, 11 (1): 387–412.

Warleigh, A. (2001) 'Europeanizing civil society: NGOs as agents of political socialization', *Journal of Common Market Studies*, 39 (4): 619–639.

Weiler, J. (1995) 'Demos, Telos and the German Maastricht decision', available at http://centers.law.nyu.edu/jeanmonnet/archive/papers/95/9506ind.html (accessed 3 August 2012).

Williams, M. (1998) *Voice, Trust, and Memory: Marginalized Groups and the Failings of Liberal Representation*, Princeton, NJ: Princeton University.

Young, I.M. (2000) *Inclusion and Democracy*, Oxford: Oxford University Press.

9 Democratic representation in transnational citizens' forums?

Dawid Friedrich

Introduction

This chapter addresses an unusual example of representation research, namely transnational citizens' forums conducted at the level of the European Union (EU) during the 2000s. Institutionally, these forums are unusual at the transnational level, as the usage of citizen panels, citizen juries, consensus conferences or deliberative polls has been predominantly the prerogative of local politics, given the proximity of the people and the shared language. Conceptually, these forums are usually discussed and evaluated in the context of participatory and/or deliberative democracy as a means of complementing the institutions of representative democracy or even moving in the direction of a 'strong democracy' (Barber 2003). In the EU context, the governance turn has specifically advanced the focus on deliberative modes of democracy, as there is (or used to be) widespread agreement that standard forms of electoral representation will not suffice to democratize the EU. Hence, citizens' forums at the EU level are peculiar institutions because of their transnational nature, especially if one looks at them from the perspective of representation.

Although the word 'representativeness' appears regularly in the context of selecting participants on such forums, there are hardly any scholarly publications that relate these forums with the concept of democratic representation.[1] Being situated at the local level, John Parkinson (2004) conducted qualitative research on the conflicting representation claims of the participants in a deliberation forum about a hospital reconfiguration in Leicester, UK. He demonstrated that the strength of different representation claims depend on the extent to which the claimants could convincingly demonstrate that they have been authorized by a constituency, and that they resemble those that they claim to represent. Furthermore, the proximity of the forum to concrete decision-making fostered its overall success. At a more general level, Mark Brown (2006) surveys the empirical literature on deliberation forums at the local level in order to locate these results in the context of representation theory, hereby focusing on what he describes as five distinct elements of representation, namely authorization, accountability, expertise, participation and resemblance. He aims at specifying the democratic potential of these forums through the lens of representation and concludes that, at the local level, the deliberative forums 'have a limited but significant role to play in representative democracy' (Brown 2006: 221).

The transnational context is a challenging environment for deliberation forums, as the proximity assumption that underlies many claims about their democratic value cannot be upheld. Furthermore, there is no lingua franca in which the deliberations can be conducted. Thus, the participation of individual citizens in deliberative practices at the transnational level seems to be at odds with the dominant logic of (electoral) representation in modern democratic politics. It was not least the question of size (Dahl and Tufte 1973) that triggered the democratic transformation from a face-to-face Agora-style democracy towards electoral representation in the modern nation state (Dahl 1989). And now it is hoped that the participation of individuals can add to the democratization of the EU?

The following contribution builds upon the above-mentioned research and aims at deepening our understanding of both the democratic potential and the limitations of deliberative citizen forums in a transnational context by adding the perspective of representation. Reflecting on deliberative experiments from a representation perspective is made possible, as I will discuss later in more depth, by the constructivist turn in representation theory (Disch 2011), which stresses the performative nature of the representative relationship between claimants, constituents as receivers and the audience of representative claims (Trenz and Michailidou 2013).

This contribution pursues the following steps:

1 The first section sets out the historical context and outlines when and why the EU has started to experiment with deliberative citizens' forums in the first place.
2 The second section introduces the cases of different deliberative forums that were implemented in the 2000s, more specifically.
3 In order to reflect upon those cases from the perspective of representation research, recent developments in representation theory are introduced, their relation to deliberation addressed and, on this basis, a tentative list of evaluative perspectives is suggested.
4 Against this background, the evaluative literature on the transnational citizens' forums is assessed.
5 The final section reflects upon the relation of these forums to representation research and gives some suggestions about the potential of these forums in the context of EU democracy.

Experimenting with deliberation: the Communication Strategy of the European Commission

The difficulties in ratifying the Treaty of Maastricht (1993) through the referenda in Denmark, France and Ireland, as well as the failure of the Constitutional Treaty of the EU in referenda in both France and the Netherlands (2005), are symbols of the end of the so-called permissive consensus on the European integration process and of a growing gap between the EU institutions and the citizens living within its confines (Kohler-Koch and Rittberger 2007). While increasingly affected by the European integration process, many European citizens believe that they have too little to say in European decision-making, a situation aptly described as 'policies without politics' (Schmidt 2006: 5). It is unsurprising, then, that research on the EU's alleged democratic deficit has developed into one of the most prominent pillars of European Studies (Bellamy and Castiglione 2003; Lord 2004; Føllesdal and Hix 2006; Majone 1998, 1999; Moravcsik 2004, 2008).

Parallel to the above-mentioned political earthquakes, and ever since, the EU has been engaged in democratic experiments in order to bridge the gap with its people. In particular, it has successively developed and/or extended four different channels of legitimacy that accompany its traditional intergovernmental core of policy-making. These four channels are as follows:

- The *parliamentary channel of legitimacy* has been strengthened in all successive treaty reforms since the Maastricht Treaty by increasing the competences of the European Parliament (EP). Most recently, with the Treaty of Lisbon (2009), the supranational parliamentary path is complemented by increasing legislative and control competences for the national parliaments in EU Affairs.
- Having gradually developed during the 1990s, the *civil society channel of legitimacy* has been extended through the establishment of a consultative regime in the EU in almost all of its policy-making processes.
- The Treaty of Lisbon sees the inclusion of a *democratic channel of direct legitimacy* for the supranational level through the establishment of the European Citizens' Initiative (ECI). The ECI came into force in April 2012 and it might yet become an important tool for transnational political actions of a European citizenry in the making.
- *A deliberative channel of legitimacy* has been experimented with in the 2000s through the initiation of a number of transnational deliberative citizen forums.

The channels for both direct and for deliberative legitimacy are reactions particularly of the European Commission, which realized that the gap between the EU institutions and the people is becoming dangerous for the integration process as such. Consequently, building upon the reform strategy formulated in its famous White Paper on European Governance (2001), the Commission used the 'period of reflection' (European Commission 2005a) after the failure of the constitutional treaty to reflect how to proceed with the integration process and the eroding legitimacy of its institutions, in order to develop a new communication strategy that aims at tackling the legitimacy crisis of the EU (for the following, see Yang 2013).

In its White Paper on European Governance, the European Commission maintained that it would suffice to better inform the EU citizens about EU legislation and to implement some reforms in the policy-making structures of the EU, in particular by establishing practices of societal consultation through the participation of civil society organizations, in order to solve the EU's legitimacy problems. Contrary to this perspective, the shock of the lost referenda seemed also to have shaken the Commission. The new Commission, presided by Mr José Manuel Barroso, established a new Directorate General on Institutional Relations and Communication Strategy (DG COMM), led by Margot Wallström, a new Commissioner. Her main and foremost task was to develop a new communication strategy – and indeed, as Yang (2013) convincingly demonstrates, the White Paper on European Communication Policy (2006) signifies a paradigmatic shift. It is envisaged that nothing short of a 'European Public Sphere' (European Commission 2006: 4) will be achieved by the shift 'from an institution-centred to a citizen-centred communication' strategy (European Commission 2006: 4). Behind this strategy lies the conviction that communication can no longer remain 'a one-way street' (European Commission 2005b: 3), but that, instead, a true dialogue, understood as a 'two-way communication' (European Commission 2006: 7), between citizens and EU institutions, must be established. The latter must become 'more responsive, open and accessible' (ibid.) in order to (re-)gain legitimacy in the eyes of the EU citizens.

This new communication strategy has a strong foundation in deliberative accounts of democracy. By stressing the interactive, dialogical nature of the communication between citizens and EU institutions, the Commission acknowledges that citizens must also become the true authors of EU legislation, that reflexive input legitimacy must be fostered, hereby superseding the earlier emphasis on output legitimacy that was to be found in the Governance White Book. In particular, the concept of dialogue in Plan D resembles very much the deliberative conceptions of public reasoning as a cornerstone for democratic legitimacy (Yang 2013; Gutmann and Thompson 1996). The process of public deliberation among citizens on European policies in itself becomes an important end that needs to be supported by appropriate democratic experiments initiated by the European Commission.

This reliance on deliberative accounts of democracy in the Communication Strategy builds upon previous attempts by the Commission to link European governance and the epistemic dimension of deliberation as a tool to improve not only the effectiveness of governance but also its legitimacy (Friedrich 2013; Magnette 2003). The Commission had already established a 'new programmatic framework for framing [its] activities and visions' (Pfister 2011: 5) of governance in deliberative terms, most prominently expressed in the Governance White Book, which was a hallmark for political and academic debates about governance and democracy in the EU. In the wake of this White Book and its preparatory working groups, often dominated by (social) scientists with a deliberative leaning (de Schutter *et al.* 2001), the concepts of deliberation and of European governance became very closely related to each other in the Euro-political discourse which, as shown above, also influenced the new Communication Strategy and the subsequent experiments with deliberative instruments of citizen involvement at the transnational level.

The cases: transnational deliberative citizen forums as examples for democratic experimentation

The most concrete output of the European Commission's new Communication Strategy is the establishment of a number of transnational deliberative citizen forums. Until 2010, 23 such truly transnational forums were initiated (see Table 9.1). Usually, it was not the European Commission itself that organized the forum; rather, a civil society actor such as the Belgian King Badouin Foundation implemented the concrete project. The transnational nature of the forum results from the fact that the participants stem from at least three countries. The deliberative nature results from the specific form of organization that allowed, at least according to the self-descriptions of the projects, for a true, reciprocal dialogue between a cross-section of people. The task of these citizens was to discuss in a deliberative manner a specified topic, which could be either fairly broad, such as the future of Europe, or could concentrate more specifically on single policy issues, such as climate change or immigration. These forums were all organized differently. Nevertheless, they do have some elements in common: usually the forums consisted of activities both at the national and the international level. Thus, participants from one country had the opportunity to prepare nationally the meeting(s) at the transnational level. These meetings were organized either online or face-to-face. Moderators played an important role during these meetings trying to assure that the rules of fair deliberation were respected. Furthermore, the participants of each forum were given the chance to deal with expertise on the topic at hand in order to deepen their understanding. The organizers of the forums tried to select the expertise so that a balanced and multi-faceted picture of the issue was presented to the lay people.

Whereas the overarching macro-aim of the forums was set out in the new Communication Strategy of the European Commission, namely to promote a European public sphere and to include the citizens of Europe in EU policy processes, each of the forums pursued additional micro-level goals that have usually been scientifically evaluated. One important goal was to assess to what extent nationality and multilingualism posed a hindrance to deliberations; another goal was to establish whether the deliberation process triggered learning processes among participants.

Table 9.1 shows that there is considerable variation among these forums despite their all sharing their transnational nature. They were funded and organized under different EU programmes and some of them were based on face-to-face-meetings, whereas others were examples of attempts to profit from the democratic potential of e-participation. Three of the projects were also designed as research projects in order to establish scientifically the (im-)possibility of citizen deliberation in a transnational, multi-lingual context. There is no reliable account for the amount spent on these forums, but since it is estimated that one of them cost approximately 1 million EUR (Euréval *et al.* 2009: 63), it seems probable that the EU has spent at least 20 million EUR on transnational deliberative citizen forums in the 2000s. Not only the sum invested in these forums is

Table 9.1 Transnational deliberative citizen forums in the EU

Year	*Name*	*EU-programmes*
2001	Futurum	Debate on the Future of the EU
2005	Meeting of Minds	Research
2005	RAISE Tomorrow's City	Research
2006	European Citizens' Panel 2006	Citizenship Programmes
2006	European Residents in Regeneration Network	Citizenship Programmes
2006	Speak Up Europe	Plan D
2006	Our Message to Europe	Plan D
2006	Radio Web Europe	Plan D
2006	Our Europe – Our Debate – Our Contribution	Plan D
2007	European Citizens Consultations 2007	Plan D
2007	Tomorrow's Europe	Plan D
2007	EUR-Action	Citizenship Programmes
2007	Virtual European Parliament	e-Participation
2007	IDEAL EU	e-Participation
2007	LEX-IS	e-Participation
2007	TID	e-Participation
2008	Online Forum Debate Europe	Debate Europe/Plan D
2008	Voice	e-Participation
2009	European Citizens Consultations 2009	Debate Europe/Plan D
2009	European Citizens' Panel 2009	Citizenship Programmes
2009	Europolis	Research
2009	Europetition	e-Participation
2009	HUWY	e-Participation

Source: Yang 2013.

impressive, so is the number of people brought together to discuss EU-related policy issues. The forums under Plan D alone included about 40 000 citizens, and the online projects even more. Thus, Yang (2013) estimates that all 23 forums have brought together at least 100 000 European citizens; despite this impressive number, the potential multiplication effect in the European public sphere of those participants remains fairly limited, given the overall size of the EU population of more than half a billion people.

However, in the light of the perhaps overly ambitious goal to initiate a European public sphere, the visible diversity hints at some important specialties and caveats of these forums: first of all, they are explorative in nature as there was no certainty for the organizers, the evaluators or indeed the participants whether intensive deliberative interaction of lay citizens from many different social and cultural backgrounds on abstract EU political issues could work. Second, it is evident that the EU does not pursue a coherent strategy of democratic innovation; instead, it seems evident that the EU did not coordinate among the different forums with which it was experimenting. The forums were not coherently organized and/or funded, but rather constituted parts of different initiatives within the Commission. The competences of the newly established DG COMM and its Commissioner Wallström were largely confined to internal communication and coordination activities. Little room for manoeuvre was given to them, and no power to demand coherent action from the other DGs was granted. Instead, the DG COMM needed to rely on its ability to persuade other DGs and Commissioners of the importance of investing in improved communication with citizens and to thus create sufficient political will. However, as Yang aptly put it, there 'simply was not enough political support to establish new participatory structures that would allow for an encompassing implementation of the demanding goals within Europe's new communication policy' (2013).

On representation in a deliberative context

The two channels of legitimacy mentioned above, for parliaments and civil society participation, are already very well researched (Crum and Fossum 2009; Raunio 2009; Rittberger 2009; Friedrich 2011; Friedrich and Nanz 2007; Greenwood 2007; Geißel 2009; Newig and Fritsch 2009; Rossteutscher 2005; Steffek *et al.* 2008), and although the ECI is still in its infancy it certainly triggers some scholarly attention. The deliberative channel with a view to transnational citizen forums, however, is still empirically sketchy and normatively focused within the deliberative paradigm.

Empirically, most of the publications engage in single case studies and try to evaluate the success or failure of individual citizen forums (Abels 2009; Boussaguet and Dehousse 2008; Culpepper und Fung 2006; Gerber 2011; Isernia and Smets 2011; Karlsson 2010; contributions in Kies and Nanz 2013; Talpin and Wojcik 2010; Wright 2007). Theoretically, the theory of deliberative democracy (Cohen 1989; Habermas 1992) is usually applied as a normative basis for normative judgements (Goodin and Dryzek 2006; Fung 2003; Gastil 2008). Of key interest has been the attempt to assess the discursive quality of the deliberation processes in these forums (Olsen and Trenz 2011). In the reading of deliberative democracy, political procedures are legitimate insofar as the processes are inclusive and truly deliberative in nature. This means that these processes need to include possibly all relevant societal positions and preferences (Goodin and Dryzek 2006: 221; Smith 2009: 20ff.). However, this notion of including all those concerned in a context of the deliberative practices of a highly selected group of people pushes the doors towards representation wide open. What are the grounds for justifying the participation of these citizens rather than others? Are substantive selection criteria for descriptive representation applied? Or, rather, are pure procedural criteria of statistical random sampling applied? And what is the effect of deliberation on such moments of representation?

Furthermore, whereas deliberative theorists tend to be content with establishing the discursive quality, the perspective of representation theory does not stop at asking for the micro-functioning of these forums but is interested in their linkages to the wider political space.[2] What position do these citizens and these forums have in the context of EU policy-making? Are these forums perceived as 'standing for' the EU citizenry? Do the participants in these forums themselves engage in representative claims-making? These preliminary questions show on a basic level that a perspective of representation is crucial in order to understand more fully the democratic potential of transnational deliberative citizen forums. But they also show that a specific conceptualization of representation is necessary; otherwise, the literatures would not be able to talk to each other. In the remainder of this section, the present understanding of representation will be elaborated. It will be argued that it is particularly the constructivist turn in representation theory that enables research into deliberative forums from the perspective of representation.

At a general level, and largely inspired by Hannah Pitkin's seminal book (1972) it is common practice to explain representation as about making present that which is absent. Furthermore, in its contemporary usage in political science as *political* representation, representation is usually closely linked to the concept of democracy, although one should be aware that democratic representation is only one form of representation amongst others (Rehfeld 2006: 2; Saward 2009).

In the context of the modern, liberal nation-state, scholars on democratic representation have interpreted electoral representation through parliaments and representative government as the dominant institutionalization and have, accordingly, put forward a definition of democratic representation that has been called the 'standard account of political representation' (Pollak *et al.* 2009: 1) or the 'traditional model of promissory representation' (Mansbridge 2003: 518). According to these authors, the standard account of democratic representation[3] is the institutionalization of a specific representation procedure that makes democracy fit for mass societies. Citizens regularly elect, equally, individual representatives and authorize them to become engaged in public decision-making. These individual representatives need to fulfil accountability requirements: they must constantly and publicly justify their actions. Through this mechanism, the electorate can decide about its judgement on the performance of the representative. In case of dissatisfaction, the representative can be sanctioned by being voted out of public office. Although this account of representation is intimately linked to electoral representation in the context of parliaments, its key characteristics of authorization and accountability can be also transposed to non-electoral contexts of policy-making.

The standard account of representation is based on a specific assumption of rational behavior in which each actor's preferences are given so that an unambiguous regime of control can be upheld. Irrespective of the fact that the sheer number of electors for each individual parliamentarian substantially challenges this idea about control possibilities, the underlying principal–agent model, where the (s)electors act as principals and the representatives as agents, dominates much of the conventional discourse on political representation to the present day. Given the centrality of the ability of the principal, the represented, to sanction the agent, the representative, Jane Mansbridge calls this model of representation the 'sanctions model' of representation (Mansbridge 2009). This sanctions model is thus based on circular processes of authorization and accountability/control. It is not only the representative's duty to act according to the preferences of the electorate, but it is also in her/his self-interest if s/he does not want to lose her/his public power position. Hence, the sanctions model purports a specific understanding of rationality that is based on maximizing self-interest, in this case the interest to remain in power.

Within theories of democracy, this specific notion of rationality upon which the sanctions model of representation is strongly based refers to a specific conception of democratic will formation, namely the so-called aggregative model of democracy (Young 2000: 18ff.). According to this model, democracy is a method to achieve specific ends, which are in line with citizens' preferences. This model is based upon equality and autonomy (Cohen 1996), and defends the idea that 'an ideally democratic procedure gives equal weight to the interests of each in arriving at binding collective decisions' (Cohen 1991: 221). Accordingly, politics is a competition among pre-politically given individual preferences that are aggregated by intermediary actors such as political parties in the political process (Nanz and Steffek 2005) and it is here that political representation, in its standard forms, plays out its key function of selection and sanctioning in modern democracies.

However, in the present context of transnational deliberative forums of citizens, a focus on this standard sanctions model of representation as well as the aggregative model of democracy would seem inappropriate. If one applied criteria from these understandings, any other form of representation beyond elections would be almost bound to fall outside the scope of democratic representation and hence to fail any normative evaluation. Thus, one needs a conception of representation that can speak to deliberative settings of policy making. Recent advances in representation theory offer this conception of representation, separating representation from the rationalist sanction model of representation and bringing representation closer to a deliberative model of democracy.

This deliberative model differs fundamentally from the aggregative model in its idea about the nature and the process of political will formation. In the deliberative conception, a reciprocal understanding that both parties can justify their positions by means of rational arguments is central, as is their capacity to change their position as a consequence of such a justificatory communicative interaction (Cohen 1996). Hence, the deliberative conception of political will formation rejects the static rationalistic idea that each rational actor possesses a set of pre-political, exogenously given preferences that cannot be changed. Contrarily, from the deliberative perspective, establishing preferences is a result of the performative function of deliberation. Social actors are capable of understanding arguments, changing their views, and thus, of learning.

Both perspectives, however, the aggregative and the deliberative, possess the conviction that the principles of equality and autonomy are central to democracy. However, policy preferences cannot, from a deliberative perspective, merely become aggregated: the process of their development is central. In order to respect demands for equality, a political process is only then democratically legitimate if these demands are 'in principle open to appropriate public processes of deliberation by free and equal citizens' (Benhabib 1996: 69).

Thus, deliberative democracy, on the one hand, stresses the epistemic nature of communicative processes and procedures, but on the other hand it also emphasizes the participation of equal and autonomous actors (Eriksen 2009). In order to achieve participatory inclusiveness, political procedures must be accessible to a diversity of actors with different positions. And it is here that the linkages to more recent advances in representation theory come into play. As David Plottke (1997) highlighted, representation and participation are not the opposite of each other, but the opposite of representation is exclusion. Thus, also representative politics relies on inclusiveness, as does deliberative politics. And non-participation consequently does not oppose representation, but would instead be an expression of abstention.

The rapprochement of representation and deliberation has, over the last years, been further stimulated by a constructivist turn in representation theory that seems likely to bridge the gap between both concepts (for the following, see Disch 2011). The standard account of representation is based on the assumption of an existing constituency whose plurality of preferences needs merely to be aggregated. Contrarily, scholars from the constructivist side do not conceptualize the representative relationship in a unidirectional manner, from the principal to the agent, but argue that it is 'only *through* representation that a people comes to be as a political agent' (Disch 2011: 5). This means that a constituency is nothing pre-politically given but constitutes itself in the representative relationship (Plotke 1997: 31). Accordingly, concepts such as *reflexivity* (Mansbridge 2003) or *claims-making* (Saward 2010) have entered the centre-stage of the theoretical discourse.

This dynamic, constructivist understanding of representation opens up the possibility of applying representation concepts to deliberative settings, as deliberative theory also stresses the dynamic character of mutual exchanges and the possibility of changing policy preferences through these exchanges. It seems to be about time that deliberative theorists start to engage in representation theory, as even one of the key figures in deliberative democracy, Jürgen Habermas, embeds his conception of deliberation within the context of established institutions of electoral representation (Habermas 1992). Unfortunately, however, the link between the 'strong' public of representative government and the 'weak' public (Fraser 1992, 2007) has not been substantially elaborated, either from the perspective of institutional theory or from democratic theory.

In the context of the transnational deliberative forums, the sanction model seems structurally incapable of functioning as the basis for a normative evaluation. At the *micro-level* of the actual organization and implementation of individual forums, the participants are neither publicly elected, nor do they possess decision-making power beyond the scope of the forums' written output. Accordingly, *selection* rather than authorization and *fairness* in the deliberative procedures seem more appropriate evaluative categories at the micro-level of a forum. Furthermore, as was argued above and in line with the constructivist turn, it seems particularly important to consider the effects of forums at the *macro-level*. Is there an audience for these forums? Do they stimulate a self-constituted

European citizenry? Do they trigger justification of EU institutions and decision-makers about how they deal with the output of the forums? Is there, thus, interaction of the forum with both citizens and policy-makers? Thus, it is equally important to consider the impotance of *accountability through publicity* rather than sanctions and the forums' *public sphere effects*, in order to understand the representative nature of the transnational deliberative citizen forums.

Certainly, these reflections do not amount to a clear measure of the democratic quality of the transnational deliberative forums. Further specification would be needed in order to establish operationalizable criteria, but such efforts go beyond the scope of this contribution. Nevertheless, the foregoing remarks should suffice to enable an understanding of the representative nature of these forums and to establish a valid picture of the democratic quality of the deliberative forums.

Moments of representation in transnational, deliberative citizen forums

In this section, the existing evaluative literature on the transnational deliberative citizen forums will be discussed in order to better understand the representative nature of the forums. In so doing, I will not outline each of the evaluative results concerning the deliberative quality of the forums. Rather, I focus only on those aspects that are relevant from the perspective of representation theory. I will distinguish the micro-level of the individual forum's internal procedures, and the macro-level of their relation to both the strong and the weak public. It will become evident that the forums possess several moments of representation, but that (1) these moments differ between online and face-to-face forums and that (2) the existing research has only very recently started to make a more explicit link to representation theory. It should be noted that the depth of research on the different forums varies considerably. Whereas for some there are, if at all, only non-academic evaluations available (Euréval *et al.* 2009), the EuroPolis Project from 2009 has been designed explicitly as a quasi-experiment, under close academic scrutiny. As both the diversity of the forums' design is substantial and the scope and quality of the evaluations differ, only a first tentative evaluation of the nature of representation of these forums can be achieved.

The micro-level of the forums

In the literature, two topics were particularly addressed at the micro-level of individual forums, namely the discursive quality of the deliberations in each forum, on the one hand, and the selection of the participants, on the other hand. From the perspective of representation theory, the latter aspect is more relevant, because all selection processes must deal with questions about the representativeness of the participants.

Although most of the articles refer to some extent to the issue of the representativeness of the participants in the forums, the discussion is dominated by reflections on the technical aspects of the selection process, and only scarce reference to representation theory is made. Nevertheless, one can distinguish two representation perspectives in the literature. A typical position, for instance, is put forward by Gabriele Abels (2009) who claims that '[t]he lay panel should rather represent a diversity of "*social perspectives*"' (ibid.: 8, emphasis in original), thus stressing an understanding of descriptive representation (similar to Gerber 2011). This conceptualization is very prominent also in the analyses of online forums, where the criticism is typically made that participants are not representative in terms of educational background and that organized groups are dominant *vis-à-vis* individual citizens (Karlsson 2010; Kies *et al.* 2013). Although there is a clear linkage between the selection of participants and the topic of descriptive representation, the literature does not engage in a theoretical discussion of this particular conception of representation. Instead, a rather intuitive assumption seems to prevail that a highly selective group of participants in a deliberative forum needs to mirror, to some extent, the most important social strata of EU society.

As a method of achieving descriptive representation, and discussed in more theoretical detail, the issue of top-down scientific random sampling appears prominent in the literature. In fact, starting with the usage of selection mechanisms by lot in Athenian democracy (Manin 1997), and referring to Robert Dahl's concept of a *minipopulus* (Dahl 1989: 340), the selection of participants in these transnational deliberation forums is usually based on statistical random sampling in order to gain a representative picture of the citizens (Carson and Martin 1999; Gastil and Levine 2005). In the wake of this *descriptive representation* (Kymlicka 2009; Sintomer 2010), or *mirror representation* (Buchstein 2009: 344), the participants of the forums are supposed to deliberate as *surrogate* (Mansbridge 2003) representatives for the whole citizenry (Dahl 1989: 340; Fishkin 1991; Fishkin and Luskin 2000). The results of these forums are perceived as legitimate because the lot is an impersonal act of arbitrariness that does not result in any systematic underrepresentation of relevant societal groups and/or interests (Smith 2009: 80).

There seems to be widespread agreement that the organizers of forums are attempting carefully to achieve descriptive representation through the application of statistical equality, and most of the commentators seem fairly content with the result, irrespective of the fact that a tendency towards stronger representation of well-educated citizens is discernible. However, this prominent conclusion is based on the counterfactual assumption that there is a homogeneous populous within the EU that can be chosen accurately by random sampling. Such an assumption, however, is difficult to maintain in the context of the EU but it is not critically reflected upon in the literature. This is not least because, as Olsen and Trenz stress, 'statistical indicators are not innocent' (Olsen and Trenz 2011: 10). It means that the reliance on scientific methods in itself is based upon assumptions about the objectivity of scientific expertise. In the light of growing awareness of the relativity of expertocratic knowledge and the political character of knowledge production, this assumption deserves, at least, deeper justification.

Furthermore, one can question whether the method of top-down random sampling is a convincing method for achieving the representativeness of the participants. This scientific method, for sure, achieves equality in the likelihood of getting selected, but it does not achieve equal opportunities for participation (Brown 2006: 212f.). Without going into a deeper discussion, one should at least reflect upon the issue whether such highly selective institutions can claim democratic legitimacy. Democracy inherently requires publicness, but the face-to-face forums are not public with respect to their accessibility.

The picture changes if one takes into consideration the online forums. Here, self-selection rather than top-down selection is the dominant method of finding participants. Indeed, in terms of inclusiveness, there are some hints that the deliberative quality of online forums might be socially more inclusive than face-to-face forums, as participants from lower educational background dare to share their opinions more openly (Talpin and Monoyer-Smith in Kies and Nanz 2013); here, the anonymity of the Internet seems to be lowering the hurdles for making statements. However, as Kies *et al.* (2013) point out, the character of self-selection, rather than top-down selection, resulted in a significantly less representative sample of participants in terms of educational background, and to a dominance of organized groups over individual citizens. Thus, online forums based on self-selection duplicate the biases known from other consultative practices based on self-selection in the EU's participatory regime (see Friedrich 2011). Once the decision to partake is made, therefore, people with less educational backgrounds are also engaged; but the hurdle to participate in the first place seems to be very high. Furthermore, as Karlsson (2010) shows convincingly, there seems to be a trade-off between the higher number of participants in online forums and the deliberative quality. Karlsson (2010) demonstrates that online forums tend to develop a majoritarian, aggregative dynamic at the cost of the deliberative quality. The result is that, in the end, it is hard to distinguish empirically between deliberative online forums and 'normal' online consultation mechanisms, which are already available at the EU level.

Particular attention was paid to the aspect of territorial representation, conceived of as a sub-category of descriptive representation. Again, an intuitive understanding about the necessity of territorial representativeness seems to dominate without being reflected upon critically. The focus on territorial representativeness supports the conviction that there is no EU-wide citizenry that could be equally selected by random sampling. This seems to be a legitimate assumption, valid for all federal polities that must come to terms with the diverging equality demands of individual citizens and territorial sub-units (see Kröger and Friedrich 2013).

However, I argue that the literature, and the organizers of the forums, underestimate the tension between the demands of representativeness and deliberation. Even if a representative sample of participants, based on whatever descriptive criteria, were achieved, the explicit aim of deliberative processes is to stimulate learning processes so that, at the end of the forums, the representativeness of the participants can be called into question, because the participants have moved away from those they are selected to represent, such as a specific social stratum or a typical representative of a given Member State. And indeed, the 'experimental setting encourages the participants in numerous ways to take the role as representatives of the larger citizenry'. This was clearly the case with Europolis, mentioned above (Olsen and Trenz 2011: 11). Either national representative claims-making or descriptive claims were frequently issued, both being examples of what Mansbridge calls 'anticipatory representation' (Mansbridge 2003). However, as Abels (2009: 13) expresses it with concerning the example of the Meeting of Minds, 'a European demos was forced into being', neglecting 'a procedural inconsistency between constructing the citizens' group based on the criterion of social diversity whereas the deliberative output should be a homogenous "single voice" – if possible' (Abels 2009: 13). As the citizen participants could not make use of a feedback loop (ibid.: 19f.), they might have 'gone European' and departed from their national 'constituency'. Thus, the underlying assumption of the transnational deliberative citizen forums seems to be in line with the deliberative polls of James Fishkin, who claims that the deliberative treatment of a randomly selected group of lay citizens establishes a kind of counterfactual, experimentally created quasi-demos under the hypothesis that the whole citizenry share the same thinking if they enjoyed the same deliberative treatment as the participants of the deliberative polls.

Overall, one can conclude that neither the organizers of the forums nor most of the evaluators engaged in substantial reflection about the representative nature of these forums. This is a lamentable state of the art because the careful emphasis on scientific selection criteria clearly demonstrates that these forums make, as such, very strong representative claims.

The macro-level of the forums

I argued above, following Olsen and Trenz (2011), that it is crucial to consider the *macro-level* of the deliberative forums if one wants to understand whether or not they are of any significance to democratic legitimacy. Given the strength of the representative claims about them, there must be an audience for these forums at both ends: the citizens (via the media and other intermediaries) and the EU institutions. It is, hence, necessary to establish whether these forums are able to stimulate a representative interaction of the forum with both citizens and policy-makers. Thus, it is equally important to consider *accountability through publicity* rather than sanctions and the forums' *public sphere effects* in order to understand the representative nature of the transnational deliberative citizen forums.

Unfortunately, this topic has scarcely been addressed directly. It is only possible to find traces of it in the context of an assessment of the policy impact of the forums' written outputs. And here, there is widespread agreement about the lacking embeddedness of the forums to both the bottom and the top. Hence, the story of the macro-level inclusion of the forums is quickly told. Typical are the findings of Abels (2009), who compared the Meeting of Minds and the

European Citizen Consultation. Considering the results of the Meeting of Minds that were distributed at the EP, she describes the report as:

> unidirectional, i.e. first the citizens presented their results and then the invited policy-makers read out their statements and votes of thanks. This public meeting did not allow for a two-way dialogue over the results and the citizens.
>
> (Abels 2009: 14)

The situation was slightly better in the European Citizen Consultation case, where several meetings with EU policy-makers took place and where some civil society organizations disseminated the final document. This difference might be an effect of the strengthened new Communication Strategy, whereas the Meeting of Minds forum took place at an early stage, when the EU's experimentation with such forums was still very much in its infancy. A lack of interest at that time on the part of policy-makers coincided with the structural fragmentation of the European media sphere, which 'constituted the main hurdle for publicizing the event and claiming general legitimacy' (Olsen and Trenz 2011: 16).

Online forums have more potential to disseminate their results publicly, as the number of people reached, and the number of participants, is by far higher than in face-to-face meetings. However, the literature gave no indication that this had led to more publicity, either for the mediated public sphere or for policy-makers of the EU institutions. Overall, thus, the strong representative claims of these forums as such did not find strong resonance, either by the constituency or by the institutionalized audience. As the EU did not initiate a viable link between the forums and the EU institutions and policy-makers, it fell short of exploiting the legitimating potential of forums. Hardly any active representative relationship was established beyond the micro-level of the forum, so for the time being the democratic contribution of these forums has been very limited.

Conclusion

In this contribution I argued that a deliberative forum that would meet micro-level requirements without any public visibility would resemble an educational exercise rather than a governance innovation with democratic potential. As was said above, the term 'public' means, in this context, two things: namely both the weak and the strong public, i.e. both the mediated public and the public of policy-makers. The wider public needs to know about these processes, as it is hoped that they could contribute to stimulating trans-European discussions about specific policy choices. If the deliberative experiments succeed in initiating public debates on EU issues, and if the participants serve as local multiplicators, citizen deliberation may become an important means of strengthening the identity dimension of European democracy, a potential outcome that appears to be of more fundamental importance to European democracy than yet another technocratic deliberative European governance arrangement.

Without any doubt, it would certainly be utopian to believe that the transnational deliberation forums will ever be very closely linked to the decision-making processes. However, if properly institutionalized, they could succeed in making use of the performative potential of deliberation. If the EU manages to push these forums enough to establish a truly effective mechanism for generating processes of transnational will formation, citizen deliberation forums could develop into the missing stone in the EU's democratic mosaic that establishes transnational awareness of commonalities and differences, and generates common visions about problems of concern to all people living in the EU.

Certainly, the challenges are high; will they successfully evade the fate of becoming a technocratic top-down exercise for a selected few to become a well-known exercise to inform all? Is it at all possible for a governance innovation, initiated by a bureaucracy, to become emancipated? This, of course, depends on the political will of the EU institutions having the political will to stop giving the impression that they can teach EU citizens lessons the value of EU integration. At the same time, it depends on the engagement of citizens in using these forums as opportunities for transnational public discussions about central issues that are of common concern. What could this mean in practice? It could mean establishing such forums on a regular basis at different places on different topics, and establishing mechanisms that require EU institutions to justify their policy choices in the light of the outcomes of the deliberative forums. Again, such a requirement of reflexive justification is only then normatively worthwhile if it goes beyond a mere summary of statements without argumentative surplus. Experience with feedback mechanisms to the online consultation, however, do not give too much reason for optimism in this respect. Yet regular forums and regular feedback could easily be taken up by the media and trigger transnational discussions.

Notes

1 But see Dryzek and Niemeyer (2008: 489), where they address the issue of authorization with view to such forums.

2 Interestingly, Olsen and Trenz (2011) use a similar argument from the perspective of deliberative democracy. They argue that mini-publics, as they call the forums, are only relevant for democratic legitimacy if, in addition to the criterion of inclusion, they can make convincing claims to represent the general public judgement (ibid.: 4).

3 Democratic representation and political representation are used interchangeably in this contribution.

References

Abels, G. (2009) 'Citizens deliberation and the EU democratic deficit – is there a model for participatory democracy?', *Tübinger Arbeitspapiere zur Integrationsforschung*, Tübingen (1).

Barber, B. (2003) *Strong Democracy: Participatory Politics for a New Age*, 3rd edn, Berkeley, CA: University of California Press.

Bellamy, R. and Castiglione, D. (2003) 'Legitimizing the Euro-"polity" and its "regime": the normative turn in EU studies', *European Journal of Political Theory*, 2 (1): 7–34.

Benhabib, S. (1996) 'Toward a deliberative model of democratic legitimacy', in ibid. (ed.) *Democracy and Difference*, Princeton, NJ: Princeton University Press, 67–94.

Boussaguet, L and Dehousse, R. (2008) 'Lay people's Europe: a critical assessment of the first EU citizens' conferences', *European Governance Papers*, 2008 (C-08–022).

Brown, M.B. (2006) 'Survey article: citizen panels and the concept of representation', *Journal of Political Philosophy*, 14 (2): 203–225.

Buchstein, H. (2009) *Demokratie und Lotterie – Das Los als politisches Entscheidungsinstrument von der Antike bis zur EU*, Frankfurt/Main (Theorie und Gesellschaft), available at http://sub-hh.ciando.com/book/?bok_id=22413 (accessed 30 November 2013).

Carson, L. and Martin, B. (1999) *Random Selection in Politics*, Westport, CT: Praeger.

Cohen, J. (1989) 'Deliberation and democratic legitimacy', in A.P. Hamlin and P. Pettit (eds) *The Good Polity – Normative Analysis of the State*, Cambridge: Basil Blackwell, pp. 17–34.

Cohen, J. (1991) 'Institutional argument … is diminished by the limited examination of the issues of principle', *Journal of Politics*, 53 (1), 221–225.

Cohen, J. (1996) 'Procedure and substance in deliberative democracy', in S. Benhabib (ed.) *Democracy and Difference: Contesting the Boundaries of the Political*, Princeton, NJ: Princeton University Press, pp. 95–119.

Crum, B. and Fossum, J.E. (2009) 'The multilevel parliamentary field: a framework for theorizing representative democracy in the EU', *European Political Science Review*, 1 (2): 249–271.

Culpepper, P.D. and Fung, A. (2006) 'Listen to the citizens: the radical way forward for the European Union', *Harvard International Review* (2), available at http://hir.harvard.edu/listen-to-the-citizens (accessed 30 November).

Dahl, R.A. (1989) *Democracy and its Critics*, New Haven, CT: London: Yale University Press.

Dahl, R.A. and Tufte, E.R. (1973) *Size and Democracy*, Stanford, CA: Stanford University Press.

De Schutter, O., Lebessis, N. and Paterson, J. (eds) (2001) *Governance in the European Union*, Luxembourg: OOPEC.

Disch, L. (2011) 'Toward a mobilization conception of democratic representation', *American Political Science Review*, 105 (1): 100–114.

Dryzek, J.S. and Neimeyer, S. (2008) 'Discursive representation', *American Political Science Review*, 102 (4): 481–493.

Eriksen, E.O. (2009) *The Unfinished Democratization of Europe*, Oxford; New York: Oxford University Press.

Euréval/Matrix/Ramboll-Management (2009) 'Evaluation of the Plan D/Debate Europe Citizen Consultation Projects' – owned by author.

European Commission (2001) European Governance, A White Paper – COM 428.

European Commission (2005a) 'The Commission's Contribution to the Period of Reflection and Beyond: Plan-D for Democracy, Dialogue and Debate', COM 0494 final.

European Commission (2005b) Communication to the Commission of 20 July 2005, 'Action Plan to Improve Communicating Europe by the Commission' SEC 985 final.

European Commission (2006) 'White Paper on a European Communication Policy', COM 35 final.

Fishkin, J. (1991) *Democracy and Deliberation. New Directions for Democratic Reform*, New Haven, CT, London: Yale University Press.

Fishkin, J. and Luskin, R.C. (2000) 'The quest for deliberative democracy', in M. Saward (ed.) *Democratic Innovation: Deliberation, Representation and Association*, London: Routledge, pp. 17–28.

Føllesdal, A. and Hix, S. (2006) 'Why there is a democratic deficit in the EU: a response to Majone and Moravcsik', *Journal of Common Market Studies*, 44 (3): 533–562.

Fossum, J.E and Schlesinger, P.R. (eds) (2008) *The European Union and the Public Sphere. A Communicative Space in the Making?*, London: Routledge.

Fraser, N. (1992) 'Rethinking the public sphere: a contribution to the critique of actually existing democracy', in C. Calhoun (ed.) *Habermas and the Public Sphere*, Cambridge, MA: MIT Press, pp. 109–143.

Fraser, N. (2007) 'Die Transnationalisierung der Öffentlichkeit. Legitimität und Effektivität der öffentlichen Meinung in einer postwestfälischen Welt', in P. Niesen and B. Herborth (eds) *Anarchie der kommunikativen Freiheit. Jürgen Habemas und die Theorie der internationalen Politik*, Frankfurt a. M.: Suhrkamp, pp. 224–253.

Friedrich, D. (2013) 'European governance and the deliberative challenge', in R. Kies and P. Nanz (eds) *Is Europe listening to us? Successes and Failures of EU Citizen Consultations, European Citizens' Deliberation: A promising path for EU governance?*, Farnham: Ashgate, 35–57.

Friedrich, D. (2011) *Democratic Participation and Civil Society in the European Union*, Manchester: Manchester University Press.

Friedrich, D. and Nanz, P. (2007) 'Europe's civil society from a normative-democratic point of view: the case of the EU's migration policy', in C. Ruzza and V. Della Sala (eds) *Governance and Civil Society*, Manchester: Manchester University Press, pp. 113–133.

Fung, A. (2003) 'Recipes for public spheres: eight institutional design choices and their consequences', *Journal of Political Philosophy*, 11 (3): 338–367.

Gastil, J. (2008) *Political Communication and Deliberation*, Los Angeles: SAGE Publications.

Gastil, J and Levine, P. (eds) (2005) *The Deliberative Democracy Handbook – Strategies for Effective Civic Engagement in the Twenty-first Century*, San Francisco, CA: Jossey-Bass, available at www.gbv.de/dms/bowker/toc/9780787976613.pdf (accessed 30 November).

Geißel, B. (2009) 'How to improve the quality of democracy: experiences with participatory innovations at the local level in Germany', *German Politics and Society*, 27 (4): 51–71.

Gerber, M. (2011) *Who are the Voices of Europe? Evidence from a pan-European deliberative poll*, paper presented at the 6th ECPR General Conference, Reykjavik, Iceland, 25–27 August.

Goodin, R.E. and Dryzek, J.S. (2006) 'Deliberative impacts: the macro-political uptake of mini-publics', *Politics & Society*, 34 (2): 219–244.

Greenwood, J. (2007) 'Organized civil society and democratic legitimacy in the European Union', *British Journal of Political Science*, 37 (2): 333–357.

Gutmann, A. and Thompson, D. (1996) *Democracy and Disagreement*, Cambridge; London: Belknap Press of Harvard University Press.

Habermas, J. (1992) *Faktizität und Geltung. Beiträge zur Diskurstheorie des Rechts und des demokratischen Rechtsstaats*, Frankfurt: Suhrkamp.

Isernia, P. and Smets, K. (2011) 'Revealing preferences: does deliberation increase ideological awareness among the less sophisticated public?' Owned by author.

Karlsson, M. (2010) 'A panacea for pan-European citizen participation? Analysis of the

2009 European citizens consultations', in E. Amnå (ed.) *New Forms of Participation. Normative Implications*, Baden-Baden: Nomos, pp. 97–112.

Kies, R. and Nanz, P. (eds) (2013) *Is Europe Listening to us? Successes and failures of EU citizen consultations*, London: Ashgate.

Kies, R., Leyenaar, M. and Niemöller, K. (2013) 'European citizens consultation: a large consultation on a vague topic', in R. Kies and P. Nanz (eds) *Is Europe Listening to Us? Successes and Failures of EU Citizen Consultations*, London: Ashgate, pp. 59–78.

Kohler-Koch, B. and Rittberger, B. (2007) 'Charting crowded territory: debating the democratic legitimacy of the European Union', in B. Kohler-Koch and B. Rittberger (eds) *Debating the democratic legitimacy of the European Union*, Lanham, MD; Boulder, CO; New York; Toronto; Plymouth: Rowman & Littlefield, pp. 1–29.

Kohler-Koch, B. and Rittberger, B. (eds) (2007) *Debating the Democratic Legitimacy of the European Union*, Lanham, MD; Boulder, CO; New York; Toronto; Plymouth: Rowman & Littlefield.

Kröger, S. and Friedrich, D. (2013) 'Political representation in the EU', *Journal of European Public Policy*, 20 (2): 171–189.

Kymlicka, W. (2009) 'Categorizing groups, categorizing states: theorizing minority rights in a world of deep diversity', *Ethics & International Affairs*, 23 (4): 371–388.

Lord, C. (2004) *A Democratic Audit of the European Union*, Houndmills; Basingstoke; Hampshire: Palgrave Macmillan.

Magnette, P. (2003) 'European governance and civic participation: beyond elitist citizenship?', *Political Studies*, 51: 144–160.

Majone, G. (1998) 'Europe's "democratic deficit": the question of standards', *European Law Journal*, 4 (1): 5–28.

Majone, G. (1999) 'The regulatory state and its legitimacy problems', *West European Politics*, 22 (1): 1–24.

Manin, B. (1997) *The Principles of Representative Government*, New York: Cambridge University Press (Themes in the social sciences).

Mansbridge, J. (2003) 'Rethinking representation', *American Political Science Review*, 97 (4): 515–528.

Mansbridge, J. (2009) 'A "selection model" of political representation', *Journal of Political Philosophy*, 17 (4): 369–398.

Moravcsik, A. (2004) 'Is there a "democratic deficit" in world politics? A framework for analysis', *Government and Opposition*, 39 (2): 336–363.

Moravcsik, A. (2008) 'The myth of Europe's "democratic deficit"', *Intereconomics: Review of European Economic Policy*, 43: 331–340.

Nanz, P. and Steffek, J. (2005) 'Assessing the democratic quality of deliberation in international governance – criteria and research strategies', *Acta Politica*, 40 (3), 368–383.

Newig, J. and Fritsch, O. (2009) 'More input – better output: does citizen involvement improve environmental governance?', in I. Blühdorn (ed.) *In Search of Legitimacy – Policy Making in Europe and the Challenge of Complexity*, Opladen: Barbara Budrich Publishers, pp. 205–224.

Olsen, Espen D.H. and Trenz, H. (2011) 'From citizens' deliberation to popular will formation: generating democratic legitimacy through transnational deliberative polling', paper presented for the ECPR Joint Sessions, St. Gallen: April.

Parkinson, J. (2004) 'Hearing voices: negotiating representation claims in public deliberation', *British Journal of Politics & International Relations*, 6 (3), 370–388.

Pfister, T. (2011) *The Epistemic Dimension of European Integration*, unpublished manuscript.

Pitkin, H.F. (1972 [1967]) *The Concept of Representation*, Berkeley, LA; London: University of California Press.

Plotke, D. (1997) 'Representation is democracy', *Constellations*, 4 (1): 19–34.

Pollak, J., Bátora, J., Morke, M., Sigalas, E. and Slominski, P. (2009) *On Political Representation: Myths and Challenges*, RECON-Online-Working-Paper, available at http://ideas.repec.org/p/erp/reconx/p0042.html (accessed 6 January 2014).

Raunio, T. (2009) 'National parliaments and European integration: what we know and agenda for future research', *Journal of Legislative Studies*, 15 (4): 317–334.

Rehfeld, A. (2006) 'Towards a general theory of political representation', *Journal of Politics*, 68 (1): 1–21.

Rittberger, B. (2009) 'The historical origins of the EU's system of representation', *Journal of European Public Policy*, 16 (1): 43–61.

Rossteutscher, S. (ed.) (2005) *Democracy and the Role of Associations. Political, Organizational, and Social Contexts*, London, New York: Routledge.

Saward, Michael (2009) 'Authorisation and authenticity: representation and the unelected'. *Journal of Political Philosophy*, 17 (1): 1–22.

Saward, M. (2010) *The Representative Claim*, Oxford: Oxford University Press.

Schmidt, V.A. (2006) *Democracy in Europe: The EU and National Politics*, Oxford: Oxford University Press.

Sintomer, Y. (2010) 'Random selection, republican self-government, and deliberative democracy', *Constellations*, 17 (3): 472–487.

Smith, G. (2009) *Democratic Innovations*, Cambridge: Cambridge University Press.

Steffek, J., Kissling, C. and Nanz, P. (eds) (2008) *Civil Society Participation in European and Global Governance: A Cure for the Democratic Deficit?*, Houndmills; Basingstoke: Palgrave Macmillan.

Talpin, J. and Monnoyer-Smith, L. (2013) 'Talking with the wind? Discussion on the quality of deliberation in the Ideal–EU project', in R. Kies and P. Nanz (eds) *Is Europe Listening to Us? Successes and failures of EU citizen consultations*, London: Ashgate, 125–152.

Talpin, J. and Wojcik, S. (2010) 'When the youth learn about political issues: A comparison of the learning effects of on-line and face-to-face discussions on climate change', owned by author.

Trenz, H. and Michailidou, A. (2013) 'Mediatized representative politics in the European Union: towards audience democracy?', *Journal of European Public Policy*, 20 (2): 260–277.

Wright, S. (2007) 'A virtual European public sphere? The Futurum discussion forum', *Journal of European Public Policy*, 14 (8): 1167–1185.

Yang, M. (2013) 'Europe's new communication policy and the introduction of transnational deliberative citizens' involvement projects', in R. Kies and P. Nanz (eds) *Is Europe Listening to Us? Successes and Failures of EU Citizen Consultations*, Farnham: Ashgate Publishing, 17–34.

Young, I.M. (2000) *Inclusion and Democracy*, Oxford: Oxford University Press.

10 Mediated representative politics

The Euro-crisis and the politicization of the EU

Hans-Jörg Trenz

Coping with crisis: the EU representative system beyond its limits

The multiple crises of Europe have stretched the idea of political representation of an integrated European social, economic and political space that is constituted by the European Union (EU) beyond its limits. Maybe for the first time in the history of European integration, the pooling of EU sovereignty cannot be justified as a 'positive sum' game with the promise of benefits for all. The new monetary policies have clear redistributive consequences 'that damage' or 'that impact on' the social and economic prospects/assets for large parts of the population. This impinges on some of the premises of the EU representative architecture,[1] which was primarily designed for the representation of constituencies, either nationally and territorially, or sectorally in the form of stakeholders or organized civil society. But is the EU representative architecture also ripe to carry out a struggle over redistribution? And how can such redistributive conflicts be channelled and turned into gains or losses of legitimacy?

In the EU multi-level political system, the representation of constituencies could rely on a couple of conflict avoidance strategies. Unitary representation could be safeguarded through high levels of aggregation in the form of national interest, specific group identities or abstract notions of the public good. Conflicts along these lines were expressed mainly in functional or identitarian terms, and less along redistributive lines. The EU representative system was thus projected upon a functional and identitarian matrix, and only rudimentarily differentiated along ideological lines (Hooghe and Marks 2004; Hooghe *et al.* 2004). Territorially, ethnically or functionally segmented groups could be allocated within the 'unity in diversity' of the Union, without necessarily entering into conflict with each other. The EU representative system was therefore intrinsically and probably also intentionally 'de-politicized'. The inbuilt conflict avoidance strategies were effective to the extent that they prolonged the low salience of EU representative politics, its technocratic character and a preference for identity ('what we are') over redistribution ('what we get'). Some integration theorists talked in this regard of an emerging post-national polity, in which redistributive conflicts were banned during the first decades in favour of a functional logic of integration (Haas 1968), which according to some observers has been replaced more recently by a 'new politics of identity' (Hooghe and Marks 2009).

Economic crisis has challenged this representation of a 'unity in diversity', in terms of accommodting different functional requirements and identitarian projects for the benefit of all and the promise of 'equal living conditions' across the territory and the polity that is constituted by the Union. The loss of credibility of positive sum games of integration predictably brings redistributive conflicts back to the fore, which can build effectively on latent structural cleavages among the countries and the populations of the Union. The return of redistributive conflicts was not only unpredicted. It also breaks with one of the doctrines of the EU governance system, which has been designed for the 'regulation' of social and political risk, rather than resource 'redistribution' (Hix 1998: 39). For many EU scholars, this inbuilt restriction of the EU to regulatory policies was not only a functional requirement, but also normatively desirable. The common assumption was that the EU is not ripe for carrying out redistributive conflicts in the double sense that the governments as national interest representatives are unwilling to concede to the redistributive effects of integration and the people as national constituents unwilling to support them (Scharpf 2009).

Under these self-imposed conditions limiting integration and democratic empowerment the negative consequences of crisis have led to a major institutional impasse and a return to intergovernmentalism as the dominant mode of 'governing' crisis and distributing costs among the Eurozone countries. De-politicized crisis governance bypasses established systems of representative democracy, transnationally and nationally. It reinforces a new *raison d'état* that allows national governments to deprive the establishment of an effective system of shared accountability and control at the EU level, while at the same time loosening the constraints imposed by national legislative authorities (Wolf 1999).

The assumption to be tested out in this chapter is that this particular mode of 'crisis governance' can be turned into an opportunity for the (re)politicizing the existing 'de-politicized' system of representation (Statham and Trenz 2012). As already observed by Brunkhorst (2007: 85), de-politicized post-national governance comes at the cost of intensifying crisis perceptions that affect the political system at large. In dealing with routines of governance, EU representative politics have been operating under conditions of low salience and restricted public attention. The economic and monetary (and previously constitutional) crisis marks the transition from the routine to the extraordinary. It is socially and politically manifested in accelerated social change that correlates with high levels of public mobilization and visibility (Holten 1987). Under these conditions, de-politicized crisis governance potentially aggravates the manifestations of public unrest and discontent. The crisis of legitimacy of the political system is related not just to economic downturn and cuts in public expenditures, but equally so to the perceived insufficiencies of political representation, accountability and control. The question then is not only how negative consequences of crisis can be 'governed' but also how they can be publically 're-presented' and translated into new and old cleavages that (trans)form the system of political representation in the EU.

My proposal for a research avenue that observes the transformation of the EU representative system is therefore to analyse the changing media dynamics through which the legitimacy of the EU is contested. The current crisis stands for the enhanced media attention under which EU politics and institutions operate. It marks the return of the public to EU representative politics, not only in the form of public unrest and the mobilization of affected parties, but even more so in the form of the public and media drama through which the crisis unfolds. In the literature on EU democracy, the role of the mass media, or of the new digital media, is discussed mainly in relation to the possibilities of enhancing more direct and participatory forms democracy (such as e-democracy) (Reedy and Wells 2009; Ward and Gibson 2009). What is rarely taken into consideration is the constitutive role of mass media as the stage of representative politics. In the following, I will approach this topic under the heading of 'EU-mediated representative politics'. In the first section, I will formulate what democratic representation is, and how it is generated through public speech. This allows me in a second step to focus on the role of the mass media as the principal arena for generating public visibility for representative politics. I will then turn to some of the intrinsic problems with ways in which EU's representative politics can potentially work in an era of 'mediated politics'. I conclude with an outlook on EU-mediated representative politics in times of crisis.

What is democratic representation?

Following Hanna Pitkin's straightforward definition, 'representing means acting in the interest of the represented in a manner responsive to them' (Pitkin 1972 [1967]: 209). Political representation thus occurs not only in a proactive strategic way but also as a response. It symbolically interlinks two positions, the agent and the principal, in such a way that the former can be held accountable for her actions by the latter. Political representation is in this sense to be seen as a *public* arrangement (ibid.: 221). It is part of *public opinion*, which is made from the preferences and opinions expressed by the voters, the rationales and justifications delivered by the representatives and the norms and expectations enshrined in the political system. Even non-responsiveness, for example of expert governance, can only be justified in the name of the *public* interest (ibid.: 224). For a theory of political representation, it is further important to note that the public is always at both ends of the process (ibid.). The representative's pursuit of public interest and response to public opinion cannot be overridden by pure self-interest, otherwise she would cease to be a representative. In equal terms, the readiness of the single citizen to vote for a candidate cannot be detached from the life world of communication, exchanges of opinions and interactions with other voters, as it is only through the latter that public opinion, which is expressed in the vote, is constituted.

This basic notion of political representation as a *public* arrangement shall be used in the following, first, to reconceptualize political representation as a triadic and mediatized communicative act, and, second, to approach the particular form and process of *democratic* representation. The reconceptualization of political representation as a triadic and mediated configuration between political agents (claimants), constituents and audiences has been prominently proposed by Michael Saward (2010). Saward defines representation as a claim to be representative for someone or something. He is however not primarily interested in the strategic act of claims-making but focuses precisely on the dynamic and performative aspects of representative claims-making, which operates through public and media discourse. From this perspective, the audience becomes decisive as the representative claims-making body with wider resonance, which accepts (or rejects) a claim as being representative of something or someone. The process of representative claims-making thus needs to be studied in relation to its capacities to create wider societal resonance and reception. At the same time, the mediatized character of a constituent–agent–audience relationship needs to be emphasized. In modern mass democracies, the formal relationship between the principal and the agent is filtered through the mass media and thus intrinsically linked to contingent processes of public reception and resonance.

Understanding political representation as a *public* arrangement is useful, in a second step, to approach the particularity of *democratic* representation both as a form and as a process. Democratic representation is not defined here by its degree of popularity or through formal aggregative procedures. It is neither externally nor internally determined,for example through the quality of particular inputs or outputs, but rather located in the generalized validity of representative claims-making to stand for the public or for the collective as a whole. As a form, democratic representation relates to any expression/symbolization of the collective will (Urbinati and Warren 2008: 391).[2] Democratic representation thus transcends the particularity of a representative–constituent relationship through its claims of generalized validity. It is in other words made by the claim of a partial subject (individual, as in the form of a representative claimant or corporate, as in the form of a Parliament) to stand for the general will. As a process, democratic representation is about collective will formation. It is made here by the contestation of all who claim to represent the collective will. As such, it is processed through public speech that meets the resonance of the general audience. Democratic representation is however not simply generated at the input side of the legislative process through public discussions, elections and referenda, but encompasses the whole process of 'law-making', its public salience and visibility.[3]

The assumption of democratic representation (in contrast to simple aggregative mechanisms) is further that this contestation substantially is not only about the accommodation of particular interests but also about the validity of norms that apply to the process of collective will formation. The underlying norms of democratic will formation are codified in the form of (1) equality (all can participate in the formation of the collective will), (2) rationality (the formation of the collective will is informed through substantive argumentative processes), (3) publicity (the underlying forms and processes need to be publically visible and accessible), and (4) effectiveness (the expression of the collective will should have a chance to become effective and empowered).[4]

My claim here is that a theory of democratic representation should analyse democratic will formation not only through the generation of inputs (the inclusive–participatory and the epistemic dimension of collective will formation) or of outputs (the dimension of efficiency and empowerment of the collective will). Crucial for the democratic representation of the collective will are further the intermediary level and processes, i.e. the question of how representative claims are channelled and made public. In this sense, the representative claim as defined by Saward (2010) can be also understood as a claim to publicity, which lies at the heart of public sphere theory. As Habermas observed as early as 1962: Organizations and delegates 'display representation'. 'The aura of personally represented authority returns as an aspect of publicity.' Representation is less an element in the internal structure of an association 'than an expression of its claim to publicity' (Habermas 1989 [1962]: 200). Democratic representation requires such claims to be publicly raised, i.e. made visible and accessible for the public. The visibility of the process means that it needs to re-present itself, create its own form that is communicated visibly. Democratic legitimation is therefore ultimately dependent on a well functioning system of mass communication to generate such representations of the collective as a body of self-legislation and control.

The point, already implicit in Hanna Pitkin, is then that political representation is generated through public speech. Democratic representation stands the publicity test through which the validity of the claims (or arguments) 'to represent' someone are publicly scrutinized and contested. The 'truth'- or 'validity'-generating potential of publicity is however measured not in substantive terms but rather in procedural terms in its capacity to mediate different positions, generalize them and make them publicly visible and accessible. Publicity is thus perceived as an effective mechanism that 'mediates' between the positions of the representative and the represented. Following John Stuart Mill's famous account, publicity is seen as a device to hold public choices accountable both from the perspective of office holders in the act of representing and of citizens in the act of voting. This 'self-disciplining effect of public speech is however of no use unless the public is not also empowered and qualified to form a "sound judgment"' (Mill 1998 [1861]: 360). The formation of the 'sound judgment' of the public is carried by an independent, self-steering mass media. Representative democracy is in this sense dependent on the mediating capacities of an autonomous mass media system.

Publicity, which is measured in the public visibility and resonance of the representative claim, relates to a neglected function of political representation perceived as a triadic relationship between representatives, represented and the audience. From this perspective, the focus is no longer on the normative quality of democratic representation but on its sociological function to generate societal visibility (Nassehi 2002). Democratic representation points to the part that needs to be held accountable for the whole. Representative democracy therefore also needs to safeguard the visibility of both the parts and their relationship to the whole in the public realm. Representation generates societal visibility, but of a particular type of society, which describes itself as a collective of self-determination. This points to a core condition of success for the establishment of representative system of democracy, which can be measured in its capacities to generate communicative spaces or to constitute a public sphere (Eder 1985). These capacities are well developed in national democracies through the institutionalization of public mediating infrastructures that guarantee continuous communication flows between office holders and national audiences or electorates. Representatives can in this sense be identified through the proceeding of publicly visible forms, arguments or discourses. In this sense, the representative system of democracy reproduces itself as a visible unit and differentiates itself into positions that can be held publically accountable.

In the EU's representative system this fundamental link between political representation and public visibility is interrupted. Not only does the EU suffer from a public communication deficit and is frequently found to be non-responsive and unaccountable to the general public – but in addition, the EU largely adopts publicity-generating instruments in the form of campaigns or the launching of public debates that remain detached from public resonance (Brüggemann 2010). In absence of a mediating infrastructure for the multiple claims of political representation that are raised in the EU setting, the community-building dynamics of democratic representation are put on hold. Democratic representation cannot be easily generated and reproduced through shared meanings and identities. There is no correspondence between the voice of the many who claim to represent and the restricted attention of the few who listen or who wish to be represented. Audiences are themselves fragmented into loose and sporadic attention cycles that can hardly be imagined as the 'body collective' of democratic representative politics. The EU has no deficit in terms of actors and institutions who can legitimately claim to represent and to channel the will of the people. It has also no deficit in terms of norms and procedures through which these claims are given public expression. Yet the EU has a deficit of amplifying these claims and of meeting the type of resonance and reception that gives the representative claim legitimacy in the eyes of the body of the citizens.[5]

The question for representative democracy in the EU (which has been described as the 'multi-level representative system of the EU': see Crum and Fossum 2009) is then how political representation, which occurs in the EU through various forms and procedures can undergo the validity test of publicity. The chances of reuniting the fragmented landscape of political representation in Europe are intrinsically linked to its capacities to draw the attention of the mass media, and to build a European public sphere of mass communication (Koopmans and Statham 2010). How can political representation in the EU be turned into a *public* arrangement of mediated representative politics?

EU mediated representative politics: its potential and limitation

In seeking to understand the potential dynamics of EU mediatized representative politics, it is necessary to analyse which particular types of audience are drawn to which of the cleavages that structure the field of political representation in the EU.[6] The party system, which focuses public attention and will formation within unitary nation state structures of political representation, is frequently found to be insufficient as a carrier of EU representative politics where possible audience–constituent relationships are multiplied and cannot rely on mediation through the established channels of unitary mass media (Hix 1999). Approaching political representation as a triadic communicative act allows us instead to analyse EU political representation not in formal terms, as constituted by and channelled through political parties, but, in more general terms, as a process of public mediation through which representative relationships (or representative claims raised by all kind of actors) are selected and amplified through the mass media. In this context, formalized representative relationships are conducive to but also constrained by public and mass media attention.

In previous projects, we have been able to observe indeed that the EU approaches a *modus operandum* of mediated representative politics (de Wilde *et al.* 2013; Liebert and Trenz 2008). The European Commission, European party groups and European civil society organizations, for example, frequently act as surrogate representatives of such groups without a direct voice in the political process: minorities, future generations, or even humanity as a whole. In these cases of surrogate representation, the representative can no longer be expected to be held directly accountable or even be responsive to the represented (Mansbridge 2003). In this sense, claimant-driven representative politics in the EU accounts for the more open and flexible ways of building principal–agent relationships in a context where clear templates for formalizing political representation are lacking and the legitimacy of political agents remains heavily contested (Trenz 2009). Legitimacy, in the sense of broad social acceptance, depends instead on public accountability, in turn achieved through the media-controlled reception of the representative claim by a third part: the audience. At the same time, there are also democratic mechanisms usually linked to mobilization from below, elections or referendums that compel representative claimants to adjust their claims to the conditions of publicness, which, however, remain confined within national public spaces.

The role of the mass media in this multi-level representative system of the EU polity, where direct links to democratic constituents are harder to establish, is crucial. Mass media has become the central arena for focusing public attention on the ways in which the legitimacy of the EU is debated and increasingly contested (Koopmans and Statham 2010). As discussed earlier, the role of the mass media in mediated representative politics has become much more decisive than merely providing and controlling the stage for representative claims. Forms of audience-driven representative politics steadily gain prominence, whereby territorially dispersed groups, who escape the communication management of representative claimants and their territorially confined constituents, raise their voice as affected parties in European and global politics. Nevertheless, the media (old or new), which constitute the main channel for expressing approval or disapproval with the performance of the political system, in most instances continue to be nationally confined and, thus, serving audiences within formalized national representative systems. This leads to an asymmetry of representation, between its old and new, national and transnational, formal and informal variants.

The above points to the relevance of mediated representative politics, but media effects remain dispersed over various arenas and can hardly account for the emergence of a unitary public sphere. The fragmented media sphere points to a mismatch between 'new' representatives in search of 'new' constituencies and 'old' representatives that respond to 'old' constituencies that coincide with nationally confined media audiences. The EU speaks for particular stakeholders, for professional groups, for minorities or in the name of the general interest (the EU constituencies) while 'the people' of Europe are rarely envisaged as an addressable entity (and if so, in the negative form, in the sense that 'the people of Europe', the European *demos*, does not exist) (Kohler-Koch and Finke 2007).

Finally, the difference between old and new media and their various ways of enhancing representation needs to be emphasized. New media technologies are not only relevant as a facilitator of e-democracy through citizens' engagement, networking or direct forms of democratic empowerment. In the public communication practices employed by EU institutions and the Parliament, new media are used, above all, to create stronger representative ties with the audience (Michailidou 2012). In our own work, we have critically scrutinized the potential of the new media to transnationalize the confined public spheres that were constituted by the old media, and to build new representative relationships with the dispersed constituents of the EU. In the context of EU Parliamentary elections, for instance, new media technologies do not simply enhance user participation through institutionalized forms of e-democracy. At a more basic level, they also confirm the trend towards an EU media democracy, in which political action becomes public action and EU representative actors operate increasingly outside the institutional and parliamentary arena to mobilize mass audiences in favour or against the the European cause. This is a relatively new development. Since early 2000, the Internet has succeeded in connecting millions of users to a mass audience. This mass audience is served by a few news organizations that regularly inform about EU politics. In particular newspapers can reach out online and focalize public opinion formation to a highly significant degree. With regard to the role of social media, the sharing of political content is paramount, not so much for the distribution of user-generated content but for the sharing of prefabricated news by professional journalists. In terms of content, these shared news stories are often found to be biased towards more EU-critical or Eurosceptical messages (De Wilde *et al.* 2013).

For understanding how the EU's representative politics can potentially work in an era of 'mediated politics' it is necessary to look at how the dispersed and episodic attention of European publics can be focused around events of shared relevance. The creative moment of representative claims-making in inventing new constituents is restricted by the rather limited options for audience formation and mobilization of public attention. The repertoire for public evaluation and scrutiny of the representative claim still remains bound to conventional schemes and traditions. While representative politics are rapidly transforming with new agents and constituents coming to the fore, the audience remains more static for the double reason that even in a 'politicized Union' public attention is to be considered a scarce resource and that audiences remain institutionally, territorially and often also culturally confined. There is thus a structural disparity between the new arenas for EU representative politics and the old media spaces of democracy (which are also replicated online).

Based on this observation of a mismatch between representative claims-making and audience attention in the European arena of representative politics, we can discuss the possibility that disempowered audiences as national electorates develop a particular way of contesting the EU not on the substantial policy issues at stake but on the character of the political system. If policies restricted to expert arenas and epistocracies are hard to challenge, a more fundamental EU resistance is mobilized (De Wilde *et al.* 2013). Audiences might thus favour a shift of EU representative politics from the restricted possibilities of authorization and control to system opposition that challenges the fundamental legitimacy of the EU (Mair 2007). These latter dynamics are best illustrated in the self-defeating dynamics of European referendums or European Parliament (EP) elections. Elections, which put the representativeness of the EU at test, lead to the formation of audiences that reject their ascribed role as constituents of the EU polity and revert to a particular form of opposition that questions the EU as a legitimate framework for democratic representation. Do such self-defeating dynamics also underlie public unrest and mobilization in response to crisis? This possibility will be tested out in the last part of this chapter with a prospective view on political representation and mass-mediated communication in times of crisis.

Mediated representative politics in times of crisis

The constitutional, institutional and monetary debt crises ('Eurocrisis') display the well known insufficiencies and lack of consolidation of the EU representative system and the potential for its public contestation through a new dynamic of EU-mediated representative politics. The public and mediated responses to crisis increase the principled uncertainty with regard to who can claim to be representative in the EU context and how these claims can be addressed to and received by the audience. In the recent literature, this trend in the polarization of public opinion and popular contestation about the ideational components of the EU political system has been described in terms of the enhanced politicization of the EU (De Wilde and Zürn 2012; Hooghe and Marks 2009).[7] These new dynamics have already become manifested in the politicization of the constitutional reform process as the background to a particular form of representative claims-making that is about the allocation of popular sovereignty in an emerging transnational polity (Statham and Trenz 2012; Trenz 2010). More specifically, the politicization of the EU is held responsible for a new salience of collective identities and of identity conflicts as an element of EU representative politics.

European integration is approached then in principled terms, expressing support or opposition not with particular policies or political agents but with the system as a whole (Checkel and Katzenstein 2009).

The public unrest and mobilization in response to the Eurocrisis might further accentuate the shift of the agenda from representative politics *within* the EU to representation *of* the EU, from interest politics to identity politics and from partisan contestation to EU-polity contestation (De Wilde and Trenz 2012; Mair 2007). In the compound system of political representation of the EU, partisan contestation along ideological cleavage lines is only one of many ways in which representative politics unfold. The potential dynamics of EU-mediated representative politics rather account for the increasing salience of pro- and anti-European cleavage lines at the intergovernmental level, within the parliamentarian arena and as a structuring element of public discourse (Marks *et al.* 2006; Taggart and Szczerbiak 2008).

In this respect, mediated representative politics in the context of crisis governance and responses concern less single actors' strategies and more the building of broader discursive coalitions with the media, where the aim is to set a 'moral agenda' that resonates within a wider audience. Political representation is then primarily structured through the polarization of identitarian projects, which help people to interpret the EU and allocate their preferences. These new identity dynamics of European integration do not simply operate on the basis of a distinction of political projects – they also divide and polarize populations into winners and losers, movers and stayers, Europeanists and national sovereignists.

In face of these new elite and audience divisions, enhanced conflicts in response to the Eurocrisis are no longer manifested purely in the form of a 'new 'identity politics'. The cleavage line is not simply drawn between pro-integrationist elites and nationalist populists (see: Hooghe and Marks 2009). The Eurocrisis is rather interpreted as a challenge to the core founding myth that integration leads to stability and growth for all (countries and citizens). Representative politics turn under these conditions first and foremost around questions of redistribution within the EU, between countries, within countries, and between social constituencies of winners and losers within and across countries, something which national executives and political elites previously swept under the carpet in the public domain, to ensure a common purpose and unity that would drive integration forward (Statham and Trenz 2012: 164). Redistributive conflicts remain in this sense closely linked to the contestation of elite preferences about the delegation of sovereignty and the popular protection of national prerogatives. Such new redistributive conflicts are nevertheless not easily translated into the old left–right cleavage, but rather seem to transcend traditional ideological cleavage lines. In all Eurozone countries, the bailout measures are contested by the protectionist left and the populist right, while a great coalition between mainstream left and right parties steps forward as the defenders of the common currency.

Another distinctive feature of political representation in this new context is that the dynamics of mediated representative politics seem to escape the control of institutional arenas and political parties. Public responses to crisis are driven by a dialectic of depoliticization and repoliticization, i.e. by the conflict avoidance strategies of mainstream political actors and the escalating reactions to crisis amplified by the mass media. The closing of institutional opportunity structures for participation as part of the official crisis responses is thus intrinsically related to the opening of new discursive opportunities for public mobilization. In the case of the Eurocrisis, the chances of access and influence for citizens through institutional opportunities are challenged by the retreat to epistocratic forms of economic and financial governance. In contrast to previous stages of integration, the pro-Europeanists carry a defensive strategy of conflict avoidance and a reversal of politicization. The Fiscal Stability Treaty, which constitutes an act of legislation outside the framework of EU law, illustrates the new constellation between epistocracy and democracy. Supranational representatives, whose mandate remains constitutionally fragile and contested, escape the constraints of public control and legitimacy by further delegating sovereignty to experts in an unprecedented way. Public choices are thus taken out of the arena of representative politics and implemented in the form of rigid regulatory action, legal obligations and automatic compliance mechanisms. Popular vote is excluded, postponed or reduced to enforced consent.

The depoliticized bodies of technocratic governance that have been set up to deal with the negative consequences of the crisis have been described mainly as bypassing the sovereign power of the people. Depoliticization is taking place however within a system of transnational law, which is already intrinsically democratic and has subscribed to the principles of representative democracy. A perspective of mediated representative politics is helpful in understanding how the depoliticized bodies of decision-making that are responsible for financial and monetary governance are externally 'repoliticized'. The displacement of democratic politics in these areas increases the feeling of impotence of the citizens, who are still formally empowered to exercise control but *de facto* are forced either to consent or to turn to populist protest votes (which, again increase the uncertainty of the whole setting of political representation). Another displacement effect is the opening of arenas for symbolic side politics that 'stage' representative democracy through the expression of identity and popular resistance. Protest actors under these conditions counter the 'politics of depoliticization' by opening up discursive opportunities for gaining visibility in the mass media, mobilizing public opinion and achieving legitimacy in the public discourse as the only 'true representatives' of the people.

This active role of the mass media as the 'organ' of popular discontent is then increasingly related to the 'depoliticization' strategies of political elites and governments. In a 'mediated politics' situation, the retreat of actors such as governments and mainstream political parties from the core of the political system to 'depoliticized' and 'epistocratic' forms of decision-making is insufficient to prevent, and in some cases might even provoke, public contestation, facilitating media access for marginal parties and less resourceful protest actors from civil society and simply giving prominence to the voice of populism.

Public contestation in response to the Eurocrisis should therefore not be seen as symptomatic of insufficiencies in the democratic design of the EU, but of the lack of political will to implement procedures and obey democratic law. Such a situation is open to criticism and control. It can develop through emancipation from within, and does not need to rely on external impulses for reform or enlightenment from the outside. It is therefore also possible that the collective resistance that is generated against the current dominance of national executives and technocratic law making are generated from within the EU system of political representation, with the potential to generate genuine processes of democratization. The question then is not so much how the Eurocrisis is transforming EU representative democracy, but how it is contributing to its implementation and to the application of the rules and procedures that have been set in place over the last decades. Enhanced visibility of the crisis and its negative consequences are the conditions for such an emancipation process to be triggered off (Brunkhorst 2012).

Conclusion

The dynamics of EU-mediated representative politics highlighted in this chapter promise insights into the justificatory resources that European integration currently draws on, as well as an understanding of the type of social constituents and media audiences with which legitimation relationships are established. The proposed research focus on mediated representative politics is primarily meant to contribute to the understanding of the 'making of' political representation not to its normative evaluation. Political representation is reconceived as a dynamic communicative process that takes place in the public sphere, filtered and shaped by the media environment. This expanded notion of political representation as a triadic configuration between representatives, constituents and the audience opens a new perspective of empirical legitimation research, which entails identifying the sequence of representative claims and the scope, conditions and directions of legitimation.

In the context of crisis governance and responses, the traits of audience democracy seem to constrain rather than to enhance the legitimacy of the EU. The perceived negative consequences of economic and monetary crisis accelerate the proclaimed shift from partisan politics to identity politics as part of the new politicized dynamics of European integration (Hooghe and Marks 2009). Representative politics shift attention from formal political representation through political parties to a form of polity contestation that questions the fundamental legitimacy of the EU. Media representations of the crisis are linked to frequent disinformation, a preference of emotional over factual content, unequal opportunities for political representatives to access the media sphere and an inbuilt nationalism of media frames and interpretations. The problem here is not so much that mediated representation unfolds mainly through emotions and symbolic side politics, but rather that it results in a populist and nationalist backlash. The politicization of European integration has in this sense thus far rather endorsed the renationalization of EU representative politics and strengthened those actors who oppose delegated authority to the EU.

At the same time, I do not want to suggest that the representative politics in times of crisis are symptomatic of a paradigmatic change from parliamentarian to post-democratic political representation. My perspective of mediated representative politics also illustrates the limitations of the post-democratic executive federalism of which Habermas (2011) speaks. Media representations of the crisis also have the potential to enhance what can be called accountability through publicity. In the sense of John Stuart Mill, the recent (re)politicization of depoliticized executive and epistocratic governance can be interpreted as a form of mediated representative politics which, through public debates, apply the validity test of publicity. Its 'disciplining effect' on executive and expert choices is hard to predict as the latter enter the media game of representative politics with a counter-strategy that uncovers the irrationality and 'populism' of the opponent. Mediated representative politics also have a decisive impact on the public choices of the voters, who are exposed to representative claims by the anti-globalists, the anti-Europeanists, the nationalists and the populists. The extent to which their public choices will also be 'disciplined' by the effects of publicity (to speak again with John Stuart Mill) depends on media performance and the quality of media coverage of the EU (which according to numerous studies is much better than its reputation).

The depoliticized official system of political representation of the EU does therefore not preclude enhanced partisan contestation, nor does it exclude alternatives of citizens' representations and deliberations. For the time being, the empowerment of the direct voice of the people remains restricted to single, though decisive, moments (like referendums), at which the legitimacy of the EU polity is subject to heavy contestations and public and media debates. In the context of EU crisis governance, such politicized moments of popular mobilization and resistance have thus far remained decoupled from the institutional structures and procedures of political representation that are in place, which renders their expression sometimes even more violent.

Ultimately, the new dynamics of EU-mediated representation and audience attention need to be understood not only in terms of the media salience and news coverage of EU representative politics but, more broadly, in terms of the general transformation of representative politics and its impact on the generation of political legitimacy of the EU. In order to understand the legitimacy impact of media communication on European integration, we need to look beyond the instrumental use of media by political actors/institutions and political parties and develop a more encompassing approach of the public sphere. With this widened focus, the public sphere can be reconstructed not merely as the infrastructure for the *mediation* of EU representative politics, but as the place where the representative claims-making of the new transnational elites resonates, meets with national (or other) counter-claimants and informs public opinion and will formation.

Notes

1 The term 'EU representative architecture' is meant to substitute the common parlance of an 'EU system of political representation'. It relates to the unfinished character of the EU building and the ongoing competition among the architects about its possible completion.
2 This idea of a symbolization of the collective is different from the Schmittian notion of an ideal representation or 'embodiment' of the collective through the representative (see: Pollak *et al.* 2009: 10). What counts is not the 'presence of the invisible', but its symbolization through public acts of speech and discourse.
3 This points to the intrinsic relationship between representative and deliberative democracy, see: Chambers (2003) and Eriksen and Fossum (2012).
4 For the trade-off between equality and rationality or what has been called the participatory and epistemic dimensions of democracy and its institutional solutions see Eder (1995) and Eriksen (2011). The condition of effectiveness or empowerment has recently been spotlighted in debates on post-democracy or post-national democracy, as it is here that the symbolic expression of the collective will is seen as increasingly detached from executive or epistocratic decision-making. See Fraser (2007).
5 This public sphere deficit is well documented by EU communication research with a number of comparative findings on the restricted scope of media coverage of the EU. See De Vreese (2001); Koopmans and Statham (2010); Trenz (2005) and Wessler *et al.* (2008).
6 The following draws on Michailidou and Trenz (2013).
7 The following draws on Statham and Trenz (2012), Chapter 6.

References

Brunkhorst, H. (2007) 'Die Legitimationskrise der Weltgesellschaft. Global rule of law, global constitutionalism und Weltstaatlichkeit', in M. Albert and R. Stichweh (eds) *Weltstaat und Weltstaatlichkeit*, Wiesbaden: Verlag für Sozialwisenschaften, pp. 63–108.

Brunkhorst, H. (2012) 'Kollektiver Bonapartismus? Demokratie in der europäischen Krise', *Blätter für deutsche und internationale Politik*, 12 (4): 83–93.

Brüggemann, M. (2010) 'Information policy and the public sphere: EU communications and the promises of dialogue and transparency', *Javnost – The Public*, 17 (1): 5–22.

Chambers, S. (2003) 'Deliberative democratic theory', *Annual Review of Political Science*, 6 (30): 7–326.

Checkel, J.T. and Katzenstein, P.J. (2009) 'The politicization of European identity', in J.T. Checkel and P.J. Katzenstein (eds) *European Identity*, Cambridge: Cambridge University Press, pp. 1–25.

Crum, B. and Fossum, J.E. (2009) 'The multilevel parlimentary field: a framework for theorising representative democracy in the EU', *European Political Science Review*, 1: 249–271.

De Vreese, C.H. (2001) '"Europe" in the news: A cross-national comparative study of the news coverage of key EU events', *European Union Politics*, 2 (3): 283–307.

De Wilde, P. and Trenz, H.-J. (2012) 'Denouncing European integration: Euroscepticism as polity contestation', *European Journal of Social Theory*, 15 (4): 537–554.

De Wilde, P. and Zürn, M. (2012) 'Can the politicization of European integration be reversed?', *Journal of Common Market Studies*, 50 (1): 137–153.

De Wilde, P., Michailidou, A. and Trenz, H.-J. (2013) *Contesting Europe: Exploring Euroscepticism in online media coverage*, Colchester: ECPR Press.

Eder, K. (1985) *Geschichte als Lernprozess. Zur Pathogenese politischer Modernität in Deutschland*, Frankfurt a. M.: Suhrkamp.

Eder, K. (1995) 'The institutionalisation of environmentalism: Ecological discourse and the second transformation of the public sphere', in B. Wynne, B. Szerszinski and S. Lash (eds) *Risk, Modernity and the Environment: Towards a New Ecology*, London: Sage, pp. 202–223.

Eriksen, E.O. (2011) 'Governance between expertise and democracy: the case of European security', *Journal of European Public Policy*, 18 (8): 1169–1189.

Eriksen, E.O. and Fossum, J.E. (2012) 'Representation through deliberation – the European case', *Constellations*, 19 (2): 325–339.

Fraser, N. (2007) 'Transnationalizing the public sphere: on the legitimacy and efficacy of public opinion in a post-Westphalian world', *Theory, Culture & Society*, 24: 7–30.

Haas, E.B. (1968) *The Uniting of Europe. Political, Social and Economic Forces, 1950–1957*, Stanford, CA: Stanford University Press.

Habermas, J. (1989 [1962]) *The Structural Transformation of the Public Sphere*, Cambridge, MA: MIT Press.

Habermas, J. (2011) *Zur Verfassung Europas*, Frankfurt a. M.: Suhrkamp.

Hix, S. (1998) 'The study of the European Union II: the "New Governance" agenda and its rival', *European Journal of Public Policy*, 5 (1): 38–65.

Hix, S. (1999) 'Dimensions and alignments in European Union politics: cognitive constraints and partisan responses', *European Journal of Political Research*, 35: 69–106.

Holten, R.J. (1987) 'The idea of crisis in modern society', *British Journal of Sociology*, 38 (4): 502–520.

Hooghe, L. and Marks, G. (2004) 'Does identity or economic rationality drive public opinion on European integration?', *Political Science and Politics*, 37 (3): 420. doi:10.1017.S1049096504004585.

Hooghe, L. and Marks, G. (2009) 'A postfunctionalist theory of European integration: from permissive consensus to constraining dissensus', *British Journal of Political Science*, 39 (1): 1–23.

Hooghe, L., Marks, G. and Wilson, C.J. (2004) 'Does left/right structure party positions on European integration?', in G. Marks and M.R. Steenbergen (eds) *European Integration and Political Conflict*, New York: Cambridge University Press, pp. 120–140.

Kohler-Koch, B. and Finke, B. (2007) 'The institutional shaping of EU–society relations: A contribution to democracy via participation?', *Journal of Civil Society*, 3 (3): 205–221.

Koopmans, R. and Statham, P. (eds) (2010) *The Making of a European Public Sphere: The Europeanisation of Media Discourse and Political Contention*, Cambridge: Cambridge University Press.

Liebert, U. and Trenz, H.-J. (2008) 'Mass media and contested meanings: EU constitutional politics after popular rejection', European University Institute: RSCAS Working Papers 28.

Mair, P. (2007) 'Political opposition and the European Union', *Government and Opposition*, 42 (1): 1–17.

Mansbridge, J. (2003) 'Rethinking representation', *American Political Science Review*, 97 (4): 515–528.

Marks, G., Hooghe, L., Nelson, M. and Edwards, E. (2006) 'Party competition and European integration in the East and West: different structure, same causality', *Comparative Political Studies*, 39 (2): 155–175.

Michailidou, A. (2012) *The European Union Online*, Berlin: Akademiker Verlag.

Michailidou, A. and Trenz, H.-J. (2013) 'Mediated representative politics in the European Union: towards audience democracy?', *Journal of European Public Policy*, 20 (2): 260–277.

Mill, J.S. (1998 [1861]) 'Considerations on representative government', in *On Liberty and Other Essays*, Oxford: Oxford University Press.

Nassehi, A. (2002) 'Politik der Staates oder Politik der Gesellschaft. Kollektivität als Problemformel des Politischen', in K.-U. Hellemann and R. Schmalz-Bruns (eds) *Niklas Luhmanns politische Soziologie*, Frankfurt a. M: Suhrkamp.

Pitkin, H.F. (1972 [1967]) *The Concept of Representation*, Berkeley, CA: University of California Press.

Pollak, J., Bátora, J., Mokre, M., Sigalas, E. and Slominski, P. (2009) 'On political representation. myths and challenges', RECON Online Working Paper 03, ARENA: University of Oslo, available at http://ideas.repec.org/p/erp/reconx/p0042.html (accessed 6 January 2014).

Reedy, J. and Wells, C. (2009) 'Information, the internet and direct democracy', in A. Chadwick and P.N. Howard (eds) *Routledge Handbook of Internet Politics*, London: Routledge, pp. 157–172.

Saward, M. (2010) *The Representative Claim*, Oxford: Oxford University Press.

Scharpf, F. (2009) 'The double asymmetry of European integration. Or: Why the EU cannot be a social market economy', working papers, Max Planck Institut für Gesellschaftsforschung, 9 (12).

Statham, P. and Trenz, H.-J. (2012) *The Politicisation of Europe. Contesting the Constitution in the Mass Media*, London: Routledge.

Taggart, P. and Szczerbiak, A. (2008) 'Introduction: opposing Europe? The politics of Euroscepticism in Europe', in A. Szczerbiak and P. Taggart (eds) *Opposing Europe? The Comparative Party Politics of Euroscepticism. Volume 1: Case Studies and Country Surveys*, Oxford: Oxford University Press, pp. 1–15.

Trenz, H.-J. (2005) *Europa in den Medien. Das Europäische Integrationsprojekt im Spiegel nationaler Öffentlichkeit*, Frankfurt a. M., New York: Campus.

Trenz, H.-J. (2009) 'European civil society: between participation, representation and discourse', *Policy and Society*, 28 (1): 35–46.

Trenz, H.-J. (2010) 'In search of the popular subject: identity formation, constitution-making and the democratic consolidation of the EU', *European Review*, 18 (1): 93–115.

Urbinati, N. and Warren, M.E. (2008) 'The concept of representation in contemporary democratic theory', *Annual Review of Political Science*, 2008: 387–412.

Ward, S. and Gibson, R. (2009) 'European political organizations and the Internet: mobilization, participation, and change', in A. Chadwick and P.N. Howard (eds) *Routledge Handbook of Internet Politics*, London: Routledge, pp. 25–39.

Wessler, H., Peters, B., Brüggemann, M., Kleinen-von Königslöw, K. and Sifft, S. (2008) *Transnationalization of Public Spheres*, Basingstoke: Palgrave Macmillan.

Wolf, K.D. (1999) 'The new *raison d'état* as a problem for democracy in world society', *European Journal of International Relations*, 5 (3): 333–363.

11 Who is the guardian of constitutionalism in Europe after the financial crisis?

Michelle Everson and Christian Joerges

1 Ceding the Constitution to the political guardian?

The issue and problem of 'constitutional guardianship' is one with a long history. It was answered starkly and infamously by Carl Schmitt during and with regard to the final, crisis-ridden, years of the Weimar Republic: The guardian of the constitution is not the *Reichsgericht*, the judicial branch, but the *Reichspräsident*, a political actor exercising the quasi-dictatorial powers defined in Article 48 of the Weimar constitution on behalf of a politically homogeneous *Volk* (Schmitt 1931). This particular understanding of constitutional guardianship has now regained a disquieting degree of topicality within a crisis-ridden European Union (EU). This dimension of our topic will be discussed in more detail in the second part of our contribution. We begin, however, with a series of reflections on the issue of constitutional guardianship within the Union in less troubled times. Even prior to the crisis, the problem was highly troublesome, albeit that very few commentators, and even fewer institutional actors, recognized the true nature of the challenge. Nevertheless, this challenge is now becoming ever more apparent, in step with a growing and critical awareness of deeply-entrenched – even growing – diversity within Europe and the obviously paradoxical nature of a voluntaristic response to diversity, which is ever more insistent in its pursuit of a future unity, but cannot explain how this project might be realized through democratic processes.

When set against this background, the relevance of our topic in the context of a debate on democratic representation should be obvious. To be sure, courts, generally speaking, are the non-majoritarian vanguard and institutions *par excellence* of constitutional democracies. Non-partisanship defines their very ethos. Nevertheless, constitutional courts, in particular, do not find their prestige and authority exclusively within the legal provisions of the constitutions that establish them. Typically, these provisions do not endow them with powers of enforcement. Instead, Constitutional courts rely and build upon a Weberian legitimacy, which they acquire to a significant degree through the modes in which they articulate and thereby 'represent' both the *normed* character, as well as, the normative *dignity* of the order in which they are situated and operate. In other words, constitutional legitimacy is founded within a tense duality of rule-bounded, but socially responsive adjudication.

This twofold – formal and social – embeddedness of constitutional courts presents its own very particular problems within a European constellation, and impacts – as we shall demonstrate – cumulatively upon the issue of the constitutional guardianship of the EU. The EU is, so the Preamble of the Treaty of Lisbon and numerous of its Articles assure us,[1] committed to human rights, freedom, equality, democracy and the rule of law. Adherence to these commitments is a condition of membership within the Union; at least in theory. Constitutional adjudication is an American, not a genuine European accomplishment, but one that has nonetheless gained the status of a common European heritage. How, however, might this legacy be understood in the context of a Union that does not comply with the conditions it imposes on its own members? What institution is in a position to exercise the function of constitutional guardianship within such a constellation? Certainly, the Court of Justice of the European Union (CJEU) springs immediately to mind. But that conclusion would be premature and far too superficial. The European Court has never been formally established as a 'constitutional' body. To be sure, its foundational jurisprudence on direct effect and supremacy, the *Cassis*-jurisprudence and its aftermath, its characterization of the Treaties as a 'constitutional charter',[2] presupposes and assumes important supervisory functions for law 'at all levels of governance', which are widely recognized by the courts and authorities of many jurisdictions and with great emphasis and near unanimity in European law scholarship. However, this power cannot be considered to be comprehensive, even in theory, as long as 'Union competences are governed by the principle of conferral' (Article 5 (1) TEU). Equally, its validity will be doubted for as long as national constitutional courts – most notably Germany's *Bundesverfassungsgericht* – refuse to make use of the preliminary reference procedure and continue to question the authority of the CJEU by determining unilaterally whether European prerogatives are being lawfully asserted. In other words, constitutional guardianship within the Union cannot yet be regarded as having been entrusted to one single body. It has both national and European masters: masters who may be in disagreement with one another.

This insight is neither new, nor particularly disquieting *per se*. It was discussed particularly thoroughly by Neil MacCormick a good while ago (MacCormick 1998). There is pluralism in Europe, he acknowledged – adding that wise solutions could and should be found where legal solutions are not conceivable.[3] MacCormick's suggestions seem to anticipate what various Courts, including the notoriously inconvenient *Bundesverfassungsgericht* have learned to do, namely to establish interactive modes of adjudication. These adjudicative modes have by now been doctrinally refined by a host of academic commentators (Viellechner 2012; Kuo 2013). We will not explore the theoretical premises and practical accomplishments of these responses in any further depth,[4] however, returning instead to the earlier conceptualization of the multiple guardian problem constellation as a contest for mastery over *Kompetenz-Kompetenz* (section 2). We suggest that the conceptualization of constitutional guardianship under this heading has, if inadvertently, disclosed a constellation of diversity in the Union that should not and cannot be dealt with through a form of hierarchical ordering, but instead requires horizontal cooperation.

The continuity that we reconstruct is a promising signal, as it indicates that the potential exists to cope constructively with Europe's diversity. In section 3, where we consider the various European transformations following the financial crisis, we will document responses to troubles of a different kind in Europe. The pragmatically legalized *comitas* among European courts, which proponents for interactive conflict resolution advocate, has now given way to a new primacy of the 'Political' in the Union *sensu* Schmitt. In section 4 we investigate the efforts of the judiciary to manage these transformations. We analyse the judicial actions of the usual suspects in relation to two judgments of exemplary importance. Both the German Federal Constitutional Court (FCC) and the CJEU retain their specific style. But the differences between them now contrast markedly with their agreement *in re.* Both courts appear to be prepared to accede to the primacy of the Political; they concur in their delegalization of constitutional adjudication.

2 *Kompetenz-Kompetenz* in a non-unitary Union?

Our argument in the following section departs from prevailing modes of European legal scholarship in a twofold manner: failing to trumpet the historical merits of the European Court of Justice (ECJ, now CJEU), it likewise appears to question them. Belief in the centrality of law and its judicial enforcement was constitutive for legal scholarship during the formative era of the integration project. Law was presented prominently as both 'the object and the agent' of European integration (Dehousse and Weiler 1990). In that vision, the ECJ necessarily figured as the incarnation of Europe's integrationist vocation. There is also more than a kernel of truth in the assertion that the Court's jurisprudence was to prove determinative, at least to the degree that it has withstood political irritations and disagreements. Similarly, the historic Court is noteworthy in that it deepened the normative quality of European law, in particular in relation to its human rights jurisprudence, and mitigated – often successfully – between competing claims and policies, all the while managing to build up an unquestioned authority. Today, however, the Court is no longer portrayed so enthusiastically, even by the most faithful of its supporters.[5] How could any judicial institution cope with the ever-increasing complexity and growth of its workload and continue to convince national legal systems throughout an ever more diverse Union with its one-size-fits-all philosophy? How might it hope ever to convince, with its highly formalistic style of reasoning in cases of fundamental conflict, which are characterized by conflicting economic interests and political disagreement? The Court's labour law judgments in *Viking*, *Laval* and *Rüffert*,[6] which assigned supremacy to economic freedoms over national labour law traditions, provide the most spectacular example of this type of failure (Joerges and Rödl 2009; Everson 2011).

Currently, the factual erosion of the Court's legitimacy is similarly converging with the ongoing, if widely unnoticed, transformation of the integration project and the ever more insistent conflict constellations that surround it. An uncompromising defence of the former authority of the Court has become both factually and normatively implausible. The once quite belligerent contest between the German constitutional court,[7] on the one hand, and the allies of the ECJ, on the other, has lost its intensity and very provocative nature (Weiler 1995; Pernice 2001; Mayer 2000, 2004). It is now largely evident that there can be no one single guardian of constitutionalism in the Union. The insistence of the Kirchhof Court on a cooperative relationship ('*Kooperationsverhältnis*') with the ECJ tells us much about the willingness of national judiciaries to engage with Europe, albeit as equal partners. By the same token, any effort to construe such constitutional dialogue as ongoing disobedience can only be substantiated with reference to the untranslatable German dichotomy between *Staatenbund* and *Verfassungsverbund*. There is nonetheless both irony and tragedy in this insight. While pragmatic responses to the *Kompetenz-Kompetenz* issue have become imaginable, the transformation of the European constellation through the financial crisis is eroding the prospects for a *legal* reconceptualization of Europe's diversity. The crisis, we will submit, is establishing a new delegalized primacy of the Political in a Union in which constitutional adjudication is losing its disciplinary functions.

3 Crisis 'law'[8]

Current responses to the financial crisis depart significantly from European law and governance as we once knew it. One extraordinary feature of Europe's new activism is its intensity. Crisis summits have become routine and the drafting of ever more ersatz-legislation, or '*Ersatzunionsrecht*' (international law substituting EU law)[9] memoranda and policy papers is breathtaking.[10] Comprehensive accounts are available (Ruffert 2011; Craig 2013b). Here, in the following, we restrict ourselves to a few highlights.

In March and May 2010, respectively, the Commission developed the 'Europe 2020 strategy'[11] and the 'European Semester';[12] followed in June 2010 by the European Financial Stability Facility (EFSF) Framework Agreement,[13] and in March 2011 by the European Council's 'Euro Plus Pact'.[14] Simultaneously, on the basis of the simplified revision procedures laid down in Article 48 (Paragraph 6 TEU), the European Council also decided, on 25 March 2011, to add a new Paragraph 3 to Article 136 of TFEU (Treaty on the Functioning of the European Union), permitting the establishment of a stability mechanism and the granting of financial assistance, effective as of 1 January 2013.[15] This was followed in November 2011 by a bundle of legislative measures aimed at reinforcing budgetary discipline on the part of Member States. The package is supposed to go down in history under the catchy title 'Six Pack' and entered into force on 13 December 2011.[16] The definite high point and cornerstone of the whole new edifice is the Treaty on Stability, Coordination and Governance (TSCG), drafted in December 2011, approved at an informal meeting of the European Council on 30 January 2012,[17] and signed on 2 March 2012 by 25 out of 27 Member States. A debt brake, designed according to the German model, will be introduced, and will be subject to judicial review by the CJEU in the form of institutional borrowing, with one Member State bringing action against another. Support from the European Stability Mechanism (ESM), a permanent crisis fund, will be available only to countries in the Euro area that have signed the pact. In March 2013 the 'Two Pack' submitted back in 2011 was adopted with parliamentary blessing.[18]

There is much to scrutinize here: legal problems as well as the way they are dealt with in legal scholarship. We will restrict our discussion here to the particular form of managerial crisis management that the new machinery has established. This management is delicate for three interdependent reasons. First, through the supervision and control of imbalances, it disregards the principle of enumerated powers, and, by the same token, does not respect the democratic legitimacy of national institutions, in particular, the budgetary powers of parliaments. Second, in its departure from the one-size-fits-all philosophy orienting European integration in general and monetary policy in particular, it nonetheless fails to achieve a variation that might be founded in democratically legitimated choices; quite to the contrary, the individualized scrutiny of all Member States is geared to the objective of budgetary balance and seeks to impose the necessary accompanying discipline. Under the conditions of monetary unity, the Member States can only respond to pertinent requests through austerity measures: reducing wage levels and social entitlements. Third, the machinery of the new regime with its individualized measures, which are oriented only by necessarily indeterminate general clauses, is regulatory in its nature, establishing a 'political administration' outside the realm of democratic politics and the form of accountability that the rule of law requires/demands.

Dariusz Adamski was among the first to highlight and underline that core concepts used by new economic governance cannot be defined with any precision, either by lawyers or by economists, and are therefore not justiciable (Adamski 2012). This implies that rule-of-law and legal protection requirements are being suspended. This type of delegalization is accompanied by a highly discretionary evaluation of Member States' performance, which economist Andrew Watt has revealed in his analysis of an in-depth review of 13 EU countries that were considered to have macroeconomic imbalances, undertaken by the Commission (Watt 2013). It is worth noting that the Fiscal Compact has entrusted the CJEU with the task of assessing compliance with the stipulation that 'the budgetary position of the general government of a Contracting Party shall be balanced or in surplus' (Article 3 1.a TSCG). This is an impossible mission that is bound to damage the Court's standing (Chalmers 2012b).

What is specific about Europe's new economic governance? Characterizations by commentators oscillate between notions such as 'executive federalism', 'distributive regulatory state', 'consolidating state', 'authoritarian managerialism', 'new sovereignty with unfettered power of rule' (Habermas 2011; Chalmers 2012a; Streeck 2013; Joerges and M. Weimer 2013; Chalmers 2013). They all acknowledge the design failures of European Monetary Union (EMU) as it was institutionalized by the Maastricht Treaty of 1992 and the Stability Pact of

1997 (Council regulations 1997[19]). They all conclude that compliance with that poorly designed framework would have disastrous consequences. Does this mean that the new regime deserves recognition? Both the FCC and the CJEU have wrestled with this problem – but neither appears to have mastered it.

4 The law or 'the political' as constitutional guardian

The German Constitutional Court has a much-contested record with respect to its European commitments and loyalty – even though signals of disobedience have always remained rhetorical. The CJEU has overruled national law in countless cases – but has hardly ever found European legal acts to be at fault. Investigating each of these Court decisions against the background of the new economic governance now evolving within Europe accordingly promises to provide us with nuanced insights into the management of the crisis.

4.1 Is the German court a 'dog that barks and never bites'?[20]

The attention which the complaints before the FCC against the ESM Treaty and the Fiscal Compact have attracted is as unsurprising as the outcome of this controversy, which the court delivered in its Judgment of 12 September 2012.[21] What the highest judicial authority of Europe's most potent economy has to say about well-argued complaints matters. And yet, it was easy to 'hazard a pretty good guess at the ending'. Paul Craig's observation concerns the Pringle Case of the CJEU,[22] but is equally valid with respect to the German case. It seemed simply inconceivable that the courts would interfere with high politics in matters of utmost importance. That, however, is not a good enough reason to close the academic files and shrug the shoulders.

On closer inspection, the judgment reveals a number of ambivalences. The most important one is the Court's defence of the budgetary power of the German Bundestag. This power is a democratic essential, protected by the eternity clause of the Basic Law. Its importance was already underlined in the previous judgment on the rescue package for Greece[23] and its validity cannot be questioned in principle. Is it a principle with bite? In both judgments, the Court underlined that the Bundestag enjoyed wide latitude, which the judiciary must respect.[24] Through this move, the rights of the Bundestag were redefined in a proceduralizing mode: the Parliament must be adequately informed, enabled to deliberate, and prevented from delegating its evaluation. This reading is in line with a principle of 'integration responsibility',[25] which the Court developed in its Lisbon Judgment; a contested notion, but one which can, in our view, be understood as a search for a response to the tensions between integration and democracy.

Such a benevolent reading is not evinced by the 12 September Judgment. To be sure, the form of judicial restraint, which the German court exercised when it gave the green light to the extensive indebtedness of the Federal Republic, is again embedded in procedural and institutional notions. The Court is not careful of 'foreign' concerns. The weight constitutionally placed upon the budgetary powers of the Bundestag, so we learn and understand, requires the German Parliament to retain the power to determine the most important conditions for future successful demands for capital disbursements.[26] In this passage, the Court once again strengthened the link between the Bundestag's budgetary responsibility and a distinctly German philosophy of stability (i.e. price stability and the independence of the European Central Bank (ECB) above all). As a consequence, the nature of the EMU as a stability community (*Stabilitätsgemeinschaft*) is even seen as being protected by the 'eternity clause' of Article 79 (3) of the German Basic Law as an unamendable core of Germany's constitutional identity.[27] After this move, the stability principles become the core of a refurbished European economic constitution.[28]

All this, the Court hopes, will protect the democratic rights of German citizens. Non-German citizens of the Union, however, should not be at all amused. Why is budgetary autonomy not understood as a *common* European constitutional legacy, respect for which is demanded by Article 4 (2) TEU? The one-sidedness of this argument is all the more disappointing as the Court, in an earlier paragraph of its judgment, had opened another and more constructive perspective, explaining that 'Article 79 (3) seeks to protect those structures and procedures which keep the democratic process open'.[29] The Court did not indicate that it would be prepared to address the tensions between democratic commitments and the integration process, which would include the concerns of all Member States. Instead, the Court's reasoning leads to a strengthening of the links between economic stability and social austerity. This form of judicial self-restraint seems even more questionable in the light of – or, rather, in the shadow of – the Maastricht Judgment.[30] In that Judgment, the Bundesverfassungsgericht had made German participation in the EMU conditional upon Europe-wide acceptance of Germany's economic and institutional philosophy. This finding has since been confirmed and developed further. While the Maastricht Judgment could be understood as an essentially legal project, this new judgment has changed the perspective from law to governmental and executive management, with requirements defined mainly by Germany and its Northern allies.

To put it slightly differently, we find it deplorable that the FCC acted as (only) the guardian of the German constitution. The qualification of financial assistance as a matter not of European monetary policy but of national economic policy,[31] as well as the somewhat euphemistic statements on the respect for the stability commitments,[32] are anything but robust indicators of truly European commitments. They are embedded in the conditionality of existing crisis management. The FCC talks about democratic essentials, Jürgen Habermas has observed, but with Germany in mind.[33] The one-sidedness of its decision seems indeed obvious – and difficult to overcome. The German Court is not entitled to act as the Guardian of Europe. What we would expect, however, is a readiness to define Germany as a Member of a Union in which the concerns of all the Member States and their democratic rights deserve recognition. Only then would the Court document an understanding, or *Integrationsverantwortung*, that might reflect common European commitments.[34]

4.2 'Let's close our eyes' – no alternative for the CJEU in Pringle

What would have happened to the EU had its Court of Justice found that Thomas Pringle's concerns about Europe's crisis management were well founded,[35] that the support mechanisms which the EFSF and the ESM have established interfere with the exclusive European competence for monetary policy, that the amendment of Article 136 TFEU was not possible under the simplified revision procedure enshrined in Article 48(6) TEU, that new policies adopted and pursued by the Member States jeopardized the primacy of price stability, that the bail-out provision of Article 125 TFEU prohibited the granting of financial assistance to Member States whose currency is the Euro, that the functions assumed by the Commission, the ECB, and the International Monetary Fund (IMF) were irreconcilable with the principles on the conferral of powers laid down in Article 13 TFEU, or that the mandate allocated to the CJEU in the ESM Treaty exceeded judicial powers? Only a fool would dare to predict the dire consequences. The same kind of uncertainty governs with regard to the success of all of these measures. Under such circumstances, the CJEU could not and should not be expected to interfere, one might conclude. Nonetheless, in so doing, one must similarly concede that this conclusion implies a complete secession of law to discretionary political power. The onus must surely be – for the lawyer at least – to commence the search for alternatives to this devastating legal default.

The search for such alternatives should allow for escape from the impasses to which Europe's crisis managements must respond, namely the design defects of EMU and its conceptually monetarist background, upon which the dedication of EMU to price stability rests, which has now become the cornerstone and sole possible value of the European economic constitution. It has by now become a *communis opinio* that European monetary policy, with its predefined objectives and institutional frameworks, cannot operate in tandem with the multitude of national actors who are pursuing economic and fiscal policies under a very loosely constructed machinery of European supervision. This insight has triggered quests for enhanced controls and generated the new machinery of authoritarian management. There is, however, a twofold flaw in the reasoning of the CJEU in the assumption that the failures of the past justify the unrestrained activism of the present.

The first flaw is the Court's failure to address the implications of its own explanation of the conceptual background to the bail-out clause:

> The prohibition laid down in Article 125 TFEU ensures that the Member States remain subject to the logic of the market when they enter into debt, since that ought to prompt them to maintain budgetary discipline. Compliance with such discipline contributes at Union level to the attainment of a higher objective, namely maintaining the financial stability of the monetary union.[36]

This is indeed a fair restatement of an ordo-liberal legacy that we can still identify within EMU. However, the Court is then silent with regard to the philosophy underlying our current cure to the failures of the past. This is by no means to suggest that the Court should have advocated an ordo-liberal renaissance. Nonetheless, what truly disappoints in its presentation of the new modes of economic governance is the lack of any kind of conceptual deliberation about their background or their adequacy. As we argued in section 3, the new modes of European economic governance amount to nothing less than a deep transformation of the state of the EU. The organizers of that transformation should be asked to explain their objectives and demonstrate the adequacy of the means that they are employing. The lack of any plausible explanation of the means–end relationship within Europe's crisis management reveals a second flaw in the judgment. Wherever the court responds to objections about the legality of the new regime, it merely parrots the orthodoxy that 'conditionality' is a justification.

Conditionality ensures respect for the exclusive European competence in monetary policy and thereby the legality of the simplified amendment procedure:

> [T]he reason why the grant of financial assistance by the stability mechanism is subject to strict conditionality under paragraph 3 of Article 136 TFEU, the article affected by the revision of the FEU Treaty, is in order to ensure that that mechanism will operate in a way that will comply with European Union law, including the measures adopted by the Union in the context of the coordination of the Member States' economic policies.[37]

Conditionality is the glue that keeps transnational actors together:

> [When granting assistance] the ESM Board of Governors shall entrust the European Commission – in liaison with the ECB and, wherever possible, together with the IMF – with the task of negotiating, with the ESM Member concerned, a memorandum of understanding ('MoU') detailing the conditionality attached to the financial assistance facility. The content of the MoU shall reflect the severity of the weaknesses to be addressed and the financial assistance instrument chosen. In parallel, the Managing Director of the ESM shall prepare a proposal for a financial assistance facility agreement, including the financial terms and conditions and the choice of instruments, to be adopted by the Board of Governors.[38]

Last, but not least, Article 125 TFEU retains its function thanks to conditionality,

> [T]he purpose of the strict conditionality to which all stability support provided by the ESM is subject is to ensure that the ESM and the recipient Member States comply with measures adopted by the Union in particular in the area of the coordination of Member States' economic policies, those measures being designed, inter alia, to ensure that the Member States pursue a sound budgetary policy.

The deeply undemocratic nature of conditionality goes unnoticed or uncommented upon. The CJEU imposes on the whole of Europe the form of discipline that the FCC has imposed on Germany's neighbours.

4.3 De-judicialization: Europe's Schmittian moment

Germany's constitutional court feels exclusively committed to the country's constitution. The CJEU is certainly motivated by its commitment to the integration project. The discrepancy between these commitments was once perceived as a threat to the European project. That risk did not materialize as anticipated. But we are now concerned with a risk of a new kind. The converging attitudes of both courts in the assessment of the *praxis* of Europe's crisis management is disquieting because it accepts the primacy of discretionary politics in the management of the crisis, and fails to develop any criteria against which the legitimacy of these practices might be assessed.[39]

At this point we return to our reference to the 'state of exception' made at the beginning of this chapter. Schmittian notions are certainly always engraved in a specific context.[40] History does not repeat itself and situational contexts remain distinct. And yet, recourse to Schmitt is anything but far-fetched.[41] Crisis management practices, which are foreseen neither in EU primary law nor in national constitutions, are justified by the argument that compliance with the letter of the law would cause more harm than its breach or daring interpretation. Even Carl Schmitt did not conceive of the state of exception as a permanent condition; his justification of a 'commissarial dictatorship' included an effort to overcome the problems that precipitated departure from the rule of law and to regain normal constitutionality.[42] In the present state of the Union, pertinent suggestions are urgent – and abound. However, they are mostly merely pragmatic and managerial, albeit that some constitutional lawyers and political philosophers have formulated some new propositions for a new constitutional architecture.

We have little room here to enter in these debates. We have presented our alternative of 'conflicts-law as Europe's constitutional form' elsewhere.[43] This is an approach that takes 'unity in diversity', the fortunate motto of the ill-fated Draft Constitutional Treaty of 2003 seriously, and rejects the notion that federalist state building is a sustainable project. We argue instead for a radical 'proceduralization' of the integration project, in which the European judiciary engages in continuous juris-generative efforts (a '*Rechtfertigungsrecht*') that seek responses to Europe's complex conflict constellations.[44] Democratization through conflicts-law constitutionalism cannot deliver ready-made responses to the financial crisis, but it can nevertheless claim to provide perspectives for a return to a constitutional European condition. To substantiate this perspective with respect to *Pringle:* monetary policy, fiscal policy and economic policy are assigned to different levels of governance in the Union. They are, however, interdependent. In the terminology of the conflicts-law approach, this generates 'diagonal' conflicts. Their 'resolution' within Europe's crisis management is currently occurring through establishment of the primacy of 'the political'.

Conflicts-law constitutionalism, by contrast, would require legally structured ('constitutionalized') cooperative deliberation.

Notes

1 Most emphatically in Article 21(1) TEU.
2 Opinion 1/91, *European Economic Area* [1991] ECR I-6079.
3 At 531.
4 Although some authors take a more sociological approach to commentary on the historic ECJ. See Everson and Eisner (2007).
5 Suffice it here to point to the introductory chapter of Dawson *et al.* (2013), 1–11.
6 C-438/05, *International Transport Workers' Federation, Finnish Seamen's Union v. Viking Line ABP, OÜ Viking Line Eesti* [2007] ECR I-10779; C-341/05, *Laval un Partneri Ltd v. Svenska Byggnadsarbetareförbundet, Svenska Byggnadsarbetareförbundets avdelning 1, Byggettan und Svenska Elektrikerförbundet* [2007], ECR I-11767; C-346/06, *Rechtsanwalt Dr. Dirk Rüffert v. Land Niedersachsen* [2008], ECR I-01989.
7 See in particular: *Bundesverfassungsgericht*, Judgment of 12 October 1993, 2 BvR 2134/92 and 2 BvR 2159/92, 89 *BVerfGE* 155 (1993) [*Brunner v. European Union Treaty*, *CMLR* 57 (1994) 1].
8 The following passages draw on Joerges (2014).
9 This term, coined by a German lawyer, was taken up in the European Stability Mechanism (ESM) Judgment of the German Constitutional Court (note 41 below) at para. 226 to denote the resort to international law for measures that European law does not foresee.
10 For continuously updated information see www.consilium.europa.eu/press/press-releases/economic-and-financial-affairs?lang=en&BID=93 (accessed 30 November 2013).
11 Communication from the Commission of 3 March 2010, European Commission (2010a) 2020 final.
12 Communication from the Commission of 12 May 2010, European Commission (2010b) 250 final.
13 Confirmed in the conclusions of the European Council, Brussels, 17 June 2010, EUCO 13/10, CO EUR 9, CONCL 2. The Framework Agreement was concluded by the ECOFIN Council and confirmed by the European Council, Brussels on 17 June 2010.
14 Conclusions of the European Council, Brussels, 24/25 March 2011, EUCO 10/11, CO EUR 6, CONCL 3 (Annex I).
15 Decision 2011/199/EU amending Art. 136 TFEU with regard to a stability mechanism for Member States whose currency is the Euro, OJ 2011, L 91/2011, 1.
16 The five regulations 1173–1177/2011/EU and directive 2011/85/EU of 8 November 2011, OJ L 91/2011, 1.
17 Cf. the Communication of the Euro area Member States as well as the TSCG in the EMU, 20 January 2012 version, http://european-council.europa.eu/media/639235/st00tscg26_en12.pdf (accessed on 30 November).
18 The 'Two Pack' provides for:

> enhanced monitoring and assessment of draft budgetary plans of Euro area member states, with closer monitoring for those in an excessive deficit procedure, and furthermore enhanced surveillance of Euro area member states that are experiencing or threatened with serious financial difficulties, or that request financial assistance.

For details see www.europarl.europa.eu/pdfs/news/expert/infopress/20130312IPR06439/20130312IPR06439_en.pdf (accessed on 30 November).

19 Decision of the European Council on the Stability and Growth Pact, OJ C 236 of 2.8.1997 (Article 12). In the Treaty of Lisbon see Article 126 and Protocol No. 12.
20 The metaphor is from Weiler (2009).
21 An incomplete English translation is available at www.bundesverfassungsgericht.de/entscheidungen/rs20120912_2bvr139012en.html (accessed 30 November 2013).
22 See his 'Guest Editorial: *Pringle*: legal reasoning, text, purpose and teleology' (Craig 2013a).
23 FCC, Judgment of 7 September 2011, 2 BvR 987/10–2 BvR 1485/10–2 BvR 1099/10 – aid measures for Greece and against the Euro rescue package; available at www.bverfg.de/entscheidungen/rs20110907_2bvr098710en.html (accessed on 30 November 2013).
24 FCC, Judgment of 7 September 2011, previous note, paras 130–132 and Judgment of 12 September 2012, note 38, para. 180.
25 FCC, Judgment of 30 June 2009, available at www.bundesverfassungsgericht.de; English translation at www.bundesverfassungsgericht.de/entscheidungen/es20090630_2bve000208en.html (both accessed 30 November 2013).
26 Judgment of 12 September 2012 (see note 21 above), para. 274; this section is not yet translated. The official translation is still incomplete. In view of the complexity and importance of this pronouncement, we add the German original:

> Da der Bundestag durch seine Zustimmung zu Stabilitätshilfen den verfassungsrechtlich gebotenen Einfluss ausüben und Höhe, Konditionalität und Dauer der Stabilitätshilfen zugunsten hilfesuchender Mitgliedstaaten mitbestimmen kann, legt er selbst die wichtigste Grundlage für später möglicherweise erfolgende Kapitalabrufe nach Art. 9 Abs. 2 ESMV;

For a critical comment, see Joerges (2012).

27 Ibid., para. 220, which reads:

> Die haushaltspolitische Gesamtverantwortung des Deutschen Bundestags wird in Ansehung der Übertragung der Währungshoheit auf das Europäische System der Zentralbanken namentlich durch die Unterwerfung der Europäischen Zentralbank under die strengen Kriterien des Vertrages über die Arbeitsweise der Europäischen Union und der Satzung des Europäischen Systems der Zentralbanken hinsichtlich der Unabhängigkeit der Zentralbank und die Priorität der Geldwertstabilität gesichert.

And 'Ein wesentliches Element zur unionsrechtlichen Absicherung der verfassungsrechtlichen Anforderungen aus Art. 20 Abs. 1 und Abs. 2 in Verbindung mit Art. 79 Abs. 3 GG ist insoweit das Verbtot monetärer Haushaltsfinanzierung durch die Europäische Zentralbank'.

28 Ibid., paras 219–220, 232–233, 239–279 and 300–319.
29 Ibid., para. 206 in the English extract, para. 222 in the German original.
30 *Bundesverfassungsgericht*, Judgment of 12 October 1993, 2 BvR 2134/92 and 2 BvR 2159/92, 89 *BVerfGE* 155 (1993) [*Brunner* v *European Union Treaty*, *CMLR* 57 (1994) 1].
31 Ibid., para. 169.
32 Ibid., paras 201–206.
33 Habermas 2012 ('Drei Gründe für "Mehr Europa" ').
34 For a similar critique cf. Deters (2014).
35 C-370/12 *Pringle v. Ireland*, Judgment of 27 November 2012.
36 Ibid., para. 135.
37 Ibid., para. 68.
38 Ibid., para. 18.
39 We should underline that we do not object in principle to the FCC's efforts insisting on parliamentary involvement. One can read this tendency as a step towards a proceduralization that seeks to engage concerned institutional 'stakeholders' in Europe's crisis management (see Lepisus (2012)); see also Deters, n. 33 above.

40 Cf. Kennedy (2011), with references to the German original writings and the translations into English.
41 E.-W. Böckenförde, formerly a judge of the *Bundesverfassungsgericht* and renowned connoisseur of Schmitt's oeuvre, was among the first to characterize the crisis of the Euro and of Monetary Union as an *Ausnahmezustand* (state of exception/emergency), which would suspend the rule of law (Böckenförde 2010).
42 See Schmitt (1938).
43 In condensed form see the introductory chapter to Joerges *et al.* (2011) with contributions by Menéndez, Rödl, Amstutz, Kjaer, Herberg and Everson.
44 See Everson, M. and Eisner, J. (2007: 13 ff) (22 ff on *Rechtsverfassungsrecht*) and Joerges (2010).

References

Adamski, D. (2012) 'National power games and structural failures in the European macroeconomic governance', *Common Market Law Review*, 49: 1319–1364.

Adamski, D. (2013) 'Europe's (misguided) constitution of economic prosperity', *Common Market Law Review*, 50: 47–85.

Böckenförde, E.-W. (2010) 'Kennt die europäische Not kein Gebot? Die Webfehler der EU und die Notwendigkeit einer neuen politischen Entscheidung', *Neue Züricher Zeitung*, 21 June, available at www.nzz.ch/nachrichten/kultur/literatur_und_kunst/kennt_die_europaeische_not_kein_gebot_1.6182412.html (accessed 30 November 2013).

Chalmers, D. (2012a) 'The European redistributive state and the need for a European Law of Struggle', *European Law Journal*, 18: 667–693.

Chalmers, D. (2012b) 'The European Court of Justice has taken on huge new powers as "enforcer" of the Treaty on Stability, Coordination and Governance. Yet its record as a judicial institution has been little scrutinised', available at http://blogs.lse.ac.uk/europpblog/2012/03/07/european-court-of-justice-enforcer (accessed 6 January 2014).

Chalmers, D. (2013) 'European restatements of sovereignty', ms. LSE (on file with author).

Craig, P. (2013a) 'Guest Editorial: *Pringle*: legal reasoning, text, purpose and teleology', *Maastricht Journal of European Law*, 20: 3–11.

Craig, P. (2013b) 'Financial crisis, response, and Europe's future', in *The Lisbon Treaty*, 2nd paperback edn, Oxford: Oxford University Press, pp. 457–517.

Dawson, M., de Witte, B. and Muir, E. (2013) *Judicial Activism in the European Court of Justice*, Cheltenham: Edward Elgar.

Dehousse, R. and Weiler, J.H.H. (1990) 'The legal dimension', in W. Wallace (ed.) *The Dynamics of European Integration*, London: Pinter, pp. 242–260, at 243.

Deters, H. (2014) 'National constitutional jurisprudence in a post-national Europe: the ESM ruling of the German Federal Constitutional Court', *European Law Journal*, 19.

European Commission (2010a) Communication on 'A strategy for smart, sustainable and inclusive growth, COM (2010) 2020 final of 3 March 2000.

European Commission (2010b) Communication on 'Reinforcing Economic Policy Coordination, COM (2010) 250 final of 12 May 2010.

Everson, M. (2011) 'From effet utile to effet neoliberal: why is the ECJ hazarding the integrity of European law?', in C. Joerges and T. Ralli (eds) *European Constitutionalism without Private Law – Private Law without Democracy*, Olso, ARENA Report 3/11/RECON Report No. 14: 37–54.

Everson, M. and Eisner, J. (2007) *The Making of the European Constitution: Judges and Lawyers in the Constitutive Moment*, London: Routledge-Cavendish.

Habermas, J. (2011) 'A pact for or against Europe?', in U. Guérot and J. Hénard (eds) *What does Germany Think about Europe*?, Berlin: European Council on Foreign Relations: 83–89.
Habermas, J. (2012) 'Drei Gründe für "Mehr Europa"' ('Three reasons for "more Europe"'), Statement at the Luca 69th Deutscher Juristentag, Munich, 21 September, as reported in *Süddeutsche Zeitung*, 22–23 September, p. 15.
Joerges, C. (2010) 'Unity in diversity as Europe's vocation and conflicts law as Europe's constitutional form', LSE: Europe in Question discussion paper series (LEQS), London, 28.
Joerges, C. (2012) 'Der Berg kreißte – gebar er eine Maus? Europa vor dem Bundesverfassungsgericht', *WSI-Mitteilungen*, 65: 560.
Joerges, C. (2014) 'The European Economic Constitution and its transformation through the financial crisis', in D. Patterson and A. Södersten (eds) *A Companion to European Union Law and International Law*, Oxford: Wiley/Blackwell.
Joerges, C. and Rödl, F. (2009) 'Informal politics, formalised law and the "social deficit" of European integration: reflections after the judgments of the ECJ in *Viking* and *Laval*', *European Law Journal*, 15 (1): 1–19.
Joerges, C. and Weimer, M. (2013) 'A crisis of executive managerialism in the EU: no alternative?', Maastricht Faculty of Law working paper 2012/7, Maastricht.
Joerges, C. Kjaer, P.F. and Ralli, T. (eds) (2011) *Conflicts Law as Constitutional Form in the Postnational Constellation, Transnational Legal Theory*, 2, Special Issue.
Kennedy, E. (2011) 'Emergency government within the bounds of the constitution: an introduction to Carl Schmitt, The dictatorship of the Reichspresident according to Article 48 R.V', *Constellations*, 18 (3): 284–297.
Kuo, M.S. (2013) 'Discovering sovereignty in dialogue: is judicial dialogue the answer to constitutional conflict in the pluralist legal landscape?', Warwick School of Law Research Paper No. 6.
Lepisus, O. (2012) 'ESM-Vertrag, Fiskalpakt und das BVerfG', *Europäische Zeitschrift für Wirtschaftsrecht*, 23: 761–762.
MacCormick, N. (1998) 'Risking constitutional collision in Europe?', *Oxford Journal of Legal Studies*, 18 (3): 517–532.
Mayer, F.C. (2000) *Kompetenzüberschreitung und Letztentscheidung*, Munich: C.H. Beck.
Mayer, F.C. (2004) 'Wer soll Hüter der europäischen Verfassung sein?', *Archiv des öffentlichen Rechts*, 129: 411–435.
Pernice, I. (2001) 'Europäisches und nationales Verfassungsrecht', *Veröffentlichungen der Vereinigung Deutscher Staatsrechtslehrer*, (60): 148–193.
Ruffert, M. (2011) 'The European debt crisis and European Union law', *Common Market Law Review*, 48: 1777–1806.
Schmitt, C. (1931) *Der Hüter der Verfassung*, Tübingen: Mohr/Siebeck.
Schmitt, C. (1938) 'Vergleichender Überblick über die neueste Entwicklung des Problems der gesetzgeberischen Ermächtigungen (Legislative Delegationen)', *Zeitschrift für ausländisches öffentliches Recht und Völkerrecht*, 6: 252–267.
Streeck, W. (2013) *Gekaufte Zeit. Die vertagte Krise des demokratischen Kapitalismus*, Berlin: Suhrkamp.
Viellechner, L. (2012) 'Constitutionalism as a cipher: on the convergence of constitutionalist and pluralist approaches to the globalization of law', *Goettingen Journal of International Law*, 4: 599–623.
Watt, A. (2013) 'Commission makes a mockery of imbalance procedure', *Social Europe*

Journal, online, available at www.social-europe.eu/author/andrew-watt (accessed 30 November 2013).

Weiler, J.H.H. (1995) 'Does Europe need a constitution? Reflections on Demos, Telos and the German Maastricht decision', *European Law Journal*, 1: 219–258.

Weiler, J.H.H. (2009) 'The "Lisbon Urteil" and the fast food culture', *European Journal of International Law*, 20: 505–9, 505, commenting on Bundesverfassungsgericht, judgment of 30 June 2009, online, available at www.bundesverfassungsgericht.de; English translation at www.bundesverfassungsgericht.de/entscheidungen/es20090630_2bve000208en.html (both accessed 30 November 2013).

Part III

Concluding essays

12 Representation as the cornerstone for efficient and legitimate governance

Beate Kohler-Koch

Representation: theory meets empirical research

The volume is systematically dedicated to the question of representation in the context of the multi-level system of the European Union (EU). It addresses both the theoretical discussion on representation and the promises and mechanisms of representation in the political life of the EU. It shows that the editor insisted on thematic coherence in the volume. Each author explains her or his understanding of (democratic) representation and examines whether or not the respective criteria are met in her/his case. In addition, the authors reflect whether the present debt and financial crisis have triggered deterioration or activated an improvement in the democratic representation in the EU. Notwithstanding the multi-faceted use of representation the authors share a broad consensus in their understanding of representation, which gives the volume a high level of coherence.

In the concluding chapter Dario Castiglione examines what we can learn in terms of theory, whereas this contribution takes a close look at the empirical case studies and aims to evaluate what they tell us about the practice of representation in the EU. The special feature of this book is that it puts into focus actors who only play a marginal role in the mainstream discussion on EU representation. Parliaments, elections and parties are the traditional focus of studies on political representation and, accordingly, there is a wealth of literature on the European Parliament, on electoral turnout and also, though to a lesser extent, on EU-level parties. This book takes a different approach insofar as it examines actors that have only recently been considered important in EU democracy but whose representation input has not yet been studied in depth: national parliaments, national parties and civil society. Furthermore, it takes a fresh look at well-known institutions such as the Commission, the Council and the Committee of the Regions in view of their contribution to political representation. By doing so, it concentrates on the interplay between the national and the supranational in political representation. Last but not least it examines the potential added value that law and expert knowledge may bring to (democratic) representation in the EU.

Upgrading parliamentary representation from bottom-up

It is common knowledge that the EU is a system of compounded representation. The Lisbon Treaty (TEU Arts 10 and 11) states in black and white that the EU is a system of representative democracy with citizens represented directly in the European Parliament (EP) and indirectly by their governments on the European Council, which is itself democratically accountable to the national parliaments. With this double system of representation citizens ought to have a good chance of channelling their interests to EU decision-makers, putting the decision-makers under close scrutiny and making them responsive to their demands. Obviously, the Constitutional Convention was not satisfied with the upgrading of the European Parliament but also wanted to involve national parliaments more actively. Better information rights and participation in the inter-parliamentary cooperation, as provided by the Treaty (TEU Art. 12) and by additional formal and informal arrangements, are seen as a promising way of fostering democratic representation. According to John Erik Fossum (Chapter 3) these have stimulated a reconfiguration of parliamentary representation and democracy in the EU so that a 'multilevel parliamentary field' is about to evolve. He sees more active involvement of national parliaments in EU-level decision-making, and more cross-level interaction and consultations. Optimistically he concludes that the development of the multilevel parliamentary field 'also opens up scope for parliaments to capitalize on their unique deliberative qualities'. In his account the present crisis has severely damaged the representative structure of the EU by sidelining the European and national parliaments in a process that has reinforced technocracy and reinvigorated transgovernmentalism. To counter these tendencies, interparliamentary coordination would be even more relevant and necessary than before. But is it realistic to assume that once the crisis abates the multilevel parliamentary field will emerge strong and vibrant?

Empirical research, unfortunately, is scarce. Whereas the changing role of the European Parliament has been studied in depth, we know much less about how the revaluation of national parliaments has affected their conduct and their representative function. This deficit makes both contributions by Johannes Pollak and by Anne Rasmussen and Gert-Jan Lindeboom (Chapters 1 and 2) particularly worth reading.

Treaty reform has given national parliaments comprehensive information rights and the right to intervene in the supranational decision-making process by subjecting legislative proposals to an *ex ante* review. The main duty of national parliaments is to defend the principle of subsidiarity, but they do not shy away from commenting on other material issues. The questions are, first, to what extent national parliaments make use of these new rights; and second, whether these rights are a qualitative improvement on pre-existing informal procedures. Johannes Pollak provides data that show that the new-won rights so far have had little bearing. The total of 64 scrutiny procedures is unimpressive and what is more telling, 'none of them came even close to a chamber majority'.

To make sense of the data we have to ask whether these new privileges are sufficient to empower national parliaments. Knowing that action always requires resources and that spending resources is a zero-sum-game, we have to know whether the enhanced status of national parliaments has been supported by additional resources. Indeed, to facilitate access to information and communication among national parliaments an online platform for EU interparliamentary exchange has been established. It draws attention to new EU proposals and expiring deadlines for comments. In addition to the relevant EU documents the platform also includes documents of individual national parliaments clarifying their positions on specific draft proposals. Members of parliament appreciate having easy access to the positions and reasoning of other parliaments as an input to their own deliberation. It strengthens interparliamentary communication and is to the benefit of resource-poor parliaments. Although the information platform is highly welcomed and used regularly, it did not noticeably increase the incentive to use the formal procedure to intervene in EU policy-making. Formulating a position still poses a considerable workload, not just for the European Affairs Committees but also for the parliament as such. In most cases also the relevant sector-specific committees and the plenary have to get involved.[1] Even then, national parliaments cannot veto a European legislative proposal. Thus, for national parliaments it is an unfavourable balance between the endeavour made and the result obtained. Consequently, national parliaments obviously prefer the less formulized and more flexible exchange with the Commission of written opinions, in line with the 'Barroso Initiative'. It is increasingly in use, documented by 622 opinions sent by national parliaments in 2011, so that Pollak comes to the conclusion that this 'points towards an extensive exchange of thoughts', and cautiously adds that '[i]n fact it can probably be termed "bavardage"'. The dark side of the new rights is that the communication process is shielded from the wider public and, although it is valued by national parliaments, its effect is minimal. The scrutiny mechanism on subsidiarity has to meet a high quorum of national parliaments in order to have a binding effect, and communication in line with the Barroso Initiative is entirely dependent on the disposition of the Commission to take up the arguments.[2] Thus we have to agree with Pollak that the new rights and procedural reforms hardly put national parliaments in the position to counterbalance the increasing powers of the executive, which have been expanded further in the current crisis.

However, when judging the democratic value of representation, impact on policy output is just one dimension and, besides, national parliaments may be more interested in keeping the national government under control than reaching out to the supra-national level. The question than is whether the new rights empowered national parliaments and made them more willing to scrutinize national EU policies; and whether they have gained autonomy from government and used it in a way that stimulates a public discourse. Given the close ties between parliamentary majority and the high level of competition between parties in many Member States we should not expect parliament as a whole to go against the government. Parliaments are not an autonomous actor but are split and the parliamentary majority being a close ally of the government will use the new instrument to ask for and receive additional information to share with their government. The intention is to bring additional weight to the national position, which explains why parliamentary resolutions sent to Brussels 'mirror' the position of the government (Jančić 2012: 84). A typical example is the House of Commons in the United Kingdom, which enjoys an extraordinarily close relationship with government. When evaluating the impact of the EU reforms, we have to remember that parliamentary control rights are defined by national law and that in this respect national parliaments vary significantly. The Danish and Austrian Parliaments have considerable scrutiny rights and Germany has been quite active in recent years to extend the rights of parliament. This happened in reaction to the deepening of integration and in response to the verdicts of the Federal Constitutional Court. According to Christian Calliess and Timm Beichelt (2013) the German Bundestag has extensive monitoring rights and has gained considerable influence on the substance of EU policies. Consequently, for these countries the new opportunities brought about by the Barroso Initiative and the Lisbon Treaty have proved to be little more than a useful complement to already existing arrangements. Also, the consensual style of politics in these countries induces members of parliament to exert influence via informal collaboration.

In other countries both the Barroso Initiative and the Lisbon Treaty have significantly changed the role of parliament. In the case of Portugal Davor Jančić has come to the conclusion that for the Portuguese Parliament 'it was a catalyst of tacit constitutional change that had a fairly palpable impact on Parliament's status' (Jančić 2012: 89). The new rights established by the Lisbon Treaty, the independent and easy access to information and the unfiltered communication with the Commission, significantly increased the autonomy of Parliament from the Government and contributed to 'transforming the Portuguese Parliament's European scrutiny into a routine business' (Jančić 2012: 89). More comparative research is needed to find out when and why EU reform initiatives have a transformative impact and empower national parliaments to increase political control of their government and even reach out to control decision-makers at the EU level.

In view of the multifaceted reality of parliamentary performance in EU Member States we ought to be cautious with general statements. Another reason to be cautious is that we know too little about the content of the communication. Is it plausible to conclude that 622 opinions sent to the Commission can be rated as 'an extensive exchange of thoughts'? Not all opinions get a formal response and even when there is a response we cannot conclude that the Commission takes the arguments presented in consideration. Also, in view of 2062 legislative acts adopted in 2011,[3] which could have been commented on by parliaments in 27 Member States, it may be a bit too optimistic to call such commentary 'bavardage'.

Apart from likely variations among countries and issues, it is important to note that striking differences exist between chambers of parliament. Comparative research[4] confirms that in majoritarian systems the second chambers, not the first, take advantage of the new openings. The German Bundesrat has a tradition of monitoring EU politics closely and so far has used its extensive rights regularly. In particular, it is dedicated to prevent any encroachment on federal rights. As to the Sénat in France, Davor Jančić records the fact that it 'takes a proactive approach to subsidiarity control' and that also the House of Lords in the United Kingdom 'has been a fairly active participant' (Jančić 2012: 88).

What does this mean for the claim of improved democratic representation? Second chambers are obviously important players to express concerns over the direction of policy and integration. They are representative bodies but, compared to first chambers, their claim of representation follows a different rationale. They do not guarantee equal representation of citizens and most of them are even not directly elected by the citizens. In view of the divergences of national representative systems it is difficult to evaluate whether the reforms mark 'a significant step in the EU's representative system', and really make 'multi-level parliamentarism' possible.

The contribution by Anne Rasmussen and Gert-Jan Lindeboom (Chapter 2) adds to the pessimistic view on national parliaments' contribution to democratic representation in EU politics. Their explorative study sheds light on an equally under-researched topic. While the Europeanization of national parties has been studied extensively, hardly anything is known concerning the relations of national parties with interest groups in EU politics. Both political parties and interest associations are transmission belts conveying the concerns and preferences of the public to decision-makers. Thus their cooperation might contribute to increasing the democratic legitimacy of EU policies. The authors argue convincingly that from a rational choice point of view we might expect parties in parliament to be very interested in working closely with national interest groups. After all, the latter are well versed in EU matters and play a prominent role in EU policy formation.

The empirical findings presented here are not at all in line with such expectations. Rather, the authors come to the conclusion that 'the focus of national parties on interaction with interest groups in areas of EU policy remains marginal despite the increased transfer of national competences to the EU level'. They explain the lack of interaction by referring to the technical nature of EU policies and the way EU decision-making works. The in-built tendency to reach an encompassing compromise takes out the political flavour that animates parliamentary controversies. Negotiations of EU policies are a back-stage affair; they are the responsibility of a small group of politicians from parliament, the government and interest groups. On top of that, a division of labour exists between party members in the national and in the European Parliament, which reduces the interest of national parliamentarians to get engaged. The main reason, however, is the lack of incentives; 'even though parties operate in an environment affected by European integration, it is still achievements in national rather than EU policy that ultimately help them secure *votes* and *office*'. Because of the depoliticized character of EU politics and the seemingly technical features of EU matters, engaging in EU policies does not benefit the politician's career.

Although these findings are based on an exemplary study including only a small sample of interviews, the result gives ample food for thought for two reasons. First, as mentioned by the authors, 'Denmark represents a "most likely" case for the EU involvement of national members of Parliament (MPs) in EU affairs, due to its high degree of scrutiny of EU matters'. Second, the low levels of contacts mirror the attitudes and the behaviour of national interest groups. In general, when it comes to EU law making, national interest groups definitely consider the national executive, be it at the political level or at the working level of government, to be more important than the parliament (Kohler-Koch and Quittkat 2013: 16). Accordingly, they have fewer contacts with parliamentary committees, with individual MPs and with party groups than with government or even with national regulatory and standardization authorities. Irrespective of some national variations, the frequency of contacts with parliamentary party groups is particularly low, and this has not changed over the years despite the fact that national parliaments benefited from the increased importance of the European Parliament.

Multi-level representation

In a multi-level system of governance such as the EU, representation is linked up with the idea of a representative chain. In this chain the representative capacity of national institutions is essential, and it determines to a large degree the representative character of EU-level institutions such as the Council and the European Council. Their representation claim is undisputed, but their mode of operation may make it difficult to fulfil their aspirations and may also constrain the representative performance of national institutions. This is especially true for the Council. In his highly informed account Daniel Naurin (Chapter 4) points out the structural reasons for the Council's aloofness, which impedes the functioning of the representative chain. The division of labour along policy fields, the delegation of intergovernmental negotiations to lower levels of the administration and the consensus style of decision-making work against a visible public representation. However, ministerial responsibility for individual policy areas and the delegation of policy formulation to bureaucrats and experts are common practice in all political systems and duplicated in the 'working parliaments'. Consequently, in the Member States citizens are also usually unaware of what is happening at the level of ministries, and neither public nor media follow closely the day-to-day business of governance. The EU may be 'an outlier in this respect', but the Council's mode of governing is not unique and thus we have to ask why it is more detrimental to the representation claim than on the national level. The decisive difference is the lack of political disputes that will catch public attention. Naurin expounds the structural reasons that political controversies are subdued in the Council and the clash of interests is not brought out in the open. First, the Council is not aligned to a majority party or party coalition in the European Parliament and, second, the main cleavage line in the Council does not run along ideological or party positions. Conflicts arise over specific issues that touch on national interests. More often than not national conflicts dominate negotiations in the Council, but they are not played out in public because of their disintegrative dynamics. Naurin supports the view that members of the Council fear that 'the Europeans are not European enough' to handle divisive debates, and that they 'will not accept being outvoted by "others" on salient issues'. Consequently, the Council avoids taking decisions by a formal vote. Governments increasingly choose to voice their opposition through formal statements that are included in the published minutes of Council meetings. This way they avoid policy gridlock and can still signal their dissent to other Member States and to domestic actors (Hagemann and De Clerck-Sachsse 2007: 14). In order to find a consensus solution persuasion is essential and this cannot happen in the plenary of formal Council meetings. Countless small and private pre-meetings are organized to seek a mutually acceptable compromise (Nugent 2012: 6–7).

Thus, it is not the sectorial and bureaucratic organization of the Council that makes it difficult for parliaments and the public to monitor and pass judgement, but the Council's deliberate strategy of hammering out compromises behind closed doors and concealing unsolved conflicts. Though the Council decides 'in the shadow of the vote', voting is not the regular mode of decision-making. However, as Naurin points out, voting is important for representation:

> The vote is the clearest and most concrete manifestation of the governments' positing-taking, which in turn can be evaluated by the voters. Without formal and explicit votes indicating the real positions taken in the process, accountability of representatives become much more difficult.

Naurin finds neither theoretical nor empirical support of the 'normal-politics thesis' advanced by Simon Hix and others that enlarged membership will cause a more frequent use of qualified majority voting and strengthen alliances that reproduce the left–right cleavages in public policy. The present crisis has triggered open dissent and moved EU policies to the centre of public attention. However, in the public perception it is a conflict between countries and not between political camps. According to Naurin the conflict management and the implementation of the fiscal union have taken the EU 'over the threshold of visibility' and 'will have altered substantially' the conditions for representation in the Councils. But what logic of representation will prevail? When controversial decisions have unequal or even redistributive effects on Member States, national parliamentarians will be alert to the position taken by their representatives on the Council and seek to keep them under control. This would reinforce the Council's image as an intergovernmental body. Obviously, members of the Council prefer to avoid divisive conflicts and they are not eager to stand for the tough regulations of the Union's fiscal policy. Thus, it is not accidental that governments – with the consent of parliaments – have established a technocratic regime, the so-called Fiscal Compact, to strengthen fiscal discipline in the Euro area, and opted for automatic correction mechanisms. The Fiscal Compact is legally binding as an international agreement and subjects Member States to rules and procedures that are more automatic than they ever been before. How does this affect the representative quality of the Council? Who will represent the Union when the crisis and crisis management hit home, and how can citizens exert accountability so that policies are taken in their interest?

The fiscal and budgetary crisis has put Member States and supranational technocratic institutions such as the Commission and the European Central Bank centre-stage. Thus, the image of European multi-level governance has been reduced to a two-tier system. The third tier, constituted by the regions and represented at EU-level by the Committee of the Regions (CoR), has not attracted public attention, even though the CoR has raised its voice on several occasions. A weak public echo is, however, not a reliable indicator of representation; it may rather indicate a weak constitutional position in the decision-making system of the EU.

From the very beginning the CoR could hardly be seen as a third representative chamber in the EU system. It originated from the pressure of regions, which were concerned that the transfer of competence from the national to the EU level could undermine their constitutional rights. Apart from institutional safeguards at the national level they asked for direct involvement in EU governance. The Committee was meant to upgrade the coordination mechanisms that already existed among the strong regions to give them visibility and voice at the European level. The idea of 'a Europe of the regions', which was *en vogue* at the time, was a convenient framing concept to support the demand and to conceal the fact that only a minority of regions had any policy-making powers that might have been at stake. The Committee was established as an advisory body that must be consulted before EU decisions are taken on matters concerning local and regional government. As Simona Piattoni (Chapter 5) rightly observes, the CoR has consolidated its position over the years and is now accepted as the main institution representing local and regional authorities. However, the heterogeneity in its composition has persisted and the vision of a Europe of the regions has withered away and given way to a more integrationist thinking expressed in the now prominent slogan 'more Europe for a better Europe'. The question then is how this development and above all how the Euro crisis, which concentrated decision-making powers at higher levels, has affected the representative function of the CoR.

It is precisely this question that Piattoni addresses in her contribution. She examines in detail the opinions of the CoR on the economic and financial crisis and on the respective measures being taken by the European Council and the Commission. By doing so she gains a profound assessment of the concerns and interests represented by the CoR. The opinions cover both institutional and material issues. By insisting on the principle of subsidiarity they call for a greater role for the regions in the process of will formation, and demand that crisis management should not encroach on regional autonomy. As to matters of substance, they point out that the crisis may result in increasing regional disparities and that in line with the principle of territorial cohesion appropriate financial and fiscal measures have to be taken. Furthermore, the relaunch of regional growth and the protection of local banks and small and medium-sized enterprises is a recurrent theme.

In order to assess whether the CoR lives up to the claim of democratic representation, Piattoni takes up Nadia Urbinati's distinction between *isegoria*, meaning the equal right of all to speak and *isonomia*, meaning the equal right of all to participate in the expression of will. She convincingly argues that the CoR's representative function is limited to articulating the rights and interests of the subnational tier and to giving voice to those it represents. Consequently she concentrates on the four criteria suggested by Nadia Urbinati to examine the quality of performing the voice function of representation: activating, proposing, receiving, surveilling. Piattoni arrives at a very positive conclusion pointing out that the CoR has managed to strike a balance among its institutional, political, economic and territorial interests that could fragment and consequently deprive it of its voice. A more sceptical observer could argue that the CoR recalled mainly well-established and undisputed principles and declared itself in favour of distributive policies which would also avoid provoking any conflicts of interest. All regional representatives are bound to agree that subnational authorities ought to have a greater say in the crisis management and to be effectively engaged in a meaningful way in the formulation and implementation of policies with direct regional impact. Also calls for an increase in funds to support cohesive growth and better cross-level coordination in managing economic policies could hardly provoke any conflict. The opinions largely reflect a self-referential consensus view, which is the traditional approach of the CoR. When it happens that a draft opinion contains a contentious statement it will most likely not be approved in the plenary and exactly this happened in the case of one of the four opinions examined.

Piattoni also prefers to see the glass half full rather than half empty concerning democratic representation. She has carefully scrutinized the texts to find evidence for the activating, proposing, receiving, and surveilling function of the CoR. In her interpretation the CoR's recommendations and requests to the Commission and the Council have a strong activating function. She considers the contributions to the debate on new policies, such as a common system of financial transaction tax, as an expression of the Committee's proposing function, and argues that the CoR is exerting its receiving and surveilling function by calling attention to the adverse effects that EU measures might have on the subnational level and by reminding decision-makers of existing commitments and fundamental principles supporting the rights of regions. When these conclusions are compared with the theoretical reasoning and intentions of the author the limits of the adopted research approach become quite obvious. It is impossible to conclude from the written opinions whether or not the CoR is expressing the constituents' interests and wishes as the constituents see them. It might also be that the CoR is acting on its own imagined version of the constituents' interests and that it gives voice to the subnational tier more in accordance with its own institutional interests than with those of local and regional actors at home, not to mention 'the man in the street'. It makes the CoR a good guardian of democratic rights when it advocates for greater equity and solidarity and defending the principles of participation, transparency, accountability and subsidiarity. But this is far from being a conception of political and democratic representation that implies a continuous dialogue between represented and representatives.

From institutional balance to multiple representation

When defining the EU as a compounded system of representation the focus is on institutions legitimized by direct or indirect elections. The Commission definitely does not belong to that category but still the representation claim of the Commission is as old as the European Communities. From the very beginning of European integration the Commission was said to represent the European interest, and this has become a persistent claim although the supporting reasons have changed over the years. It started with attributing the Commission a special role in the institutional balance of the European edifice. According to the constitutional logic of the Treaties of the 1950s the Commission was part of 'l'équilibre des pouvoirs' ('Gleichgewicht der Gewalten') or rather of the 'tandem' driving the integration project forward. The *raison d'être* of the mutual dependence of Council and Commission was to secure the long-term objective of a working system of peace without violating short- and medium-term interests of the Member States. While the Council, composed of member governments, had the dual obligation to represent distinct national constituencies and at the same time compromise in the interest of the common good, the Commission was the representative of the European interest. This interest was assumed to be defined by the treaties, and the Commission's legitimacy was founded upon its role of being the guardian of the treaties. This logic was only valid as long as the treaties not only defined common objectives but also set out the road map to reach the agreed upon goals. In the meantime the situation has changed dramatically. The treaties are far less precise in describing concrete actions, and give the European institutions wide discretionary powers. In so-called ordinary law-making they endow the Commission, the European Parliament and the Council with close to equal political power. More political power means more pressure on legitimacy. The upgrading of the power of the European Parliament is legitimate as it is based on direct electoral representation. The Council's representational legitimacy remained unchanged; governments represent Member States and are themselves democratically accountable to their national parliaments. The Commission still claims to represent the European interest, but rather than legitimizing this claim by referring to its role as guardian of the treaty the Commission now boosts its positive ratings in the EUROBAROMETER and other public surveys.

In Chapter 7, Nieves Pérez-Solórzano Borragán and Stijn Smismans reject the idea that political representation is asserted by claims-making and indications of public acceptance. They point out that Michael Saward's concept of political representation founded on processes of 'representative claims-making' (Saward 2010) entails the risk of empiricism and of lacking criteria that will have a 'normative guiding function' for institutional design. In their contribution they focus on the institutional dimension of representation; in their own words on 'the features of the institution itself and … its relations with other institutions'. With regard to the Commission they single out four essential features that constitute its representational quality. They refer to the traditional elements, namely the Commission's role as guardian of the treaties, and its constitutionally defined composition and autonomy. The additional factors are the institutional position of the Commission as broker between the Council and the European Parliament, and the Commission's central role in the institutionalized consultations with a wide range of stakeholders. They argue that the treaty-based powers, in combination with a well-functioning system of wider consultation, make the Commission 'a promotional broker of "the general interest of the Union"', by 'balancing a plurality of interests'. Consequently, the authors dedicate a full section of their chapter to the consultation regime of the Commission.

Since the early 1990s the Commission has introduced general principles and norms of consultation that have promised openness, inclusive participation, transparency and accountability. It has put rules and regulations in force to underline its willingness to institutionalize a system of encompassing and balanced interest representation. These, however, have not lived up to their stated objective. The authors mention the changing objectives of transparency. While at first intended to facilitate the input of civil society organizations and to make the Commission more accountable, the more recent Transparency Initiative has introduced a register that is rather a governance instrument adjusted to the interests of the Commission. It is meant to provide systematic information on who aims to influence EU policy-making, who is active in specific policy fields, and how many resources actors have at their disposal. Borragán and Smismans underline the positive aspect of the register, which offers an overview of all sorts of interest groups and gives clues as to the representativeness of individual groups. Indeed, this kind of information could facilitate balanced consultations with representative organizations. It would be a helpful instrument if it were incorporated in an obligatory and effective system of interest intermediation. In my assessment the weak point in the Commission's claim to represent the European interest is that the system of interest intermediation has severe shortcomings. It does not guarantee a balanced representation of the divergent views; it does not promote a discursive exchange of views and it lacks the mechanisms of political responsibility. The Commission is not obliged to consult in a given case, procedures for feedback and the justification of deviating decisions are weak and insufficient, and for institutional reasons the Commission is exempt from CSO accountability. Also the introduction of new consultation instruments is not a success story. Interest groups of different kinds consider them to be the least effective when comparing them with traditional instruments of interest representation (Kohler-Koch and Quittkat 2013: 16). And though the Commission tried to improve access to consultations for a broad constituency by fostering 'weak interests' and providing easy access, the institutional arrangements did not and for structural reasons cannot really improve actual accessibility (Quittkat and Kohler-Koch 2013: 58). The result is an enduring inequality in interest representation.

What does this tell us about the legitimacy of the Commission's claim to represent the general interest of the Union? Our own research suggests that consultation deficiencies have structural reasons pertaining to lacking capacities in the organization of societal interests and to institutional constraints in the multilevel system of EU governance. If this argument is valid and if we accept the authors' suggestion that representation should be judged on the basis of institutional design and not on social acceptance, then the Commission's claim to represent the European interest has to be discarded.

This conclusion is made even more evident by the crisis management of recent years. The general impression is that the Commission has been sidelined to an unusual degree and in an extraordinary way, whereas EU documents[5] convey the impression that the Commission's input to the new strategies of economic and fiscal governance was not at all negligible. But the documents do not disclose where the ideas came from, who designed the road map or who put it on the agenda. For those who know the publications and policy briefs of the European Round Table of Industrialists (ERT), where around 50 chief executives and chairmen of major EU-based multinational companies gather,[6] of BUSINESSEUROPE, the European umbrella association of business,[7] and of the Group of Thirty (G 30), a club of leading international bankers and presidents of Central Banks,[8] the arguments sound very familiar. This is not a coincidence, given the successful lobbying record of these organizations and their extensive activities on showing a way out of the current crisis. Their influence, past and present, on course-setting decisions in economic affairs is well documented.[9] Even when the Commission has organized broad consultations with civil society it can hardly prevent the position of business from prevailing owing to the quality of expert reasoning, the omnipresence of the actors in European elite circles, and the positive resonance of their arguments in the quality press.

Only if the Commission's position were backed up by consultations with a wide range of stakeholders that end up in a truly balanced consideration of diverging interests would it have the legitimacy of acting as a broker between the European Parliament and the Council, which both enjoy electoral legitimation. This vision, however, overestimates the Commission's institutional capacity to constrain market forces, to gain independent economic expertise, and to balance the plurality of interests in Europe. Consequently, its claim to act in the European interest stands on shaky ground.

Representation through participation

The involvement of civil society in EU governance may not have resulted in empowering the Commission to play the role of a true representative of the European interest. But its consultation policy has activated the representation of a broader range of societal interests than ever before, and has thus added to the plurality of interests voiced at the EU level. This then begs the question as to whether civil society organizations do speak in the interest of their constituencies. Though the image of the transmission belt is very present in the literature, empirical studies on the interaction between EU-level organizations and the grass-roots are rare. In her contribution Sandra Kröger (Chapter 8) provides both theoretical arguments and empirical data to shed new light on the representative quality of EU-level civil society organizations. Her main point is that the constituencies have to be involved in the development of policy positions; at least they should have the opportunity to consent to or to reject the positions of the EU association. Thus, she investigates whether and to what degree nationally grounded civil society organizations are actually linked to and communicate with their respective EU umbrellas.

The case selection is based on the assumption that modes of representation will differ according to the type of constituency and purpose of the organization. She takes up the differentiation made in the literature between organizations representing (1) members, (2) a cause, and (3) weak interests. The term 'members' should not be taken literally because, with only few exceptions, all EU associations have members. EU associations are at the top of a multi-level system of organizations and have to pay tribute to the concerns and demands of the national, regional or local associations that constitute their membership. The concept of 'members' does not refer to this organizational structure, but highlights the properties of the constituency at grass-roots level. It is composed of self-interested individuals or corporate actors, and consequently the organization has to act in favour of the well-being of these members. If the organization is dedicated to a cause it has a mission, and this mission unites the organization and its supporters. People tend to be loosely connected and often support the organization not by becoming members but by responding when called to donate money, sign a petition or disseminate information. The representation of weak interests is close to acting for a cause but it is different insofar as the respective organizations aim at descriptive representation by at least partially involving the disadvantaged people. For the 'members' ' organizations Kröger has selected the COPA-COGECA family, for the cause organizations the European Environmental Bureau (EEB), and for the weak interests the European Anti-Poverty Network (EAPN). The questionnaire and the interviews generate data that seem to confirm the expectations derived from the theoretical models:

> The analysis showed that the 'members' ' organizations, here sectoral agricultural groups, are very active over the different governance levels and consistently involve their constituencies in EU affairs.... Less involvement with EU policy-making was found for the constituencies of the umbrella representing a 'cause', and comparatively little involvement was found for 'weak interests' groups.

Hence Kröger concludes that in the light of the demands of democratic representation the democratic legitimacy of 'cause' and 'weak interests' organizations 'seems somewhat limited'.

But can we attribute the comparatively weak performance of the EEB and EAPN to the type of constituency and purpose of the organization? Kröger presents the three factors that have been mentioned chiefly in the interviews: the nature of the policy field, the unequal endowment of resources and the high degree of heterogeneity between member countries, which make it difficult to find a common denominator for interest representation. In the explaining the three cases she demonstrates that the factor 'policy field' is of high importance and comes in different variations. On the one hand it is the level of integration that affects the relevance of EU policies. On the other hand it is the type of policy (regulative, distributive, re-distributive) and the kind of interest affected by these policies (concentrated, diffuse).

One can clearly see the relevance of these factors in the case of COPA-COCEGA. The Committee of Professional Agricultural Organisations and the General Confederation of Agricultural Cooperatives have a dual character. They are advocates of the interests of their members and they are service organizations for their members. The CAP directly concerns the economic well-being of members: without the lobbying efforts of their association farmers would have to face policy reforms with a strong negative impact, and without the advice of their association they could not take the most profitable decisions concerning production and marketing. Environmental policy is quite a different case. Though protecting the environment has become a European competence and has a considerable impact on people in Member States, it is a different type of policy. It is mainly regulative and touches not on existential but on diffuse interests. Anti-poverty, again, is different because it is a case of advocacy in the interest of others and it is a policy field with limited EU rights and resources. Another difference can be seen in the availability of additional channels of representation. While COPA-COCEGA have established a dominant position close to a monopoly, the EEB and also the EAPN are just one – though an important – advocacy group among others at the EU level, and their national membership is composed of heterogeneous organizations that are also members in other EU umbrella groups. They can choose between different associations to voice their interests in Brussels or decide to go it alone.

It is interesting that another important variable has not been mentioned in the interviews. Research concentrating on the organizational properties of associations has revealed that these make quite a difference with respect to communication and interaction within the association.[10] At first sight, the formal organization of EU umbrella associations is very much alike. Brussels-based associations have to be registered and thus are subject to Belgian law and statuary provisions on governance and accountability. But apart from the formal procedures of representation and mandating, the actual involvement of members differs widely. In a larger-n study it can be shown that the variations can best be explained by the legacy of the past, the divergence of interests among members, power play within and between associations, and by the involvement of the Commission (Kohler-Koch and Buth 2013: 124–126). Whereas some umbrellas have a hierarchical structure and only accept one member organization per country or region, others have a network structure with a heterogeneous membership that sometimes overlaps with other umbrella organizations. The policy field does not produce homogeneity as can be demonstrated by the example of the environment. The Group of 10 represents the environmental NGOs and each of these EU-level associations, including the EEB, is representing a different organizational model.

In other words, if we want to know whether cause groups are different from other types of interest groups it would be advisable to extend the research so that the variations in organization can be covered. Nevertheless, the research findings presented here give an instructive confirmation of the hypotheses that organizations serving the self-interest of members are more open to vertical communication than cause groups and groups working for weak interests. This is in line with the observation that the latter are more interested in discourse and, accordingly, encourage the direct participation of activists who sometimes bypass the intermediate levels between grass-roots and EU umbrellas.

Involving civil society organizations in EU governance has been just one strategy among others to redress the democratic deficit of the Union. Another one was to experiment with direct citizens' participation. The European Commission and also the European Parliament initiated citizens' conferences and citizens' forums, which either brought a selected group of citizens into direct face-to-face interaction or mobilized Europeans to participate directly in online communication. Many of these forums were appraised in evaluation reports and examined in academic research. Nevertheless it is difficult to assess what has been achieved and what these endeavours contributed to strengthening the democratic legitimacy of the EU. First of all, neither the Commission nor the European Parliament developed a coherent concept and also the programmatic approach was haphazard. Citizens' forums were neither part of a strategy of democratic innovation, nor did they profit from coordination between individual activities. After a few years the EU institutions lost interest and this impaired a learning process. Also, only few Directorates General of the Commission launched corresponding programmes and those commissioned the implementation to external actors and the latter often engaged sub-contractors, who partly pursued their own agenda. The diversity of the forums' objectives and design make it all the more difficult to arrive at general conclusions.

Dawid Friedrich has screened available publications to make an assessment from the perspective of representation theory. This is no easy endeavour taking into account that comparative research is rare, that the evaluation of individual cases varies in depth and that an explicit link to representation theory is the exception. Scholars have mostly evaluated citizens' forums from the perspective of deliberative democracy. As many observers have had considerable doubts that communication and deliberations could be achieved in a transnational, multilingual setting some of these forums have been launched explicitly to test the feasibility of this instrument in the EU context.

The issue of representation is not absent but it is primarily related to the question of representativeness. Because online forums have been based on self-selection and representativeness could not be controlled, biased representation has been common. In contrast, the organizers of the face-to-face forums have paid great attention to achieving balanced representation in the composition of the forums. They aimed at a mirror representation of the European societies in terms of country origin and social position. Also evaluation reports and academic publications mostly reflect the concept of descriptive representation. The benchmark has been that forums should represent a diversity of social perspectives and territorial diversity. I disagree with Friedrich that this benchmark was based on 'a rather intuitive assumption'. After all, electoral studies have produced sound theoretical arguments and overwhelming empirical evidence concerning the relevance of social categories to political opinions and behaviour. Why rehearse what is now academic conventional wisdom? In addition, the micro-analysis was in no way restricted to examining representativeness in statistical terms. Some authors also brought up the issue of the 'activity bias' and investigated the distorting effects of internal rules and procedures in the management of the forums. They explicated that some procedures were not even meant to bring out clashes of opinion and, accordingly, did not result in the representation of dissenting voices but rather produced a harmonious view.[11] This is a far cry from the ideal world of deliberative democracy, which postulates the autonomy of the individual to justify her/his own position and the unrestrained exchange of arguments.

Friedrich goes beyond the usual approach by extending the analysis from the micro- to the macro-level. Indeed, this is crucial to examining the external effects of the forums, if one wants to assess their democratic potential. Since systematic research is lacking, one can only conclude from the reports on single cases that EU institutions were at best passive recipients of presentations and that the forums' written output had no traceable policy impact. The same sobering conclusion must be reached with respect to the resonance of the forums in the media or among other intermediaries. As there is no interaction with a public audience the representative claim is unfounded. Friedrich's analysis suggests that it will be less difficult for a deliberative forum to meet micro-level requirements than to reach out to citizens. He nevertheless ends on an optimistic note arguing that citizens' forums 'if properly institutionalized … could succeed in making use of the performative potential of deliberation'. Proper institutionalization would mean 'establishing such forums on a regular basis at different places on different topics, and establishing mechanisms that require EU institutions to justify their policy choices in the light of the outcomes of the deliberative forums'. This is a very ambitious strategy, which under present institutional conditions does not sound very realistic. But if we assume that it could be successful, we face the same question that relates to the wider involvement of organized civil society: how do we conceptualize complementarity with the representation claim of parliament?

Representation and guardianship of constitutional courts and experts

Two contributions differ substantially from the other chapters of the book. When examining the role of parliaments, of EU institutions or civil society actors, representation is always linked to the idea that people are represented. It is a concept of democratic representation in line with that of Hanna F. Pitkin, who understands that representation ought to be 'acting in the interest of the represented in a manner responsive to them' (Pitkin 1967: 209). In her contribution Simona Piattoni emphasizes expressly that the representation of 'unattached interests' is clearly not democratic, and quotes Hanna F. Pitkin, who says that such a technocratic notion of representation 'leaves the realm of representation altogether' (Pitkin 1967: 210). How then do the contributions by Michelle Everson and Christian Joerges (Chapter 10) on constitutional guardianship and by Martino Maggetti (Chapter 6) on independent regulatory agencies fit?

Everson and Joerges address the challenge of constitutional development aiming at political unity in a Europe that is characterized by deeply entrenched and even growing diversity, and where already in pre-crisis time it was hard to imagine that a sustainable compromise could be achieved through democratic processes. They examine critically the potential and actual exercise of constitutional guardianship by the constitutional courts, which in their view are not only powerful but also legitimate actors for dealing with the challenge. Constitutional courts enjoy legitimacy founded on authority and this authority is not just derived from the legal provisions of the Constitution but also acquired in the application of the constitutional norms, which, in their reading, are a process of socially responsive adjudication.

The trouble with constitutional guardianship within the EU is that it is entrusted both to national and European courts and that they are not placed in a hierarchical ordering. Thus disagreements have to be dealt with through horizontal cooperation. Such interactive modes of adjudication encounter their limits in the present crisis, as can be shown in the judicial actions of the German Federal Constitutional Court and the Court of Justice of the European Union.

The problem at heart is that both courts have accepted delegalization in the management of the crisis and by acceding to the primacy of 'the political' they represent what they consider to be the true (economic) interest of their own constituency. It is not just that the responses to the financial crisis depart significantly from European law, or that neither the Court of Justice of the European Union nor the German Federal Constitutional Court have shown clear opposition. Rather, the readiness of both courts to give in to the political-economic reasoning both in Brussels and in Berlin erodes the disciplining functions of law, and it also erodes the prospects for a legal reconceptualization of Europe's constitutional situation, which could help to find a way out of the given impasse.

So far the German Federal Constitutional Court has been 'narrow-minded' insofar as it has acted as the guardian of the German constitution without giving recognition that Germany is part of the Union and that the democratic rights of other Member States also deserve recognition. Now, by accepting the practice of the crisis management, it has also legitimized the German economic orthodoxy in substance. Consequently, cleavages are more pronounced than before and constitutional adjudication will become even more difficult.

Everson and Joerges do not bring it up explicitly, but their reference to Carl Schmitt and the 'state of exception' suggests that they also wonder if the courts have not lost their legitimacy as 'institutions *par excellence* of constitutional democracies'. They point out that the courts have failed to develop any criteria against which the legitimacy of the crisis management practices might be assessed, and that they have not insisted on reasoning and justification in view of constitutional norms. By accepting the argument that compliance with the letter of the law would cause more harm than its breach, the courts have traded the primacy of discretionary politics against the normative dignity of the constitutional order.

The same logic also applies in the case of European regulatory agencies. They are independent from national governments and from European institutions and enjoy a high degree of autonomy. The legitimacy of these agencies such as the Committee of European Securities Regulators (CESR) is founded on the (assumed) superiority of expert knowledge, which can be mobilized in transnational network arrangements. In his research Martino Maggetti found confirmation that the members of the Committee, in the meantime transformed into the European Securities and Markets Authority (ESMA), combine independence with shifting claims of representation. At the beginning they saw themselves as representing their national regulatory authorities and as acting in the national interest. Over time they increasingly developed a team spirit and defined themselves as representatives of the European interest. According to Maggetti the financial crisis was a critical juncture that caused an Europeanization of financial supervision but then prompted Member States to retain supervisory powers. It is not clear from the text if and in what way this affected the representative understanding of the Committee, and whether the strong emphasis on acting in the interest of a particular constituency devalued the neutral expert image and consequently degraded the legitimacy of this regulatory body.

Mediated representative politics

Hans-Jörg Trenz's contribution deviates from all the others, as he is not studying the representation claim and function of individual institutions and actors but is rather interested in the European representation system in general. He follows Michael Saward's (2010) argument that representation is not just a relationship between represented and representatives but, as he puts it, 'a triadic and mediated configuration between political agents (claimants), constituents and audiences'. Accordingly, the quality of representation, and above all democratic representation, cannot be assessed by examining the representativeness of a parliament, a government or other governing bodies but needs to be studied with regard to the public visibility and societal reception of representation claims. Further, Trenz emphasizes strongly that 'democratic representation is about collective will formation.... As such, it is processed through public speech that meets the resonance of the general audience'. Consequently, the deficiencies of EU representation do not result from a lack of representative institutions or the disregard of the principles of democratic representation. Rather, the trouble with EU representation is that it lacks the capacity to generate communicative spaces. The processes of representation claims-making do not produce the kind of wider societal resonance and reception (or contestation) necessary to gain generalized validity. The EU does not have the well-established public mediating infrastructure possessed by the national democracies, and, to make things all the more difficult, it has to compete with these national democracies. The media serve the audience in the Member States; they give input to nationally well-established public spheres, and in this way they reproduce the existing fragmentation. EU-level institutions and actors may advance in representativeness and new constituencies may form and find representation in Brussels, but audiences do not follow suit and remain nationally confined.

Does this change in times of crisis? The recent crisis has definitely enhanced the visibility of the EU and attracted the attention of a broad audience. Another question is whether the representative claims-making in the European arena has now found a better match with an emerging European audience and can be transformed into transnational responses. The crisis management and the newly established economic and monetary policies have substantial redistributive effects which have provoked a paradox: EU institutions have continued to pursue a depolitization and conflict avoidance strategy, whereas the media and national political actors, in particular in the debtor countries, have stressed the damaging effects. Conflicts have emerged not so much on traditional ideological cleavage lines but between countries imposing, and those having to suffer from, budgetary discipline. EU policies and the EU system have become politicized, and this has resulted in popular discontent and open public contestation simply because European representatives have been hiding behind so-called economic necessity. The optimistic view is that crisis perception and public resistance against the costs imposed by technocratic politics will trigger an emancipation process. A more critical view sees public contestation as decoupled from the European structures of representation, which accelerates the shift to identity politics and a renationalization in political representation.

Conclusion

The chapter by Hans-Jörg Trenz shows that the contributions to this volume are less coherent than it appears at first sight. Authors dealing with specific institutions and actors conceptualize representation as a relationship between represented and representatives. They examine constellations of interaction and participation and consider whether these live up to the standards of democratic representation. The empirical investigations look into the responsiveness of institutions to the constituents' interests and disclose the structural conditions that make democratic representation difficult. By looking at them all together it becomes obvious that institutions and actors legitimize the representation claim on different grounds, and that representation claims shift over time.

Since nearly all contributions look at only one institution or representation mechanism it is difficult to tell what it contributes to EU representation. The systemic view is not only missing in the empirical parts of the contribution but also in the theoretical reflections. Consequently, important questions are not addressed: do we have to imagine that representation claims complement each other, or that they overlap and compete? The European Parliament, the Council, the European Council, and the Committee of the Regions are all representative institutions based on the principle of territorial representation. They represent the same citizenship though according to different logics of aggregation. Do we have to look for a Pareto optimum of representation, or could representation deficiencies of one institution be compensated by a better representative performance of another one? On what normative ground could one of these institutions claim to possess superior representation legitimacy? Equally important and difficult to answer is the question whether an additional representative institution, for example a European Civil Society Committee supplementing the European Economic and Social Committee, adds to the democratic quality of EU representation. Furthermore, it has to be decided if the new institutional positions created by the Lisbon Treaty, namely the semi-permanent and full-time European Council President, the High Representative of the Union for Foreign Affairs and Security Policy and the reformed troika system, have to be taken into consideration when evaluating the representative performance of the Council and of the Commission. In other words, a comprehensive assessment of the overall constellation of EU representation is needed in order to fully exploit the lessons we can draw from the individual contributions.

Notes

1 Information on the procedures of national parliaments can be accessed at www.ipex.eu/IPEXL-WEB/parliaments/neparliaments.do (24 June 2013).
2 For quantitative data see the yearly report by the Commission on positions submitted and answered by the Commission http://ec.europa.eu/dgs/secretariat_general/relations/relations_other/npo/index_en.htm (24 June 2013).
3 See http://eur-lex.europa.eu/Stats.do?context=legislative&date=2011 (28 April 2013).
4 Davor Jančić (2012) analyses the effects of both the Barroso Initiative and the new rights arising from the Lisbon Treaty. He argues that this is justified because 'the Barroso Initiative has blended with the early warning mechanism into one hybrid procedure" ', and because in the understanding of the Commission both procedures are 'two sides of the same coin' (Jančić 2012: 83).
5 See the Commission's Communication 'A blueprint for a deep and genuine economic and monetary union' (Brussels, 28 November 2012 COM(2012) 777 final) to be compared with the report 'Towards a Genuine Economic and Monetary Union', presented by the Presidents of the European Council, in close collaboration with the Presidents of the Commission, the Eurogroup, and the European Central Bank (Brussels, 5 December 2012), available at www.consilium.europa.eu/uedocs/cms_data/docs/pressdata/en/ec/134069.pdf (accessed 12 May 2013).
6 See www.ert.eu/ (accessed 12 May 2013).
7 See www.businesseurope.eu/ (accessed 12 May 2013).
8 See www.group30.org/index.shtml (accessed 12 May 2013).
9 For the Round Table of Industrialists see Maria Green Cowles (1995); for the Group of Thirty see Eleni Tsingou (2012) and for BUSINESSEUROPE see Corporate Europe Observatory (2013).

10 For more details see Beate Kohler-Koch and Vanessa Buth (2013).
11 See for example Thorsten Hüller (2010).

References

Calliess, C. and Beichelt, T. (2013) *Auf dem Weg zum Europäisierten Bundestag: Vom Zuschauer zum Akteur?* Berlin: Bertelsmann Stiftung.

Corporate Europe Observatory (2013) *Business Europe and Economic Governance*, available at http://corporateeurope.org/publications/businesseurope-and-economic-governance (accessed 25 March 2013).

Cowles, M.G. (1995) 'Setting the agenda for a new Europe: the ERT and EC 1992', *Journal of Common Market Studies*, 33: 501–526.

Hagemann, S. and De Clerck-Sachsse, J. (2007) *Old Rules, New Game: Decision Making in the Council of Ministers After the 2004 Enlargement*, Brussels: CEPS Special Report.

Hüller, T. (2010) 'Playground or democratisation? New participatory procedures at the European Commission', *Swiss Political Science Review*, 16: 77–107.

Jančić, D. (2012) 'The Barroso Initiative: window dressing or democracy boost?' *Utrecht Law Review*, 8 (1): 78–91.

Kohler-Koch, B. and Buth, V. (2013) 'The balancing act of European civil society. Between professionalism and grass roots', in B. Kohler-Koch and C. Quittkat *De-Mystification of Participatory Democracy: EU Governance and Civil Society*, Oxford: Oxford University Press, pp. 114–148.

Kohler-Koch, B. and Quittkat, C. (2013) *Interest Intermediation in the European Union Revisited: Report on a Survey Study*. Mannheim: MZES Working Paper 151.

Nugent, N. (2012) 'Enlargement policy and its impact on EU decision-making', paper presented at the *Sixty Years of European Governance* conference, 13–14 September 2012, York University, Toronto.

Pitkin, H. (1967) *The Concept of Representation*, Berkeley, CA: University of California Press.

Quittkat, C. and Kohler-Koch, B. (2013) 'Involving civil society in EU governance: the consultation regime of the European Commission', in B. Kohler-Koch and C. Quittkat *De-Mystification of Participatory Democracy. EU Governance and Civil Society*, Oxford: Oxford University Press, pp. 41–61.

Saward, M. (2010) *The Representative Claim*, Oxford: Oxford University Press.

Tsingou, E. (2012) 'Club model politics and global financial governance: The case of the Group of Thirty', PhD Thesis, Faculty of Social and Behavioural Sciences, University of Amsterdam. http://dare.uva.nl/record/418085 (accessed 25 March 2013).

13 Concluding notes

Rethinking political representation in a supranational context

Dario Castiglione

Introduction

Modern democracy is *representative* in form. The basic institutional structure of what we call democratic government is founded on a system of political representation, generally operated through elections, which allows citizens to select (and occasionally renovate) a political class, who is in charge of the main legislative power and, through various other mechanisms, the government of the state. Democratic power does not operate in institutional isolation. Modern 'democratic' states are complex systems of social and political governance where legal, economic, and administrative institutions operate with a degree of autonomy and self-referentiality, according to principles and mechanisms that are rarely – and in any case, only marginally – 'democratic', and which also tend to check the power of the political system and the political class. In Bourdieuian terms, these different institutional systems could be considered as separate, though often overlapping, 'fields' of governance, with distinctive structures of power and domination (Bourdieu 2012). But modern 'democratic' states owe their legitimacy in large part to the democratic quality of their political system, and to the latter's capacity to imbricate, when not to give basic direction, to the operations of the other fields of governance.

Because of the way in which democracy and representative government have become intertwined in the past 200 years, the mechanisms of political representation play a fundamental role in both the conception and justification of democratic legitimacy. As a consequence, the historical process of constitutionalization of the modern democratic state has consistently engaged with ways of establishing the principles and the appropriate institutional mechanisms according to which citizens can be 'represented' politically – even though this process has resulted in a variety of local solutions. But, insofar as the citizens are given 'voice' through their representatives, and these representatives are accountable to them, the democratic system is said to guarantee basic autonomy (capacity to give themselves their own rule) and influence (capacity to exercise power over one's life chances) for the citizens. Given the similarity of their respective dual structure (of authorization/control, and autonomy/power), representation and democracy could almost be considered to be identical – as indeed, they have often been taken to be, at least in their modern sense (cf. Pitkin 2004).

This conception of modern representative democracy has, however, grown in close symbiosis with other political 'languages', such as that of sovereignty, the people, the nation, all of which have variously contributed to defining the paradigmatic modern political form of the nation state, in either its unitary or federal variants. It is no surprise, therefore, that one of the causes for recent dissatisfaction with representative democracy may have something to do with the alleged weakening of the nation state (cf. Pollak, Chapter 1 in this volume; Urbinati and Warren 2008, Castiglione and Warren 2006). The growing internal differentiation and the external over-determination of the nation state challenge both its interest-aggregating capacity and problem-solving ability, weakening at the same time the legitimacy of the political system, for this becomes less effective in 'representing' (i.e. giving voice and guaranteeing power to) the citizens. Democratic representation in an increasingly internationalized politics, and in more institutionally embedded supranational contexts, is therefore problematic. Its forms and manifestations can no longer be reduced to the familiar and well-established operations that characterize nation-state democracies. The case of the European Union (EU) – here meant both as its supranational and intergovernmental structure, and as the sum of its Member States – is perhaps the best example for assessing some of the shortcomings of democratic representation in general, and for the possibility of rethinking it in an international and supranational context. As explained in the introduction, this is indeed the originating idea of the present volume, whose main scope is as much to offer a state-of-the-art view of the way in which political representation takes place within the EU (its agents, its levels, and its more informal channels), as to assess whether an examination of representation in the EU provides us with useful theoretical and empirical insights to understand the transformation of political representation, and whether the latter is still at the centre of the process of democratic legitimation in contemporary societies.

In these concluding notes, it is my intention to reflect in particular on the second of the volume's aims, and to do so by examining several related questions:

- the possibility of democratic representation to operate beyond the national context, especially in a situation in which multiple political systems need to be coordinated;
- the kind of constituencies that are represented and through which processes of authorization, claims-making, and control in multilevel systems of governance, in the absence of a single hierarchical structure;
- more generally, whether the European integration process is contributing to changing representative theory and practice, and whether we may need to revise our normative conception of democratic representation in the light of the internationalization of our political systems.

In the remainder of this piece, I shall address these various questions by making use of the analyses offered by the contributors to this volume, in an attempt to see whether we can draw some conclusion from their reflections.

The complexity of representation

There is broad agreement in the recent literature on democratic theory that the return of interest in representation is a result of the decline of interest in more participatory and deliberative approaches to democracy, and perhaps to a slight disappointment that their promises to renovate democratic institutions failed to materialize in any significant way. It may be suggested that something similar has happened in the theoretical literature on EU democracy, where a growing number of scholars have started reflecting on the longstanding issues of the democratic deficit and democratic legitimacy in the EU, by looking at them through the lenses of political representation (not exclusively in terms of a greater role for the European Parliament), rather than those of either citizens' participation or deliberative democracy, which had dominated previous discussions and proposals for reform. Many of the contributors to this volume have been part of this new trend and are drawing insights from the new theoretical literature on political representation in order to make sense of what representation is, or what it may become, within the EU context.

In truth, such new interest in representation does not do away with either participatory or deliberative theories of democracy altogether, indeed building instead upon their achievements, while incorporating them in a renewed vision of the relationship between democracy and representation. Contrary to previous commonplaces, political representation is no longer seen as the opposite of participation, but as a form of it (cf. Plotke 1997); while the aristocratic interpretation of representative government, as a way of countering more radical forms of direct democracy, has been challenged by stressing how representative processes offer a more 'mediated' and deliberatively inclined form of democratic politics (Urbinati 2006). These strategies of re-description have been associated with and supported by an attempt to redefine representation conceptually, and to pay more attention to some of its micro-mechanisms. All this has resulted in what Lisa Dish (2011 and 2012) has called the 'constructivist turn' in political representation. This is seen as a move away from considering political representation as being synonymous with electoral representation, and most importantly, towards a view that constituencies 'do not precede acts of political representation but are, rather, figured by them' (Dish 2012: 115).

There are two aspects to the 'constructivist turn'. One is the way in which it is a reflection on past theories of representation (with an eye in particular to the path-breaking work of Hanna Pitkin in 1967), and how such theories are criticized for over-emphasizing a more objectivist understanding of pre-existing constituencies and interests, so that they can be transposed into the political arena; the other is the implicit acknowledgement of the fact that increasingly, in contemporary politics, representation takes place outside the more formal and official channels traditionally identified with parliaments and parties, and without formal processes of authorization. These two aspects of the 'constructivist turn' are particularly useful for analysing representation in the EU, and more generally in international contexts, since the more opaque, indirect, and often informal character of political representation in such contexts seems well suited to an analysis that insists on the importance of the way in which representation depends primarily on the efficaciousness of the 'claims' made by the representatives, rather than on a more formalistic conception of the relation between represented and representatives as principals and agents (Saward 2010). The theoretical and analytical appropriateness of the 'constructivist turn' as a way of accounting for representation in the EU is therefore a common theme to a number of contributions in this volume (Pollak, Kröger, Friedrich, Trenz, Piattoni, Pérez-Solórzano Borragán and Smismans) – even though these authors do not always agree with each other on its validity.

As Johannes Pollak in particular argues in Chapter 1, the 'constructivist turn' challenges what can be taken as the 'standard view' of political representation. This is a rather abstract and simplified model, offering a theoretical synthesis of democratic representation in most constitutional states throughout the past two centuries. In sum, there are four main features to it (Castiglione 2012b: 24–26; see also Castiglione and Warren 2006). First, from a more structural perspective ('formal', in Hannah Pitkin's analysis: Pitkin 1967), political representation can be thought of as a principal–agent relationship, encompassing both the processes of authorization and accountability, whose combination is constitutive of the very relationship of representation. Second, modern political (and particularly democratic) representation has developed territorial and electoral bases, both of which, in different ways, have provided a basis for political equality, progressively reinforced by the diffusion of the universal franchise and the tentative equalization of constituencies. Third, political representation offers a focal point (a deliberative space) for decision-making, which has both symbolic and procedural significance, and which is meant to facilitate the task of reducing the differences of opinions, interests, and identities within the body politic, while directing decision-making towards an approximation of the common interest. Fourth, political representation (unlike legal representation, for instance) provides a flexible channel through which it gives substance (Pitkin's 'substantive' conceptions) to both influence and responsiveness. In their simplicity, electoral mechanisms are blunt, yet economical means for this operation; but more subtly and efficaciously, the processes of opinion formation, interest aggregation, leadership and mobilization give social representativeness to the workings of the political system, and democratic legitimacy to its substantive decisions.

Each of the four features of the 'standard view' is problematic when looked at from a constructivist perspective. Both the principal–agent and the territorial features fall foul to the first aspect of the 'constructivist turn': its insistence that 'claims-making' as a social construction is at the core of the phenomenology of political representation. On the contrary, the formal rigidity of the principal–agent relationship, and the fixity of interests often attributed to territorial constituencies tend to obscure the social dynamics of representation. Moreover, in increasingly complex and diversified societies, the sole criterion of territoriality fails to provide a strong basis for the kind of equality that rests on the principle of one-person-one-vote. The other two features of the 'standard view', the way in which parliamentary institutions and the political system provide both focus and representativeness, are partly undermined by the constructivist insistence that political representation is more diffuse and informal in its operations than the 'standard view' allows.

We find a number of illustrations and supporting arguments for such criticisms of the 'standard view' in many of the contributions to this volume. Let's take the two aspects of the constructivist critique in turn. First, the formal and naturalistic account of the 'standard view' seems to be challenged by the fact that none of the main institutions involved in the European decision-making process presents a clear chain of authorization and accountability, while the multilevel structure of governance makes it difficult to identify precise and distinct constituencies at the European level, except perhaps the Member States. Traditionally, parliaments have a primary place in the politics of representation. As Pollak's contribution explains, this is not the case in EU politics. Although increasingly powerful, the European Parliament's role in legislation remains limited, not just because it is still subordinated to other institutions such as the Council and the Commission, but above all because of the 'weak' and unfocussed mandate it receives from the European citizens. Moreover, as Pollak also remarks, parliamentary politics in the EU has a compound structure that has grown piecemeal and that comprises both a vertical (the EP) and a horizontal structure (national parliaments). Neither of the two, however, provides an effective and unequivocal channel for the representation of the interests of the European citizens and the European peoples, so that, as Pollak suggests, this is a case where 'voice' is manifested, but has no real efficacy within the decision-making process of the EU.

The process of vertical and horizontal representation is no less fraught with problems when one looks at the role of the European Council and the Council of Ministers. Daniel Naurin (Chapter 4) offers an illuminating analysis of the limits and conditions that the internal organization and the modus operandi of the Councils impose on their representative role. The most obvious limit comes from the fact that the official representatives of the Member States, who are on the Councils, are too high up in the chain of representation, so that both the chains of authorization and accountability are too loose to work properly. National elections rarely give a clear mandate to governments for the more detailed European legislation in which the European Council and the Council of Ministers are involved; while the lack of transparency characterizing Council negotiation and decision-making procedures makes it almost impossible for national electorates to hold governments to account for the role they play in the EU.

Political representation in the EU is further complicated by the lack of a proper political parties system at the European level. In their contribution (Chapter 2), Anne Rasmussen and Gert-Jan Lindeboom question the degree of Europeanization of political parties, which, as they argue, still tend to operate within the national context as their main point of reference (in search for votes and office), thus failing to provide those typical functions of public opinion orientation, coherent and responsible policy elaboration, and problem-solving capacity that are needed for an effective political system to be truly representative. None of the channels here examined – parliaments, government officials on the Councils, and political parties – offer a robust enough link with the citizens for these institutions to be said to represent them at a European level according to the model suggested by the 'standard view', with clear authorization and effective accountability.

If we move to the second aspect of the constructivist critique, we find that there are a considerable number of agents and institutional actors in the EU whose representative function is neither clearly sanctioned nor entirely formalized, but which nonetheless advocate to themselves representative roles and a representative 'mission' within the European decision-making process. As explained in each of the relevant chapters, the European Commission (Chapter 7: Borragán and Smismans), the Committee of Regions (Chapter 5: Piattoni), but also the European regulatory agencies (Chapter 6: Maggetti), the European Constitutional Court (Chapter 10: Everson and Joerges), civil society organizations (Chapter 8: Kröger), and citizens' Forums (Chapter 9: Friedrich), all claim to represent the opinions and best interests of either part or the whole of the European public. In each of these cases, the agents' understanding of their own representative role and scope is independent of any direct process of authorization, or indeed from ex-post accountability. We shall see in the next section how the various contributors characterize the way in which these agents and institutions interpret their own role and the scope of the claims they advance on behalf of those they wish to represent; for the time being, we only need to observe the self-referential character of such an understanding. This would seem to confirm the 'constructivist' intuition that political representation is increasingly dependent on the agents' own claims (cf. Saward 2010) that they are acting as representatives, and on the way in which the agents themselves 'construct' the social identity and the interests of the represented, rather than on any precise mechanism or chain of authorization from principals.

Overall, the image that the 'constructivist turn' gives of representation in the EU is that of an extremely complex system, where there are many channels through which the 'voice' and interests of the citizens are brought into the political process of decision-making, but where such channels are not subject to the discipline provided, for instance, by electoral authorization and accountability, nor are they always directed towards collective will formation, both of which figure prominently in the 'standard view'. The constructivist analysis seems to have the advantage of offering a more realistic account of the complexity of representation in a multilevel and supranational context, and a more perceptive description of the dynamic way through which agents construct, while they interpret and give voice to, the needs and demands of their 'constituencies'. Moreover, the constructivist analysis brings to the fore two further elements of political representation. One is that representation cannot be exclusively confined within the process of collective will formation and legislation, and the institutions presupposed to it. There is more to political representation that escapes this process narrowly defined – something that is particularly true in multilevel systems of governance. Political representation takes place through a variety of forms and channels, which contribute to the democratic system of checks and balances, and more broadly to that of opinion formation and deliberation, rather than the legislative process itself (cf. Chapters 5, 10, and 7). The other element is that the legitimacy of the representative claims depends also on a system of social validation that involves not just representatives and represented, but also the public as a distinct 'audience' (cf. the Chapter 9: Friedrich; Chapter 11: Trenz). In some respects, this idea challenges democratic sovereignty, but it is important in order to understand the way in which public opinion formation relates to legislation and the operations of the political system in modern, complex societies.

It must be said, however, that, even though the 'constructivist turn' seems to be right in pointing out that representation is both a dynamic and complex process, neither of these elements was entirely absent from previous theoretical accounts, which tried to make sense of the 'standard view'. Hanna Pitkin, for instance, stressed the dynamic and reciprocal way in which represented and representative participate in the process of representation, insofar as this is making present something that is not (cf. Pitkin 1967, Castiglione 2012a, but also Young 2000). Moreover, as we shall explore further in the next section, the complexity of political representation, and the need for it to be judged from a more holistic and systemic perspective, is something that is true as much for modern, nation-state-politics as for politics in the post-national constellation.

But if the 'constructivist turn' offers some refreshing ways of looking again at political representation, particularly at the added complexity and informality that comes from supranational contexts and multilevel forms of governance, it is less convincing as an account of democratic representation. As Sandra Kröger, for instance, notices in her analysis of different types of civil society organizations, and of the way in which they relate to either their membership or their self-defined scope, the question remains how such 'claims' to represent constructed identities, interests, and issues (cf. Saward 2010) can contribute to the democratic quality of decision-making, and ultimately to its legitimacy. As the contributions from both John-Erik Fossum (Chapter 3) and Hans-Jörg Trenz (Chapter 11) seem to emphasize, in the complex context provided by the different processes and agents of representation in the EU, democratic legitimacy might depend more on the way in which the overall system of representation operates, rather than on simple mechanisms of authorization and accountability. This is, at the same time, a test for the more 'constructivist' theories of representation, and for democratic representation in the EU.

The representative system

The democratic legitimacy test for representation in the EU and more generally in multilevel and internationalized forms of governance raises two separate issues, to which the chapters in this volume offer interesting material for reflection, even though neither of them can be answered conclusively at this stage.

The two issues can be neatly presented as the macro- and micro-mechanisms of political representation.

I start with the macro-level, since this has often remained implicit, even in the literature on democratic representation, which has tended to concentrate on the particular rules or norms defining the role of the representatives and the nature of their relation with the represented. Democratic representation has a systemic aspect to it (Pitkin 1967; Weale 2007; Mansbridge 2009; Castiglione 2012b), which cannot simply be reduced to the individual operations of representing – in the sense of making politically present or relevant – the views, interests or identities of the citizens, or of particular groups of citizens. The 'standard view' was perhaps better attuned to capturing this aspect of democratic representation insofar as it emphasized the way in which political representation was an intrinsic part of the process of both collective will and opinion formation in democracies. From such a perspective, political representation's main role was that of providing a moment of mediation, filtering, and self-reflectivity as part of democratic decision-making; but at the same time to guarantee specific mechanisms through which the community could arrive at collective decisions with a relative degree of coherence across issues and time. As already mentioned, the 'standard view' also allowed for a broad conception of political representation, which was meant to consist of a variety of institutions and political processes, comprising parliaments, parties, public opinion, public debate and consultation, but also more informal, dispersed, and more socially rooted processes of deliberation and opinion formation. Historically, during what Manin (1997) calls the age of 'party democracy', this was the role of mass parties, workers' organizations, and social movements. Nowadays, such a role tends to be taken by civil society organizations, mini-publics, and citizens' assemblies, or even more professional organizations operating in civil society. But in the present conditions of internationalized politics and multilevel governance, the two distinct moments of public deliberation and collective will formation, which the representative system tried to bring together, often remain apart, so that the system of political representation becomes more tenuous, informal, dispersed and disaggregated. This is partly the message that one finds in many of the contributions to this volume, a problem that the constructivist approach tends to illustrate, but to which it seems to have no definite answer.

Both Pollak's and Fossum's contributions highlight how the horizontal and vertical parliamentary systems operating in the EU offer many opportunities for representing both territorial and functional constituencies, the views and interests of national and European citizens, but the overall system remains ineffective when looked at from a democratic perspective: i.e. in terms of the actual influence that such a system of representation can exercise on the decision-making process in the EU. For their part, Rasmussen and Lindeboom notice how the parties' function of 'gate-keepers', helping to transmit the views of the public and of pressure groups to the political system, does not work effectively at the European level, thus weakening public opinion influence on EU policy-making. Friedrich and Trenz are, however, more sanguine in their assessment of the way in which the more traditional process of political accountability does take place through publicity and public discourses, rather than through sanction-based forms of representation (cf. Mansbridge 2009). A similar view is partly advanced in the chapters on the Committee of Regions (Chapter 5: Piattoni) and the Commission (Chapter 7: Borragán and Smismans), whose proper function is seen respectively as the receptors of representative claims and the broker of a common European interest. In both cases the institutions are seen as being primarily part of the opinion formation process, and less functional to the process of will formation, which remains undetermined. Indeed, the disjunction between these two moments seems to be the main problem for political representation in multilevel and supranational systems of governance. A disjunction that nation state democracies were able to overcome at least in part by their more centralized and hierarchical structure of power, which placed the legislative process at the centre of a web of representative instances. The question, from a democratic perspective, is whether what is lost at a systemic level can be gained at a micro-level, by the promotion in the public sphere of different democratic instances and by the diffusion of more democratic practices operating autonomously.

This is where the micro-analysis of the nature of the representative relationship comes into its own. The 'standard view' of political representation had concerned itself mainly with the traditional delegate–trustee distinction in relation to the way in which representatives interpret and conduct their role. But, of late, a more sustained attempt has been made to revaluate a more trusteeship-based conception of the role of the representatives. Amongst the various attempts, the most imaginative is Jane Mansbridge's (2009), for her nuanced analysis of the way in which the relationship between represented and representatives can be characterized in ways that escape the straitjacket of the simple dichotomy between delegates and trustees. Mansbridge's introduction of new classifications such as 'promissory', 'anticipatory', 'gyroscopic', and 'surrogate' shows the variety of roles that representatives can play, and the different forms that the relationship between represented and representatives can take. More importantly, I think, her rescue of the 'selection model' of representation points to a series of mechanisms and strategies that can inject virtue and commitment in the representative body, without this relying on some aristocratic view of what representation is about. As she says, 'the characters of the representative and the constituents are also formed in the representative–constituent relation' (Mansbridge 2009: 392). This is perhaps problematic from an empirical perspective, but normatively, such a defence of the 'selection model' is of a piece with a more deliberative conception of a democracy, and with the constructivist emphasis on claims-making, which Saward (2010) and others place at the core of the process of representation. Both the 'selection model' and the idea of 'claims-making' seem to emphasize the way in which representative agents can be made both responsible and responsive by the way in which they take their own roles seriously.

This self-disciplining function that comes from taking on a particular conception of one's own representative mission is something that emerges from a number of chapters in the book. Both Kröger and Friedrich (Chapters 8 and 9 respectively) investigate whether certain kind of civil society organizations and citizens' forums can have representativeness, even when they do not perform a delegated function, either subject to sanctioning or determined by their own status as 'descriptive' representatives of a particular group or cause. The importance of the way representatives see their own role is also emphasized in the chapters on the Council (Chapter 4: Naurin), the Commission (Chapter 7: Borragán and Smismans) and the regulatory agencies (Chapter 6: Maggetti). Naurin suggests that the way in which ministers take on their role as members of the Council in some cases make them less, rather than more, responsive to their natural constituency, insofar as they see themselves in the first instance as members of the Council, something that may determine a certain propension to compromise. Maggetti, on his part, notices a certain tension in the way in which regulators tend to take on different personas, as either 'national' or 'European' representatives within the regulatory agency, and how this may determine their choices. In all these instances, representativeness is mainly dependent either on understanding one's own role or on how one conceives the scope of the institutional context within which one operates. But, in this case, representativeness becomes subordinate to the idea of being responsible towards one's role rather than responsive (either through sanction or selection) to those one represents. Overall, the message that comes from the various chapters of the book, with regard to the micro-mechanisms that determine the functioning of political representation in the EU, is a mixed one. Nonetheless, the general impression is that the emphasis on trust and responsible role-playing presents considerable dangers from a democratic perspective, tending to encourage the insulation of the representatives from the represented.

Conclusion: the supranational dimension and the 'test' of the financial crisis

It is precisely such a danger that most of the contributors remark on when they reflect on the current financial crisis. There is general agreement that, in some way, the crisis offers an opportunity for democratic renewal in the EU, insofar as it gives salience to European issues, and therefore makes the EU and European politics an issue for public debate at the national level. But the general view is that, so far, the crisis has weakened, rather than strengthened, the channels of democratic representation in the EU, while the fundamental legitimacy of the policies pursued in relation to the crisis have been called into question. The more vital the decisions at the EU level have become for the citizens of Europe, the more the distance between them and the European institutions seems to have grown. This is the current challenge for democratic representation in the EU: a challenge that will require not only a closer analysis of how political representation works at a supranational level, but will also involve new institutional imagination and experimentation.

In conclusion, and returning to the questions mentioned at the beginning. It would seem that current theories may help us to make sense of the way in which political representation works in the EU, or more generally in multilevel systems of governance, as a complex, and sometimes intricate web of institutions and agents who make claims on behalf of both territorial and functional constituencies. Conversely, the analysis of representation in the EU may help us to sharpen some of our theoretical tools, and this has been shown by the productive way in which the contributors to this volume have both used and tested the 'constructivist turn' in their attempt to make sense of representation in the EU. From a more substantive perspective, many of the chapters of this volume show that political representation in supranational politics is more diffuse, informal and fragmented than it is in the context of nation state democracies, though it would be wrong to assume that these are entirely new features of representation. Political representation, particularly in its democratic form, has always operated at a systemic level. But it is true that in post-national politics, there is an increasing disjunction between opinion formation and will formation that comprise the overall system of political representation. As the current financial crisis has shown, this poses a democratic problem to the way in which political representation works in the EU: the European public has a 'voice', but risks having no 'influence'. To remedy this problem is both a theoretical and a practical task.

Acknowledgements

I would like to thank all the contributors to this volume and the participants to the originating conference in Exeter for the many ideas they gave me in preparing this concluding note, and particularly to Sandra Kröger for her comments.

References

Bourdieu, P. (2012). *Sur L'État. Cours au Collège de France 1989–1992*. Paris: Seuil.

Castiglione, D. (2012a) 'Giving Pitkin her due,' in 'Critical Exchange on Michael Saward's *The Representative Claim*', *Contemporary Political Theory*, 11 (1): 118–22.

Castiglione, D. (2012b) 'La rappresentanza informale e il sistema della rappresentanza politica', *Parolechiave*, 47: 23–35.

Castiglione, D. and Warren, M. (2006) 'Rethinking democratic representation: eight theoretical issues', working paper, Conference on Rethinking Democratic Representation, Centre for the Study of Democratic Institutions, University of British Columbia, Vancouver.

Disch, L. (2011) 'Toward a mobilization conception of democratic representation', *American Political Science Review*, 105 (1): 100–14.

Dish, L. (2012) 'The "constructivist turn" in political representation' in 'Critical Exchange on Michael Saward's *The representative claim*', *Contemporary Political Theory*, 11 (1): 114–18.

Manin, B. (1997) *The Principles of Representative Government*, Cambridge: Cambridge University Press.

Mansbridge, J. (2009) 'A "selection model" of political representation', *Journal of Political Philosophy*, 17 (4): 369–98.

Pitkin, H. (1967) *The Concept of Representation*, Berkeley, CA: University of California Press.

Pitkin, H. (2004) 'Representation and democracy: uneasy alliance', *Scandinavian Political Studies*, 27 (3): 335–42.

Plotke, D. (1997) 'Representation is democracy', *Constellations*, 4 (1): 19–34.

Saward, M. (2010) *The Representative Claim*, Oxford: Oxford University Press.

Urbinati, N. (2006) *Representative Democracy*, Chicago, IL: Chicago University Press.

Urbinati, N. and Warren, M. (2008) 'The concept of representation in contemporary democratic theory', *Annual Review of Political Science*, 11: 387–412.

Weale, A. (2007) *Democracy*, 2nd edn, Basingstoke: Palgrave Macmillan.

Young, I.M. (2000) *Inclusion and Democracy*, Oxford: Oxford University Press.

Index

For Product Safety Concerns and Information please contact our
EU representative GPSR@taylorandfrancis.com Taylor & Francis
Verlag GmbH, Kaufingerstraße 24, 80331 München, Germany